# SIGN AND CULTURE

## A Reader for Students of American Sign Language

edited by
William C. Stokoe

Published by

Linstok Press, Incorporated
9306 Mintwood Street
Silver Spring, Maryland 20901 USA

ISBN 0-932130-07-0
Library of Congress Catalog No. 80-82122

Manufactured in the United States of America

Except for "Pidgin Sign Languages"
and "The Study and Use of Sign Language,"
the chapters in this book originally
appeared in SIGN LANGUAGE STUDIES
copyright ©by William C. Stokoe, Editor in
1972, 1973, 1974, 1975, 1976, 1978

Cover design by Caroline Lee

# PREFACE

Students of sign language need, along with vocabulary drills and conversational practice, some knowledge of the world as signers see it. Academic decision makers may admit petitions to use sign language as a foreign language or as a doctoral working language, but they also need to know of the cultural nexus—those intricate connections between a signed or a spoken language and the society that uses it. Teachers of deaf pupils facing the choice of one or another manual communication method as one component in "total communication" need a background for intelligent choice— or for adjusting to a choice already made for them. Parents of deaf children face an agonizing decision: whether to accept the negative view of deaf people and their signing as represented by oralists or to look for some evidence that the use of signing has a positive side.

A single book can hardly satisfy such diverse and deep needs, but this selection of papers that have appeared in Sign Language Studies between 1972 and 1979 has been made to give students, educators, teachers, and parents as well as the intellectually curious useful information. Following an introductory essay "The Study and Use of Sign Language" the chapters are arranged in four sections.

The first section addresses the broad question "What is sign language?" Woodward and Markowicz show how gestural-visual behavior communicating in language continuously merges manually encoded English with American Sign Language, two quite different languages; and they go on to show how these two languages in contact lead to another, Pidgin Sign English, formed in the same way as other pidgins. Clifford Abbott restates the question and

asks and answers how grammars of spoken and signed languages encode information variously. Dennis Cokely and
Rudy Gawlik describe a fascinating language variety not
often studied in formal language courses: Childrenese, the
age-graded language of children and adolescents, whose
signing in metropolitan Washington is little different from
that of deaf contemporaries in suburban Oak Park. In "Wit
and Poetry in American Sign Language" Edward Klima and
Ursula Bellugi display the relations of sign language expression to the humor and imagination of its deaf signers.
Robbin Battison and King Jordan, with first hand evidence
gained from dozens of signers from as many countries,
point out what is fact and what fancy in "Cross-Cultural
Communication with Foreign Signers," and find that signed
languages are as localized and as regionally special as
are spoken languages. Susan Fischer and Bonnie Gough
discuss in detail some of the central grammatical features
in "Verbs in American Sign Language."

The second section, on "Learning and Using Sign
Language," gets deeply into a psycholinguistic vein. Judy
Williams describes what may be the ideal way for a deaf
child to grow up knowing two languages equally well, the
natural sign language of the family and friends and the manually encoded English of school and deaf-hearing interaction.
Marina McIntire describes the typical stagewise learning
by a deaf child to control the formation of the words of her
parents' sign language. Ray Stevens looks at the larger
learning scene, the school, and finds the discoveries of
Piaget and other leading psycholinguists still not being used
as they deserve—deaf children in school are being taught
English as if they were adults who must learn by rule and
logic, not by doing. Marvin Sallop recounts a personal and
successful teaching experience: his pushing and pulling his
pupils up a series of steps by his willingness to accept
appropriate use of gestural language output. John Bonvillian,
Keith Nelson, and Veda Charrow consider in depth the value
of signing for deaf children as well as for children with
other language learning needs.

The third section, "(Sign) Language and Culture," relates sign language use and public attitudes and policies to
the deaf community. Harry Markowicz presents the whole
panorama in a remarkably prophetic (1972) essay. William

Stokoe, Russell Bernard, and Carol Padden focus on a small
elite group in the deaf community and find some remarkable
indications of the power of sign language to link and to separate members of social networks.

Three chapters in the fourth section reinforce two basic
truths that enthusiasts sometimes forget. Language is not
all biological, although a capacity for and a necessity for
language use are part of being born human. And, language is
not all socio-cultural, although innate capacity withers
without human interaction and the born-human individual
does not gain full humanity. Pat Siple shows how the phys-
iology of seeing constrains sign aspects (What Acts, Action,
Place) to conform to the requirements of the visual field,
the interactive distance, and the central importance of faces
and eyes in sign language and face-to-face interaction. Adam
Kendon relates sign language to Language by his microanalysis
of gesticulation, the system all speakers use along with their
speech; he finds gesticulation a deeper, earlier learned way
of expressing inner language structures. Finally Susan Goldin-
Meadow and Heidi Feldman describe what may be the ultimate
experiment, after Herodotus, in language origin. Children
they observed had no spoken language input and were allowed
to see no sign language; and yet the children developed,
stage-by-stage, out of their innate language capacity and
their interaction with attentive investigators, a workable language of gestures that they and no one else devised.

The differing lengths of the four sections do not indicate
the relative importance of the four themes, but they do show
approximately the relative amount of study, research, and
writing that has been devoted to sign language itself, to
learning and teaching it, to the society that most uses it,
and to the implications that sign languages of deaf people
have for biological, linguistic, and socio-cultural theory.

Selecting these eighteen studies from the more than
one hundred which have appeared in Sign Language Studies
has not been easy. I have been guided of course by numbers
of requests for reprints and offprints from fellow teachers,
but I am deeply conscious that a great many of the papers not
chosen might have served as well to develop the themes of
this selection or other pertinent ideas. As a corrective to

my editorial choice the wise reader of this selection will
keep at hand the whole run of <u>Sign Language Studies</u>, the
journal that has published since 1972 more than ten times
the number of studies of sign language than have appeared
in other periodicals.

I am sincerely grateful to the twenty-four authors of
the following chapters and to their fellow authors in <u>SLS</u>.
Together, they constitute a group of scientists as likely to
change the world significantly for the better as any. A
longer debt of gratitude is owing to my earliest sign language
teachers and collaborators—the late Elizabeth Benson,
Richard M. Phillips, Rex Lowman, Carl and Eleanor Crone-
berg, Dot Casterline, Jack Gannon, Vilas Johnson, Ben
Schowe, Roy Stewart... If I have been able to give some
shape to an idea of the language and culture of the American
Deaf Community, credit goes to those already named and to
other colleagues: Leon and Hortense Auerbach, Allen and
Florence Crammatte, Don and Agnes Padden, Bill and Babs
Stevens, Tom Berg, Sully Bushnaq, Fred Schreiber, Terry
O'Rourke, Gene Bergman, Boyce Williams, Barbara Kannapell,
Larry Fleischer, Larry Berke, Tom Humphries, Gil and June
Eastman, Yerker Andersson, Bernard Bragg, Katie Brown, Bob
Davila, Bob and Kitty Dillman, Hal Domich, Merv Garretson,
Lin Smith, Jerry Jordan, Marybeth Miller, Ron Nomeland,
Al Pimentel, Debbie Sonnenstrahl, Frank Turk, John Schrœdel
— the list could go on for pages more, and I hope those un-
intentionally omitted will understand and accept my thanks
as well; for this is just the beginning of an enumeration of
the members of a community whose language, culture, and
shared experiences have greatly enriched the life of an
outsider, an outsider humbly grateful for their hospitality
and shared wisdom.

SIGN & CULTURE

A READER FOR STUDENTS OF AMERICAN SIGN LANGUAGE

◇      ◇      ◇      ◇      ◇      ◇      ◇

△          △          △

(Complete contents next page)

# CONTENTS

8

PART TWO (Continued)

INTRODUCTION:

# THE STUDY AND USE OF SIGN LANGUAGE

William C. Stokoe

Formal education of deaf persons in America was at its
outset in 1817 synonomous with sign language use. The
method of teaching in signs of the natural sign language
used by deaf persons themselves and augmented with signs
invented to represent grammatical and lexical signals was
easily adapted to the American scene by Laurent Clerc, the
deaf teacher who learned it in France. As in France and many
other countries to which it had spread, this method produced
in a few school generations an educated deaf elite that urged
its continuance with vigor. However, for reasons that would
require a good sized history to explain, the educational use
of sign languages in the United States and in most countries
declined. During most of the twentieth century signing has
been strictly prohibited in some schools, discouraged and
neglected in many, and even if permitted for out of classroom
use has been studiously ignored by teachers and staff in
most schools for the deaf.

Beginning about 1970, an educational philosophy known
now as "total communication" (Denton 1972) has been adopted
in a growing number of schools. It permits the deaf pupil to
use manual as well as vocal and written means of expressing
English, and at least encourages the teachers to use their
hands for signing and fingerspelling; but its implementation
has seldom included recognition of the distinct natural and
complete sign language used in the American Deaf Community.

Now linguists and sociolinguists have joined deaf people
—who of course never stopped signing—to insist that the
natural language for interaction among those who cannot hear

be given a central role in their education. Increasing dis-
content with the low achievement of the average deaf child
in school has also turned attention to sign language. There
are more than 70,000 pupils in schools and programs reporting
to the Annual Survey of Hearing Impaired Children and Youth.
Some studies show a superiority on standard tests of deaf
children whose instruction and early experience included use
of manual means of communication; but as yet there are no
large numbers of deaf children with a natural sign language
as their primary language to support the commonsense view
that a bilingual approach may work better than a mixture of
means or the prohibition of some channels outright. The few
case studies are impressive (see Chapters 7 and 8 below),
but sign languages remain too little studied and used.

Sign language is a central fact in the life of deaf individuals and groups, and this essay will treat it as a natural
focus as well for educational efforts. This will require looking
at the relation of Sign to English, for English is another
central fact in the lives of American deaf people. "Sign" is
used here as a short and pronounceable abbreviation for the
proper name, American Sign Language, sometimes abbreviated
ASL or Ameslan (with the disadvantage in the first case of
adding to "alphabet soup" and in the latter of being pronounced
variously to rime with Pakistan, homage slang, dristan, and
almost gone).

While sign languages generally and Sign in particular
make excellent objects for scientific study—e.g. by anthropologists, linguists, and psychologists; the present intent
is to treat Sign as a prime educational medium and as a language
that can make a deaf person both a sharer in general American
culture and also a member of a special group with its own
self awareness and pride. To treat Sign in this way requires
first to look at some of the different ways that languages are
presented to the eye instead of to the ear. Second, it requires
an examination of bilingualism and its special place in the
life and education of deaf persons. Third, we will look at
ways for concerned teachers to apply research findings in
their own work. Finally, teachers will be shown ways to ask
and answer questions of importance about Sign; i.e. to do
practical research in the study of sign language for themselves.

Sight, language,     Education for deaf children confronts
and speech.          a central fact: sight instead of hearing
                     is the sense that conveys language
symbols to the person who cannot hear. In the history of
systematic education this fact has not always been faced
squarely. The French pioneers, Épée, Sicard, and Valade,
in harmony with the empirical and scientific spirit of the
Enlightenment (Seigel 1969), founded their teaching on this
fact; visibly distinct signals for French grammatical features
were built into their programs of instruction. But even in
Épée's lifetime, Heinicke challenged the French approach,
insisting that words and the ideas they stood for could never
be presented inside the mind without sounds. The controversy,
in letters, between Épée and Heinicke began in 1780, and
Paris, Leipzig, Vienna—the whole intellectual world of Europe—
became embroiled. The decision of the Rector and Fellows of
the Academy of Zurich in Épée's favor in 1783 did not end this
controversy (Garnett 1968). The fact remains, however, that
eyes and not ears are the deaf person's prime symbol receivers.
     Heinicke and his modern heirs follow a train of reasoning
that turns away from this central fact; he began by teaching
"deaf-motes" to make sounds, thence "to read and speak
clearly and with understanding." At least that is his claim.
Like all readers, his pupils had to use their eyes, but he
contended that the written symbols had meaning for them only
through association with the sounds that they had been taught
to produce. He and teachers of the deaf before and since his
time also try to have their pupils associate the sounds that
they make (and that they must suppose others are making) with
visible facial movements—in a word, to read lips.
     Language taught by these procedures is expressed in
speech, but speech with a difference: receptively it is seeing
the facial activity of persons speaking; expressively it is
making the sounds one has been taught to make. This way of
teaching is not marked by its success, as many compelling
reports are pointing out (e.g. Denmark 1973, Conrad 1979).
Yet various ways of using these procedures dominate American
education of the deaf. Users of the "pure oral" method insist
on postponing instruction in reading and writing until lip
reading and voice production have been in use for some time.
Proponents of the "natural method" do not teach language
either analytically or synthetically but as situations arise in

its use in a classroom of deaf pupils with a hearing, speaking teacher, not notably a natural environment. "The oral method" differs from these first two chiefly in that reading and writing instruction accompany instruction in lipreading and in making speech sounds. In theory, when any of these procedures is in use, there is nothing for the deaf child to see except for the lip and face movements of the teacher and other pupils. In fact, there is a wealth of information being presented to their eyes. Besides the inevitable gesticulation of the teacher (see Chapter 15), there are the teacher's other actions, the room itself, and all the objects in it, not to mention the activity of a handful or double handful of brighteyed children.

American educators of the deaf have gambled that all this and more information, of a linguistic kind, can be integrated and understood by means of spoken English taken in and interpreted from the visual inspection of a speaker's face. For a hearer and possibly for some profoundly deaf children spoken language (and all the nonverbal communication that surrounds it) does perform this function. Many readers will have had some interaction with a three or four year old hearing child and the spoken question "Why?" and the count-less repetitions and variations on the theme. The child is asking for spoken explanation or verification of what the child's mind is constructing. But oral methods of teaching a deaf child at the preschool stage concentrate on getting a few syllables produced and lipread; and even after the child is in school, the expectation holds that in one full year the average deaf child will have gained a lipreading and speaking vocabulary of fifty words—fifty against the average five year old's five thousand! One wonders what the three year old deaf child thus educated is creating with his or her mind to compare with the why-asker's (again see Chapter 7).

The question is whether a deaf child's eyes and mind are being put to anything like efficient use in any setting that excludes sign language. It is this question above all other considerations that has turned attention back to the sign languages used by deaf people. Sign, American Sign Language, is directly related to the language of signs used by the gen-erations of deaf people Épée and Sicard and their successors instructed in France. It is the language of deaf adults in North America and has been their language for more than a century and a half. It has been put to special uses recently by hearing

persons where speech will not work: in noisy locations, in
airless space, under water, and in communication with
chimpanzees and gorillas. It is also the language in which
most deaf persons who get a higher education acquire that
valuable prize—not that the hearing teachers or the deaf
teachers at Gallaudet College use ASL in formal instruction,
though the latter may indeed use it in intimate tutorial
sessions, but it is the language in which those highly
educated deaf persons interact with one another and into
which they translate anything of real importance (see
Chapter 13).

The nature of a    A sign language uses sight, as lip-
sign language.     reading speech also does, but uses
                   it in a special way. Sounds—vowels
and consonants along with differences in rate and intonation—
are the elements of language received by the normal ear.
What is "read" by a deaf person who has learned to do so
is the position changes of the lips, teeth, and tongue in the
act of producing sounds. But the elements of a sign language
are actions seen exactly as they are performed. They do not
divide air from the lungs into sounds contrasting as vowels
and consonants. The elements of a sign language are actions
that can be seen composed of two complementary but almost
simultaneous aspects: what's acting, and what it's doing.
One hand or both hands of a signer usually will be seen to
act, but at this point in the study of sign languages it is not
possible to say with certainty if the hands are major or minor
actors in sign language. A signer's eyes, face, head, shoulders,
trunk, and whole body also act to transmit sign language signals. It is certain, however, that when a hand acts or when
both hands act, the arms as well take part.
    Thus the first aspect, what acts, in a manual sign is
recognized by signers because of what two sets of muscles
have done. These muscles are (a) the distal muscles, which
can open and close the hand, can extend, bend, and clench
any finger, can spread or abduct two or more fingers; and (b)
the proximal muscles, which can flex, straighten, and bend
back the wrist, can bend or straighten the elbow, can rotate
the forearm bones and can rotate and swing the upper arm.
What these muscles are sensed to have done presents what
acts (although it may be necessary to stop the action by fast

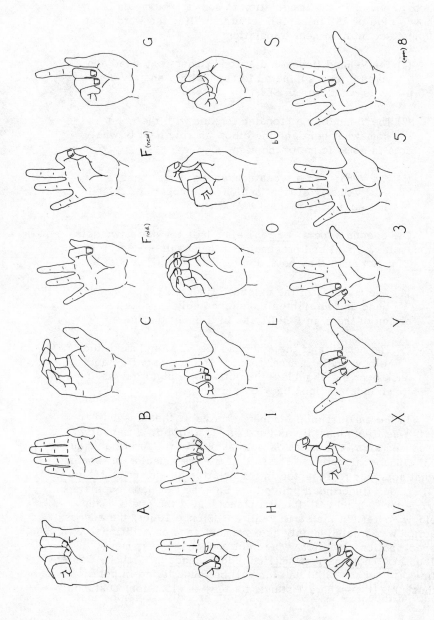

photography or in the imagination to see it). Examples below
show a sign of ASL in capital letters spelling the word most
signers accept as a near translation:

> (1) The V-hand (index and second fingers extended and
>     spread) on a supinated forearm with a sharply bent
> elbow is what acts in SEE;

> (2) The V-hand on a pronated forearm with the wrist
>     somewhat bent and the elbow sharply bent is what
> acts in some forms of the sign LOOK-AT;

> (3) The V-hand on a pronated forearm, wrist bent,
>     elbow nearly at right angles, and upper arm raised
> is what acts in (someone) WALKING.

The second aspect, action, also uses the same two sets
of muscles, distal and proximal; but under this aspect what they
are doing not what they have done makes the difference; e.g.

> (4) The muscles of the extended fingers of the V-hand
>     bend and straighten them repeatedly to make the
> action of the sign DOUBT, as in 'I doubt that';

> (5) The muscles of the arm bend the wrist and make the
>     elbow angle sharper to move the supinated V-hand
> back over the shoulder—the action of a sign that means
> 'reminisce' or 'look back on'.

In the earliest sign language analysis, the aspect what
acts was treated mainly as hand configuration in a manually
produced sign, and notation was taken from the American manual alphabet (Figure 1). The role of the arm muscles in forming
what acts was represented in the notation by subscripts (e.g.
$G_\wedge$ - index finger hand pointed up; $B_a$ - the flat hand supinated;
$\sqrt{Y}_v$ - the Y-hand with forearm pronated and the angle of the
elbow acute). In the same treatment (Stokoe 1960), the aspect
action was treated mainly as movement, and an additional
specification, location (where action focuses) was made.
Thus in A Dictionary of American Sign Language (Stokoe, Casterline, Croneberg 1965), a sign will be found listed in notation
thus: $TD_{\check{s}}^{s(s)}$ —where T stands for tab, the location; D stands

for what acts (but only as the hand configuration), with a
subscript to show what the arm muscles have done (sometimes called orientation but without reference to muscle
action); and ˢ stands for <u>sig</u>, the action—two sig symbols
on the same line indicate successive actions, one above
the other indicate actions performed simultaneously.

The two complementary aspects, what acts and action,
can thus be further analyzed—if activity is manual. A hand
that acts is distinguished by configuration (or handshape)
and by what the proximal muscles have done. (If the latter
is called "orientation," the analyst is caught in the problem
of relating the hand, the palm, a finger, which finger, etc.
to the signer's body, the addressee's view of the signer,
the three dimensions of space as seen by one or the other...)
When it is a hand or both hands that act, action can be
distinguished as motion and location. Hence, for manual
signs a dez symbol and a subscript provide notation for what
acts, and sig and tab symbols provide notation for action.
When current and future research establish precisely the role
of other than manual activity in sign language expression, it
will be sufficient to consider simply what acts (e.g. the nose)
and its action (e.g. wrinkles)

There is an epistemological and a biological basis for
looking at gestural signs under two aspects—and for avoiding
the loose, often misleading use of terminology and thinking
that applies to analysis of the sequential production of language sounds. Human vision of something acting can render
accurate information about the movement but requires the action
stopped before detailed information about what is acting can
be gained. The reason for this is that the retina of the eye
has cells of two kinds: those adapted to tracking movement,
and those adapted to resolving fine detail. Signers can tell
us the exact configuration and angle of a hand in a sign because they know the language and are able to produce that
sign; but watching either a live performance or a filmed or
videotaped record of signing does not present enough actual
visual information for any viewer to be certain about details
of configuration at any instant.

Just as vowels and consonants are assembled in some
orders but not in others to make syllables of English, the
elements of Sign combine to make signs: some forms of what

acts and some forms of action go together, others do not.
Signs are considered to "have meanings" just as words are,
but here some of the common misunderstandings about sign
languages have their beginning. The usual notion, fostered
by many English-to-Sign handbooks, is that a sign represents
a word of English with the same meaning, and conversely
that each English word "has a sign." The facts are different.
The study of languages as systems complete in themselves
has shown that no word for word translation of any language
into another will result in grammatical output. Among signers
a sign may have some of the meanings and uses of an English
word used to translate it but not others. Likewise, a word
may translate a sign as it occurs in some contexts but fail
completely to translate its meaning in other contexts. This
being so, the phrases and sentences of English and Sign
may be even more different in structure than the words and
signs of the two languages.

Here it is necessary to stop a moment and look more
closely at the notion of languages as systems "complete in
themselves." This idea is really a convenient fiction of
linguists. Far from being complete in themselves, languages
mingle with other systems at either end. At the meaning end, a
language connects to everything in the world that its users
do and say and think; at this end there is an interface between
language and the user's whole culture. At the other end, the
physical world of sights and sounds, the structures of language in order to get expressed must connect with some bodily
mechanism to produce an output that sight or hearing can
receive. For most of the human race, the primary output is
speech sound and the input sense is hearing. For the deaf,
a minority often estimated at about one one-thousandth of the
total population, the primary output is bodily activity, also
called gestural, gesticulational, motor, nonverbal, or mimic
activity.

The notion of languages as "systems complete in themselves" also fails to describe languages in real life in all
those instances when people, individually or in groups, use
more than one language. Both in the larger, social sphere
and inside the language habits of one individual, two or
more language systems can mingle with each other and so
lose their absolute completeness. The possibilities, however,
when one of the competing or combining languages is English
and the other is Sign are different from the situation when

both are spoken languages. Signing activity and speaking activity can in some respects be carried on at the same time. Of course when that happens, the signing is not at all likely to be the output of Sign as a language system. Instead, the signing speaker, or an interpreter shadowing the speaker, will be using signs as code substitutes for the words being spoken.

Much of what is called sign language, and indeed most of what is taught in so-called sign language courses, is this kind of signing; in such uses signs are not a language but a word encoding system. Nor is this a precise code like finger-spelling, in which one hand configuration and only one stands for one letter of the alphabet. In word-encoding signing there is no one-for-one matching, but some word-sign pairs are familiar to all the deaf and hearing people who use them, while other words of English do not have familiar and unique sign representatives. When saying one of these less familiar words, the speaker or interpreter may then fingerspell the spoken word or may perform some sign usually paired with a word somehow similar in meaning to the one spoken.

This way of using signs as an encoding device is the entry point for most people who learn signs to teach or work with or converse with deaf persons. It has the advantage of being easily learned—as an expressive medium— because the learner does not have a whole new language to learn. The sign-for-word code can be memorized in a fairly short time, and with practice it enables the learner to make normal spoken utterances visible to deaf persons who have a reasonably good command of English at the encoder's level, and who also have practice in using this double output system.

Like Morse telegraphy and fingerspelling, the process of encoding spoken words as signs allows its learner to gain skill and speed in transmitting before any receptive skill can be developed. Unfortunately, many hearing persons who have learned it thus never do learn to receive signing from deaf signers with facility. All this is quite characteristic of secondary language codes. Learning a true language works the other way around: the learner gains the ability to produce grammatical phrases and sentences in the language being learned only some considerable time after gaining the ability to receive and understand what its users are expressing.

The latter process, learning Sign as a language, follows
normal language learning patterns. Those hearing persons who
do succeed in learning how to sign in a way approaching that
of deaf native signers reach that level only after a long period
of watching and understanding signers. Deaf people also, who
move to a place where another sign language is in use, report
that they spend much time watching and trying to understand
what the others are signing before trying to make any sign
utterances of their own in that language. (See Chapter 5)
Moreover, interpreters, who very fluently encode the words
of a speaker they are listening to, find it very difficult and
anything but fluent to watch a signer and to put the Sign output into spoken English—the latter task is genuine translating,
the former is secondary encoding. Much of the difference in
difficulty for the simultaneous interpreter arises in this system
difference.

System differences.   When the two systems, English
                      and Sign, are considered, the
possibilities of difference in structure between something
that is said in standard English and the same idea expressed
in Sign have often been exaggerated and misrepresented
(Tervoort 1968). It is quite possible for an expression in ASL
to be exactly parallel to an expression in English, as we shall
see. It is also possible for the constructions in the two languages expressing the same idea to be quite different. This
has led some users of Sign as well as some of its detractors
to claim that Sign is "ungrammatical" or has "no syntactical
rules." Unfortunately this false notion, uncorrected by any
real knowledge about language, is repeated in many textbooks
used in training teachers of the deaf.
    The signs in a Sign sentence may occur in the same
order as the words in an English sentence, or they may occur
in different order. A Sign sentence may seem to omit signs
for words that are essential in the English sentence. Again,
the Sign sentence may have signs for which the English sentence shows no equivalent word. Sign language grammar has
its own rules as well as its own lexicon of signs with their
meanings; and the rules and lexicon of American Sign Language
differ from the rules and lexicon of English.
    Seen as a whole system, then, Sign is quite like English
or any other langauge. Its elements contrast with each other—

what acts and action in one sign with what acts and action in
another; but the contrast is visible not audible. The elements
combine in certain ways and not in others. These combinations, the signs, "have meaning" as words in other languages
do. Constructions combining signs, like constructions combining words, express meanings more competely and complexly
than can single signs or single words. These constructions
or syntactic structures are systematic, rule-governed structures.
There is a unique set of rules for making ASL constructions just
as there is another unique set of rules for making standard
English constructions, various non-standard English constructions, and the constructions of any language.

Before looking at the extreme differences that may occur
between Sign and English constructions, we will look more
fully into the possibility of similarity. One thing that makes
parallel constructions in the two languages possible is the
general agreement that many signs and words do form pairs
for practical purposes (which include contact between deaf
and hearing persons at least partly familiar with signs).
Another reason that constructions signed may duplicate the
order of constructions in English is really incidental to Sign
as a language. There is a third way for language to be directly
presented to sight, different both from the changing appearance
of a speaker's face and from the different elements of signs.
This third way is fingerspelling; it is usually closely associated with ASL by deaf signers in America, but it may also be
used as a way of encoding English or any language written
without using Sign at all (see Carmel 1975).

Fingerspelling works by virtue of the pre-existence of
alphabetic writing. There is some evidence that its use—
perhaps more for secret communication than for the needs of
deaf persons—is as old as the practice of scratching, carving,
and writing letters (Abernathy 1959, Stokoe 1974). When
fingerspelling is incorporated into signing, differences between
Sign and English grammar and vocabulary may grow less. Words
that have no counterpart in ASL, like the, a, an, of, and the
forms of be, are fingerspelled when the encoder wants to make
the manual expression follow English rules more closely.

Fingerspelling also serves as an important link between
the two languages for the bilingual American deaf person. New
signs are coined, and many old ones have been, by using the
manual alphabet "hand" as the configuration of what acts and

moving it in a sign-like action. Thus the first letter of the
borrowed English word becomes the configurational part of
what acts in the new sign. Signs for days of the week,
color names (except RED, WHITE, BLACK) are made this
way, as are personal name signs and other signs.

   To the linguist interested in grammar, English and Sign
may seem to differ enormously because of their different
transmission modes, but with the link fingerspelling gives,
the deaf American signer shifts from one to the other (i.e.
ASL and manually coded English) with ease. Two sociolinguistic distinctions need to be made, however. First,
the deaf signer who is seen sometimes to use a sign, sometimes to fingerspell an equivalent word is likely to have
reached a higher educational level than one who uses the
sign only. Second, there are many signs the forms of which
are derived from short frequently occurring English fingerspelled words, but these are not used by deaf persons in
their conversation with hearing persons. These and the very
interesting changes in form, meaning, and grammatical coding
they have undergone are described by Battison in Lexical
Borrowing in American Sign Language.

   The conditions, then, under which a Sign sentence will
preserve the order of an English sentence are: (a) the free
use of fingerspelling; (b) the signer's and the sign addressee's
competence in English; and (c) communication situations that
call for the use of English-like signing instead of ASL. Such
a situation may be the signed interpretation for a deaf audience of a formal lecture or may arise from the natural tact of
a deaf signer conversing with a hearing partner who knows
sign-encoded words but is unfamiliar with ASL structures. If
the communication situation does not call for this kind of
adjustment of the output to English-like structures, Sign
sentences may show a wide departure from the patterns of
standard English. Two examples of such divergence will be
examined in detail.

Surface similarity      The first example comes from
in Sign sentences.      one possible way of signing a
                        simple and basic sentence in
English: "He saw me." It is simple and basic because its
syntax may be described by a small number of explicit rules.
Leaving aside all explanation of meaning and the sound out-

put of the English original, we may use three rules and a
brief lexicon to generate this sentence's syntactic structure:

|     |                        | Lexicon |
| --- | ---------------------- | ------- |
| 1.  | S → NP + VP            |         |
| 2.  | NP → Pro               | Pro: he (1st time), |
| 3.  | VP → VT + NP           | me (2nd time) |
|     |                        | VT: saw |

Below is a diagram of the structure these rules generate and
the word string that results from replacing the symbols generated
by the rules with lexical entries:

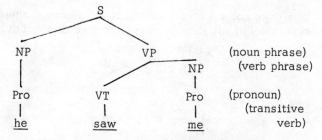

|        |                  |
| ------ | ---------------- |
| NP     | (noun phrase)    |
| VP     | (verb phrase)    |
| Pro    | (pronoun)        |
| VT     | (transitive verb)|

There should be no difficulty in reading this description by
rule and diagram in terms of usual parsing: Rule 1 describes
the structure as Subject followed by Predicate, and Rule 3
describes the predicate as Transitive Verb followed by Object.

The difficulty arises when the same sentence in Sign is
put beside the English sentence or the English-like way of
signing it. All that an observer will see is what manuals of
sign language call one sign, but the sign is not one to be
found in any of the manuals. The sign given for the meaning
'see' in sign language books is described something like this:
"The V-hand, held up so that the fingertips are near the eyes
of the signer, back of the hand outward, is moved away from
the face a short distance." But instead of this, a signer who
is expressing the meaning 'he saw me' in Sign holds the V-hand
pointing obliquely out at about shoulder level (forearm supine,
elbow near right angle, upper arm rotated outward), and while
looking at it, bends the wrist sharply so that the fingertips
point at the signer's own face.

Using the rules and diagram for this sentence, we are
forced to observe that two of the three symbols are not given
lexical entries:

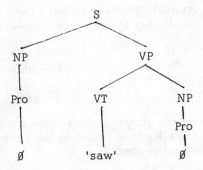

This does not seem very satisfactory, although there is a
sentence in English with something like this structure:

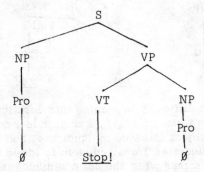

Speakers and hearers of English understand perfectly that
"Stop!" may be expanded as "You stop" or "Stop that" or "You
stop that"—any of which in fact may occur instead of the one
word form. Thus, all four of these English sentences have the
same underlying structure of the diagram, and all four share
the meaning command.

    In the case of "He saw me" spoken or written and its
signed translation (at the top of the page), the utterer and the
addressee understand: 'A masculine person, not either of us
(but whom we both could identify were it necessary), saw me.'
In the English version (or one fully fingerspelled), there are
two other bits of meaning given surface representation. Saw
has a form that indicates the seeing happened in the past; me
redundantly indicates what its position in the string also tells,
that it is the object. When an example like "He saw me" is

used in a discussion such as this, we must suppose that the
sentence was spoken in a situation in which the speaker and
hearer both can indicate and understand all the meaning of <u>he</u>
through glances of their eyes. (Just how much of this gesticulation or nonverbal communication is necessary for efficient
communication in speech is another subject.) If we turn from
speech to written English, we must suppose that the sentence
<u>He saw me</u> has been taken out of a sequence of sentences
that more or less exactly identify who <u>he</u> is. In the example
from Sign the same kinds of supposition are needed. Because
the Sign sentence translates into 'He saw me', the meaning
'past' must have come from some signed indication earlier in
the signed conversation or narrative that a past time is being
talked about. Although we can thus account for the element
'past' in the Sign sentence by the same explanation used to
account for the reference of <u>he</u> in the English sentence, the
problem remains, how does a signer make this one sign sentence mean 'He saw me'? The signer does so: (a) by a change
in the way of producing the sign SEE (which in uninflected
form also means 'I see' or 'seeing' in general); (b) by starting
the changed sign SEE with the signing hand held where it
would be held to make the sign meaning 'he' or 'him' or 'her';
and (c) by moving the signing hand's two extended and spread
apart fingers by wrist action to point toward the signer's self.
   To sum up this comparison, or more properly this contrast,
of Sign and English sentences more rules are needed. First,
for the English sentence, tense and object-marking can be
specified by rules:

      1.   S   →   NP + VP
      2.   NP  →   Pro (+ Obj, in context of VP)
      3.   VP  →   VT + NP
      4.   VT  →   V  + Past

The lexical choice and the form change in the verb are now
managed by rule instead of in the lexicon; thus, V becomes
<u>see</u>; Past is rewritten as a vowel change, <u>see</u> to <u>saw</u>; and
Pro becomes <u>he</u> (or <u>him</u> if obj) first time and I (or <u>me</u> if object)
second time. But the structure changes very little, as the
diagram on the next page shows.

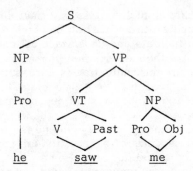

This is still a simple structure, but the one-sign sentence
in Sign is not exactly described by this tree diagram. To describe it requires more and different categories, as the next
diagram shows:

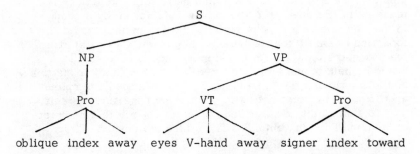

If these elements at the bottom of the diagram are put together
in a Sign way, the result is a three-sign sentence with the same
order as in the English sentence, but the one-sign sentence that
we have been considering can only be derived by transforming
this structure. The elements, or aspects, of a sign occur simultaneously, as can be shown by writing them vertically, with the
sign shown in capitals as a gloss below:

| oblique | near eyes | signer | |
| index | V-hand | index | ⇒ |
| away | away | toward | |
| | | | |
| HE | SEE | ME | |

The double arrow to the right indicates that a transformation

takes place at the sign formational level: the meanings of
each of the three signs are preserved, but after the transformation only the aspects shown below are visible:

$$
\Rightarrow \quad
\begin{array}{l}
\text{oblique} \\
\text{V-hand} \\
\text{toward}
\end{array}
$$

HE-SAW-ME

Other grammatical analyses of this sentence in ASL may
be made, but two points should be quite clear from the analysis
just made: (a) Sign has just as much regular grammatical structure as English; and (b) Sign sentences convey precisely as
much meaning to one who knows Sign as English sentences
convey to a native speaker of English. One point further: just
as such emphatic productions as HE saw me! and He saw ME!
and He SAW me! may have different meanings for speakers of
English, so the Sign sentence can be varied, especially with
head and eye movements and with modulations in the manner
of the hand's action (see Baker & Padden 1978, Klima & Bellugi
1979).

**Simultaneous major constituents in Sign sentences.** The second pair of sentences to be compared seems to show more complication of syntax on the English side. Grammarians who speak of generation of structures by rules and transformations would say that there is a base structure underlying the sentence There's a man in there and point out that a transformation of the base has made it what it is on the surface. They might write rules like the following to generate the base:

$$
\begin{array}{llllll}
1. & S   & \rightarrow & NP     & + & VP \\
2. & NP  & \rightarrow & Det    & + & N \\
3. & VP  & \rightarrow & Copula & + & Adv \\
4. & Adv & \rightarrow & Adv    & + & Adv \\
\end{array}
$$

These rules generate the structure shown in diagrammatic
form on the next page:

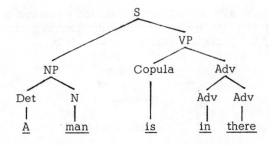

Various transformational rules have been proposed to derive a <u>there</u>-sentence from such a base as this. (Part of the educational value of this kind of grammar is the practice it gives the proposer of rules.) One proposal is to consider that there are two bases and that they are transformed by <u>embedding</u> one within the other. This requires the generation of another base: *<u>There's something</u> (The * marks the sentence as suppositious and non-appearing as surface expression.) Then the part represented by <u>something</u> is replaced by the whole original base structure. The rule for this transformation may be: <u>Something</u> ⇒ S. The diagram below shows the first stage in this embedding transformation:

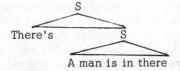

A deletion rule then effects the removal of the extra <u>is</u> to give: <u>There's a man in there</u>. The Sign sentence that "says" the same thing seems to be much simpler in structure. It uses only two signs, MAN and THERE (which is actually a pointing rather than a lexical sign). It has no determiner and no copula. Sign, like most of the world's languages, does not translate <u>be</u> overtly. In this sentence—which is one actually observed as the output of a signer in a specific situation—the sign that equates with the English adverb <u>there</u> means 'in there', because the signer was pointing to a closed door; the man referred to was not in sight. In English, <u>a man there</u> has to be translated as 'a man where you can see him too'. Thus the actual situation

in which it is used determines whether this sign means 'there'
or 'in there'. This is not an unusual way for a language and
its situational meanings to relate.

Despite the absence of articles and copula, despite its
having just two signs, the Sign equivalent of 'There's a man
in there' is a difficult structure to describe in current linguistic
terms. What makes it so is that the system of rules we have
been using specifies the order of the elements as well as the
nature of the elements (NP, Pro, or the words that replace them).
But in the Sign sentence both the signs composing it, its two
major constituents, appear at exactly the same time!

The rule, S → MAN + THERE, will not do, because any
rule of the form S → X + Y means that Y must follow X, must
appear later. Neither of the diagrams shown below can catch
the basic structure if they also specify time order first-second
by their left-to-right order:

Order has meaning in Sign of course as it has in all languages. The difference in ASL between YOU FORGOT and
FORGOT YOU may be just like the difference if these signs
are translated into English spoken words. Sign like English
has XY and YX as possible orders in its syntactical system,
but nothing in our normal or special conventions for writing
can show the third kind of order that only Sign normally uses. X Y
If we write the elements one above the other as in fractions— Y X
—the usual implication is that the upper element occurs
before the other. We might try what looks like a typist's
strikeover: X. But microscopic examination of this symbol
might show which key was struck first. Two signs performed
at the same time contain no clues to help one decide priority
in time. A speaker of English might cry out, "In there! In
there!" And a listener might respond: "What?" and get the
answer, "A man!" With only this much context to go on,
grammarians may argue that beneath all this excited talk lies
the English language competence of speaker and listener,
that this competence has quietly generated the base, a man
(is) in there, and that two deletion rules have operated to
produce the repeated first outcry.

Rules, however, of the usual deletion, substitution, combination, and permutation kind do not describe the Sign sentence

|         | MAN     |    | THERE |
|---------|---------|----|-------|
|         | MAN     | or | THERE |
|         | THERE   |    | MAN   |

The point is not that generative-transformational grammars are inadequate for Sign—"All grammars leak" is a common linguistic saying. No theorist of language has yet adequately described the way languages work inside their own systems, let alone the way they work socially, in human groupings. The point is instead that Sign, far from having no grammar, has such interesting structure and so unusual a system that it challenges all theories of grammar based only on spoken languages. The differences we have seen in just two pairs of sentences should warn us that everything we know about English, right or wrong, must be questioned all over again before we apply it to a sign language and what its users do with it.

   Equally important is the fact that languages are much easier to learn and use than to describe or explain. Every spoken language used (now or in the past) has been learned and learned quite thoroughly by every child, bright or normal or dull, that is born among its users—provided of course that the child can hear it being spoken. Children who cannot hear learn sign languages in the same way if given the chance. Moreover, the elements of a sign language can with exposure and use become clear and understandable to anyone who can see. The combinations of these elements—what acts, its action, and its location if it is as moveable as a hand—are signs that have meaning for all who use the particular language the signs belong to. Having meaning, these signs can also be used to translate English words—but to translate them no better or worse than the words of any language can translate the words of any other. The combinations of these signs are used by signers to make sentences in Sign. Signers or nonsigners also may use the signs and others to make a reasonable fac-simile of an English sentence. Therefore it is possible to encounter signing in which signs are arranged exactly as if they were words of a standard English sentence, but it is also possible to encounter signing mildly or wildly different from English yet still quite faithful to its own grammatical rules.

Social implications    In the preceding section we saw
of a sign language.    that the structure of Sign senten-
                       ces is sometimes like and some-
times unlike the structure of English sentences. Education of
the deaf is both like and unlike American education in general.
Of the latter William Labov has said, "...the fundamental
role of the school is to teach reading and writing of standard
English" (The Study of Non-Standard Dialects, 1969). But the
schools that Labov looks at in the aggregate play their roles
on the solid stage of language competence: a hearing child
in America comes to school after four or five years of very
intensive language learning and use. The child has the rules,
i.e. the competence, to generate and understand countless
sentences—which may be in standard English or in some non-
standard dialect of English. Others might put it somewhat
differently: the child has completely learned the sound subsystem by school age, is nearly done learning the inventory
of grammatical forms and combinations, but is only well
started on learning the whole semantic system of the language
spoken in his or her environment.

Most deaf children probably will not have learned any of
these subsystems of English. The school for the deaf child
undertakes to teach literacy of course, but it assumes an
additional role: to teach the child English so that it will be
the child's native language. But hearing children learn English
naturally; they do not have to be taught their native language
(see Chapter 9). Language formally taught is either a second
language or else something as unrelated to real language as
the can/may distinction drilled into every American boy with
negligible results.

What surprises linguists like Labov when they learn of
it and shocks compassionate teachers like Herbert Kohl (1966)
is that no school for the deaf uses a natural sign language to
perform either the role of teaching literacy or the role of
teaching English as a second language. Even in an era of
"total communication" the usual school for deaf children
allows a multitude of modes for expressing language structures—
speech, signs, fingerspelling, cues, etc.—but only when
"straight" or "correct" or "grammatical" English is the language
in which the structures are generated. It would take too much
time away from the study of sign language to go into the
language teaching methods in use and the various rationalizations

offered for not using Sign, which children of any degree of
hearing impairment can see and quickly learn.

One of the most important uses of language is in the
formation and preservation of social groups. The term group
can be given its widest range of meaning, for language has
critical functions in the intimate group of two persons (if
we disregard the possibility that the smallest group is one
person thinking), and language also has tremendous power
in the largest possible groups: e.g. Western Civilization,
The Free World, Socialist Peoples' Republics. If these last
seem too large and remote to be convincing, one has only to
recall the inclusive and divisive effect of just one word,
black, as used in American society in the sixties.

The most notable outward effect of Sign is to make deaf
persons using it immediately visible and visibly different.
Conversely, not using it hides the deaf person from detection
as different by a casual observer. An unreasonably high valu-
ation put upon this effect has worked along with outmoded
language and social theories to keep Sign out of schools.
Nevertheless, this fact remains: those who cannot hear must
use eyes instead of ears to receive language information,
and in this respect they are very different from hearing
persons.

Deaf people constitute a social group both by the difference
of not hearing and even more by the social working of language.
But this is grouping by separation from hearing, "normal,"
society; yet deaf people form groups as people of all kinds do,
and in large part this is by the operation of language. Having
a common language joins people by the strongest of bonds
(see Chapter 5).

Using sign language, however, does not make a single
and homogeneous group. Just as among users of any of the
world's languages, there are all kinds of subgroupings also
determined by language and its use. One of these subgroupings
is that made by age and language (see Chapter 3). Children,
teenagers, adults who use sign language are in far more
complete communication within these and smaller age groups
than across them. The case of infants is somewhat different,
as in any language community. The fortunate among the deaf
infants—from a language standpoint—have deaf parents and
perhaps deaf brothers and sisters with whom sign language
use puts them into perfectly natural communication at the

earliest possible age. Once the sign language user moves
out of infancy and joins a group of agemates using sign (and
those who do not acquire Sign in the family become signers
by joining such a group later), this user's language is that
of the age group and stays so for a lifetime (see Chapter 13).

Another kind of grouping by language, found among
speakers of all spoken languages, is typical of Sign users
too. Persons of the same age group sign alike, except that
those of the same sex sign more alike. Obviously there are
physiological causes, such as vocal tract size, for the
difference between men's and women's voices; but when the
focus is language, not speech, the differences in vocabulary,
grammatical structures selected, and every other part of the
system can be observed. Here the observer who comes new
to the sign language is at an advantage. One of the first
impressions will be of the difference between the signing of
men and of women, a difference that may also be attributed
ultimately to physiological difference in skeletal structure.
The reader may doubt that there is a similar difference to that
of men's and women's signing among the speakers of English
unless he or she has heard and noticed the difference in
speakers of other dialects.

A third kind of grouping, a more precisely interpersonal
relationship that language accomplishes, is done through
style levels. Martin Joos calls these levels "the five clocks"
in his book of the same name. As five clocks can be set to
tell different times, so the style levels of language can be
set, and are set, to tell different things of importance about
the relationship of speaker to listener. These levels Joos
names "intimate, casual, consultative, formal, and frozen."
Consultative is the central norm with opposite tendencies.
Consultative style joins two people through language use,
despite their differences, because as Joos says, "two heads
are better than one" for consulting about most subjects. The
vocabulary, structure, manner of production, and information
content of this style can be taken as standard for the language.
In casual style, the next less formal, the language used
implies 'we're friends', and therefore much information may
be left out that has to be in place in consultative style. Also
in casual style, slang is not only permitted but required. In
the other direction, formal style treats the addressee as if
he or she is not there—in fact the addressee is not able to

reply when addressed in formal style by virtue of being one
member of an audience to a lecture or of some other formal
group. All the connections must be clear in formal style and
every bit of information must be in place. Because interrup-
tions are not expected or allowed, "careful" is the obvious
characterization of formal style. Formal is the speaking style
of course that comes closest to written style of the kind that
gets published in formal works. Ironically, it is also the
kind of English style that is often taught to deaf children
despite its being one or two style levels away from what is
most appropriate.

Two levels away from consultative, intimate style comes
very close to being a contradiction to some familiar old
definitions of language, because it is a social vehicle, a
possession, shared only by those who know its special rules.
Intimate style is private language. Husbands and wives, to
take one kind of intimate group, have a special vocabulary
known only to one another. It includes pet names, as many
observers have noted, but it has other features as well; for
instance, a clearing of the throat or a grunt or a word that
would have no obvious meaning in other settings—things
like these have more force sometimes in an intimate group
than whole paragraphs of formal language could have.

Frozen style is the imaginative label Joos gives to the
style of (good) prose and poetry. He does not call it "literary"
perhaps because in casual or consultative exchanges we
sometimes take the word literary to mean artificial or artsy-
craftsy. Frozen may seem a chilly label for artistic language
until we think of how our standard of eating has improved
since the invention of frozen food processing. From his discussion of the level of frozen style, Joos launches into a
description of literature, its nature, uses, and production,
by actually creating some. This is also pertinent to the study
of sign language and is of the utmost importance to every
person who has contact with a deaf child.

Sign language is not written, but it has a literature.
Careful language characterizes formal style, but artistic
language, frozen style, has more than just care behind it.
Many peoples whose culture does not include writing have
songs, poems, dances, charms, histories, and liturgies that
use frozen language style. Sign language users too have
artistic forms of expression and themes to express in them.
Two of the most intensively developed forms are fortunately

accessible to non-signers. One is a union of Sign and modern
dance in which signs seem naturally—but really with consum-
mate artistry—to merge into the total movement of the dance.
As in any artistic movement many individuals have made con-
tributions to this art form, but much credit is due to the very
early inspiration of two deaf signers, Carolyn Bateman and
Colette Foley, and to their dance teacher Peter Wisher. The
second Sign art form widely visible is Theater of the Deaf.
To be seen on television and in national and international
tours as well as in local deaf communities, this also is a
natural-seeming development, from pantomime and from the
pioneering of the Gallaudet Dramatic Club in the fifties and
sixties. The "Director's Note" by Gilbert Eastman in the
playbill for the Gallaudet College Theater's production of
"Hands" in November of 1975 contains an excellent brief
history of this development of the art of theater.

All five of the styles that Joos describes, then, are also
found in the uses signers make of Sign, and recognizing them
has tremendous importance for the study of sign language.
First of course is the conviction that recognizing them brings:
if a sign language, say ASL, works intimately, casually,
consultatively, formally, and artistically, even as it unites
and divides its users by age and sex, and as its structures
come from its self-contained system—then surely it is a
language of the depth and social complexity that only natural
languages have and a language well worth study. Second,
when its "frozen style" embodies artistic achievements that
make (hearing) critics of drama and dance jump to their feet
in applauding, then parents and teachers of deaf children
need to realize that using signs in their own grammatical
systems does not cut off the heights of intellectual and artistic achievement but opens new ranges to be surmounted. And
third, for the study of sign language itself, the five styles
are indispensable instruments.
Elizabeth McCall attempted in 1965 to explain the syntax
of Sign in "A Generative Grammar of Sign." She writes phrase-
structure rules and transformational rules to generate some
sentences of sign language that she had observed in use.
One problem in this work is that the signs themselves, the
physical elements of signing behavior, are not described.
Instead the sentences collected are recorded as sequences

of English words used to translate the signs she observed.
The use of Joos' five clocks would have prevented a more
serious flaw. The signing was observed at picnics and other
social gatherings of deaf persons. Those signing to each
other were friends, fellow workers, immediate relatives, and
intimates of one another—as is learned from McCall's introduction and from the internal evidence of the sentences
themselves. It is a safe bet, then, if not a certainty, that
the signing observed was all on the casual and intimate
level, never even rising to the consultative; since persons
not on casual terms do not go to such gatherings with each
other, of if they do, as Joos points out, they stay on strangers'
footing for a few seconds at most—the time for a formal introduction and one response. Therefore, since the characteristics
of casual style are ellipsis and slang, and those of the intimate style are extraction (of information that the intimate
already knows) and jargon, any attempt to write the grammar
of ASL and its (partial) lexicon from the data collected is
bound to describe something quite different from the standard
(consultative or formal) language, the sign language that
might be used to advantage in schools.

Indeed, the first two rules of the McCall grammar show
more things left out (parentheses) than left in the base Sign
structures:

$$1. \quad S \to \{ \; {}^{G^1}_{(Adv_e)} + (NP) + Pred + (T) \; \}$$

$$2. \quad G \to \{ \; {}^{(Adv_e)}_{G_2} + G_1 \; \}$$

Using this same procedure would result in a much elided
or extracted English sentence structure. Suppose an overheard
conversation between husband and wife is transcribed by a
writer of fiction:

> "Dear?"
> "Engh?"
> "Checks."
> "N't goin' that way."

After much study, a panel of experts on English as it is spoken

---

[1] G, any gesture or sign used alone as complete utterance.

might translate the passage as follows (material in the parens
is supplied to show what has been left out because the person
spoken to already knows it):

'<u>Dear</u> (are you listening; I want to remind you of something)?'
'(throat sound for 'yes; I'm listening; what is it)?'
'(I'm almost out of blank) <u>checks</u> (as you know, and you
    also know I do the accounts tonight. Would you please
    stop at the bank on your way to work and pick up some
    for me)?'
'(I have to drive Charlie to the airport this morning, and
    I wo)<u>n't</u> (be) <u>going that way.</u>'

If we were to write rules to generate English sentences like
those utterances transcribed on the preceding page, with
parentheses to show what elements were left out, we might
possible get a generative grammar of (intimate) English much
like the first generative grammar of Sign.

Language and     Two other ranges that Martin Joos
the community.   relates to the range of five style levels
               are those of <u>scope</u> and <u>responsibility</u>.
A speaker or user of a language may be understood only by
persons in a small isolated locality, in a wider provincial
region, or anywhere the language is used. Scope widens then
from local to provincial to standard, but it narrows to conservative or all the way to puristic. Education and variety of
experience are usually the means of changing one's way of
using language to standard; but personal preference usually
accounts for later narrowing of scope, if it occurs. There is
frequent reference among Sign users to other signers' "home
signs" and much condescension in discussing these strictly
local and provincial manners of signing. Ironically, the
makers of handbooks and some teachers who teach signs to
hearing adults (since children are usually not permitted to
use them) miss the standard scope and take a conservative
or even puristic attitude. Their description of the "right way"
to make signs and put them together can depart in one direction from standard as home signers depart in the other. Of
course standard is not a matter of legislation but of currency.
When leaders of national organizations discuss standardization
of Sign in, e.g. the National Association of the Deaf or the

Jewish Deaf Association, they are not trying to halt the tides
of natural language change but only to recognize that there
are local, provincial, standard, conservative, and puristic
kinds of Sign, and to indicate that the signer who studies,
practices, and uses standard Sign is on surest ground.

The second range Joos treats is responsibility. Just as
in a person's way of speaking we detect character, so it is
in Sign use. The smooth operator, the promoter, the born
loser, the show-off, and all the other types that we instantly
associate with a particular way of using language are all to
be found in the signing community too. One does not have to
be a native signer or an expert in sign language to recognize
the general indications of character in sign language use.
This kind of language difference is what Joos calls responsibility. We judge it of course by the way a person talks,
looks, and acts, so that it is a language difference closely
linked to many other indications of character.

Bilingualism  The constant use of two languages—bi-
in Sign and   lingualism—may be looked at from either
English.       end of a sociolinguistic telescope. In the
                broad view, it is a complicated social and
political problem, with a linguistic center and a very explos-
ive potential when peoples of two language stocks must live
under one government. It is also, if looked at closely, a very
valuable skill of an individual person. The study of sign
language requires looking in both directions. The deaf population of the United States may suffer the same irritation,
frustration, even loss of basic rights and privileges suffered
by members of other minority language groups. The deaf
individual, however, faces a unique problem: one of the two
languages to be used is not oral —the full definition quoted in
part at the beginning of this paragraph reads: "Bilingualism
is the constant oral use of two languages."

The broad social aspect of bilingualism has many facets
when looked at worldwide. Canadian bilingualism involves
two languages of high prestige, and the rivalry of French,
British, and Canadian cultural values complicates the sociolinguistic situation. In other bilingual areas only one of the
languages may have the prestige of worldwide use, while the
other remains little known and perhaps is unwritten. In the
past, obviously, the world language would become the one

official language in such a situation, and the local language
would remain the tongue of the governed classes. In the
present world, however, it is possible to find the language
of the emerging nation made official, and the world language
reduced to secondary status.

These are but a few of the possibilities when languages
are in contact, but for the deaf the pattern is still most like
that of the colonial past. Sign language is not written, though
now it may be. Sign is little known, either to the general
public or to those whose professional study is language. Sign
is excluded from official school and religious instruction—
though it should be noted that several religious groups have
been and continue to be its strongest supporters. For the
deaf individual and population in other countries, the bilingual
situation can be even less advantageous. Colonialism, im-
perialism, and racism—words that occur as often now in hot
debate as in cool study—still summon up a social attitude
that can be discerned in much official policy regarding Sign,
ASL and other sign languages. Here, for example, are the
words of a British royal commission to examine "the place if
any of 'manual communication' in the education of deaf
children" (emphasis added):

> Clearly the major risks associated with the use of a
> combined method which includes signing would be
> eliminated if the signs were themselves chosen from
> a systematic language with normal grammatical
> structure. (Lewis 1968)

The chairman of this commission later amplified his remarks
in an address to teachers and others in Britain concerned
with teaching deaf children:

> Everybody knows what is commonly said about signing,
> that it may impede, may retard, the development of
> language. I think there is some misunderstanding about
> this, if I may give my personal opinion. The notion is
> that signing is more natural, that signing is easier than
> the mother tongue [whose?]. Up to a point this is true,
> but if signing is to be a means of educating the children,
> the question is whether it is in the hands of teachers
> who understand what they are doing and have the skill
> to put it into practice; and how far the signing itself is
> linguistic. (Lewis 1969)

The commonly held notion that "the mother tongue" is the sole repository of "normal grammatical structure" is a concept well known to anthropologists, who have called it ethnocentrism. When ethnocentrism is used to deny that some other language is systematic and to impute to some out-group who use that other language a deficiency of mental functioning, this notion comes periously near to racism. The study of the grammatical systems of sign languages as well as their semantic and symbolic or expressive systems is the best way to replace such ethnocentrism and linguistic chauvinism with useful knowledge. To begin, one may read with profit the essays "The Linguistic Community" and "Sign Language Dialects" by Carl Croneberg in A Dictionary of American Sign Language (1965, 1976). More recently, several articles by James C. Woodward appearing in the quarterly Sign Language Studies show how all of these subsystems of language relate to the special social dimensions of the Deaf community. (See also especially Chapters 1 and 12 below)

Social bilingualism is important to understanding education of deaf persons in America, but the bilingual development of the deaf individual is crucial (for an excellent case study of such development, see Chapter 7). In truth, a deaf person faces more than the classic bilingual dilemma. The member of a minority language group has the choice of staying monolingual and so staying a second or third class citizen, socially and economically. Or if that person tries to shift to the language of the dominant majority, he or she may either succeed and shut off all background contact and incur social and psychic costs, or fail and be rejected by the dominant group, with equally serious consequences. Ideally, of course, one should grow up where one can learn and use both the languages with about the same amount of time for each. But that is a situation hard to realize.

The person who cannot hear does not even have these hard choices. The chances are ten to one against growing up in a family using sign language naturally, and so the deaf child must come to school age without knowing any real use of spoken language or of standard (or provincial but community supported) sign language. Even with sign language learned at home or from association with older deaf children, the deaf person cannot receive any formal education in this language, because schools and teachers, if not parents, reject signing.

Instead, this person will be taught in school to make sounds and perhaps to lipread them, to recognize and write letters, and even in exceptional situations, to fingerspell. All of this activity has an English language basis of course, and it is designed to make this person into a monolingual user of English. Early resistance or failure on the person's part to function like a native speaker of English despite profound hearing loss consigns the person to worse than a depressed social and economic status. Dropping out early, either by volition or through the "reassessment of learning aptitudes" in repeated psychological testing, consigns the signer to sheltered institutions instead of school.

Fortunately the good sense and adjustment to reality on the part of many members of the signing linguistic minority exceeds that of well-meaning officialdom. None or very few of those whose native language is Sign suppose that a monolingual life in a sign-using deaf community is an open option; although there was a short-lived movement early in this century to set aside some of the Southwest Territory to form a deaf state, which would have made the language of signs its official language. While the authorities in school try to force deaf children to function as monolinguals in a vocal-symbol language, wiser heads in the deaf community strive for a maximally effective bilingualism. The higher the level of competence in reading and writing English the deaf signer can attain, the better his life chances in the bilingual situation. Acquired speech and lipreading skill are highly rewarding assets that no deaf person despises. The deaf person does object,though,to a formal educational program that concentrates on the two "oralist" skills alone at the expense of all learning else. All evidence shows that reasonable proficiency in speech and lipreading is attainable by very few profoundly deaf persons, while for most even a dozen years of full-time effort brings only frustration and non-success. The extent of this non-success is fully exposed by Dr. R. Conrad's recent book, The Deaf School Child (1979). Meanwhile, the language competence in English that could have been fostered through bilingual use of the deaf child's Sign competence has been lost.

From the point of view of one who cannot hear, bilingualism can be more a challenge than a dilemma. Direct personal communication with one's friends will naturally be in sign language; one does not have the same kind of relationship with foreigners, and all speakers of spoken languages will in a sense always

be foreign to those who must listen with eyes not ears. But
consultative and formal participation with others is almost
exclusively for the deaf person to be carried on in English,
the language of the general culture and the language that
affords the only way into that culture and all its benefits.
Therefore the person who cannot hear will learn just as much
English just as well as circumstances allow. Until now the
circumstances provided by formal education have been less
than optimal. The real issue is not oralism versus manual
communication, as much time has been wasted arguing; instead the issue is whether the true bilingual situation of
the deaf person—Sign and English is to be recognized.

The question to be faced by all who have a hand in
shaping the life circumstances of deaf persons is this: will
the deaf person reach maximum competence in English better
if forced into apparent monolingual use of English or if the
need for bilingual development is acknowledged and met?
This question is a somewhat different way of looking at the
old controversy: linguistics and sociolinguistics, that is,
provide a way of saying not "one language or the other"
but of saying "both." Linguistics as an anthropological science
begins from the view of language as central in total culture.
From that it follows that differences in the way people communicate, in the things that they do, and in their languages are
taken as data to be studied and not as deviation, error, deprivation, primitivism, or degeneracy (All of these have in the
long or recent past been invoked to explain the failure of the
society to enculturate deaf people). Sociolinguistic studies
have shown repeatedly that bilingualism, diglossia, and other
intimate combinations of languages in the individual and in
society are facts of life. From a sociolinguistic viewpoint the
bilingual competence of deaf persons may be compound or
complex; i.e. they may be more at home in Sign than in English
or may be better in English than in Sign (rarely) or may be
equally competent in both (also rarely). In contrast, the
psychological model behind much current educational policy
for deaf children treats deafness and the language of deaf
persons as a pathological condition to be treated clinically.

Fortunately, some teachers' practice is better than their
theory, but bad theory can corrupt practice. A teacher may
understand a complicated statement, an explanation, or a
request that a pupil presents entirely in Sign and may respond

appropriately. Yet this teacher is all too likely to tell an
observer that the pupil who has just communicated in Sign
"has no language"! What we are to understand from this
amazing statement requires careful explanation:

1. By "language" the teacher really means 'competence in English needed (a) to understand those
   sentences presented in the teacher's speech or
   in writing, and (b) to produce grammatical sentences in the pupil's own voice or writing.'
2. By "no language" the teacher means: '(a) the
   pupil's responses to written or spoken sentences
   are inappropriate or are lacking; (b) the pupil's
   production is not grammatical; or (c) both of
   these.'
3. By "has no language" the teacher implies that the
   pupil is as much out of place in his or her classroom as a two-year-old would be in third grade.
4. By using "language" as the token for 'correct
   English' and by not allowing "language" to stand
   for Sign, the teacher is guilty of falsely condem-
   ning the pupil to a subhuman, socially inferior
   status.
5. By the statement, the teacher is also unconsciously
   confessing and excusing failure—who could be
   blamed for not teaching anything to a child who
   "has no language"?

But such a teacher is still on the side of the angels. At least
the pupil's communication in Sign may be responded to and
understood adequately. What the teacher says and thinks
about "language" are the residue of teacher-education courses
and textbooks. That this teacher does not use Sign to address
the pupil and to help pupils learn English and literacy is in
most cases simply the policy of the school—to act counter to
such policy is as much as many teaching positions are worth.
Yet the study of sign language could free this teacher from
the fear and ignorance that equate all knowledge and thought
with a single language or dialect—from ethnocentrism.
   Unfortunately, the teacher who can understand the pupil's
Sign utterances is not typical nor even part of a substantial
minority. The usual teacher response to the first appearance

of a deaf child's signing is often such utter rejection that
signing is ever afterward hidden from teachers. This does
not keep the teachers from saying however that this pupil
"has no language." Sociolinguistics could at least inform
these teachers that even in a "one hundred percent American"
community there are other languages than English in use and
other varieties of English than the standard of the school.
Teachers and others in special education programs who will
become teachers of deaf children can find other benefits also
in the study of sign language and in the findings of linguists.

The greatest obstacle to successful second language
learning seems to be lack of opportunity. There must be a
great many persons, among them teachers, who would like to
know another language if only they could find someone to
teach it and use it with them. The good fortune of finding a
person one spends minutes or hours with every day to learn
from as a native speaker of an exotic language seems remote.
Nevertheless, most teachers of deaf children are blessed
with such riches to the point of embarrassment. An older deaf
pupil knows far more sign language (both vocabulary and
structure) than any hearing teacher is likely to imagine. The
pupil indeed has probably become extremely skillful in hiding
this knowledge because of the attitude of the school and its
teachers.

So, if a teacher of the deaf has a genuine desire to learn
Sign, the problem is not to find someone who knows it but to
persuade those who know it that using Sign is permissible and
will not be punished overtly or subtly. A pupil who is at a
loss and halting and inarticulate in English may be fluent,
imaginative, even eloquent in Sign. Of course one who resolves
to learn the pupil's language must first accept the fact that it
is a language, must remain undisturbed by its differences from
English, and must make the pupil-informant comfortable in the
new situation. In some cases it may be easier to find an informant not in the pupil-teacher relationship. Many teachers in
schools for the deaf can find a colleague (perhaps in the voca-
tional department), a dorm supervisor, or another staff member
easier to approach and to learn from. After all, learning the
pupils' language requires of a teacher a difficult reversal of
the normal roles, and some teachers may not be able to bend
enough to learn. There are many references in the writing of
deaf persons to the kind of response (often unconscious) from

hearing persons that effectively and finally checks their
attempts at speaking. The looks on the faces of those who
are standing near when they venture to produce their version
of hard-learned speech sounds are often mentioned in these
personal histories. Just as clearly, the deaf person is quick
to note the kind of effect his use of signs has elicited in a
strictly oral school environment. The classroom teacher who
is at least open to being convinced that sign language might
be studied has only to be attentive, sympathetic, and en-
couraging. But such an attitude may go directly against the
policy of the school and so needs to be carefully considered.

Classroom research     Once contact is made with a
and application.       willing informant-instructor and
                       a teacher is in a situation where
the study of sign language can begin, progress can be rapid.
Besides being in more direct communication with pupils, the
teacher who learns to sign and understand signing and to be
well disposed toward signs and signing can engage in research
of a directly applicable kind. Contrastive study of Sign and
English has barely begun as a formal linguistic activity, so
that any teacher with a classroom of deaf children is able to
anticipate the professional researcher. The first kind of contrast noted by everyone who encounters a new language is
contrasting vocabulary pairs. What is the sign for this word?
is a question asked hundreds of times by all who start out to
learn a sign language. But the kind of information this question
can produce has only very limited usefulness. If there were
really a definite answer each time this question is asked,
if there were to be exactly one sign and only one for each
English word, there would be no sign language—only a simple
one-for-one substitution code of signs to represent English
words.

A more effective way to study contrasts may be put like
this: If sign A and word Z each translates the other, what are
the differences in the way that the word and the sign can be
used? This question is open-ended. A complete answer asks
for a full description of both languages. Nevertheless, much
useful information can be discovered by asking it.

Take for example the word to and the sign TO: the third
word in "from Chicago to New York" is equivalent to the third
sign in FROM CHICAGO TO NEW-YORK. The sign here written

as TO is made by touching one index fingertip to the other.
However, in translating "He forgot to pay," no sign is used
for the third word; HE FORGET PAY is perfectly grammatical
standard Sign. It is also a Sign sentence that may be translated into English in various ways:

|  |  |
|---|---|
|  | * Him forget pay |
|  | * He forget paid |
| HE FORGET PAY | * He forgot pay |
|  | * He forgot paid |
|  | He forgot to pay |

The first is likely to occur when a hearing translator has an
open or hidden animosity toward sign language and all who
use it. The next three translations are more likely to occur
when the translator is more at home in Sign than in English—
the English native speaker in a billion or so patterns like this
one has never failed to hear, and to produce, a /tə/ or at
least a /t/ between the two verbs. The deaf translator may
never have heard this very low energy manifestation of spoken
English. The last translation, the only one in grammatical
English, is the translation made by a person seeing the Sign
sentence HE FORGET PAY in a context where past time has
been indicated and having the capability, from study of sign
language, to make a full translation out of one language into
the other.

　　To return for a moment to vocabulary study: the contrast
usually found between mutually translatable vocabulary items
can be broken into more detailed questions—to which the
teacher who studies sign language can apply answers at once.
One thing to look for is a one-to-two pairing. Some of the
signs in ASL need two words to translate them properly in
English; e.g. SEARCH (the cupped hand circles in front of
the signer's face) equates with English 'search for'. Conversely,
some words of English need two signs for their translation; e.g.
discuss goes into ASL signing as DISCUSS ABOUT.

　　No one has yet made a full study of these contrasting
sets of singles and doubles; consequently the teacher of deaf
children with a real interest in sign language is in a better
situation for studying them than are most graduate students in
linguistics. The teacher may also be the most important user of
this kind of research result, just as this teacher's pupils are in

line to receive the most benefit. Two-word to one sign and two-sign to one word pairings present obvious contrasts for anyone who is studying sign language; the bilingual deaf signer whose English proficiency is classed as "native" also finds these pairs clearly contrasting. But to deaf pupils in a classroom or doing homework, there is no such clear cut contrast between the patterns of one language and the patterns of the other. They will persist in writing "I searched the word in the dictionary" or "we discussed about Vietnam." Any experienced teacher of the deaf can list a great many more examples of mixups of these opposite kinds. The teacher who makes a study of sign language, however, will know how to take steps toward reducing the frequency of such pattern interferences and increasing the frequency of grammatical combinations that the pupils can produce. The algorithm here is a bilingual one; the teacher points out: "See here is the way that we sign it; but if we want to write or say it in English, we put in this word for these two signs (or we put in these two words for this sign)."

How much and how fast the English language production of pupils so taught will improve may be viewed optimistically or pessimistically, but there is evidence that simply having a teacher who knows and who makes known to the pupils that they are dealing with two languages not one will pay educational as well as social dividends. And something can be said in favor of actually having a teacher in two-way communication with the pupils. Another approach is to look for pairs of English words that occur in the same order in normal English usage but when translated may take the opposite order in Sign (e.g. plane reservation / RESERVATION PLANE). The same may be done for word pairs that cannot be separated in English but are used apart from each other in Sign translations, and vice versa.

Besides these syntactic contrasts, which are relatively easy to discover and deal with, there are other system differences between the two languages that need study. English has a unique tense system. Every finite verb in English must be marked for past tense or remain unmarked; sign language, however, does not use verb forms as indicators of time. Of course signers like everyone else must deal with time. Here too the classroom teacher is in a position to do front-line psycholinguistic research; e.g. How do children who use Sign deal with time while their understanding of time and sequence,

their concepts for dealing with time, and their language symbols for the concepts are developing? The work of Piaget on
children's growth in handling time, space, equivalence, proportion, and other matters is of use here, as is the application
of it Hans Furth has made in his studies of deaf school children.
Children must have reached a certain stage in cognitive development to treat such operations effectively in language, and Furth
has found that this stage occurs at about the same chronological
age whether the children are native hearer-speakers of English
or born deaf and so used to using gestural instead of vocal
signs for thought and communication.

To move from these syntactic contrasts to semantic differences, so common a matter as degree is treated in quite dissimilar ways in the two languages. The English speaker has
command of resources of paralanguage and kinesics shared
with other users of the same dialect. For instance, a speaker
can say "Good!" and use intonation and voice features and
facial expression and body gestures that will modify the effect
of the word spoken in several ways. But in addition to these
modifications, which are paralinguistic or "nonverbal", the
speaker usually has a wide range of words similar but slightly
different to choose among for slightly modified message. Instead
of good, the speaker might have said: fine, right, ok, excellent,
super, wonderful, first rate, etc. A different choice of word,
equally with the use of paralinguistic and kinesic modifications,
will alter the effect—it will also indicate style, scope, and
responsibility. Then, besides, all the users of English that
the speaker usually talks with are also in complete control
(although the control may be outside their awareness) of both
these scales of modification, the word choice and the nonverbal.
Like the speaker these others with the same language habits
know how to interpret the result of change along both ranges
at once; e.g. to decide whether "Wonderful" with lower than
normal voice pitch, falling intonation, and a grimace of resignation indicates a more or less negative reaction than "Good"
spoken with false heartiness, speeded-up tempo, clipped
resonance, and a frown.

In contrast with all of this is the sign language users'
communication of similar ranges of meaning. The first and
most striking difference is vocabulary size. Sign languages
generally have many semantic areas covered by what appears
to outsiders as a single sign; while the same or similar areas

of meaning are covered by a number of different words of
English. Everyone who first begins to study the communication
of persons using sign language notes with surprise the great
subtlety and precision of their interchanges. Sign language
has no need for large numbers of closely related separate
items of vocabulary, because one sign can be easily modified
to express many degrees of meaning. Sincerity, intensity,
interest, and other nuances are portions of meaning that a
signer can use modulations of action to build into the production of a single sign. The size, speed, tension, precision,
and duration of the actions involved in sign performance are
variable at will yet rule governed; and all are used and understood as message-bearing fractions of the visible signal. But
most of this is outside the awareness of sign users, just as
speakers need not think consciously about the tone of voice
or the gesticulations they are using as they speak.

What has just been hinted at—the different manners of
"making signs" and signs themselves—is certainly expressed
in the way that one uses in speaking of languages generally.
Looking at facial expressions, timing, size, and other features
of signing as variable elements of "making a sign" has already
proved useful as an alternative way of speaking of signing. A
particular facial expression or eye movement or tempo change
might not have occurred without a specific accompanying
manually made sign, but it still might have a definite grammatical
role in expressing meaning. In this case, the facial action or
manner of performance would be similar to a spoken language
grammatical feature, say the -s of English, which does not
occur except with a word, but which may make a noun plural
or may mark a non-past verb used with gender-marked subject.

The contrast between English and Sign vocabulary size
and function finds a rough analogy in two mechanics' tool-
boxes. One has a complete set of wrenches, each of a fixed
size to fit just one different size of bolt head or nut the mech-
anic expects to work with. The other has just one adjustable
wrench, which will open wide enough for the largest and can
be made to fit anything smaller. But this contrast of English
and Sign needs more study. In fact it would be best to treat
it as a hypothesis; the testing of its truth by observing sign
language and English in operation is research that any teacher
working with deaf pupils may undertake. Here too the opportunity to apply what one finds out is large. Those pupils who

are adept at conveying to each other finely shaded meanings
have real semantic skills and may prove to be apt learners,
if they are shown how to put the same message
in standard English. This can be done once the teacher
has worked out the full details of the contrasting patterns. For
the teacher engaged in this contrastive study there are several
accessible materials in the classroom: what the pupils are
saying to each other is by all odds the most interesting of all
possible material to them. What the lesson is about, what
Dick said to Jane, what the teacher is trying to say—these
things do not come near in pupil interest to what the pupils
are signing to each other. One real objective of the study of
sign language is the ultimate ability of the teacher to take
part in the real, intimate, vital communication of deaf children, and after that to impart to them all the knowledge and
experience and understanding that a teacher has to contribute,
and to show the pupils that what they have to say and know
how to say in Sign may be put into English that is appropriate
also to their messages.

Interesting as sign language is as a system, tantalizingly
like other languages and fascinatingly different, the real value
to be found in the study of sign language is a human, not an
abstract scientific value. Every language is unique, but the
study of sign languages reveals that language is both abstract,
independent of speech and of gestural expression, and biologically concrete because of its expression. Language depends
on the human brain, not on the naked or the electronically
assisted human ear.

Abernathy, Edward R.
    1950    An Historical Sketch of the Manual Alphabet,
            American Annals of the Deaf 104, 232-240.

Baker, Charlotte L., & Carol A. Padden
    1978    Focusing on the Non-Manual Components of ASL,
            in Understanding Language through Sign Language
            Research, Siple ed. (New York, Academic), 27-57.

Battison, Robbin M.
    1978    Lexical Borrowing in American Sign Language
            (Silver Spring, MD, Linstok Press).

Carmel, Simon J.
    1975    International Hand Alphabet Charts (Rockville, MD,
            Author).

Conrad, R.
    1979    The Deaf School Child (London & New York, Harper).

Croneberg, Carl G.
    1965    Appendix C, Appendix D, in A Dictionary of ASL,
   [1976]   Stokoe et al. eds. (Washington, Gallaudet College
            Press; revised 1976: Silver Spring, MD, Linstok
            Press), 297-319.

Denmark, John C.
    1973    in Hearing (Royal National Institute for the Deaf)
            28.9, 284-293.

Denton, David M.
    1972    A Rationale for Total Communication, in Psycho-
            linguistics & Total Communication: The State of the
            Art, O'Rourke ed. (Washington, American Annals of
            the Deaf), 53-61.

Furth, Hans
    1966    Thinking without Language: Psychological Implications
            of Deafness (New York, The Free Press).

Garnett, Christopher B.
    1968    The Exchange of Letters between Samuel Heinicke and
            the Abbé Charles Michel de l'Épée (NY, Vantage).

Joos, Martin
    1967    The Five Clocks (New York, Harcourt Brace).

Klima, Edward, & Ursula Bellugi
    1979    The Signs of Language (Cambridge, MA, Harvard).

Kohl, Herbert R.
    1966    Language and Education of the Deaf (New York,
            Center for Urban Education).

Labov, William
    1969    The Study of Non-Standard Dialects (Washington,
            Center for Applied Linguistics).

Lewis, M. M.
    1968    The Education of Deaf Children (London, Her
            Majesty's Stationery Office).
    1969    Speech at the RNID Conference, Hearing 24.4, 102.

McCall, Elizabeth
    1965    A Generative Grammar of Sign. Unpublished M. A.
            thesis, University of Iowa.

Seigel, Jules Paul
    1969    The Enlightenment and the Evolution of a Language
            of Signs in France and England, Journal of the
            History of Ideas 30, 96-118.

Stokoe, William C.
    1960    Sign Language Structure, Studies in Linguistics:
   [1978]   Occasional Papers, 8; revised 1978 (Silver Spring,
            MD, Linstok Press)
    1974    The Classification and Description of Sign Languages,
            in Current Trends in Linguistics, Sebeok ed. (The Hague,
            Mouton), vol. 12.1, 345-371.

- - - - -, Dorothy S. Casterline, & Carl G. Croneberg
    1965    A Dictionary of ASL on Linguistic Principles (Wash-
   [1976]   ington, Gallaudet College Press; rev. Linstok Press).

Tervoort, Bernard M.
    1968    You Me Downtown Movie Fun?, Lingua 21, 455-465.

PART ONE

# WHAT IS SIGN LANGUAGE?

More than three-quarters of the way through the
twentieth century it has become almost impossible to be
educated and yet to hold opinions of the kind that were
prevalent in print and in lecture halls as late as the
1950's. Sign language is not a way like writing to represent English or another spoken language for the eyes,
although sign language elements can be so used. Sign
language is not a simple multiplication of the kinesic or
gesticulational behavior by means of which speakers of
all languages supplement their vocal utterance with
emblems, batons, illustrators, pointers, emphasizers,
and other "nonverbal" activity. Sign language is not a
universal language with rules of grammar and a lexicon
instantly and without learning available to anyone so un-
fortunate as to be in a situation where no spoken language
will work. And most emphatically sign language is not a
grammarless collection of vague, approximate, yet concrete
symbols used by persons lacking in the power of abstract
thought or other cognitive skill.

All these baseless charges have until recently been
leveled at sign languages used by deaf people. None are
worth detailed rebuttal; instead, the reader will find in the
next six chapters that the authors have much more interesting
information to impart than that slanders of sign language and
its users stem from ignorance at best or from a vested interest
in maintaining a profitable monopoly on hearing and speech.

53

A brief introduction to Part One has already been sketched
in the Preface, but the question that this part addresses is so
large that some further indication of its scope may be helpful.
The six chapters range from the specific sociolinguistic process
called pidginization to the general linguistic and semiotic
nature of encoding information into sense-perceptible output
(Chapters 1 and 2); from the age-specific variety of American
Sign Language (ASL) that children and young people use to
the human universals of wit and humor in (here signed) language
expression (Chapters 3 and 4); and from the realities of sign
language differences across political and cultural boundaries
to the detailed grammar of part of the ASL verb system (Chapters
5 and 6).

PART ONE: 1

# PIDGIN SIGN LANGUAGES

James Woodward
Harry Markowicz

Introduction. The study of pidgin and creole languages
has offered many insights into the nature
of language, especially language as an observably dynamic
phenomenon. Like most linguistic studies, studies of pidgins
and creoles have concentrated on spoken language codes, but
because the transmission channel used directly influences
the surface form of the language output, natural gestural language codes, which are not dependent on vocal language codes,
have expanded our knowledge of the nature of language. Pidgin
sign languages can also serve as ideal testing grounds for
the ideas of universality and uniqueness in languages, because
code structures of such pidgins are relatively unexplored and
because the diverse channels of the languages that are pidgin-
ized heavily influence surface code structure, especially in
the phonological component.

This paper will concentrate on one pidgin sign language,
Pidgin Sign English (PSE) to discuss: (a) an overview of the
language situation in the Deaf community; (b) sociolinguistic
reasons for the existence of PSE, including social functions
of and attitudes toward PSE in the U.S. Deaf community; (c)
linguistic characteristics of PSE, especially suprasegmental
features; and (d) the relationship of these matters to a dynamic
theory of pidgin and creole languages.

---

1
    Revision of a paper (Some Handy New Ideas on Pidgins &
Creoles) presented at the January 1975 International Conference
on Pidgin & Creole Languages, Honolulu. Support from National
Science Foundation Grant SOC 74-4724 is gratefully acknowledged.

The Language Situation
in the U.S. Deaf Community

Sign language        Language is a cohesive force in a deaf
diglossia.           community as in most communities, but
                     the language situation in the U.S. Deaf
community is similar in many ways to a special language situation called "diglossia." Stokoe (1970) first wrote of diglossia
in the Deaf community. Using Ferguson's classic paper (1959)
as model, Stokoe defined the public or H variety of signed
language in use as Manually Coded English (MCE), and the
domestic or L variety as American Sign Language (ASL). MCE
used with or without a spoken or voiceless show of speaking
is a combination of manual signs and fingerspelling intended
to represent spoken English word for word; e.g.

> (1)  I went  TO  the  STORE (signs in CAPS, fin-
>                              gerspelled words ex-
>                              panded)

If all the words in (1) had been fingerspelled, as they might
have been, the result would be what is known as the Rochester Method or sometimes as Manual English. ASL, however,
is a language in and of itself. ASL has a different grammatical
structure from that of English. For example, the English question, "Have you been to California?" (composed of Auxiliary,
Subject, Verb, Locational prepositional phrase), is translated
into ASL as,

                                        QUESTION
> (2)   TOUCH FINISH CALIFORNIA  YOU

(composed of Verb, Auxiliary, Locational noun, and in last
place, Subject and Question simultaneously presented).
    In the article cited (Stokoe 1970) MCE and ASL are
seen to pattern sociolinguistically like the H and L varieties
respectively of a language in a diglossia. H is used in more
formal situations and with more formal topics and participants. L is used in less formal situations. H is generally
felt to be superior to L by the users, and some will claim that
L does not exist; i.e. they will tell outsiders that L is not a
language or is a "broken" language or a "short" language. L

is generally acquired in the home, H in the formal educational
system. H is generally studied in school as part of the curric-
ulum; L is not. Much formal grammatical description has been
made of H (English), but usually not much research has been
done on L (this is especially true in the case of signed varieties). Some signers feel that standardization is necessary,
but sign language diglossia appears as stable as other diglossic situations.

One major difference between diglossia in the U.S.
Deaf community and other instances of diglossia is the manner
in which the language varieties are acquired. In typical diglossic situations L is learned at home from parents and sib-
lings and H is learned later in school. But fewer than ten per
cent of deaf children have deaf parents to learn signing from,
so that the typical pattern is not followed. However, if we
consider that the home is the initial locus of enculturation
for hearing children, while the residential school has served
as the initial locus of enculturation for many deaf children of
hearing parents, this difference is seen to have a sociolinguistic explanation. We can now say that L generally is learned
in the initial locus of enculturation. The deaf children of
hearing parents learn ASL from their peer-group deaf children
who do have deaf parents or from older deaf children already
enculturated into the Deaf community. The acquisition of ASL
takes place always in informal situations. English (spoken or
written) is learned so far as it is learned in formal classrooms,
and MCE may be used there, but more often it too is excluded
from the formal educational setting, at least in the earlier grades.

This diglossic situation is not the typical diglossia, for
the language varieties H and L described by Ferguson (1959) are
varieties of one language. However, Fishman (1967) extended
the definition of diglossia to include the situation in bilingual
communities. Fishman pointed out that it is possible to have
diglossia with bilingualism, diglossia without bilingualism,
bilingualism without diglossia, and neither bilingualism nor
diglossia. The relationship between ASL and English is thus
diglossia with bilingualism—as is the case with Guarani and
Spanish in Paraguay (Fishman 1967).

More recently several researchers have added to the
definition of diglossia by pointing out how H may be determined
in a community and by the notion of a language continuum.
Meadow (1972) and Stokoe (1973) showed that for some signers

a formal variety of ASL may serve as H. While we have no
exact knowledge of which groups of deaf signers use a form
or variety of ASL in formal situations, we can hypothesize
that the members of them are probably deaf themselves, have
deaf parents, and learned signs before the age of six (or
that their closest associates have these characteristics).
Woodward (1973a,b,c, 1974) has shown that these variables
predict which signers function nearest to "pure" ASL in informal situations.

It is also possible that some signers use special
varieties of manually represented English for informal conversations. This would probably be true of those signers who
function primarily near the English end of the diglossic continuum, as will be explained.

The Sign-to-English       The notion of a language con-
continuum.                tinuum in the Deaf community
                          was first pointed out by Wood-
ward (1972). Varieties of ASL were seen to be at one end of
this continuum—which as Stokoe (1973) suggests, probably
is multidimensional; with varieties of Manually Coded English
at the other. Woodward (1973d) also demonstrated that intermediate varieties along this continuum had the linguistic and
sociological characteristics of a pidgin language and called
these varieties Pidgin Sign English (PSE). Battison, Markowicz, and Woodward (1973) and Woodward (1973a,b,c,d,
1974) have shown that variation along this continuum is non-
discrete, but regular, rule-governed, and describable in
terms of modified scalogram analysis (Guttman 1944, Bailey
1974, Bickerton 1972) as well as by use of variable rules
(Fasold 1970, Labov 1969). The variation in language choices
made by ASL signers also correlates with gross social variables: whether a person is deaf, has deaf parents, learned
signing before the age of six, and attended college (Woodward
1973a).

Sociolinguistic Background of Pidgin Sign English

The Deaf          Formation of a Deaf community, a special
subculture.       subculture, resulted largely from two pat-
                  terns of behavior, the attendance of deaf
children in special residential schools, and the use of sign
language by these children (Croneberg in Stokoe et al. 1965

[1976]: 297-312). Barth (1969) suggests that ethnic groups
should be viewed as a form of social organization, in which
membership is determined both by self-identification and by
identification by others. Residential schools for the deaf
provide the environment in which most deaf children "begin
to develop feelings of identity with the deaf group and to
acquire the group attitudes which tend to set them apart"
(Lunde, in Stokoe 1960 [1978:22]). After leaving school, the
deaf person continues to associate socially with other deaf
persons, both informally and through formal organizations
(Schein 1968, Stokoe, Bernard, & Padden below pp. 295-317).
        Barth states that ethnic group boundaries specify
patterns of behavior and social relations within a group as
well as between interacting groups. Membership in the same
ethnic group "implies a sharing of criteria for evaluation and
judgment" (Barth 1969: 15). On the other hand, for individuals on opposite sides of an ethnic group boundary there exist
different criteria for judging values and performance, and
interaction is restricted to common areas of understanding
and interest. Restricted ability to communicate with hearing
people thus accounts only partially for the fact that deaf
people prefer the company of other members of the Deaf community to that of outsiders, as hearing persons almost in-
variably are. Membership in the Deaf subculture is not strictly
limited to the deaf, because it includes hard of hearing persons
and hearing children of deaf parents (Furth 1963), at least
until outside forces enculturate them as hearing (Nash & Nash
1978). In these cases it is clear that inability to communicate
with hearing persons is not the principal criterion for membership in the Deaf community.
        With regard to the claim that deaf signers constitute
an ethnic group, Meadow states:

> The group definition is strengthened further with the
> knowledge that deaf persons are characterized by
> endogamous marital patterns. In the survey of the
> deaf population of New York State, for example, it
> was found that only 5 per cent of women born deaf,
> and about 9 per cent of women who became deaf at
> an early age, were married to hearing men.
> (Meadow 1972: 20)

It should be pointed out that not all the women in the survey
cited by Meadow were necessarily members of the Deaf

community, so that the percentages for marriage across the
ethnic boundary may actually be even smaller.

The first school for deaf persons to survive and set a
pattern for residential schools was established with Thomas
H. Gallaudet as its head, in Hartford, Connecticut. Laurent
Clerc, a deaf native of France who had been highly educated
by Sicard and taught in the original National Institute in Paris,
became the first teacher in the Connecticut school. There, as
well as in similar schools which soon began operating in other
states (most of them with Clerc's aid and advice), a variety of
sign language served as the medium of instruction. [Harlan
Lane, in an address at Gallaudet College on 19 February 1980,
identified Clerc's variety as the methodical signs of Sicard
and Épée—a kind of manually coded French—modified so that
it did the like for English.] The language of signs and these
schools flourished "to the point where a national college for
the deaf was deemed necessary and established by Act of
Congress in 1864 for the higher education of the graduates of
these schools" (Stokoe 1960 [1978: 9]).

Functions of language     ASL has served three primary
in the Deaf community.     purposes in the Deaf com-
                           munity: (a) communication
on the interpersonal level, (b) socialization of the individual
into the Deaf subculture, and (c) identification of members
of the subculture. In all three functions, ASL acts as a powerful cohesive force in the Deaf community (Croneberg op. cit.,
Meadow 1972, von der Lieth 1978).

The Deaf, in many national communities, flourished
in the 19th century; however, in 1880 an international conference of teachers of the deaf meeting in Milan passed the
following resolution:

The Congress, considering the incontestable superiority of speech over signing in restoring the deaf
mute to society, and in giving him a more perfect
knowledge of language, declares that the oral method
ought to be preferred to that of signs for the education and instruction of the deaf and dumb. (Quoted
by Denmark 1973: 285, emphasis added)

As a result, sign language in the schools was abandoned in
the U.S. as well as in European schools, and the oral method
of instruction replaced it. Nevertheless, ASL in some variety

has continued to be used by pupils of American schools, but
until recently not "in school"—thus ASL for a long time has
been an "underground" language.

Cokely and Gawlik (See Chapter 3)   show that the
language of deaf school children differs, in some regular ways,
from that of the adults in the Deaf community, perhaps because
of the limited contact between the age groups. With the exception of a very small number of deaf teachers of deaf children,
deaf children of deaf parents are the only cultural brokers between the adults and children in the community. Upon leaving
school the young deaf person joins the adults in the subculture, adopting then the community's linguistic standards. ASL
has continuously remained the language of the Deaf community
where its use cannot be ruled or legislated against by outsiders.

The acquisition of a spoken language by a person who
is born profoundly deaf presents difficulties of such magni-
tude that only a small minority has been found to have achieved
competence in English as demonstrated by writing (Furth 1966).
Among deaf persons competence in written English ranges from
the totally incomprehensible to (for a few) fully native skill.
With few exceptions, English remains a foreign language for
a deaf person.

Interaction between the Deaf              Members of
and English-speaking communities.  of the Deaf
                                                          community
tend to associate socially within their own ethnic group. On
the other hand, they have formal relations with those outside
the group; e.g. parents, teachers, doctors, speech therapists,
counselors, psychologists, religious workers, and employers.
In spite of the fact that the deaf person feels a complete and
competent member inside the community, in encounters with
outsiders he or she may be treated as a pathological individual.
Membership in a minority culture is ignored, nor does the outsider know of the existence of that culture with its own rich
language. Instead the deaf person outside the community is
viewed as a defective hearing person.

Unfortunately for deaf persons, their schools are controlled by hearing outsiders. The school opposition to ASL may
find some of its basis in the empirical tradition, with its contemporary manifestation in behaviorism, which equates vocal

(miscalled "verbal") language with thinking (Markowicz 1972).
A psychological explanation has been suggested by Vernon
(1972), who bases the rejection of ASL by hearers on the inherent linking of signing with nonverbal communication,
because signing makes the signer's deep feelings, of aggres-
sion, sexuality, etc., more apparent in social intercourse
than does speaking. The imposition of English at any price
on the deaf child and adult can also be seen as an attempt to
impose the cultural values of the dominant majority on the
members of a minority group.

Development of PSE.    Pidgin Sign English has devel-
                      oped as a result of this cultural
clash. Communication is necessary for the interaction that
necessarily takes place between deaf people and those
hearing people who come into contact with them through the
professional activity of the latter. This situation is remini-
niscent of the commercial relation between Europeans and
natives of other lands. According to Barth (1969), the interaction between members of different ethnic groups is so
structured as to retain the boundary that separates them.
To maintain the integrity of the deaf subculture as well as
that of the dominant hearing culture, two rules promote the
use of PSE as the medium of communication between deaf and
hearing people: (a) within the Deaf community sign language
diglossia accounts for the use of the H variety, i.e. PSE,
as the correct form  with outsiders; and (b) the dominant
culture requires the use of its own language (or an approximation if the real thing is not feasible) in order to maintain
its dominance.
        PSE may be learned at almost any age by a deaf per-
son, but there are social restrictions on who learns PSE at
what time of life. Although fewer than 10 per cent of the deaf
population has deaf parents, only a tiny proportion of the
deaf parents are highly educated and competent at a native
or near native level in English. In this tiny minority, PSE
may be learned along with ASL from infancy (see Williams,
Chapter 7, Pt. Two). In this situation, PSE may be incipiently
a creole language; i.e. what a pidgin often becomes when
passed on from one generation to another. For the majority
of deaf children of deaf parents, however, it is more likely
that PSE will be a second language, learned from interaction

with hearing people and educated deaf people in formal, i.e. English-mediated, situations.

Until recently the majority of deaf children of hearing parents were not formally exposed to any variety of signing until high school age. It was believed by those in charge of their education that signing in any variety would inhibit the development of speech production; all research studies, however, show the opposite (e.g. Stuckless & Birch 1966, Meadow 1966, Moores 1972). Deaf children of hearing parents picked up ASL from deaf children of deaf parents, because ASL is preferred for informal conversations and children, by definition, have informal conversations. PSE was then later learned in some high school classrooms. Thus until recently, for the majority of deaf persons, PSE has been a second language, as is normally the case with a pidgin.

At the present time, the use of PSE is generally limited to formal occasions. For most deaf people signing in PSE only remotely approaches the H variety on the diglossic continuum described by Stokoe (1970) and Woodward (1972). As the signing approaches PSE, the grammatical features of ASL are replaced by such English features as grammatical markers and word order. The loss of ASL features sometimes decreases redundancy in the system without any compensation from the introduction of spoken language features. For example, the loss of suprasegmentals, which in ASL are expressed by facial expression and body movement, cannot be replaced by English suprasegmentals such as intonation, stress, and accent. PSE is no doubt sufficiently complex for communicative purposes, but it lacks the integrative and expressive functions of a natural language (Smith 1972). The deaf choose ASL over PSE as a vernacular language despite the low status of ASL in educational circles.

It is sometimes claimed that PSE allows the deaf person to acquire English in a normal manner. This is like claiming that knowledge of a spoken English-based pidgin is equivalent to competence in standard English. What the Deaf community members classify as PSE when signing among themselves often remains somewhat incomprehensible to hearing signers fluent in the H variety (MCE) of signing. Transcripts of signers conversing in PSE make clear that whatever their competence in ASL it is not competence in standard English.

## Some Linguistic Characteristics of PSE

This section will present some grammatical and formational (phonological) characteristics of PSE. Because of the comparative recency of linguistic interest in PSE (since 1973), the account cannot be complete, but reductions and hybridizations that characterize many pidgin languages have been noted in PSE. Because of the wide variation already observed in PSE and because of the complex nature of the Sign-to-English diglossic and bilingual continuum of which PSE is a part, many of the linguistic characteristics are here stated in terms of relative tendencies (i.e. not that so and so is true of PSE and not of ASL, but that it seems to be more often in one than the other). The appearance of these tendencies have been found to correlate with social variables in the case of those grammatical characteristics that have been studied in some depth; i.e. verb reduplication, negative incorporation, and agent-beneficiary directionality. It is probable that the other constructions discussed are also implicationally ordered and correlated with social variables.

It should be remembered that PSE comes from two quite different languages—ASL, a language channeled through the gestural-visual modality, and English, a language channeled through the vocal-auditory modality. Deaf signers who learned signs before the age of six and especially those who have deaf parents, come from ASL backgrounds. Those signers will retain more ASL structure in their PSE. Hearing signers approach PSE usually with an exclusively English base; but because PSE is channeled through the gestural-visual modality like ASL, hearing signers cannot carry as much of their native language into PSE, since linguistic information (especially formation of units, phonology) from a vocal language cannot be directly carried by a gestural-visual channel. As a result, the hearing person's PSE suffers much more reduction in structure than does the deaf person's PSE. There is about the same amount of reduction of English structure and admixture for both hearing and deaf signers' PSE; however, deaf PSE signing includes much more ASL redundancy than does hearing PSE signing. In fact hearing signers of PSE may in acquiring PSE learn none of the manual and other than manual activity that gives ASL its normal language redundancy.

Grammmatical characteristics of       In ASL the progressive
PSE: a. Progressive aspect.           aspect is represented
                                      by reduplication in the
sign verb—all or part of the action of the sign is repeated; see
Fischer & Gough below, Chapter 6.      Verb reduplication in
varieties of signing along the Sign-to-English continuum is
ordered implicationally; i.e. the presence of one reduplicating
verb regularly implies the presence of one or more others or
of none in a signer's language, depending on which verb it
is (Woodward 1973b). Table 1 shows the implicational relationship of nine ASL verbs in six lects (patterns into which
a number of individual signers' language knowledge and performance falls). Lects 6 through 10 in Table 1 use verb reduplication in fewer environments and are characteristic of PSE.

|  |  | 1 | 2 | 3 | 4 | 5 | 6 | 7 | 8 | 9 | 10 |
|---|---|---|---|---|---|---|---|---|---|---|---|
| | Lects: | | | | | | | | | | |
| | MEET | + | - | - | - | - | - | - | - | - | - |
| ASL | MEMORIZE | + | + | - | - | - | - | - | - | - | - |
| | SEE | + | + | + | - | - | - | - | - | - | - |
| Verbs | WANT | + | + | + | + | - | - | - | - | - | - |
| | STUDY | + | + | + | + | + | - | - | - | - | - |
| | READ | + | + | + | + | + | + | - | - | - | - |
| | KNOW | + | + | + | + | + | + | + | - | - | - |
| | RUN | + | + | + | + | + | + | + | + | - | - |
| | DRIVE | + | + | + | + | + | + | + | + | + | - |

Table 1. Implication in verb reduplication in ASL (and PSE).

For the progressive aspect, MCE also makes use of a PSE sign
for uninflected copula, or uses inflected forms of be plus a
main verb, to render standard English be + ing. PSE, however,
drops the redundant -ing. Deaf persons, persons with deaf parents, persons who learned signing before age six, and persons
who attended some college all use more verb reduplication
than do persons who do not have these characteristics; e.g.

(3)   ASL: HE DRIVE DRIVE DRIVE      [with reduplication
      PSE: HE BE DRIVE DRIVE DRIVE   transcribed as the
                                     repetition of the
      Eng: He is driving             whole verb sign]

(4) ASL: LESSON HE MEMORIZE MEMORIZE
    PSE: HE BE MEMORIZE the LESSON
    Eng: He is memorizing the lesson.

b. Negative        Several verbs in frequent use in ASL may
incorporation.     be made negative by action within the
                   performance of the sign itself; this neg-
ative component is a bound, outward twisting movement of
the active hand or hands from the place where the sign is
made. Verbs that undergo this transformation are also implicationally ordered. Table 2 shows the implicational ordering
for five of these verbs (Woodward 1974). Half of the lects
shown, 4 through 6 in Table 1, tend to show PSE characteristics, with negative incorporation used in fewer environments.

| Lects | HAVE | LIKE | WANT | KNOW | GOOD |
|-------|------|------|------|------|------|
| 1     | +    | +    | +    | +    | +    |
| 2     | −    | +    | +    | +    | +    |
| 3     | −    | −    | +    | +    | +    |
| 4     | −    | −    | −    | +    | +    |
| 5     | −    | −    | −    | −    | +    |
| 6     | −    | −    | −    | −    | −    |

Table 2. Implicational patterning of negative incorporation
in ASL verbs (and PSE in lects 4-6).

Surveys of signers show that deaf signers use more negative
incorporation than do hearing signers.

(5) ASL: ME KNOW        (6) ASL: ME LIKE
    PSE: I  KNOW            PSE: I NOT LIKE it
    Eng: I don't know       Eng: I don't like it.

c. Agent-beneficiary     ASL has a large number of verbs
directionality.          that express the relationship
                         between agent and beneficiary
by direction of the signing hands' movement. The hand(s) that
form the sign begin at the agent (or at a point in the agent's
direction) and move toward the beneficiary. Although directionality may be used for all three persons, only second person

agent-to-first person beneficiary use of directionality has
been studied in a dynamic framework. Verbs that may take
agent-beneficiary directionality are also ordered implicationally. Table 3 shows the ordering of nine of these verbs.
Again approximately half of the lects, 6-10 in the table, represent more PSE-like signing. Some of the verb directionality characteristic of ASL has been retained in PSE, but
most of it has been lost.

| Lects: | 1 | 2 | 3 | 4 | 5 | 6 | 7 | 8 | 9 | 10 |
|---|---|---|---|---|---|---|---|---|---|---|
| Verbs | | | | | | | | | | |
| FINGERSPELL | + | - | - | - | - | - | - | - | - | - |
| HATE | + | + | - | - | - | - | - | - | - | - |
| HIT | + | + | + | - | - | - | - | - | - | - |
| FORCE | + | + | + | + | - | - | - | - | - | - |
| SAY-NO-TO | + | + | + | + | + | - | - | - | - | - |
| ASK | + | + | + | + | + | + | - | - | - | - |
| TELL | + | + | + | + | + | + | + | - | - | - |
| SHOW | + | + | + | + | + | + | + | + | - | - |
| GIVE | + | + | + | + | + | + | + | + | + | - |

Table 3.   Implication in ASL (and PSE, 6-10) verbs that
           undergo  agent-beneficiary directionality change.

Deaf persons, persons who learned signs before age six, and
(deaf) persons who attended some college are more likely to
use directionality than are hearing persons, persons who
learned signs after age six, and (deaf) persons who attended
no college. Examples:

(7) ASL:  SHOW        PSE: YOU SHOW ME   Eng: You show me
          (with inward movement for 'show')

(8) ASL:  HATE        PSE: YOU HATE ME   Eng: You hate me
          (moves in)              (moves out: citation form)

d. Copula.  ASL does not have a copula. PSE used by older
            persons has an uninflected sign as copula—
the same sign as ASL TRUE. More recently several new signs

to stand for English forms of <u>be</u> have been developed for use
in the contrived MCE systems. Some of these new copula
forms have been accepted by users of PSE, especially the
younger users. The presence of past tense copula forms in
a user's PSE implies the presence of present tense forms; e.g.

(9)  ASL: GOOD HE      PSE: HE BE (= TRUE) GOOD
                                             Eng: He is good

(10) ASL: DOCTOR HE    PSE: HE IS A DOCTOR
                                             Eng: He's a doctor.

e. Perfec-       ASL has a marker for perfective aspect in
tive aspect.     a verb phrase; it is the ASL sign FINISH.
                 PSE also makes use of FINISH. In PSE the
verb follows FINISH and remains uninflected (contrived MCE
codes may have a sign for the -en ending of English or use
the same sign indiscriminately for past tense and perfect par-
ticiple). For example,

(11) ASL: HE EAT FINISH    PSE: HE FINISH EAT
                                             Eng: He's eaten.

f. Articles.  ASL does not have an article system like
                 that of English. PSE has variable use of
articles that is probably conditioned by environments. For
older and less educated users, articles appear to be used
with less frequency. PSE has a sign for English a/an (10)
and fingerspells the. The limited data that we have on
written Deaf English shows use of the more often than a;
however it should be remembered that if Deaf English (Charrow
1974) is a written analog of PSE, it approaches standard
English more closely than signed varieties normally do, and
so it should not necessarily correlate with signed varieties
of PSE. The variable use of constructions in written Deaf
English and in conversational signed PSE may be quite
different quantitatively and possibly qualitatively as well.

g. Number       In ASL numbers are often incorporated
incorporation.   into pronoun signs (e.g. WE-2, signed
                 with K-hand which has two extended
fingers upright; THEY-3, signed with 3-hand). Most signers

use numbers from 1 to 5 for incorporation, although some may incorporate higher numbers. There are probably restrictions, e.g. environments, on the incorporation of higher numbers. Some deaf signers of PSE may incorporate 1 and 2 in their signs, but most PSE signers do not incorporate higher numbers into pronouns.

Selected phonological characteristics of PSE. Because PSE shares a number of the phonological characteristics of ASL, and because readers may not be aware of some of the recent research in ASL phonology, we have included a short summary of the research done by Woodward and Erting (1974).

There is a level of sublexical structure in ASL analogous to but not dependent on the phonological components of spoken languages. In preliminary structural analyses of ASL Stokoe (1960 [1978], 1965 [1976]) showed that sign phonemes (there called "cheremes") could be categorized in three major aspects: tabs, the places where sign action occurs; dezes, what acts in a sign; and sigs, the actions or movements made by the active element. Bellugi (1972, Klima & Bellugi 1979) using short-term memory tests found that sign phonemes were processed by signers in the same way as phonemes of spoken languages are processed by hearing speakers.

There is no previous research on the phonology of PSE. Battison, Markowicz, and Woodward (1973) have discussed certain gross overmarkings in artificial MCE systems (such as Seeing Essential English, Signing Exact English); however, this overmarking is a result of poor language planning and does not appear in PSE, a natural pidgin language.

The limited data we have viewed on PSE phonology suggests an interesting relation and interaction between channels and codes (Hymes 1964, 1968). PSE is channeled through the gestural-visual modality as is ASL. This channel cannot carry vocal phonological information directly, nor can the vocal channel carry gestural-visual phonological information directly. PSE, because it is channeled through the gestural-visual modality, like ASL, has many more of the phonological characteristics of ASL than of spoken English. PSE handshapes are basically the same as ASL handshapes. PSE tabs and sigs (locations and actions) and suprasegmentals are somewhat reduced in the PSE of deaf signers and are greatly reduced in the PSE of most hearing signers, for these have little or no knowledge of ASL.

Influence on PSE from English phonology appears to be limited to fingerspelled words and initialized signs, i.e. signs with a dez handshape more or less exactly that of the fingerspelling handshape for the letter which begins the English word. The influence from English phonology is thus quite indirect, since English phonology reaches PSE only through the intervening medium of spelling. Influence from English vocabulary, however, is another matter; fingerspelled words are borrowed and become changed in many ways into signs of ASL (Battison 1978).

PSE handshapes.   PSE retains all of the handshapes used in ASL and does not have any additional handshapes not found at the phonetic level in ASL. Because of the influence of English phonology on initialized signs in PSE, the pidgin sign language makes some distinctions at the phonological level that are not made in ASL: A, T, S, G, and D are distinctive handshapes in PSE at the phonological level. These handshapes are distinctive in ASL only on the phonetic level. Examples,

(13)   ASL: TRY (using either a-like or s-like form of A-hand)
       PSE: ATTEMPT (using A-hand)
       PSE: STRIVE (using S-hand)

(14)   ASL: TALL (G-hand slides up palm of B-hand as tab)
       PSE: TALL (Identical with ASL)
       PSE: DEVELOPMENT (D-hand makes same action on B-hand)

Although ASL has initialized signs (some of which go back mutatis mutandi to French SL)[1] and therefore shows some influence from English phonology, there is considerably more use of initialized signs in PSE than in ASL. For this reason there are also more signs using marked handshapes (e.g. R-hand and T-hand) in PSE than in ASL (cf Boyes 1973, Battison

------------

[1]   E.g. For 'blue' (bleu) a B-hand is vibrated in ASL and FSL; for jaune FSL shakes the j (i) hand; 'yellow' uses Y-hand.

1974). Relative markedness of R-hand and T-hand has no
relation to English phonological marking, but only to the
relative overall complexity of these handshapes in comparison to the other handshapes of ASL. The R- and T-hands
require crossing of fingers, which is more complex than the
other actions, such as extending or bending, that compose
a handshape. Chinese SL does not appear to have either R-
or T-hand in its native signs. Moreover R-hand and T-hand
are learned comparatively late by children acquiring ASL from
parents (Boyes 1973, McIntire, Chapter 8, below).
    Although a number of signs using these relatively
marked handshapes have been introduced into PSE, natural
phonological processes seem to be leveling out some of the
markedness. For example, many signs made with R-hand are
being produced with the thumb extended (Woodward & Erting
1974). Phonetically similar handshapes like G and H have
also been found to be undergoing the same (historical) change
(Battison, Markowicz, & Woodward 1973).

PSE locations     Although ASL handshapes are not reduced
& actions.        in PSE phonology, locations and actions
                  are. Deaf signers of PSE tend to keep a
good deal of ASL phonology intact in location and action;
however, the actions are generally made smaller than in ASL,
and the locations tend to be moved toward the central region
of the body. Frishberg (1975) has pointed out that centralization is one strong process in ASL phonological change over
time. She states

    The center of the signing area seems to be the hollow
    of the throat. Signs move down the face, in from the
    side of the body, and up from near waist level.
    (Frishberg 1975: 701)

    The tendency toward centralizing the locations and
actions of signs is seen in extreme form in hearing signers
of PSE. Their signing space is limited as much as possible
to the area from just above the eyebrows to the upper chest.
Lateral movement is restricted even more, so that hands only
rarely move beyond the shoulders.
    While centralization is a natural historical process in
ASL, and probably in other natural sign languages as well,
extreme centralization is viewed negatively by a number of
deaf persons in the ASL community. Some ASL singers have a

derogatory sign for those who sign with extremely restricted
location and action; the sign suggests an analogy with the
habit of mumbling among speakers.

Suprasegmental              "Intonation" is distinctive at the
phonology in PSE.          phonological level in ASL; i.e. in
                            true sign languages like ASL,
facial expression serves a function analogous to intonation
in spoken languages. A change in facial expression, for instance, can convey a change of an ASL sign string from a
statement to a question (Stokoe 1960 [1978: 69-77]). In PSE
the use of facial expression is much restricted. Deaf signers
who use PSE will use facial expression more than will hearing
signers, who are often said to sign without expression.

        In PSE facial expression is not distinctive at the phon-
ological level, as it is in ASL. Changes from statements to
questions are signalled in PSE by an English question word-
sign, by English word order, or by a question-marking sign
at the end of the question. Facial expressions may accompany these devices, especially among deaf signers, but the
use of facial expression alone to signal a question is not
found in PSE. Similarly, other ASL facial, head, eye, or body
movements may be used by deaf signers in PSE—e.g. negation with head or facial action alone; but these are not characteristics of PSE and do not make distinctions at the level
of phonology. It must be remembered that English intonation
cannot be directly conveyed in PSE because of the incompatibility of the gestural-visual channel to carry such vocally
produced information.

PSE and written       Thus far PSE has been discussed only as
Deaf English.        a language variety put into expression
                     by signing. Charrow has suggested that
written (non-standard) Deaf English is PSE's "written analog,
but is closer to Standard English in the continuum" (1974:
56). Because of the limitations imposed by the writing channel,
Deaf English cannot express certain purely ASL constructions
such as directionality in three dimensional space. There is a
great deal of grammatical variation in the Deaf English Charrow
studied, and also "elimination of number, gender, tense markers and other essentially redundant features" (1974: 50).
Such constructions in Deaf English as the variable use of

articles and copula forms indicate further similarities between Deaf English and PSE.

Along with the restriction and admixture in grammatical structure characteristic of DE, there goes a socially restricted use and an apparent lack of registers. The apparent lack of registers may be more an effect of the limitations imposed by the writing channel than of the pidginization process. PSE, while socially restricted, appears to have registers based on degrees of formality. This variation, however, may occur more for those whose use is more characteristic of a creole (i.e. learned as an infant from older users) than of a pidgin signed English. At this time it is impossible to know the exact relation of PSE to written Deaf English, but Charrow's hypothesis deserves further investigation.

### Pidgin Sign Languages and Linguistic Theory

In the preceding sections we have discussed some of the sociological and linguistic characteristics of PSE. The variation and dynamism observed in PSE is describable in terms of recent developments in Variation Theory (Bailey 1974). PSE, while having some unique salient characteristics of a signed language (e.g incorporation, directionality), appears also to have characteristics considered substantive for all pidgins (Samarin 1971); these include reduction (ibid.) and admixture and restricted inter-group use (Hymes 1971).

Reduction & admixture. Reduction of grammatical and phonological characteristics of ASL and English and their admixture can be seen in all the grammatical and most of the phonological characteristics discussed above. One exception is that PSE handshapes are phonologically more complex than ASL handshapes. Reduction and admixture can be seen as paralleling the simplification found in pidgins of spoken languages. Reduplication of words and the use of a copula and a verb to represent progressive aspect can be found in several spoken pidgins. Implicationally ordered variation of these constructions would be as expected in a vocal as in a gestural pidgin.

Other reductions and admixtures appear to be a result of incompatibility of vocal and gestural channels and not

of the usual working of the pidginization process. This seems
especially true of phonology. English suprasegmentals cannot
be carried in a gestural-visual channel. Thus there is more
reduction and less admixture in phonology than in grammar, as
we have seen. Deaf PSE signers are able to keep suprasegmentals, but hearing PSE signers cannot keep English suprasegmentals (nor for that matter segmentals) because of channel
incompatibility. Hearing signers cannot utilize ASL suprasegmentals—usually they do not know they exist—because they
are effectively culturally isolated from the deaf community.
This situation appears to be unique to pidgin sign languages
arising from contact between a natural sign language and a
spoken language.

Restricted inter-        Hearing signers, unless they are
group use of PSE.        children of deaf signing parents,
                         will undoubtedly prefer English
(in spoken or signed expression) for all types of communication. Most deaf signers prefer and use ASL for communicative,
integrative, and expressive interaction with other deaf persons.
Interaction between hearing persons and deaf persons is often
limited to a purely communicative level. Different (sub)cultural
values and beliefs as well as language differences hinder if
they do not utterly bar any integrative and expressive interaction between members of the two groups. Deaf people are
prevented from total integration with hearing society not only
because of their inabilty to hear but also because of the predominantly negative attitude of many hearing people toward
any disability. Conversely, hearing people are often prevented
from acculturation in the deaf subculture because of language
differences as well as the diglossic situation, which ensures
that most deaf persons will move or shift towards a signing
variety more like English immediately on discovering that a
person is hearing, even if the person has been signing to them
in ASL. Besides this language situation there is a strong feeling of group solidarity in deaf communities. This solidarity,
which is often coupled with a distrust of hearing people, is
extremely hard for an outsider to penetrate.

PSE allows communication between the deaf and the
hearing groups, but perhaps more importantly it helps the Deaf
community maintain its identity by not allowing extensive integrative and expressive communication between members of

the two communities across the boundary. This language barrier thus helps to prevent significant intrusions of the dominant language community's values and language patterns into the Deaf community.

Although Woodward (1973d) stated in an earlier study that PSE might be short-lived as a number of other pidgins have proved to be, it appears that this prediction is erroneous in the light of the discussion above. ASL helps the individual deaf person to maintain identity as a member of the deaf subculture. PSE fosters development of the subculture, providing means for beneficial contact with, but preventing long-term cultural interference from, the hearing community. With such a vital function to perform, it is extremely doubtful that PSE will disappear, unless a better means can be found for the maintenance of cultural boundaries and therefore promulgation of cultural traditions.

## REFERENCES

Bailey, Charles-James N.
  1974    Variation and Language Theory (Washington, Center
          for Applied Linguistics).

Barth, Frederick
  1969    Ethnic Groups & Boundaries (Oslo, Johansen & Nielsen).

Battison, Robbin M.
  1974    Phonological Deletion in American Sign Language,
          Sign Language Studies 5, 1-19.
  1978    Lexical Borrowing in American Sign Language (Silver
          Spring, MD, Linstok Press).

- - - - -, H. Markowicz, & J. Woodward
  1977    A Good Rule of Thumb: Variable Phonology in ASL,
          in New Ways of Analyzing Variation in English, II,
          Shuy & Fasold eds. (Washington, Georgetown U.).

Bellugi, Ursula
  1972    Studies in Sign Language, in O'Rourke (1972), 68-84.

- - - - -, & Susan Fischer
  1972    A Comparison of Sign Language & Spoken Language,
          Cognition 1, 173-200.

Bickerton, Derek
    1972    The Structure of Polylectal Grammars, Georgetown
            University MSLL 25.

Boyes, Penny
    1973    An Initial Report, WIP on a Developmental Phon-
            ology for ASL. MS, Salk Institute, La Jolla, CA.
            (see Lane et al. 1976).

Charrow, Veda
    1974    Deaf English—An Investigation of the Written English
            Competence of Deaf Adolescents. Ph.D. dissertation,
            Stanford University.
    1975    A Psycholinguistic Analysis of Deaf English, Sign
            Language Studies 7, 139-150.

Cokely, Dennis, & Rudy Gawlik (=Chapter 3, 95-104)
    1974    Childrenese as Pidgin, Sign Language Studies 5, 72-81.

Croneberg, Carl
    1965    The Linguistic Community, in A Dictionary of ASL,
    [1976]  Stokoe, Casterline, Croneberg, eds. (Washington,
            Gallaudet College Press), 297-312. (Rev. ed. 1976)

Denmark, John
    1973    The Education of Deaf Children, Hearing 29:9, 284-293.

Fasold, Ralph
    1970    Two Models of Socially Significant Linguistic
            Variation, Language 46, 551-563.

Ferguson, Charles
    1959    Diglossia, Word 15, 325-340. (repr. in Language
    [1964]  in Culture & Society, Hymes ed. NY, Harper & Row)

Fischer, Susan, & Bonnie Gough (=Chapter 6, 149-179)
    1978    Verbs in American Sign Language, Sign Language
            Studies 18, 17-48.

Fishman, Joshua
    1967    Bilingualism with & without Diglossia: Diglossia
            with & without Bilingualism, Jour. of Social Issues, 29-38.

Frishberg, Nancy
  1975    Arbitrariness & Iconicity: Historical Changes in
          American Sign Language, Language 51, 696-719.

Furth, Hans
  1963    Conceptual Discovery & Control..., Journal of
          Educational Psychology 54, 191-196.
  1966    Thinking without Language: Psychological Impli-
          cations of Deafness (New York, The Free Press).

Guttman, Louis
  1944    A Basis for Scaling Qualitative Data, American
          Sociological Review 9, 139-150.

Hymes, Dell
  1964    Towards Ethnographies of Communication, in The
          Ethnography of Communication, Gumperz & Hymes
          eds., American Anthropologist 66, 1-34.
  1968    The Ethnography of Speaking, in Readings in the
          Sociology of Language, Fishman ed. (The Hague,
          Mouton).
  1971    Introduction to Section III, Pidginization & Cre-
          olization of Languages, Hymes ed. Cambridge,
          Cambridge University Press), 65-90.

Klima, Edward, & Ursula Bellugi
  1979    The Signs of Language (Cambridge, MA, Harvard).

Labov, William
  1969    Contraction, Deletion, & Inherent Variability of the
          English Copula, Language 45, 715-762.

Lane, Harlan, P. Boyes-Braem, & Ursula Bellugi
  1976    Preliminaries to a Distinctive Feature Analysis of
          American Sign Language, Cognitive Psychology 8, 263-89.

Lunde, Anders
  1960
  [1978]  The Sociology of the Deaf, in Stokoe (1960), 21-28;
          (1978), 16-24.

Markowicz, Harry
1972    (1st publication of Chapter 12), Sign Language Studies
        1, 15-41.
1973    What Language Do Deaf Children Acquire? (Review
        article), Sign Language Studies 2, 73-78.
1974a   Sign English: Is It Really English? Paper, Sign
        Language Conference, Gallaudet College, April.
1974b   Review: Psycholinguistics & Total Communication,
        Sign Language Studies 5, 82-89.

Meadow, Kathryn P.
1966    The Effect of Early Manual Communication & Family
        Climate on the Deaf Child's Development. Unpublished
        Ph.D. dissertation, University of California at Berkeley.
1972    Sociolinguistics, Sign Language, and the Deaf Sub-
        Culture, in O'Rourke (1972), 19-33.

Moores, Donald
1972    Communication: Some Unanswered Questions and
        Some Unquestioned Answers, in O'Rourke (1972), 1-10.

Nash, Jeffrey, & Anedith Nash
1978    Distorted Communicative Situations, Sign Language
        Studies 20, 219-250.

O'Rourke, Terrence J., ed.
1972    Psycholinguistics & Total Communication: The State
        of the Art (Washington, DC, American Annals of the Deaf).

Rainer, J. D., K. Altshuler, & F. Kallmann, eds.
1963    Family & Mental Health Problems in a Deaf Population
        (New York, N.Y. State Psychiatric Institute, Columbia).

Samarin, William
1971    Salient & Substantive Pidginization, in Hymes (1971),
        117-140.

Schein, Jerome D.
1968    The Deaf Community (Washington, Gallaudet College).

Smith, David
1972    Language as Social Adaptation, Language & Linguistics
        Working Papers, No. 4 (Georgetown), 61-77.

Stokoe, William
    1960    Sign Language Structure, Studies in Linguistics:
    [1978]  Occasional Paper 8 (revised 1978, Silver Spring, MD,
            Linstok Press).
    1970    Sign Language Diglossia, Studies in Linguistics 21,
            27-41.
    1973    Sign Language Syntax & Human Language Capacity,
            Florida Foreign Language Reporter 11 (1-2).
- - - - -, C. Croneberg, & D. Casterline
    1965    A Dictionary of American Sign Language on Linguistic
    [1976]  Principles (Washington, Gallaudet College Press);
            revised (Silver Spring, MD, Linstok Press).

Stuckless, Ross, & Jack Birch
    1966    The Influence of Early Manual Communication in the
            Linguistic Development of Deaf Children, American
            Annals of the Deaf 111, 452-460; 499-504.

von der Lieth, Lars
    1978    Social-Psychological Aspects in the Use of Sign
            Language, in Current Trends in the Study of Sign
            Languages of the Deaf, Schlesinger & Namir eds.
            (NY, Academic Press).

Vernon, McCay
    1972    Non-linguistic Aspects of Sign Language, Human
            Feelings, & Thought Processes, in O'Rourke (1972),
            11-18.

Woodward, James
    1972    Implications for Sociolinguistic Research among
            the Deaf, Sign Language Studies 1, 1-17.
    1973a   Implicational Lects on the Deaf Diglossic Contin-
            uum. Ph.D. dissertation, Georgetown University.
    1973b   Some Observations on Sociolinguistic Variation &
            American Sign Language, Kansas Journal of Sociol-
            ogy 9, 191-200.
    1973c   Interrule Implication in ASL, Sign Language Studies
            3, 47-56.
    1973d   Some Characteristics of Pidgin Sign English, Sign
            Language Studies 3, 39-46.

PART ONE: 2.

ENCODEDNESS and SIGN LANGUAGE

Clifford F. Abbott

Everyone knows what a language is. Most people have
one in working order before they even start school. And since
everyone knows what language is, it should be possible to
determine the principles that underlie that knowledge. But to
come up with a clear-cut, precise definition of language is
something of a problem. Clearly we would want that definition
to distinguish language in particular from communication in
general. There are many systems of communication or ways
of conveying meaning, which we metaphorically call languages; e.g. body language, the language of flowers, the
language of art. But they are not really true languages like
English, French, or Chinese. Many previously proposed
definitions of language are lists of criteria for judging if a
given communication system is a true language or not. Dual-
ity of patterning, the possibility of metalanguage, a way to
express temporal relations, and other features or traits are
often included in such lists. These definitions are useful for
distinguishing, for example, a body language as a communication system from Greek as a true language.

There are, however, grey areas where we are less sure
of that distinction. Suppose A and B are in a room and B is
sitting next to a closed window that he could open. If A says
"It's hot in here," then under normal circumstances two
things have been communicated: (1) A has made a comment
on the relative temperature of the room, and (2) A has made
a request for B to open the window. The first communication
was surely done by the English language, but was the second
communication part of that language or part of a separate
communication system? This second kind of communication
is typical of a whole range of meanings that linguists and
philosophers have labelled 'pragmatic' as opposed to

81

'semantic.' There is currently a debate among linguists as to whether pragmatic meaning should be incorporated into linguistic descriptions.

In certain situations a raised eyebrow can communicate a lot of information. It is a good example of body language, really a non-language communication system. Again, if the situation is appropriate, a certain tone of voice can convey the same information as the raised eyebrow—information, incidentally, that may not be easy to put into words. Is that tone of voice then part of the grammar of its user's language, or is it like the raised eyebrow, part of a separate communication system? The situation is even more perplexing when we consider that in some languages the relative tone on which a word is pronounced is very much a part of the grammar. In Chinese, for example, a different tone may change a word meaning 'blue' (high rising tone) into a word meaning 'lazy' (low-dipping tone) (Chao 1968). Yet in other languages such changes in lexical meaning are impossible with tone changes. Even within a single language like English, the kind of phonological juncture used around relative clauses distinguishes restrictive from non-restrictive clauses, while the same junctures elsewhere have no such semantic effect.

Tones of voice, junctures, and prosodic features generally, where they signify various nuances of attitude rather than concrete semantic differences, are often labelled paralinguistic. Like the pragmatic features, these paralinguistic features are part of that grey area between language and non-language communication (Lieberman 1973).

Among many people, especially non-signers, there is confusion as to whether sign languages are true languages or are non-language communication systems. There is by no means as much agreement on the classification of sign languages as there is on the classification of English or of body language. Part of the reason for this is the heavy use in sign languages of the very same mechanisms that serve most people for pragmatic and paralinguistic systems. Ultimately, the answer to the question "Are sign languages real languages?" is less important and less productive than the way in which we attempt to answer the question.

This paper proposes a different kind of measure or question. Instead of seeking a criterion of language, let us look

for a measure of how language-like, or linguistic, any part of
a communication system is. Not all parts of English are equally
linguistic; the same is true of sign languages. If we have a
measure for how linguistic a feature, a construction, a level,
or any other part of a communication is, then we have a more
insightful answer than saying "Yes; sign languages are
languages;" or "No; they are not."

     The basic processes of language are encoding and de-
coding. A semantic message is encoded into a form suitable
for transmission, e.g. speech, and then is decoded into the
same or an equivalent semantic message. In non-language
communication the message is either delivered holistically
(a yellow rose means the sender is 'jealous' in the "language"
of flowers), or is simply enciphered unit for unit (each letter
has a unique representation in the cipher of semaphore or
morse). The guiding principle then is that the more encoded
a message is, the more linguistic or truly language-like the
system encoding it must be. To illustrate the measure of
encodedness, let us first look at a paradigm case, determine
the features which characterize that case, and then try to
find analogues of those features in other parts of the structures of the English Language and American Sign Language.

     The paradigm case we will examine is the speech code.
There are a number of reasons for choosing this particular
part of language as our paradigm. First, we know more about
the encoding and decoding of speech than we do about the
other levels of language, primarily because those other processes are less observable than speech. Another reason is
the specialization of speech to language. On the encoding
side, there is some evidence that the anatomical evolution
of the human vocal tract has resulted in a shape that produces
a larger repertoire of sounds (than the non-human vocal tract)
at the expense of some more obvious survival features; e.g.
it is easier for a human being to choke today than it was for
Neanderthal man (Lieberman et. al. 1972). And on the decoding side, it is now clear that the perception of speech
sounds in speech context is quite different from the perception of other sounds (Liberman et al. 1967). It seems then
that both the production and the perception of speech have
become specialized to facilitate language. The assumption
being made here is that whatever the particular characteristics

of the speech code are, they are likely to reflect more general
principles of language, since the speech code has so clearly
accommodated itself to language.

The paradigm case.   The task of the speech code is to
                              convert a string of phones (con-
sonants and vowels) into a succession of sound waves. Traditionally the former is represented in a phonetic alphabet
and the latter by plotting of sound frequencies over time
(usually resulting in a pattern of bands or formants). One
might expect a fairly simple and direct relationship between
the phones (or the phonetic level) and the formant patterns
(or the acoustic level); i.e. ideally each phone would have
one and only one corresponding pattern of formants. If the
phonetic and acoustic levels were connected by such a
direct relationship, it would not be a code at all, but a
simple cipher, a one-to-one matching. The actual relationship, however, is much more complicated. It is indeed a
code, or if you will, a grammar (Liberman 1970, Cooper 1972).
We can isolate at least the following four characteristics of
that coding: (1) context conditioned variation,
(2) categorical perception, (3) parallel processing of information, and (4) abstractness of
signal.

Context conditioned   The first simply means that the
variation.                    code matches up different ele-
                              ments in different environments.
For example, the phone /b/, a voiced labial stop, is matched
up with one formant pattern in the syllable /ba/, with another
in the syllable /bi/, with another in the syllable /bu/, and
so on. In each of these syllables, if the formant pattern for
the vowel is removed, what remains of the acoustic signal is
not a single formant pattern identifiable as /b/, but instead
several different patterns. In other words, an element of the
phonetic level, in this case the phone /b/, is encoded into
one of several varying patterns on the acoustic level. Which
of these variants is chosen is a function of, or is conditioned
by, the environment or context, in this case the following
vowel. So the first characteristic of the speech code is that
it produces context conditioned variation in its output.

Categorical    If context conditioned variation compli-
perception.    cates the encoding of speech, categorical
               perception is the process that simplifies
the decoding of speech. It is essentially our built-in key to
decoding speech, so that when confronted with one of the
context-conditioned variants of /b/ our very perception of
it classifies it into a single category with the other variants
of /b/. As a result, we hear one sound for /b/ regardless
of the actual acoustic differences. We cannot hear those
differences. This is rather amazing, for there is no such
thing as categorical perception in our hearing of non-speech
sounds. If we are presented with a gradually changing musi-
cal tone, we recognize and hear the gradual change; but if
we construct, artificially of course, an acoustic pattern
gradually changing from the acoustic signal of /pa/ to the
acoustic signal of /ba/, then we perceive no gradual change—
only the two categories of sounds /pa/ and /ba/.

Parallel processing    Another prominent feature of the
of information.        speech code is the parallel pro-
                       cessing of information. Since the
acoustic pattern for /b/ has a unique variant if the vowel /a/
follows, it stands to reason that this pattern supplies information not only about the /b/ but also partly identifies the
following vowel as /a/. In general, the cues for decoding will
be scattered throughout the syllable, the normal unit of encoding in speech; and the cues for the several phones in a
single syllable are transmitted in a parallel, overlapping
fashion.

Abstractness.    A fourth characteristic of the speech
                 code is abstractness. The form of the
acoustic pattern and the ways in which it can be modified
bear no direct relation to its meaning and the ways in which
meaning can be modified. There is no inherent link between
any sound and any meaning in speech (onomatopoetic words
being possible exceptions); and varying any acoustic parameter (e.g. loudness, pitch) does not result in a corresponding change in some semantic parameter. It is thus not a
characteristic of language coding for a word meaning temperature to mean 'hot' if said loudly and 'cold' if said softly
and degrees between if said with moderate force. The ele-

ments of encoded language are abstract in the sense that they
are removed from such correspondence with their expression
in the real world.

All these characteristics can be directly and objectively
observed in the coding of speech, our paradigm case. By
using these characteristics as our criteria, it should be possible to determine which parts of English and which parts of
ASL are highly encoded or highly linguistic, and which parts
are less encoded. First, however, it should be pointed out
that even in the speech code itself not every element is as
highly encoded as every other; i.e. not every element shows
the characteristic features of encodedness to the same degree.
For example, pure or steady state vowels (those without on- or
off- glide) are far less encoded than are consonants; they
show less variation in different contexts; they can be perceived more continuously (like non-language sounds) and
less categorically; and they can be transmitted alone without
any other sound segments. If encodedness is a measure of
linguistic structure, we can say that these vowels are less
linguistic than the consonants. Some of the prosodic features
of speech are less encoded still. Emphatic word stress, to
take one example, is a relatively unencoded prosodic feature.
It is not conditioned on context, since the way speakers
stress any one word is not particularly different from the
way they stress any other. Their perception of stress is not
categorical. One might claim that there was parallel transmission of information because in order to use emphatic
stress one needs something to use it on, but this is rather
vacuous parallelism, because almost any sound one can
make is stressable. Finally, emphatic stress is not very
abstract—the amount of stress is more or less directly correlated with the meaning of emphasis. Emphatic stress is
one of the features that often serves a paralinguistic function
and it is important to note that though part of every language
it is relatively unencoded.

Encodedness      One feature of English grammar that is
in English.      highly encoded is the subordination of
                 relative clauses. The first indication of
their encodedness is the context conditioned variation. The
conditions on the syntactic transformation of relativization

provide evidence of this. One condition on the choice of relative pronoun involves the position of a preposition. If a preposition precedes the relative pronoun, <u>which</u> is a possible choice as in (1), but <u>that</u> in (2) is not; both are permitted as choices in (3) and (4), where the preposition does not precede:

    (1)  the school from which I graduated
    (2)  *the school from that I graduated
    (3)  the school which I graduated from
    (4)  the school that I graduated from

      Another condition involves a semantic element of the head noun (the word to which the relative pronoun refers). The forms <u>who</u> and <u>whom</u> require that the head noun refer to an animate being; <u>which</u> generally requires an inanimate head noun; and either is possible with <u>that</u>:

    (5)  the man | whom | I saw yesterday
               | *which |
               | that |

    (6)  the building | *whom | I saw yesterday
                  | which |
                  | that |

This latter condition is a kind of grammatical agreement, which can be taken wherever it occurs as a sort of context conditioned variation.

      Still another indication of the encodedness of relative clauses would be their categorical perception. There is little direct evidence on how we perceive whole clauses, and it is commonly held that we perceive and process language in smaller segments. Nevertheless there is evidence from repetition tasks that clauses with the same meaning have a psychological sameness regardless of their syntactic form. When asked to repeat a sentence under certain noise conditions, a subject may frequently offer the sentence in an altered form, but with the original meaning preserved. As for parallel transmission of information, relative clauses are more clearly encoded. A relative pronoun carries information that the following clause is subordinate and often also information as to the role of the noun phrase deleted from the dependent clause. In the clause itself, the deletion site provides cues for the same information. And the abstractness of a relative clause is obvious, because there is no continuous way to modify its form and so create a corresponding modification in its meaning.

Contrast the highly encoded relative clauses just considered
with a rather unencoded simple main clause such as

(7)  John kissed Mary.

Here the context conditions no variation. The information is
presented in three discrete elements without overlapping
(subject, verb, object), and presumably that is how we perceive them. There seems to be very little, if any, parallel
processing of information. Abstractness is the only clue to
the linguistic nature of (7). The encodedness is thus minimal.
       In the deictic (pointing out) and referential system of
English syntax, some uses of pronouns are more linguistic
than others. Apart from their various lexical forms, which are
themselves fairly encoded, the ability of a pronoun to refer
is sometimes dependent on a simple, unencoded method of
reference. When a speaker says (8) and picks out a real-
world immediate reference by pointing directly at someone,
the case relation of the pronoun <u>him</u> is encoded, but the
reference by pointing is not.

(8)  I've never seen him before.

The pronoun's reference is not conditioned by the context,
for no matter where the pronoun occurs in the sentence, the
direct deictic reference is the same. There is no parallel
processing of information; the pointing is used for reference
only. Again, there is no direct evidence on perception, but
one would assume that far from being categorical, a listener's
perception of direct deictic reference is dependent on how
the listener understands the pointing. Even the abstractness
is lost here, since a change in the form (the direction of the
pointing) will cause a corresponding change in the meaning
(the intended reference of the pronoun).
       There are also pronouns whose reference is dependent
on rather encoded linguistic variables. The reference of the
anaphoric pronouns in examples (9) through (12) is conditioned
by the command relations, defined in terms of order and subordination.

(9) Before I met him, John never worked very hard.
(10) John never worked very hard before I met him.

(11)  He never worked very hard before I met John.
(12)  I met him and John never worked very hard.

In (9) and (10) the antecedent 'John' commands the pronoun
him, but in (11) and (12) 'John' does not command the pronoun
him or he. The exact definition of the command relation need
not detain us here. What is important is that him refers to
John only in the first two sentences, when the command relation holds. In the second two sentences him or he must
refer to some other person also male. Certainly this mode of
reference is context conditioned. Both the meaning and the
reference of the pronoun are processed together, and surely
this type of anaphoric reference is abstract. We can conclude
that while direct deictic reference is rather unencoded, anaphoric reference constrained by the command relation is considerably more encoded.

 Prosodic features, as mentioned earlier, are not generally very much encoded, but in certain syntactic functions
they do become part of the encoded linguistic structure. Restrictive and non-restrictive relative clauses are usually distinguished by particular junctures (changes in the intonation
of the voice speaking the clauses). Those same junctures at
different points in the grammar are not distinctive, do not
make any important difference in meaning; but with relative
clauses they are distinctive. This means that a normally unencoded feature of a language can be encoded for a particular
function.

 This measure of encodedness is very likely to show us
that not every part of every language's system is encoded to
the same degree. A language with a highly encoded morphology
—such as certain American Indian languages have—may well
have a somewhat unencoded syntax, but that hardly implies
that it must lose its status as a language.

Encodedness  Some investigators of American Sign Lan-
in ASL.    guage (most probably those who have noted
        especially the relatively unencoded parts
of the linguistic system) have declared that ASL is not a real
language, is not linguistic, although they grant that it may be
used as a means of communication. Other investigators, who
have looked at the more highly encoded parts of ASL have argued

strongly that it is a real language. It is probably pointless to
argue whether or not a particular means of communication is or
is not a language because we do not have a nonarbitrary definition of language. But it may be illuminating to discover how
the elements of ASL measure up to the criteria of encodedness.

The basic encoding unit of ASL is the word. There are
exceptions, but in large measure the word formation rules of
ASL are highly encoded. Each sign consists of a certain hand-arm
configuration at a particular location in the signing space. In
addition each sign consists of action, normally movement, of
that configuration. Many of the hand-arm configurations have
slightly different variants conditioned by the context. Locations
and actions also have variants conditioned by context, although
some of these variants may also be conditioned by the speed
of signing (Stokoe 1960 [1978]). Unfortunately information on
the perception of these features is unavailable and awaits
further research (but see McIntire below and reference to Lane
et al.).

Because the three aspects of a manual sign—hand-
arm configuration and presentation, location, and action—
are all combined in a single sign, there is clearly parallel
processing of information. With regard to abstractness,
there is a wide variation in signs. A few signs have the properties of an index; e.g. me, you. A large number of signs
appear to be icons only after one knows their meaning; i.e.
jump, cat, sun, meet. Another large number of signs are
truly abstract, although in some cases folk etymology may
attribute some iconicity to them; e.g. man, happen, summer.
Thus, while individual signs may be highly encoded, not
all signs necessarily are.

The device of negative incorporation is an example of
a highly encoded part of ASL grammar and syntax (page 66
above). A class of predicates—including the signs for 'good'
and 'with'—are made negative by an outward turn of the hand
in making the positive sign, thus incorporating the negative
meaning without adding another sign. Depending on the formation of the particular sign, this outward turning will be
made slightly differently, so that there is necessarily context conditioned variation. There is also parallel transmission
of information, since two formerly separate signs (one for
the predicate and one for the negative) are now combined in a
single sign. As with the higher levels of structure in any

language, it is difficult to test directly the perception of ASL
negative incorporation, but impressionistic reports indicate
that the different forms of negative incorporation are perceived
as the same; i.e. they are perceived categorically. Furthermore, negative incorporation is fairly abstract, since a modification of its form does not correlate directly with any change
in its meaning. E.g. the sign GOOD is made by the upright,
central, supinated (palm-in) forearm extending forward with
a simple straightening of the elbow angle. The sign with negative incorporation meaning 'bad' is identical except that the
forearm makes a pronating rotation as it extends. This pronating motion can be made to any degree (turning the palm to
the side or out and down), but no matter how far it is turned,
the sign means 'bad' and the sign without the pronation means
'good'; there is no intermediate meaning such as 'fair' with
some degree of rotation between little and much.

We should take pains here to distinguish the abstract
feature of negative incorporation from a similar feature of
emphasis that is not abstract. When the sign GOOD is made
quickly and forcefully it may mean 'very good'. With this
feature of emphasis a signer can vary the degree of meaning
from 'good' to 'very very good' with the strength of the sign's
performance; in a similar way English speakers may use emphatic
stress on good. Both emphatic processes are relatively unabstract
and unencoded. Similarly the negative-incorporated sign BAD
may be made to mean 'very bad' by the same feature of emphasis.
The important difference between the abstract negative incorporation and the non-abstract emphasis is that the non-abstract
feature is capable of expressing a continuous semantic range—
from 'good' to 'wonderful' or from 'bad' to 'terrible'—but the
abstract feature expresses either one semantic category or the
other—'good' or 'bad' but nothing in between.

In ASL as in English, pronominal reference is sometimes encoded and sometimes not. Real-world deixis, i.e.
pointing to an object or person, is a rather unencoded feature
of signing. Direct pointing does not vary in different contexts, there is no parallel transmission of information, and
it is far less abstract than the English pronominal system; it
is thus less encoded. Friedman's finding (1975) that real-
world deixis takes precedence over any other type of reference makes the whole reference system of sign pronouns
relatively less encoded than English pronouns.

But there are other kinds of reference in ASL that are
more encoded. For example, certain verbs incorporate the
pronominal reference to certain nominal arguments (the agent
'I' in SEE, the object looked at in LOOK) in their unmarked,
citation form. So the sign TEACH incorporates reference to a
first-person agent and often second-person beneficiary in its
citation, dictionary listed form. By reversing the directionality
of TEACH a signer makes the second person the agent and the
signer the patient. Both case role references are incorporated
into the (changeable) direction of the sign's action. Here is
parallel transmission of information: the verb, its agent, and
its patient are all given in a single sign. Here too is context conditioned variation. The incorporation of case roles is
consequently an encoded part of sign language structure, a
linguistic part of that structure.

Reduplication is generally an encoded feature whenever it occurs in a language. By its very nature any reduplication is context conditioned and transmits information about
two semantic elements simultaneously. In ASL a good many
verbs (among them SEE, WANT, READ, KNOW, DRIVE) may re-
duplicate, i.e. repeat part of or all of their characteristic
action; and the semantic force of such reduplication is to
signal continuing action, the progressive aspect (see above,
Chap. 1 ). Two different kinds of reduplication have been
noted in ASL: a habitual aspect (meaning 'all the time') is
signalled if the sign is repeated quickly with a horizontal
sweep; and a continuous aspect ('for a long time'), if the
sign has a slow, drawn out repetition (Fischer & Gough, below,
Chapter 6). There is also simple repetition that generally
translates the same meaning as using a form of be in English
followed by the -ing form of the main verb.

Another feature of ASL grammar is that many verb signs
allow some adverbial modification so that the way the sign is
made is directly related to the action or process or state that
it represents. Thus the sign ACCIDENT may be signed gently
for a little bump and more vigorously for a more serious col-
lision. Although there is parallel transmission of information
indicating some degree of encodedness, these adverbial modifications are not very abstract, because the amount of force
used in making the sign correlates continuously with the force
implied in the meaning. This is a good example of a partially

encoded feature. [Here the reader is reminded that Abbott's discussion of encodedness was written in 1975 and that much research on the encoding of information in ASL has been done in the relatively short time since; see especially chs. 11 and 12 "Aspectual Modulation on Adjectival Predicates" and "The Structured Use of Space and Movement" in The Signs of Language by Klima and Bellugi (1979).]

Conclusion.  If the notion of encodedness as developed and illustrated here captures some important organizing principles of linguistic structure, both from a biological viewpoint and from a structuralist viewpoint, then it is a valuable guide in the investigation of linguistic structures—more valuable it is to be hoped than trying simply to determine whether a particular communication system should rightfully be called a language. The illustrations here demonstrate at the very least that both English and ASL encompass a range of encoded and relatively unencoded features. It remains for further research to put together the total picture and to determine the exact extent of encodedness in ASL as compared with other languages.

## REFERENCES

Chao, Yuen Ren
    1968    Language & Symbolic Systems (Cambridge, Univ. Pr.).

Cooper, Franklin S.
    1972    How is Language Conveyed, in Language by Ear & by Eye, Mattingly & Kavanagh eds. (Camb., MA, MIT Press), 25-45.

Friedman, Lynn
    1975    Space, Time, & Person Reference in ASL, Language 51, 940-961.

Liberman, Alvin M.
    1970    The Grammars of Speech & Language, Cognitive Psychology 1, 301-323.
- - - - -, Cooper, Shankweiler, & Studdert-Kennedy
    1967    Perception of the Speech Code, Psychology Review 74, 431-461.

Lieberman, Philip
    1973    On the Evolution of Language, a Unified View,
            Cognition 2, 59-94.
- - - - -, E. S. Crelin, & D. H. Klatt
    1972    Phonetic Ability & Related Anatomy of the Newborn,
            Adult Human, Neanderthal Man, & the Chimpanzee,
            American Anthropologist 74, 287-307.

Stokoe, William
    1960    Sign Language Structure, Studies in Linguistics:
            Occasional Paper 8 (revised 1978, Silver Spring,
            MD, Linstok Press).
Woodward, James
    1973    Implicational Lects on the Deaf Diglossic Continuum.
            Ph.D. dissertation, Georgetown University.

PART ONE: 3

# CHILDRENESE as PIDGIN

Dennis R. Cokely
Rudolph Gawlik

Perhaps one of the most frustrating experiences for parents and educators of deaf children is being unable to understand fully the sign language behavior of the deaf child. This frustration is echoed in statements like, "That's not what the book says;" or "That's not how we learned it in sign class;" or "My child's signing seems to be different!" This communication gap is experienced even by parents and educators who have been using signs for several years. The explanation that the children "just sign too fast" does not account completely for this gap, for there are many parents and educators who have gained proficiency in the use of American Sign Language (ASL) and who are not bothered by the speed of deaf adults' signing, yet they still confess a lack of understanding of children's sign language. The feeling is that perhaps the children are signing a totally different language—different from what is taught in the numerous sign classes throughout the nation.

The thrust of what follows is that in fact deaf children are using a different variety of sign language. This language, c h i l d r e n e s e , is neither adult ASL nor is it signed English.

This fact should not be surprising. There are many factors which would lead children to develop a sign language that is neither ASL nor standard English recoded in signs. First, it should not be surprising that childrenese is not ASL. Most of the children currently enrolled in schools for the deaf (with the exception of deaf children of deaf parents, a tenth of them at most) do not know and use adult ASL because:

    a. hearing parents and educators for the most part lack the skills to be effective models of ASL

    b.  in most schools for deaf children there are
only a few deaf teachers who consistently
use ASL

    c.  in most schools for the deaf child the pressure
is to model English and <u>not</u> to model ASL.

It should not be surprising that childrenese is not
English either, because:

    a.  few schools have a fully implemented policy
of consistently signing English (this applies
also to the homes of the deaf children)

    b.  few teachers have the skill to present English
clearly and correctly in signs at various linguistic levels and to monitor and adjust to
the individual child's attempts at English

    c.  only a small percentage of English is visible
on the lips of those nonsigners (parents,
teachers, etc.) who have regular contact
with the child.

**C h i l d r e n e s e**    If childrenese is neither ASL nor English,
**a s  a  p i d g i n.**    what is it? In an attempt to describe
                            childrenese it is useful to draw upon the
linguistic notion of pidgin languages. In a paper entitled
"Some Characteristics of Pidgin Sign English" Woodward says:

> It is generally agreed that pidgin languages are reduced
> in structure, contain a partial mixture of structure of
> two to several languages, and contain structure common
> to none of the languages in the communication situation.
> (1973: 39; see also Ch. 1 above)

Figure 1 may be helpful in understanding the notion of this
mixture in pidgins.

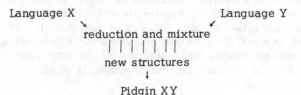

Language X                                        Language Y

reduction and mixture

new structures

Pidgin X Y

F i g u r e  1 . Diagram illustrating pidgin languages generally.

Stokoe (1970) and others have noted that there is a continuum of language varieties between ASL and English expressed or encoded in signing. Woodward (Chapter 2) calls this "the deaf diglossic continuum" and proposes that some of the language varieties, between ASL and English, on this continuum may properly be called Pidgin Sign English (PSE). PSE is illustrated in Figure 2.

American Sign Language          English (manually expressed)

reduction and mixture

| | | | |

new structures

Pidgin Sign English

Figure 2. Diagram illustrating pidginization of ASL and English.

Bernard Bragg says that adult users of sign language often sign a mixture (use a variety on the continuum) of ASL and English, which he calls "Ameslish" (1973: 673). He adds:

> The crux of the whole thing, however, is that neither of us, high verbal or low verbal (deaf persons), really utilize English or Ameslan (alias ASL) in its purest possible form. Our true vernacular is always made up of varying percentages of literal and nonliteral aspects of expression, which works exceedingly well for us as individuals—both expressively and receptively. For some of us who are high verbal, it is always English that dominates over Ameslan; for others, who are low verbal, it is the other way around...[Ameslish] embraces actual speaking, or word-mouthing, fingerspelling (abbreviations and "slurrings" tolerated), gestures, ASL grammar, pantomime, SEE-devised signs, body English, facial expressions, acting, and what have you.

Childrenese may now be placed in the context of Pidgin Sign English and the changes and expression modes Bragg has indicated. Figure 3 may serve to suggest relationships between the language varieties already mentioned.

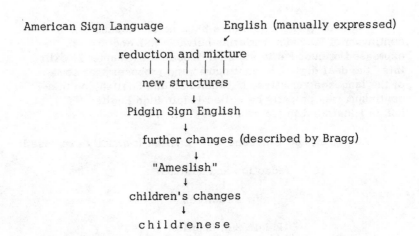

Figure 3. Diagram illustrating further changes in Sign-
English pidgins.

Characteristics   The following examples of childrenese
of childrenese.   have been gleaned from two years of
                  observation and approximately 50 hours
of transcribing videotapes of children's signing at the Kendall
Demonstration Elementary School (Gallaudet College, Washington, D.C.). Perhaps what is described here would more properly be called "Kendallese;" however, some of the following
characteristics and patterns are found in the signing of children in the vast majority of schools for the deaf in this country.

(In the four sections below, the same spatial design used in
the diagrams of Figures 1-3 is used. The characteristics of
ASL are on the left, those of English on the right, and those
of childrenese centered below. Following the descriptions
of the characteristics are examples in the same spatial relationship: top left ASL, top right English, and below center
Childrenese. In the examples of the two signed languages,
capitalized words represent signs that by a convention well
distributed in the sign linguistics community relate to the
English word so appearing. Hyphenated capitalized words
give the approximate meaning of a single sign (or a repeated
sign). Words in lower case with extra spacing between the
letters indicate a fingerspelled item in an example.)

1. Question forms

ASL has signs to ask who,          ENGLISH has specific words
what, when, where, why,            for questions and also uses
how, etc. Facial express-          pitch, intonation, stress, and
ions also mark questions           facial expression

> CHILDRENESE uses two signs
> almost exclusively for its
> questions: FOR-FOR, DO-DO

E.g.
WHY (YOU) HIT LARRY ASK-YOU    Why did you hit Larry?
        FOR-FOR HIT LARRY FOR-FOR
2. Time expressions

ASL has signs meaning 'past,   ENGLISH has all of the ASL
during, since, before, after,  possibilities plus periphrastic
future, tomorrow, yesterday,   constructions and verb tenses
next year, last year, last
week, everyday, every week,
etc.

> CHILDRENESE for the most part
> uses only the following:
> TOMORROW = 'any time in the future'
> YESTERDAY = 'any time in the past'
> EVERYDAY = ' something that happens regularly'
> NOW

E.g.
LAST-WEEK TUESDAY (I) SICK    Last Tuesday I was sick.

> YESTERDAY TUESDAY ME SICK

Because of the limited range of time signs there is a tendency
(and a need) to relate incidents in chronological order. Thus,
an entire series of events may have to be related before a main
point can be made. Childrenese also lacks time connectors
other than THEN and FINISH. Ideas are related only chrono-
logically; there is little or no subordination of ideas.

3. Negation

ASL has signs equivalent to          ENGLISH has all the ASL choices
no, not, don't, nothing,             plus headshake, pitch, stress,
none, not yet, can't,                and intonation.
don't care, no matter,
refuse, etc. Also uses
headshake and negative-
incorporating signs (Ch. 2)

    CHILDRENESE has NO, NOT, NONE
    and also headshake. Often an entire
    utterance is made negative by ending
    it with NOT

E.g.
I LATE STEAL CANDY (with          I didn't steal the candy.
headshake)

    LATE-LATE ME CANDY STEAL NOT

4. Suprasegmentals

ASL tends, according to Fant,        ENGLISH has very definite
to place the visually most im-       word order, uses pause or
portant item first or last in        juncture to aid in clarity of
the utterance; also uses pause       phrasing; dialogue is indi-
or juncture to make meaning          cated by pitch, intonation,
clear and positioning of signs       stress, and juncture.
on "sight line" (1972: 2, 62)

    CHILDRENESE has few fixed patterns;
    visual importance seems not a factor;
    little pause or juncture appears; no use
    of the "sight line" to clarify dialogue

E.g.
(Examples of the three-dimen-     I didn't. (You) Think I did?
sional use of space cannot be     I'll ask Ira. I don't hit Glenn
captured in print or 2-D dia-     everyday of the week, do I?
grams)                            Ira says, "No, you're right."

ME LATE-LATE THINK ME ASK-TO
WHEN ME HIT ME EVERYDAY EVERY-
DAY WEEK HIT g l e n n  SAY i r a
RIGHT-TALK YOU  (English example above is
   a translation of this videotaped passage)

5. Lexical items.

In childrenese, we note that specific lexical items, although
they may be authentic signs of ASL, sometimes have very
limited meanings or take on entirely new meanings. In the
example above, for example, LATE-LATE is a denial (instead
of having its ASL sense 'haven't' or 'not yet'); THINK-ME is
a common sign meaning 'do you think that I'd...'; and
RIGHT-TALK is the most emphatic affirmation of a statement
(often only a mild 'true' in ASL). Other examples in Kendall
School childrenese show an even greater departure from ASL
lexical meanings—    TEMPT (tapping the underside of the
elbow with the index finger of the opposite hand) here means
'talking behind someone's back'; and the common ASL sign
BRIBE has come to mean 'going off the point' or 'changing the
subject'. Of course some idiosyncratic vocabulary is found
in every school for the deaf; it is usually referred to as
"local" sign.
        In addition to these characteristics, which may or may
not be peculiar to Kendall Demonstration Elementary School,
there are other obvious qualities of children's signing that
could be pointed out. There is in children's signed conversation variable and inconsistent use of articles, plurals,
forms of the copula, and verb inflections—all depending on
the degree to which the children attempt to incorporate some
of English structure into their language. Woodward cites these
same characteristics as common to pidgin languages:
    In most pidgins, articles are deleted; the copula is
    usually uninflected; inflections such as the English
    plural are lost; and most derivations are lost just
    as they are in PSE. Perfective aspect in pidgins is
    often expressed by finish or a similar verb like done.
    (1973: 42; and chapter 1 above)
Teachers and parents of deaf children will surely recognize
the ever present sign FINISH to show completed action in
children's signing.

The above examples are enough to suggest that children-
drenese is linguistically different both from ASL and from
English. It is worth noting that while some of the structures
in childrenese may occur in ASL, the latter offers more variety, specificity, and precision of expression. In childrenese
there is evidence of reduction and admixture of the structures
of both ASL and English; there is evidence of a limited choice
of expressive structures; and there are new structures that
are common to neither English or ASL. It is therefore reasonable to conclude that childrenese as described does fall
within the category of a Pidgin Sign English.

Perhaps notice should be taken of a kind of development in children's language; in that case "home signs" are
still further from the two major languages in the communication situation and could be shown as a line below childrenese in Figure 3.

Implications         Identifying childrenese as a pidgin
of childrenese.     and placing it on the deaf diglossic
                    continuum is hardly enough. The fact
that childrenese is a different language variety has, or
should have, several important implications for any school
with deaf pupils. Obviously someone in every such school
should study the everyday language the children use and do
some basic analysis of it, so that the teachers, staff, and
parents will have a working knowledge of the language actually used by the children—the language in which they are
comfortable and presumably most able to understand fully.
Teachers who are unfamiliar with the structures of childrenese
cannot adequately   model   or teach appropriate English
equivalents.

For example, a six year old hearing child says,
"Maybe we will get thirsty or eaty!" The expected reply by
teacher or parent would be, "Yes, maybe we will get thirsty
or hungry." But suppose that the teacher or parent in this
situation did not understand what the child meant by the odd
form "eaty." In that case the reply might have been, "Yes,
maybe we will get thirsty or hot." Similarly, when a deaf
child signs, ME FINISH BATHROOM, FINISH ART, FINISH EAT,
if the teacher replies, "No, you can't go;" it becomes obvious
that the teacher's lack of understanding of the sign FINISH

as it is used in childrenese not only destroyed communication but also eliminated the opportunity for teaching a correct English way of expressing what the child wanted to say (that he had been to the bathroom, finished his art work, and had eaten lunch, and most important, wanted to know what the teacher wanted of him now).

Besides the fact that pidgin languages have attracted the attention of linguists interested in language structure, the simple truth is that pidgins work—they are useful in the situations where they are used. Persons who do not understand the native language of those with whom they must communicate have need of a common language (perhaps while one or other of the parties learns the other's language) and so they readily (and unashamedly) turn to a pidgin. Considering the current situation—deaf students may not be able to communicate satisfactorily in English or in ASL—teachers, parents, and school staff members should enthusiastically utilize childrenese as an aid toward the child's mastery of English and ASL.

At the very least, each school for the deaf should discover and inform teachers, staff, and parents of the local vocabulary, idioms, and patterns in the children's language. Such knowledge is a necessary and invaluable tool for communication and instruction. This is merely to follow a widely accepted principle of effective communication and instruction —meet the student at his or her own level—linguistically too.


## REFERENCES

Bragg, Bernard
    1973    Ameslish: Our American Heritage, American Annals
            of the Deaf 118, 673.

Fant, Louie J.
    1972    Ameslan, An Introduction to American Sign Language
            (Silver Spring, MD, National Association of the Deaf).

Stokoe, William
    1970    Sign Language Diglossia, Studies in Linguistics 21, 27-41.

Woodward, James C.
    1973    Some Characteristics of Pidgin Sign English, SLS 3, 39-46.

Woodward, James
    1974    Implicational Variation in ASL, <u>Sign Language
            Studies</u> 5, 20-30.
- - - - -, & Carol Erting
    1974    Synchronic Variation & Historical Change in ASL,
            Paper at summer meeting, Linguistic Society of
            America, Amherst, Massachusetts.

PART ONE: 4

# WIT & POETRY IN
# AMERICAN SIGN LANGUAGE

Edward S. Klima
Ursula Bellugi

Abstract.    One measure of the psychological reality of
more abstract linguistic categories, for native
users of a language, is the extent to which those categories
are manipulated in such "secondary" uses of language as
poetry and wit. The authors are particularly interested in how
wit and poetic form in sign language are determined by the
visual-gestural mode. A dichotomy will be developed between
those properties of the heightened use of sign language that
are involved more essentially with the structure created by
aspects of movement in general and those that are involved
more purely with the grammatical code itself.[1]

In terms of propositional or referential content, it matters
little that in English, for example, worst ( the superlative of
bad) and wurst meaning 'sausage' sound the same; or that
June, moon, croon, swoon have the same vowel and final
consonant; i.e. that they rhyme. But there are functions of
language outside of the purely referential for which such otherwise incidental similarities become significant in terms of the
totality of what is communicated—in terms of the total import
of an utterance. Among cases where this is obviously true for
the English speech community are puns; such a punning ad-
slogan for mustard as "It brings the best out of the worst
(wurst)" derives its full import from the wurst/worst ambiguity in English. And of course just such rhymes as June, moon,
swoon, croon provide the basis for a superimposed structure
of sound whereby mere sentences take on, in addition, that
special significance of the patterning embodied in verse—
albeit the sentences may express inanities and the verse may
be doggerel. What is special about puns, verse, and poetry

in general is a heightened awareness of linguistic phenomena
as linguistic phenomena. As Jakobson (1960) puts it: "the set
toward the message as such, focus on the message for its own
sake, is the poetic function of language" (p. 356).

Like "art for art's sake" l a n g u a g e   f o r   l a n g u a g e ' s
s a k e would be pure poetic function. While the poetic function
certainly dominates in various forms of language-based art—
and certainly very much so in lyric poetry—the poetic function
is also represented in everyday language use, though in a
less structured way.

In what follows, we shall attempt to show that the
poetic function is represented also in the linguistic activities
of the Deaf community's use of its primary visual-gestural
language, American Sign Language (ASL).

I: AN ANALYSIS OF WIT AND PLAYS ON SIGNS

We have often been asked whether puns and other
sorts of linguistic play are possible in ASL. Sometimes the
question arises along with the much older question of
whether or not the gesturing of deaf persons does or not
constitute a "language" in the sense that English, say, is
a language. [see Chapter 2 above] Perhaps, or so this question sometimes implies, the existence or non-existence of
the special form of wit known as punning could give us clues
to the status of ASL as a language, since punning relies so
heavily on the form of a language. Certainly the older literature on signs and signing contains much that would lead the
uninitiated to question whether such possibilities exist. Tervoort (1961) claims that the spontaneous use of signs in an
ironical or metaphorical way is rare to non-existent.[2] One
might be led to suppose that linguistic creativity in the form
of punning and other playful manipulation of linguistic units
is also absent. One might even be led to ask if the general
sort of structural properties present in all spoken languages
that provide the basis for such linguistic play might not
somehow be absent from sign languages. Thus, since punning and rhyming can inform us about significant structural
properties in spoken languages, it is relevant to ask whether
or not punning and other forms of linguistic play are possible
in ASL.

By 'punning' we mean the calculated use of one word

in an utterance in such a way as to suggest, at the same time, the different meaning of another word having the same (or nearly the same) sound. To say, "If you take care of your peonies, the dahlias will take care of themselves," is to play on the similarity in sound of peonies and pennies and of dahlias and dollars, as well as on speaker's and listener's knowledge of an old saw. When a critic talks of a new series on TV as "The bland leading the bland," he is playing on the similarities in sound between bland and blind, and on another cliche (although such cliches are not essential to punning).

What are the ingredients required in ASL—aside from a kinky imagination bent on verbal punishment? The basis, it seems, is the occurrence, and the awareness on the part of signers, of homonyms or near homonyms. These there are in plenty in ASL, as we have found from the typical errors made in short-term memory experiments we have conducted (cf Klima & Bellugi 1979). Among many others there are pairs like the sign CHAIR and one of the signs meaning 'salt'; the sign FURNITURE (Western U.S.) and the sign translated as 'nothing to it'; the sign THIRTEEN and the sign EJACULATE. Thus the ingredients are certainly there within the language. And we can report that the awareness and the quirky imagination required to make use of them (and, with mock disdain, to recognize them) is present among deaf signers using ASL. One deaf person signed the equivalent of, 'You know he's a man when a boy ejaculates (becomes 13).' Is there the possibility of punning in ASL? Yes, there is, and punning does occur as wit in the communication of deaf persons.

Those who ask us such questions may not realize, however, that there is a rich and abundant use of sign-play by deaf people in ASL —a use that does not depend on the general principles of punning but rather on principles that are special to sign language itself. We shall examine here some of these special principles of sign-play used for wit and humor in ASL. We find that such sign-play frequently involves one of three basic processes:

Process 1. The overlapping of two signs: this can occur in different ways: (a) by making the two signs simultaneously, or (b) by holding a sign (or part of it) while making another sign. The overlapping of two signs relies on a possibility that exists in sign language but not in speech.

Because we have two hands we can, in principle, make
two different [manual] signs at the same time—one with
either hand. Our impression is that the desired goal of
some of these overlappings in ASL wit is to achieve the
ultimate compression of meaning into a minimal number
of units.
Process 2. The blending of two signs: this can occur (a)
by making one sign and then blending it into another sign
so that the two form a complex unit, or (b) by blending
together at the same time properties of two signs—again
the result is a kind of compression.
Process 3. The substitution of one regular ASL "prime"[3]
for another in a sign—such substitutions can occur in
any of the major parameters: hand configuration, place
of articulation, movement, orientation of the sign. The
resultant gesture, in such substitutions, is not an existent ASL sign, but rather a possible sign—one closely
resembling a particular ASL sign in all but one prime of
one parameter. The particular changes in primes generally
have morphological or other symbolic or iconic significance.

In the following sections we will spell out with examples these
three basic processes, which by no means exhaust the possibilities of linguistic play in ASL. The examples are from our
daily association with deaf people and from our videotapes of
everyday signing.

1. The overlapping    In signing, because of the existence
of signs.             of two autonomous articulators
                      (i.e. the two hands), there is the
logical possibility of producing two independent [manual] signs
simultaneously. Moreover, such simultaneity would not be inconsistent with some of the facts and impressions about ASL
that have been mentioned in the past: the weakness of order
of signs alone as a clue to grammatical function (Fischer 1975);
the apparent tendency to compress information into single
units (see Klima & Bellugi 1979: ch. 8); and the use of simultaneous (rather than sequential) modifications of signs to
modulate meaning (Chapter 6 below). In everyday signing, in
fact, one class of signs does occasionally manifest this sort
of simultaneity: the deictic signs in which the pointing hand

is directed to a locus in signing space to be used as a basis
of "pronominal" reference—glossed as (THERE), (HE), (SELF),
etc. (see Friedman 1975). Aside from the simultaneous production of a deictic sign with one hand and a nominal sign
with the other, there are many other logical possibilities; e.g.
the simultaneous signing of a subject with one hand and its
predicate with the other. However, we have found no such
instances in our data of conversational signing. Although the
visual mode could theoretically accommodate such simultaneity,
sentences in conversational ASL are not composed of simultaneous signs. [Editor's note: The failure to find such sentences may be due to limiting the search to manually produced
signs. In conversational signing such a question as 'Are you
interested?' is usually simultaneous in ASL, with a manual
sign expressing the adjectival or state-verb predicate and
head, face, and eye action expressing at the same time the
subject and question indication. Some simultaneous two-sign
manual sentences have also been observed—pp. 27 - 30 above.]
        Overlapping of signs does occur, and quite frequently,
in selfconscious signing of preplanned material, in the plays
on signs that deaf people love to make, and, as we shall see
later, in poetic signing as well. Let us examine a few cases
of overlapping (simultaneous) signing in wit.
a    Making two signs simultaneously. Strict simultaneity is
    best defined as having the movement of a sign being
made by one hand coincide with the movement of a second
distinct sign being made with the other hand. Certainly there
are restrictions on this type of simultaneity, having to do
with the difficulties of making two different motions, one
with either hand. The least complex movement of ASL signs
is that of making a contact with some part of the body or
with a point in space. This is not difficult to combine with
the movement of other signs. However, we have seen other
types of simultaneity in plays on signs.
    E.g. 1: We asked a young deaf man how he felt about
    leaving a place he loved for a new situation and a new
    job. He summed up his feelings eloquently by making
    simultaneously the signs for EXCITED and DEPRESSED
    (Figure 1, Plate 1). Ordinarily each of these signs re-
    quires two hands operating symmetrically. Instead, this
    signer made "half" of each sign with either hand. Not
    only are the signs antonyms, they are also related for-

"EXCITED/DEPRESSED"

Figure 1

"CLEVER/EMPTY-HEADED"

Figure 2

EYES

"EYES/EXPERT"

Figure 3

PLATE I:  THE OVERLAPPING OF SIGNS

mationally, differing only in the direction of movement
(upward brushing of the chest, downward brushing of the
chest). Thus the signer compressed into a single new
sign-creation his ambivalence of emotions.

b    Holding one sign (or part of it) while making another.
    This involves making one sign and holding the final
position and handshape of that sign while making another
sign with the other hand. The final positions of both signs
are then held. Again, this depends on either choosing
signs that are made with one hand only, or on changing a
sign so as to make it as a one-handed sign.

    E.g. 2: A deaf person signed to us that she is clever at
reading signs but poor at remembering them long enough
to write them down. She first made the sign CLEVER with
her right hand, and then held that while she made
EMPTY-HEADED with the other hand (Figure 2, Plate I)—
thus indicating her mixed evaluation of her competence.
These are both one-handed signs, with different handshapes but with a simple contact for movement, and
thus are easily combined in this way.

    E.g. 3: A young deaf man was seen each day with a
different girl. When we commented that he had an eye
for pretty girls, he twinkled and signed what could be
rather freely translated as, 'Yes, I'm an expert (girl-)
watcher.' He first made a sign for EYES, one that
mimics the eyes with two hands. Then holding the final
position of "half" the sign with one hand, he made the
sign EXPERT with the other (signing "eyes-pert" as it
were—Figure 3, Plate I). The combination is particularly
effective in ASL because the two signs he chose use the
same handshape.


2 . The blending      There are various ways of blending
of two signs.         two signs into one unit. One can
                      make one sign and then add the move-
ment of another sign so that the two signs become one unit.
One can take, say, the handshape of a name sign and make
it with the movement, location, and orientation of a different
sign blending the properties of the two into one unit. One can
make a sign and continue its movement throughout what would
normally be the transition to the next sign, allowing for slight
changes in orientation or location, until one sign has been
transformed into another.

E.g. 4: One day we were particularly inept in our attempts
to sign. Our deaf teacher good-humoredly signed to us
that ordinarily we are clever, and then by blending the
sign CLEVER with the sign DEFLATE and the formationally
related INFLATE, she suggested playfully that today the
cleverness was deflated but that tomorrow—after a good
rest—the cleverness would become inflated again. She
made the sign for 'clever' on the forehead as usual with
one hand. At the same time she blended that with the
movement of another sign, usually made with one hand on
the other and meaning 'deflate'. She then "re-inflated" the
sign back to CLEVER again (Figure 1, Plate II).

E.g. 5 (not illustrated): Name signs are often blends of
two signs (See also Meadow 1977). Name signs often begin
by forming the handshape corresponding to the fingerspelled
initial of a first or last name and choosing a location and a
movement for the hand in that configuration. The name signs
for people in our research group were all given to us by deaf
people who work with us. It happens, not infrequently,
that as people become better known, deaf people begin to
blend that name sign with some other sign that refers to
a special characteristic of the person, often originally as
a joke or to differentiate several people with the same
simple name sign. The name sign for Ursula Bellugi is a
U-hand on the side of the mouth with a soft repeated contact. Because she always jots down with great excitement
any new sign she sees, one deaf person dubbed her 'Ursula
the Copier', by blending the U-hand of her name sign with
the location and action of the sign COPY.

E.g. 6: We do not know the history of the next sign, but
its combinatorial properties are very clear. Long before
the impeachment issue arose, deaf people had a name sign
for (former President) Nixon, which was used commonly on
the signed interpretation of TV news. This name sign consists of the handshape (the same as U-hand but horizontal)
representing the letter 'N' made across the chin with a
brushing motion. This sign is a blend of a name sign with
'N' and the ASL sign LIAR, which is made by an index or
G-hand brushing across the chin. Thus the name sign had
indicated, long before the scandal and resignation, that
he was 'Nixon the Liar' (Figure 2, Plate II).

"CLEVER + DEFLATE"

Figure 1

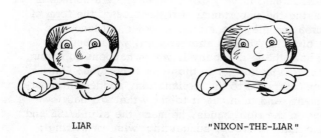

LIAR                          "NIXON-THE-LIAR"

Figure 2

PLATE II:  THE BLENDING OF TWO SIGNS

   There are other kinds of blends. In some plays on
signs, a sign is made and the movement continued throughout
what would be the transition to the next sign, while allowing
changes in orientation to take place until one sign has "become" another. In the examples we have found, these depend
on choosing signs with the same handshape and similar location:
   E.g. 7 (not illustrated): There is a sign of recent coinage
   that means 'total communication'; it is made with the hands
   alternately moving away from and toward the signer at neck
   level. In one play on signs involving this sign, as the
   movement of the sign repeats alternately, the hands gradually move closer and closer to the mouth, until finally the
   signer is making the signs for 'drinking' with one hand and
   'smoking marijuana' with the other. Here we have a case
   of double blending.[4]
   E.g. 8: One time we were explaining to deaf colleagues
   that the blending of signs depends in part on the felicitous
   choice of signs in the first place. There is a sign meaning
   'wise', another meaning 'brilliant', and a third meaning
   'clever'—all formed in very different ways. We non-deaf
   were stressing the importance of the choice of the _form_ of
   signs in creating plays on signs. In order to blend the
   movement of DEFLATE with another sign, we argued, a
   particular handshape is required, which happens to occur
   in the sign CLEVER but not in the other two signs. One
   deaf persons listened to the explanation, nodded in apparent agreement, and then, as if to show that wit has few
   restrictions in the right hands, he made the sign WISE and
   allowed the hand to droop, suggesting 'wisdom wilting';
   then he made the sign for 'brilliant' and made it shatter
   into the sign DUST; and for good measure, made the sign
   WISE again, continuing the movement of the sign while
   changing the orientation of the hand slightly, until WISE
   had turned into PUZZLED.
   These, then, are various ways of overlapping and
blending two signs. Linguistic jokes involving these mechanisms depend on the choice of particular combinations of
meaning and form (as does punning); some of them also depend on making deliberate use of a rarely used possibility in
sign language—forming two signs simultaneously, one with
each hand.

3 . Substitution of       The third general process we
one regular ASL prime    will illustrate used in plays
for another in a sign.   on signs is a change in one
                          of the basic parameters of a
sign so that there is simple substitution of one prime of that
parameter for another. This is essentially a distortion of a
sign so that all but one of the basic characteristics of the
sign are retained. The result of this sort of linguistic play is
a possible but not an actual sign of ASL: neither a citation
form nor a standard modulation of a sign. But it differs from
an actual ASL sign in a way that is significant and meaningful—either in terms of ASL morphology, or in terms of more
general spatial-gestural symbolism. Appreciating the wit
(and often, in fact, recognizing the actual sign behind the
distortion) usually depends on knowing the context in which
the new sign was created.

      It is important to distinguish the differences between
various phenomena all characterized by the substitution of
one prime for another. In the memory experiments previously
referred to (Klima & Bellugi 1979: ch. 4), intrusion errors—
signs that deaf subjects "misremembered"—were frequently
formationally similar to the original sign presented, and often
only a prime away. However, unlike the sign-plays referred
to here, the intrusion errors were actual signs of ASL. We
also find substitution of primes in one other class of phenomena that are not sign-plays: exchanges of primes may occur
in slips of the hand when some aspects of an intended sign
message are transposed. These are analogous to slips of the
tongue or "spoonerisms" in speech, and Fromkin (1971, 1973)
has show how these can provide clues to the way in which
language is organized. For example, if two signs are made in
sequence so that, by mistake, the handshapes are transposed,
perseverated, or anticipated, the result is a slip of the hand
—a prime in one sign being exchanged for a prime in another
sign. Slips of the hand are inadvertent, unplanned, and though
they may arouse a laugh, they differ from wit (see Klima & Bellugi 1979: ch.5). The examples of ASL wit given below were
deliberate, planned changes in signs depending on the linguistic parameters of the language, and they caused that special
type of response triggered by linguistic play.

a   Change in handshape prime.
    E.g. 9: On one occasion a complex technical point about

transformational grammar was being explained in sign language. When asked, "Do you understand?" a deaf person
replied with the sign UNDERSTAND, but instead of using
the index finger (G-hand), the signer made the sign with
the little finger (I-hand). The basis for this distortion is
clear: the little finger occurs in a symbolic way in some
signs where it conveys the notion of thinness (e.g. SPA-
GHETTI, THREAD, SKINNY-PERSON) or extreme smallness
(e.g. TINY, INFINITESIMAL). The substitution of the little
finger for the index finger in UNDERSTAND clearly carried
the meaning 'understand a little' (Figure 1, Plate III).

b   Change in orientation.
E.g. 10: The sign for 'New York' is ordinarily made with
Y-hand brushing sideways [the active forearm is rotated in
pronation bringing the bent fingers of the active handshape
in contact with the other hand, and the action is rotation
of the entire arm at the shoulder joint] along a flat open
palm-up base hand. New York as a city has become a place
where corruption abounds. This distinguishing characteristic
is sometimes playfully expressed within the sign itself by
making the sign, but changing the orientation of the base
hand [i.e. the location marking hand is pronated instead of
supinated before the sign's action begins] so that it is
palm down instead and the active hand is below it. The
significance of this playful change in orientation is made
clear by the fact that the standard citation forms of a few
signs in which the palm of the base hand faces downward
[or in which the action is below the forearm whichever way
the non-active forearm is rotated] have a common semantic
component; e.g. the signs STEAL, KILL, BRIBE, SNEAK-A-
WAY. Thus, making the sign for 'New York' with this change
in orientation of the base hand [and the relative position of
the two hands] can be interpreted as adding to the meaning
of the sign some of the "underhandedness" of life in the
big city (Figure 2, Plate III).

c   Changes in movement.
E.g. 11: After an explanation, which may have been more
confusing than enlightening, a deaf person responded with:
"Yes, I understand." But the sign UNDERSTAND was made
with a backwards movement. Instead of starting from a

UNDERSTAND          "UNDERSTAND-
                     a-little"

Figure 1

COLLEGE          "non-COLLEGE"

Figure 4

NEW-YORK     "underhanded-
              NEW-YORK"

Figure 2

DEAF          "sight-DEAF"
[to sound]

Figure 5

"un-UNDERSTAND"

Figure 3

"B-O-Y-S on-the-mind"

Figure 6

PLATE III:   THE SUBSTITUTION OF ONE ASL PRIME FOR ANOTHER

closed position and flipping open, the hand started from
the final position [i.e. G-handshape] and changed to what
should have been the initial closed position. This resulted in something that was not a sign of ASL, but could be
construed to mean, 'I un-understand' (Figure 3, Plate III).
E.g. 12: One deaf person was asked if she had attended
college. YES she signed, and made the sign for 'college'
with the movement downward instead of upward, conveying
if it can be translated at all, something like 'non-college'
(Figure 4, Plate III). Such sign play is similar perhaps in
spirit—but certainly not in form—to a play on words in
English in which the actual English word upbringing (in the
sense of 'education') might serve as the basis for the playful coining of such a form as downbringing. Certainly not
all movements can be made forwards or backwards and not
all signs with upward or downward movement have predictable
meanings. However, there are some sign pairs which are
opposite in meaning and similar in form except for a predictable difference in, say, direction of movement. The existence of pairs of signs like EXCITED/ DEPRESSED, shown
in Example 1 above, helps in the interpretation and creation
of the plays on signs involving such changes in movement.

d   Changes in location.
E.g. 13: Ordinarily the sign RELAX is made with the hands
crossed on the torso. One time a person claimed that her
eyes were tired, and so suggested that she should 'relax
her eyes', making the sign with her hands crossed over
her face and resting under her eyes instead of on the torso.
E.g. 14: Another person told of the time he bumped into
a door and his eye became bruised and swollen shut so
that he could not see through it. He summed up the situation by signing the equivalent of 'My eye is deaf', making
the sign DEAF across his eye instead of on his cheek.
These changes depend on iconic [indexic] values of the
new locations (Figure 5, Plate III).
E.g. 15: A related phenomenon is characterized by the
change of location of the hand fingerspelling words,
which are ordinarily signed in the space in front of the
chest. One person signed that her daughter was obsessed
with thoughts of young men. She conveyed that by spelling
b o y s , but with the spelling hand on her forehead; i.e.
literally, 'boys on the mind' (Figure 6, Plate III).

The processes of sign play that we have been describing involve manipulations of signs that are, on the whole,
special to the form of sign language itself. The overlapping
of two signs, for example, depends on the use of the two
hands independently to create special kinds of simultaneity
of signs. This is made possible by the existence of two
articulators—the two hands—in producing [the manual signs
of] the language. The blending of two signs, as another example, may involve the fusion of properties of two signs.
Lewis Carroll attempted to achieve something similar in
speech in his blends of, e.g., _furious_ and _fuming_ into
_frumious_. But the essentially sequential nature of word segments does not lend  itself in quite the same way to the
creation of fusions as does a visual-gestural language
based on _simultaneously_ occurring parameters.

Perhaps, we may speculate, a language based on
gesture and vision lends itself to particular kinds of playful extension and distortion of the shape of its basic units
a little more readily than our spoken, more "frozen" words,
which cannot so easily blend, overlap, or otherwise change
shape. In any event, we consider it indicative of the inventiveness and linguistic creativity of the deaf people we have
met that wit and humor abound in the everyday communication
we have observed and captured on videotape.

## II: AN ANALYSIS OF POETIC STRUCTURE IN ASL

The poetic function figures most complexly, of course,
in poetry itself, where linguistic form becomes the basis for
the patterns constituting the multiple layers of structure underlying a poem. In spoken language, we distinguish several
major types of poetic structure. The first of these we shall
call "internal poetic structure," by which we mean structure
that is, as in spoken language, constituted from elements
that are completely internal to the language proper (i.e. in
the case of sign language, constituted from the form of standard signs in ASL—constituted from parts of the grammatical
code itself). The two sub-types of internal poetic structure
to which we shall address our attention here we refer to as
conventional poetic structure (provided or even demanded by
tradition) and individual poetic structure (individual to the
particular poem). In the English literary tradition, such metrical

schemes as iambic pentameter constitute the basis for a kind
of conventional poetic structure. For this structure, the fact
that a syllable has greater stress than the syllables immediately surrounding it becomes significant, as do the number of
significantly stressed syllables. Similarly, various end-rhyme
schemes that establish recurring sound patterns (e.g. aabb,
abab, abba) are part of conventional poetic structure in the
English tradition, as are larger designs like the Elizabethan
sonnet form.

        In structurally complex poetry, however, conventional
structure will be overlaid with more innovative individual poetic structure, consisting of more subtle patterning of not only
sound texture but also of other linguistic elements—syntactic,
semantic, and thematic. Blake's "Infant Sorrow," analyzed
thoroughly by Jakobson (1960), exemplifies the distinction
between conventional and individual poetic structure—both
constructed from aspects of the grammatical code itself.

        In sign language "art-sign", we have discovered
three different types of poetic structure. It seems to us that
there is an Internal Poetic Structure, corresponding to internal
poetic structure in the poetry of spoken languages, but the
patterning of linguistic forms in art-sign is by and large individual rather than conventional. In addition, we have discovered
two types of external structure, different from poetic structure
in spoken language, and special to sign language poetry. One
type can be distinguished as External Poetic Structure, in
which the basic principles include, (a) creating a balance between the two hands, and (b) creating and maintaining a flow
of movement between signs. Then there is yet another kind of
structure, an External Kinetic Superstructure, a kind of design
in space, which may be superimposed on the signs and the
signing, just as in song we may have melodic structure superimposed on the words of a poem.

        The sources for our discussion of poetic or art-sign
structure are varied, but our primary source is from deaf
persons who are or have been associated with the National
Theater of the Deaf,[5] a remarkably talented group of deaf
actors (with an occasional hearing person, often one who has
deaf parents). Several of the actors have worked with us in
our research at one time or another, generously giving of
their time and enormous creative talents. The members of the
National Theater of the Deaf have been developing a poetic

tradition in sign language within our own time. This blossom-
ing tradition involving the heightened use of sign language is
based, as we shall see, on the inherent structural properties
of signs and on special characteristics of signing. Aside
from formal poems, we have also videotaped "songs" that
deaf children invented in sign language, lullabies, children's
sign games, and other aspects of what might be called "folk
art" in sign language.

In order to illuminate some of the basic principles of
poetic signing, we shall present an analysis in depth of a
single line of poetry. Bernard Bragg, a master signer of the
National Theater of the Deaf, has spent many days with us
in our work and has greatly enriched our research. In order to
study the creative process in the development of poetic signing
we gave him as a problem a poem which he had never worked
on before. We asked him to translate it into everyday signing,
and then to show us the process of changing it into poetic
form in ASL until he found what was to him a satisfying solution.
The poem was one by e. e. cummings, "since feeling is first,"
and is peculiarly apt, we feel, for linguists and artists to work
on together, since it juxtaposes "syntax" and "feeling." The
first four lines are:

>               since feeling is first,
>               whoever pays any attention
>               to the syntax of things
>               will never wholly kiss you...

We shall present here only the first line, and study
the change from "straight" (i.e. everyday non-poetic) signing
to poetic "art-sign," in Bernard Bragg's capable hands. The
drawings in Plate IV represent the signs which he chose to
represent the meaning of the first line in straight non-poetic
signing. This version is a direct literal translation of the
words into signs of ASL, as can be seen from the English
glosses of the signs illustrated in Plate IV.

As in normal everyday signing, we find examples of
three formational classes of signs:

a    signs involving both hands, both active and
     operating symmetrically—SINCE[6]
b    signs made with one hand only—FEELING, TRUE
c    signs made with one hand acting on the other—FIRST

A Line from e. e. cummings:  "since feeling is first . . . "

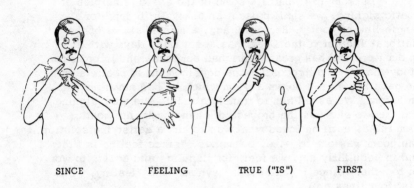

SINCE            FEELING         TRUE ("IS")         FIRST

PLATE IV:  STRAIGHT AMERICAN SIGN LANGUAGE (NON-POETIC STYLE)

BECAUSE          FEELING          ITSELF          "MOSTEST"

PLATE V:  POETIC STYLE IN AMERICAN SIGN LANGUAGE

Because Bragg is right-handed, the one-handed signs are
made with the right hand. In this "straight" version, during
those signs, the left hand is by his side or otherwise not in
use. In this sequence of four signs, there are changes in
handshape from one sign to the next as follows:

| Sign | Right hand | Left hand |
|------|-----------|-----------|
| 1. SINCE | G | G (active) |
| 2. FEELING | 8 | (unoccupied) |
| 3. TRUE | G | (unoccupied) |
| 4. FIRST | G | Å |

The "G" hand                The "8" hand                The "Å" hand

The right hand, then, starts with a G-handshape,
switches to an open 8-handshape, and back to a G-handshape
for the last two signs. The left hand starts with a G-handshape,
then drops down to the side of the body and returns with a
thumb-up Å shape. Note that the hands not only perform the
movement of the signs themselves, but also move in making
the transition between signs. As one sign is finished and before the next sign begins, the hands move from one place of
articulation to another, changing handshape if necessary
during that transition. For example, at the conclusion of the
two-handed sign SINCE, the left hand relaxes and drops to
the side, and the right hand changes from a "G" to an "8"
as it is moving in the transition from the final position of
SINCE to the initial position of FEELING. When signs are
viewed in slow motion (60 fields per second), we might mention that they are observed to be held slightly in their initial
and final positions so that it may become possible to identify
notions like "the initial position of a sign","the movement of
a sign", "the final position of a sign", and "the transition to
the next sign", by objective measurements.

Internal poetic    In moving from conversational style to
structure.         the poetic style of art-sign, Bragg
                   made special changes (see Plate V).
(While the changes he made are interrelated, we will artificially separate them for purposes of analysis.) Consider
first those changes that are associated with the choice of
signs—with "internal poetic structure."

Bragg replaced three of the four signs in changing
from a "straight" to a "poetic" version. The only sign that
remained the same in the two interpretations is FEELING.
Instead of signing SINCE, he chose the sign BECAUSE;
instead of TRUE, he chose the sign ITSELF; and instead of
FIRST, he created a new sign in which a one-handed rendition
of MOST (normally a two-handed symmetrical sign) blends
with the superlative marker -EST. He himself "re-translated"
the resultant blend as "MOSTEST." While not precisely like
the citation form of any single ASL sign, it is certainly inter-
pretable by a deaf viewer. Note that the three signs he chose
for the poetic interpretation all have the same handshape, "A",
and furthermore, that they are, in the way he made them, all
made with one hand only. And as we shall see, aside from
handshape similarities, there were other characteristics
manifested in his particular choice of signs.

In this first line of the art-sign version of the poem,
then, we have four signs, each of which is made with one hand
only. The three made with the right hand share the same handshape. We have come to feel that this notion of shared handshape is analogous to such phenomena as consonance (alliteration) or assonance in the poetic tradition of spoken language.

External poetic    External poetic structure is character-
structure.         ized not by the choice of signs, but
                   rather by their style of presentation.
One general principle of art-sign seems to be that of maintaining a balance between the two hands. Signers, like
everyone else, are generally either right-handed or left-
handed, and sign accordingly in everyday signing; the signer
will use his dominant hand to make one-handed signs; the
dominant hand also is the active hand in signs in which one
hand acts on the other (the base). This means that for the
majority of signs there is an imbalance in the use of the two
hands by any individual signer.[7] But whether, in the act of

signing, it is the right hand that is active or the left is irrel-
evant to the grammatical code of ASL (and no two signs are
distinguished by one being made with the right hand and the
other with the left hand or one with the dominant hand and
the other with the non-dominant.)[8] However, in the poetic
tradition being developed by the National Theater of the Deaf,
an external poetic structure is imposed on art-sign which
includes that of maintaining a balance between the two hands.
There are several ways in which we have observed ASL poets
achieve this balance:
a   Alternating hands in making consecutive signs. After
    signing BECAUSE with his right hand, instead of signing
FEELING also with the right hand, as he would in ordinary
conversation, Bragg uses his left (non-dominant) hand for
that sign.
b   Overlapping, or making (parts of) two signs simultaneously.
    In this one line, we note that Bragg engages both hands
at all times after the first sign. He holds the sign BECAUSE
(right hand) in its final position while making the sign FEELING
(left hand). He holds the sign FEELING (left hand), and in
fact uses it as aim or base for the sign ITSELF (right hand
active). He continues to hold the final position of the sign
FEELING (left hand) while making the final sign-blend MOS-
TEST (right hand). It is in this sense that in art-sign (as
opposed to straight signing) there is a balance of the two
hands—providing a basis for poetic structure external to the
grammatical code proper. It will be recalled that in ASL wit
we have also noted occurrences of overlapping signs.
        Let us look at the use of the hands in the poetic style
of signing the first line, below:

|    | Sign      | Right hand | Left hand |
|----|-----------|------------|-----------|
| 1. | BECAUSE   | A          |           |
| 2. | FEELING   | (A)        | 8         |
| 3. | ITSELF    | A          | (8)       |
| 4. | "MOSTEST" | A          | (8)       |

        parens ( ) indicate handshape held during other
        hand's active signing

There is a second quite general principle of external
poetic structure exemplified by the signing in the presentation

of this one line, and that is the creation of a <u>flow of movement</u>
or a <u>continuity between signs</u>. Creating flow of movement goes
beyond the general principle of internal poetic structure whereby signs are chosen so that, for example, the handshapes
(part of the grammatical code of ASL) of two consecutive signs
are the same. Creating a flow of movement or continuity between signs is often accomplished by interesting sorts of
distortions imposed on the form of the signs themselves, again
going beyond the grammatical code proper. This, for the most
part, is different from what we have found in plays on signs,
in spoonerisms, in regular meaningful modulations of signs,
or in the memory errors we collected from our short-term memory experiments, and is quite specific to art-sign. The distortions associated with flow of movement involve not only
the form of the signs themselves, but also the <u>transitions</u>
between signs. One way of considering this aspect of poetic
style in ASL is to say that an effort is made to utilize the
transitions between signs in such a way as to avoid "wasted"
movement. In distorting transitions between signs, the sign-
poet may attempt to make every movement—even that involved
in the transitions betweens signs—"meaningful," displaying
in some instances the formational properties of the preceding
or following sign. We might mention that poetic signing is, in
our experience, decidedly and markedly slower than signing
in everyday conversational style. One might speculate that
because of this decrease in rate, sign-poets may distort the
shape of signs and the transitions between them without losing
all comprehensibility.

 The sketches in Plate IV of the straight ASL signing of
this line of the poem show the position of the hands at the
initial and the final stages of each sign. The movement from
the final position of one sign to the initial position of the
next sign would be what we are calling the "transition" between signs, and is not represented in the sketches.

 Consider the sequence of signs SINCE and FEELING
in straight signing (see Plate IV). The initial position of SINCE
is represented by the dotted lines near the shoulder, and the
final position is represented by the hands in the solid lines
in the space in front of the shoulder. Similarly, the initial
position of FEELING is represented by the lower drawing of
the hand, which is a dotted line at the mid-line of the lower
torso. The transition between SINCE and FEELING, then,

involves dropping the left hand to the side since it is not in
use; and, at the same time, moving the right hand from the
final location of SINCE to the initial location of FEELING
while changing the handshape from the "G" to an "Ꝿ" hand
during this movement. This is what we mean by the transition between signs.

In the poetic version of the line, Bragg manipulates
the form of the signs so that the final position of the hand
after making each sign is precisely the starting position of
the next sign. The final position of BECAUSE, which is held
throughout the signing of FEELING, becomes the starting
position of ITSELF, and the final position of ITSELF is also
the starting position for "MOSTEST." This would not be the
case in the conversational style of signing the same sequence
of signs. So we see that the internal and external structures
of the line have been made to work together: (a) there is a
simple patterning (repetition) of an element of the grammatical
code—the three signs made with the right hand all share the
same handshape; and (b) the continuity between the signs,
already expressed in the similar handshape, is enhanced by
making the final position of one sign coincide with the initial
position of the sign following it, without the usual blurred
transition or "wasted" movement between signs.

In additional poems we have analyzed there are also
other ways of creating a flow—a continuity—of signs. Some of
these involve blending consecutive signs; occasionally one
finds a distortion of a sign in the form of the substitution of
one prime of a formational parameter for another so that, for
example, consecutive signs maintain similar handshapes,
even if the citation forms of the signs are different. In art-
sign we have also found other ways that signers manipulate
what would normally be the transition between two signs;
i.e. prolonging a handshape throughout a transition, prolonging the handshape and movement of a sign, anticipating
a handshape and place of articulation, etc. This does not
exhaust the means of creating a continuity or flow of movement between signs.

External kinetic          There is yet another type of external
superstructure.           structure which we will consider,
                          and that is external kinetic super-
structure. We consider this somewhat analogous to the com-

bination of melodic and poetic structure which occurs in songs. The melodic structure is superimposed on the words which may as a result undergo certain kinds of distortions from the point of view of the linguistic code, though aspects of melodic and poetic structure may coincide and interact as well.

In the single line of poetic signing under consideration, it may be a little difficult to separate clearly the superimposed kinetic structure from some of the other principles we have discussed. If one looks at the flow charts of the movement of the hands (Plate VI below) in the non-poetic and poetic styles of signing that one line, it becomes clear that in the latter style there has been a further distortion of the signs which creates an enlarged pattern of movement. This is enhanced by other types of distortions we have discussed (such as those eliminating "wasted" movement in transitions), but this further, grosser distortion clearly seems an aim in its own right as well. Bragg has superimposed a special design in space on the signs chosen for the poetic style of signing, a design in space characterized by large, open, non-intersecting movement as shown on the right in Plate VI.

Thus we have illustrated three principles of poetic structure in examining closely one poetic line, and the way in which it has been molded, shaped, and changed in passing from non-poetic straight signing to poetic art-sign. There is internal poetic structure involving the choice of signs—in this case, perhaps, an analogue of alliteration. There is external poetic structure, involving a balance between the hands (by alternating hands in making one sign after the other and by holding one sign while making another) and involving a flow of movement, a continuity from one sign to another throughout the line (distortion of the transition between signs, in this case making the final position of one sign coincide with the initial position of the next). And there is external kinetic superstructure, having to do with creating a design in space, superimposed on the signs themselves.

We have found such principles occurring quite generally in the poetic signing of the members of the National Theater of the Deaf and also in the art-sign of other poet-signers. There are of course other principles of poetic signing which happen not to be represented in this one line. For further analysis of art-sign see Klima and Bellugi (1979).

Clearly there is developing now a rich and fascinating
tradition of poetic style in American Sign Language, highly
sensitive to the special characteristics of a visual-gestural
language and to the possibilities inherent in performing in a
visual-gestural mode.

## NOTES

[1] This research was supported in part by National Science
Foundation Grant GS 42927X and by National Institutes of
Health Grant NS 09811 to the Salk Institute for Biological
Studies. Our thanks to the many deaf people who have fur-
nished us with examples of the sign-play presented in this
paper in the course of our research.

[2] Our experience in communicating with deaf people certainly
contradicts Tervoort's claim. The usage of signs in ironical
or metaphorical ways occurs frequently and freely. These
special uses of signs can often be recognized by very slight
changes in the manner in which they are produced.

[3] We refer to the particular values of the major parameters
(Hand Configuration, Place of Articulation, Movement, Point
of Contact) as the primes of each of those parameters. Thus,
the pointing index hand—a "G" hand—is one prime of the
parameter Hand Configuration.

[4] Robbin Battison furnished this example.

[5] Among those who have helped us by discussing and creating
poetry for us on videotape are: Bernard Bragg and Lou Fant,
both of whom have spent many sessions with us in our work;
also Jane Wilk, Linda Bove, Pat Graybill, Joe Castronovo, Ed
Waterstreet, and others. Members of our research group
(either deaf or hearing people of deaf parents) have also
shared in interpreting, performing, and discussing poems,
including Bonnie Gough, Carlene Pedersen, Ted Supalla,
Sharon Neumann, and Shanny Mow.

[6] The sign SINCE is a direct translation of the English word
since, but its use in ASL would be restricted to the temporal
sense.

[7] In a study of more than 2,000 signs of American Sign Language, we found that only 35% involve the use of both hands where both hands are active. About 40% of the signs are made with one hand only, and another 25% are made with one hand acting on the other hand which remains stationary as a base. Thus for almost two-thirds of these signs, one hand is used as the dominant hand.

## REFERENCES

Bellugi, Ursula, & Susan Fischer
    1972    A Comparison of Sign Language & Spoken Language, Cognition 1, 173-200.

Bellugi, Ursula, Edward S. Klima, & Patricia Siple
    1974    Remembering with & without Words, in Current Problems in Psycholinguistics (Paris, CNRS).

cummings, e. e.
    1923    since feeling is first, in A Selection of Poems (New York, Harcourt Brace & World).

Fischer, Susan
    1975    Influences on Word-Order Change in American Sign Language, in Word Order & Word Order Change, Li ed. (Austin, University of Texas Press).

- - - - -, & B. Gough (=Chapter 6, pages 149-179)
    1978    Verbs in American Sign Language, Sign Language Studies 18, 17-48.

Friedman, Lynn
    1975    Space, Time, & Person Reference in American Sign Language, Language 51, 940-961.

Fromkin, Victoria
    1971    The Non-Anomalous Nature of Anomalous Utterances, Language 47, 27-52.
    1973    Slips of the Tongue, Scientific American 229, 110-117.

Jakobson, Roman
    1960    Linguistics & Poetics, in <u>Style in Language</u>, Sebeok
            ed. (Cambridge, MA, MIT Press).

Klima, Edward S., & Ursula Bellugi
    1979    <u>The Signs of Language</u> (Cambridge, MA, Harvard
            University Press).

Meadow, Kathryn P.
    1977    Name Signs as Identity Symbols in the Deaf
            Community, <u>Sign Language Studies</u> 16, 237-246.

Stokoe, William, Dorothy Casterline, & Carl Croneberg
    1965    <u>A Dictionary of American Sign Language</u>, (Wash-
            ington, DC, Gallaudet College Press; rev. ed.
            1976, Silver Spring, MD, Linstok Press).

Tervoort, Bernard M.
    1961    Esoteric Symbolism in Communication Behavior
            of Young Deaf Children, <u>American Annals of the
            Deaf</u> 106, 436-480.

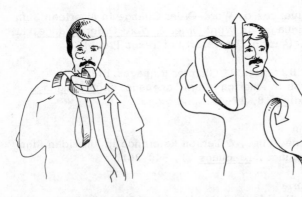

NON-POETIC STYLE                    POETIC STYLE

PLATE VI:   FLOW CHARTS OF SIGNER'S MOVEMENT

CROSS-CULTURAL COMMUNICATION WITH FOREIGN SIGNERS:
FACT & FANCY

Robbin Battison
I. King Jordan

According to popular belief, sign language is very different
from spoken language in several ways. Many people believe that
the signs of sign language are always iconic; i.e. that sign language is a "picture language". Others believe that sign languages
have no grammar, no "proper" ways of expressing things, but merely
"throw together" gestures and pantomimic actions; or they believe
that sign languages abridge and corrupt correct spoken language
grammar. These myths have been treated in recent years by other
researchers, who find that the formal structures and communicative
functions of sign languages used by deaf people are comparable to
those of spoken languages used by hearing people (Stokoe 1960,
1970; Woodward 1973; Battison 1974; Bellugi & Klima 1975; Baker
1975; Frishberg 1975; Chapter Five, above; Liddell 1975; Padden &
Markowicz 1975; Stokoe & Battison 1975).

What we choose to examine in this study is the global and
international nature of sign language. We shall examine briefly
some popular beliefs or myths about sign language in the world,
formulate some questions for study and research, discuss some
past work, and present some of our own research findings relevant
to these questions. We will deal with some very basic questions
about the nature of sign languages used here in the U.S. and in
other countries. We will certainly not exhaust the topic, since our
own investigations are limited in scope and duration, and are still
continuing.

Popular beliefs. There are two related popular beliefs about sign
languages on a global scale: (1) Sign language is universally the
same throughout the world; (2) Deaf signers everywhere have little or no difficulty understanding each other. Naturally if the first
statement is true, the second must be true also, but not vice-versa.
What we would like to do is break down both these beliefs into
statements which can be shown to be true or false.

These beliefs are directly evident in the things that people
write and say when they discuss sign language, and indirectly in
the manner of their discussions. Consider such innocent things
as the word the. It was especially popular in the 19th century to
include "the sign language" in titles of books and articles written
on deaf communication, and the practice has even continued into
the 20th century. We can cite Long (1918), The Sign Language,
and Michaels (1923), A Handbook of the Sign Language of the Deaf.
The misleading implication  of these titles and many others like
them is that there is only one sign language. A very observant
writer of the 19th century, Garrick Mallery, even stated that the
sign language of Indians and of deaf people and everyone else
"constitute together one language--the gesture speech of mankind
--of which each system is a dialect" (1881: 323).

Berthier, another 19th century writer, who was deaf himself,
made a statement typical of his time: "For centuries scholars from
every country have sought after a universal language, and failed.
Well, it exists all around, it is sign language" (1854: 5).

Michaels proposed a somewhat more moderate position: "The
sign-language is universally used by the deaf people, and though
all nations do not use the same mode of signs, one having a
knowledge of the signs herein delineated will experience little, if
any difficulty in understanding other modes, and of being understood by those who use a different mode" (1923: 6f).

Even in very recent years, scholars have made proposals that
sign language could become a universal language for all of mankind
in principle— although no concrete analyses or proposals have
recently been made.

There is abundant evidence that deaf signers themselves believe in the universality of sign language or at least in its potential
easily to become universal. One can cite the efforts of the World
Federation of the Deaf in creating a 323-item list of signs, primarily designed for use during international meetings (Magarotto & Vukotic 1959), and the more recent international sign language Gestuno
(1975). A list of signs designed by a committee, however, should
not be confused with a sign language.

There are also many stories circulating among deaf people regarding communication with foreign signers. The main elements of
these stories seem to be that: (1) Deaf people communicate with
deaf foreigners better than hearing people do with hearing foreigners;
(2) Deaf people throughout the world are united by one basic sign

language;   (3)  Sign Language will eventually become a world
language for everyone, both deaf and hearing.

Issues.  Of course, there is also information which contradicts
these beliefs, and this is one of the things that initially guided
us into the present study. After considering the many things people
say and write about the issue, we formulated a basic set of
questions:
1.  Do deaf people around the world use the same signs?
2.  Can signers understand each other's sign languages?
3.  Can signers from different countries communicate with
    each other even if they don't know each other's sign
    languages?
4.  Do signers have a clear idea of the separateness of dif-
    ferent sign languages, or do they feel and act as if they
    are all basically the same thing?
5.  What attitudes do people have about their own sign lan-
    guage and about foreign sign languages?

While some of these questions seem to overlap, the distinctions will become clear in the discussion which follows.

Procedure.  From a number of sources, we began to collect information on interaction with foreign signers, including:  (1) published
material on the subject;  (2)  Interviews with both American and
foreign signers about their own language background and experiences;
(3)  Our own observations of and participation in sign conversations
involving American and foreign signers;  (4)  Videotaping unstructured
conversations among foreign signers; and (5)  A referential communication experiment by Jordan & Battison (Sign Language Studies, 1976).
      Most of these activities took place in July and August of 1975,
when several thousand foreign deaf signers visited Washington, D.C.,
primarily in order to attend the 7th Congress of the World Federation
of the Deaf. We also had ample contact with foreign students attending
Gallaudet College, which primarily serves deaf students, and with
Americans who had travelled abroad or who had interacted with foreign
signers during the W.F.D. meetings. Whenever possible the longer of
these interviews were videotaped.
      A total of 53 interviews were conducted with people from the
following 17 countries: Australia, Canada, Denmark, Finland, France,
Germany, Great Britain, Hong Kong, India, Italy, Malaysia, Mexico,
Poland, Portugal, Sweden,  U.S.S.R., and U.S.A.

Findings. The first question, concerning the uniformity of signs throughout the world, is easy to answer, because there is much published information on the specific individual signs used in various countries. Some of the many available dictionaries include: American (Stokoe et al. 1965), French (Oléron 1974), Australian (Jeanes et al. n.d.), British (British Deaf & Dumb Association 1960), Swedish (Bjurgate & Nilsson 1968), American Indian (Mallery 1881 [1972]). See also Bornstein & Hamilton(1972). From examining these dictionaries it is evident that there is a great variety of signs used by people to denote the same thing. Signs are not uniformly the same throughout the world, nor are they necessarily standardized within many countries.

One example we can offer to show this variety is from a comparison of French and American signs done by Woodward (1976). He performed a detailed comparison of the 872 signs in a recent French dictionary (Oléron 1974)[1] with current American signs. One would expect a high correspondence between these French signs and American signs for two reasons: (a) French and American Sign Languages are historically related--they share a common ancestor, and (b) Oléron purposely chose for his dictionary those signs which are most easily explainable in "iconic" and "pictographic" terms (Woodward, personal communication), and thus one would expect more correspondence between American and French signs simply because with the more "iconic" signs there would supposedly be less chance of arbitrary symbolism entering into the formation of the signs and creating a difference. What Woodward found in his comparative study was that in spite of these two conditions (the historical relationship and iconic signs), there was only 26.5% shared vocabulary; i.e. only 26.5% of the signs were highly similar or identical in both the French and the American versions. Of course the question of mutual intelligibility does not depend solely on the amount of shared vocabulary, since mutually intelligible dialects of the same language may have a great many lexical differences, and vice-versa.

As a concluding note on this question, it should be noted that earlier researchers on these problems sometimes emphasized (and perhaps exaggerated) the similarities between sign languages rather than noting their (random or systematic) differences. Sometimes the nature of the similarity and the total number of signs involved in the comparison were vague. For example in speaking of deaf signs and Plains Indian signs, Mallery says simply, "Many of them show marked similarity, not only in principle[2] but often in detail" (1881: 323).

Let us take up the next two questions simultaneously, for the
evidence bears on both of them: Can signers understand each other's
sign language? and Can signers from different countries communicate with each other even if they do not know each other's sign
languages? We would like to keep these two questions separate,
because communication can take place without sharing a natural
language--through mime or nonverbal communication, for example.

We quoted Mallery earlier as saying that the signs of Indians,
deaf people, and everyone else really made up one language; however, he later notes that not all Indians can understand each
other's signs (1881: 82, 86-90 passim.). What Mallery meant by
language in these contexts is hard to determine, as he never attempts a concise definition. Certainly he missed one of the basic
distinctions between Indian and deaf sign languages--that deaf
sign languages are learned by some deaf children as native or
first languages, and must necessarily serve all the social functions
of a complete language; whereas Indians primarily used signs with
people who did not speak the same language, and in limited social
situations like hunting, trading, etc. Interestingly, though Mallery
discusses at length the signs of both Indians and deaf people, no-
where does he mention deaf Indians and how they might have used signs.

Let us go back ninety-five years to an early experiment in sign
communication that took place in Washington, D.C., on March 16,
1880.[3] Colonel Garrick Mallery brought seven Ute Indians to
Gallaudet College, where they met with seven deaf students, the
college's president, E.M.Gallaudet, and a number of the staff. A
"testing procedure" was used in which the two groups, Indians and
deaf signers, alternated telling each other individual signs and connected narratives. Mallery describes six of the short narratives and
describes seven of the "signs" in detail.[4]

Interestingly, four of the seven "signs" he describes were not
understood. The six short narratives were understood without much
difficulty, although it is apparent that much of it was simply miming
scenarios involving hunting, gathering food, and eating specific
foods. Two examples will illustrate the ad hoc nature of the communication on that day:

Among the signs was that for squirrel, given by a deaf-
mute. The right hand was placed over and facing the
left, and about four inches above the latter, to show
the height of the animal; then the two hands were held
edgewise and horizontally in front, about eight inches
apart (showing length); then imitating the grasping of

a small object and biting it rapidly with the incisors,
the extended index was pointed upward and forward
(in a <u>tree</u>).
   This was not understood, as the Utes have no
sign for the tree squirrel, the arboreal animal not
being found now in their region (1881: 321).

We need only point out two things: (a) The supposed "sign"
was really a sequence of at least four separate mime elements;
(b) The Utes probably did understand what was being described
(not named)--a small arboreal animal which gathers and chews
small objects.
   The second example indicated another weakness in these experiments. Despite Mallery's expertise in observing, collecting,
and describing gestural communication, he neglected to fully take
into account the effects of social context on intelligibility:
When the Indians were asked whether, if they
(the deaf-mutes) were to come to the Ute country
they would be scalped, the answer was given,
"Nothing would be done to you; but we would be
friends," as follows:
   The palm of the right hand was brushed toward
the right over that of the left (<u>nothing</u>), and the
right hand made to grasp the palm of the left,
thumbs [sic] extended over and lying upon the
back of the opposing hand.
   This was readily understood by the deaf-mutes
(1881: 322).

We are not given the details of the students' interpretations
of these two signs, but we can reasonably assume that the Utes
were expected to say something of a friendly nature, thus it is
not surprising at all that the students "readily understood" them.
A report of a more modern experiment is given in Jordan and
Battison (1976).
   But now let us move to more recent events with other trans-
ported signers. From our interviews with deaf signers from America
and other nations, we obtained a range of self-reports on communication with members of other deaf cultures. First, examining the
question <u>whether sign languages are understood by foreigners</u>, we
have the following information:

1. A German actor, whose company performs in mime (not in any variety of German Sign Language), complained that one of the reasons they could not perform a stage show in their own sign language was that they would not be understood when they travelled to other German cities.

2. A young woman from Lyons reported that she refuses to visit Paris without her friend who has been to Paris more often and understands the Parisians' sign language better--Lyons and Paris are 250 miles apart.

3. A standard story, repeated by travellers and natives alike, holds that if you travel 50 miles in Britain you will encounter a different sign language that cannot be understood in the region you have just left.

4. An Italian and a Pole who have both travelled widely were in a casual conversation with five Americans. They made no attempt to imitate or use American signs; they stated flatly that they did not understand American signs; and they relied the entire time on an American who was skilled in using international signs and signs from various European countries.

5. From Swedish, Danish, and Finnish informants we learned that the four Scandinavian countries have separate sign languages, but that people from Sweden, Denmark, and Norway can undertand one another with only moderate difficulty. On the other hand, interaction between Danes and Finns frequently requires the use of an interpreter.

6. An American who has a reputation for being a highly skilled communicator reported that when he was with the Israeli groups during the W.F.D. Congress: "They signed so fast, I felt like I was hearing!"[5]

7. Both an Australian learning American signs and a Dane learning Finnish signs reported that their comprehension of the new language exceeded their abilities to express themselves correctly in it. The Dane said, "After many visits, I can understand it with almost no problem, but I can't sign it myself." The Australian said, "I don't feel comfortable using ASL; I can understand it, but not express myself."

What we conclude from these reports and others like them is that: (a) Not only do people use different signs in different parts of the world but also these signs are largely unintelligible to foreign signers when used in connected discourse; (b) Geographical

boundaries of sign language intelligibility do not always correspond to the boundaries of spoken languages--while many of the
deaf in Scandinavia can understand one another with only moderate
difficulty, we also have the opposite situation, that cities or
regions within small countries (e.g. Britain, Germany, France)
determine linguistic boundaries;[6] (c) As with spoken languages
that are learned informally (in a normal communicative situation
rather than in a classroom), comprehension of a second sign
language surpasses correct expressive usage of that language.

Now we shall again take up the question Whether deaf
signers can communicate with each other, and if so, how?

Most of our non-American informants, particularly the
Europeans, say that communication with foreign deaf people is
not a problem. Depending on past experience and amount of
interaction with the foreigners, most people say that after two
or three days they can understand each other pretty well.

This does not at all contradict the previous findings that sign
languages are unintelligible to foreigners, because, when asked
specifically about how they communicate with foreigners, many
of them say specifically that they stop using their own sign language and start using mime and gesture. Other features of such
communication are that it is slower than signing, very repetitious,
and involves a lot of back-and-forth bargaining and checking about
the meanings of various gestures. Gradually, a shared meaning for
various signs emerges through the conversation. The composite
description of cross-cultural communication matches Mallery's
(1881) very insightful discussion of interaction among different
tribes of Indians.

The general consensus of our well-travelled informants was
that this type of communication is a skill that can be improved
with the experience of a great deal of foreign interaction. The communication may be augmented by other means: E.g. using agreed-
upon international signs, fingerspelling familiar words from a spoken
language, speaking occasional words which are thought to be well
known. In this preliminary report we shall not attempt a detailed
description of how these cross-cultural communications take place,
but we would like to consider briefly the factors of topic, situation,
and motivation.

Many contacts between deaf foreigners take place when people
are travelling, and are therefore concerned with the basic necessities
of food and shelter. Also, when meeting foreigners for the first time,

much basic personal and social information is exchanged--Where
are you from? What do you do? Are you married? Is your husband
with you? Where are you going next? Etc. etc. In other words,
there is a high expectancy that certain topics will come up again
and again before interaction is allowed to move to more intricate
and less superficial interactions.

Motivation is higher in these interactions, partly because when
one is tired, cold, hungry, or bored, one tries very hard to alleviate
these situations by establishing communication with those who live
in the area. A consensus among our informants was that it is difficult to discuss very weighty or "deep" subjects with foreigners.
Politics, religion, and philosophy are difficult, while travel, food,
school, jobs, family, and entertainment are much easier. Also, it
is much easier to discuss things in a dyad than in a larger group.
One other motivational factor which may contribute to successful
communication is the patience and perseverance of deaf people,
most of whom have a great deal of practice dealing with weak communicative situations involving hearing people.

Moving to the fourth question: "Do signers have a clear idea
of the separateness of different sign languages, or do they feel and
act as if they are all basically the same?"--most of the evidence
says they do keep languages separate in spite of the fact that an extensive mixing of languages and styles takes place when in contact
with foreigners.

The evidence regarding this separateness is of five kinds:

1. When native signers (those with deaf parents) are asked what
their first language was, they almost always answer, "Sign Language"--not Swedish Sign Language or French Sign Language, or
any other national or regional type. It seems as if they are under-
differentiating or confusing various sign languages that they know
(or know about), but when pressed further, they make it clear that it
was a sign language, as opposed to a spoken language, that they
learned first.

2. Some signers in America tend to think of all European sign
languages as being vaguely the same entity and are often surprised
at the complexity and differences among European sign languages;
while Europeans themselves are more experienced with languages.
We have two illustrations of this contrast: (a) In the course of intro-
ducing a Dane to some Americans, the Canadian introducer used a
few Danish signs. One of the Americans remarked to him, "Oh, you
know International Sign Language!" (b) A European teacher of the
deaf, who is deaf himself, spent a year as a graduate student at

Gallaudet. An American student asked him if he planned to take
American Sign Language back to his country. The teacher looked
surprised and said, "No, what for? We have our own sign language
in my country." The student was astonished. Prior to his departure
for the U.S., the same teacher had announced to his class of ten-
year-old deaf pupils that he was going to America for a year of
study. The class erupted with expressions of dismay. When asked
why they thought it was so terrible, the pupils answered, "Because
you'll have to learn American Sign Language!" These European
youngsters, who had seen many foreign deaf people come and go,
had a clear idea of the separation of different sign languages; while
the older American college students did not.

3. We have two other major kinds of evidence to show that people
keep their sign languages "separated." The first involves people
who move to a different country. By all reports they forget their own
signs rapidly as they acquire the sign language of their new country.
We can report only one exception to this, a Finnish woman who
moved to Denmark. Other foreigners in Denmark were surprised that
she retained her native Finnish Sign Language.

4. It is also interesting to note what happens when one of these
expatriates has visitors from his native country. All of them report
that they have difficulty readjusting to their first language and that
it takes several days of interaction with their guests before they
begin to feel normal. They also report that they can understand but
not express themselves very well in these situations.

5. Another type of evidence which shows that signers are capable
of keeping their languages separate is what happens when a multilingual person mistakenly substitutes one language for another. We
can illustrate this with an event which occurred two separate times:
Two Finns, a Dane, and an American were travelling in a car. The
two Finns were father and daughter and were having a conversation
in Finnish Sign Language. The Dane was multilingual and attempted
to interpret from Finnish to American signs for the benefit of the
American. However, in the confusion he started signing to the American in Danish signs, and went on like that for a minute before the
American stopped him and asked him to interpret into a language he
could understand!

Attitudes. Finally let us consider attitudes toward language and
language users. Since much of our material on language attitudes
is from European signers collected during a three-week period in
the United States, these generalizations are not without limitations.

Europe consists of many small countries whose deaf people interact extensively through travel and emigration. The United States is large, relatively homogeneous, and linguistically isolated from the rest of the deaf world. Possibly because of this isolation, deaf Americans seem to mirror the language attitudes of the American hearing majority culture. This involves ethnocentrism, language chauvinism, and linguistic naïveté.

Europeans claim that Americans are rigid and inflexible in their language and hard to understand. One deaf couple from Europe had to resort to pencil and paper to communicate with deaf people when they first arrived in the U.S. They could make themselves understood, but could not understand the Americans when they signed, because they claimed, the Americans did not modify their language or slow down at all.

There were several reports of American students being surprised that foreigners had different sign languages, and also that deaf people needed interpreters to go from one sign language to another. When asked how foreigners communicate with each other, Americans would describe their communication with labels like "home signs", "all pictures", "basic gestures", "mime", and "poor sign language". Europeans who knew about these American attitudes suggested that the Americans were not judging them on their own national sign languages but on the gestures and mime that they used when communicating with foreigners.

To illustrate how language-related attitudes can affect cross-cultural interaction, we offer the following story of two foreign deaf students at Gallaudet College. Although they came from two separate countries, they had very similar backgrounds. Both were profoundly deaf, had deaf parents, and were native signers of their own national sign language. They learned English before arriving in the United States, and they had an excellent command of written and spoken English. Possibly because of this prior knowledge, and possibly because they first were exposed to American signs in a classroom, they used American signs with English syntax, just as most hearing people do. As a result, the other students thought they were either hearing or orally-oriented, awkward signers. The American students were not willing to believe that they had deaf parents, because they did not sign like the children of deaf parents should. Because of this "suspicious" behavior, one of these foreign students was falsely labelled as a narcotics agent and briefly ostracized.

Mistaken identity worked the other way, too. In spite of the fact that they had been signing all their lives, several foreign students said they could not distinguish deaf Americans from hearing Americans on the basis of their signing, for the first six months or so. To them, "Everyone signs the same."

For the European visitors during the W.F.D. Congress, America was full of pleasant surprises also. Most of them were awed by the fact that people from California could really understand people from the East Coast without any problems, and that the U.S. had a truly national Sign Language. Many people from the European drama troupes, all of whom perform in mime, dance, and gesture, were astonished at the National Theater of The Deaf's performance in American Sign Language. Several of them had previously commented that a play in real sign language would be impossible to stage. And finally, many Europeans commented on how well sign language was accepted here in the United States--it was used in the schools; hearing people learned it; and deaf people could sign on the street and not feel ashamed. These people were surprised, since these contrasted with their own experiences in their own countries.

Conclusions. We have established and examined a number of questions relating to sign language communication between deaf people from different countries. From personal interviews and observations we can suggest partial answers to some of them.

From examining some of the many sign language dictionaries available and from our records of communication with deaf foreigners, we do know that signs vary considerably from country to country. This much is certainly not in dispute.

From the personal reports of travellers and immigrants alike, we know that sign languages are not understood by signers who are not familiar with them--certainly not as easily understood as some stories would have us believe. Comprehension of a second language exceeds correct expression in that language; receptive skills exceed expressive skills.

The fact that deaf signers can and do communicate despite not sharing the same sign language is interesting, and it bears more investigation. While being skilled in sign language may prepare one for dealing with mime and for communicating in difficult cross-cultural situations, the two should not be confused. Signers consider them separate tasks.

The data we have gathered gives us little reason to believe that sign languages are much different from spoken languages as regards

cross-cultural communication. To the extent that sign languages
are separate entities, communication is hindered between groups.
We need more information about the limitations and potentials in
communication between foreign signers. We also feel that there
is a need for intensive linguistic investigation of national sign
languages everywhere.

## NOTES

[1]  The signs in Oléron (1974) are taken from the same corpus
of data Oléron examined twenty-two years earlier (1952).

[2]  We interpret Mallery's "in principle" to mean that the
general image evoked by the sign is the same, but not
necessarily the actual formation of the sign. This is
another example of the notion of iconicity clouding the
investigation of formational structure.

[3]  Mallery gave the date as March 6 (1881: 321). It is identical of course in the facsimile reprint of 1972. The date,
however, for the event given in E. M. Gallaudet's diary
is March 16, undoubtedly the more reliable dating.

[4]  Seeking corroboration of Mallery's account of the meeting,
we looked in the Gallaudet College archives at the personal
records of E. M. Gallaudet. Apparently the event was not
as impressive to him as to Mallery; his diary entry that day
is:
>          March, Tuesday 16. 1880
>          Cold raw day, a little rain. We had a visit
>          at the Inst.[itute] from Col. Mallery
>          & a party of Ute indians [sic]. I took a
>          Fr.[ench] lesson. Called on Mr. W. K. Rogers
>          the Prnts. [Pres. Rutherford B. Hayes'] Pri. Sec.
>          Rev. John Chamberlain of N.Y. arrived & was
>          quartered at the inst.

In his report of the event Mallery records the names of none
of the deaf students but names five of the Indians.

5.  In other words, he was made to feel like an average hearing signer, who always has great difficulty following a normal deaf sign conversation.

6.  One might begin to look for an explanation for these geographic discrepancies in national attitudes toward sign languages. The two groups of countries named are at extreme ends of a continuum as regards public and educational acceptance of signing among deaf people. Signing in public and in schools is becoming widely accepted in Scandinavia, while it is forbidden in schools and heavily stigmatized and suppressed in many countries of the world. One could argue that the public and institutional acceptance of signs has a standardizing influence, since people communicate more freely under these conditions and tend to interact over social and regional differences and in a greater variety of situations.

## REFERENCES

Baker, Charlotte
    1975    Regulators and Turn-Taking in American Sign Language. Paper presented at the 50th Annual Meeting of the LSA.

Battison, Robbin
    1974    Phonological Deletion in American Sign Language, Sign Language Studies 5, 1-19.

Bellugi, Ursula, & E. Klima
    1975    Aspects of Sign Language & its Structure, in The Role of Speech in Language, Kavanagh & Cutting eds. (Cambridge, MIT Press), 171-205.

Berthier, Ferdinand
    1854    Observation sur la mimique considérée dans ses rapports avec l'enseignement des sourds-muets. A M. le Président et a MM. les Membres de l'Academie Imperiale de Médecine. Paris, L. Martinet.

Bjurgate, Anne-Marie, & M. Nilsson
    1968    Tekenspràk för döva. Stockholm, Sö-Förlaget;Skolöverstyrelsen.

Bornstein, Harry, & Lillian Hamilton
    1972    Recent National Dictionaries of Signs, Sign Language Studies 1, 42-63.

British Deaf & Dumb Association
     1960     The Language of the Silent World (Paisley, Scotland).

Frishberg, Nancy
     1975     Arbitrariness and Iconicity: Historical Change in Ameri-
               can Sign Language, Language 51, 696-719.

Gallaudet, E. M.
     1880     (Personal diary for the year 1880) Archives of the
               Gallaudet College Library, Washington, D.C.

Jeanes, D., R. Deanes, C. Murkin, & B. Reynolds
     n.d.     Aid to Communication with the Deaf (Melbourne,
               Victorian School for Deaf Children).

Jordan, I. King, & R. Battison
     1976     A Referential Communication Experiment with Foreign
               Sign Languages, Sign Language Studies 10, 69-80.

Klima, Edward
     1975     Sound and Its Absence in the Linguistic Symbol, in The
               Role of Speech in Language, eds. Kavanagh & Cutting
               (Cambridge, MIT Press), 249-270.

Liddell, Scott
     1975     Restrictive Relative Clauses in American Sign Language.
               Working paper, the Salk Institute, LaJolla, California.

Long, J. Schuyler
     1918     The Sign Language: A Manual of Signs (Reprinted 1962,
               Washington, D.C., the Gallaudet College Library).

Magarotto, Ceasare, & D. Vukotic
     1959     First Contribution to the International Dictionary of Sign
               Language--Conference Terminology (Rome, World Feder-
               ation of the Deaf).

Mallery, Garrick
     1881     Sign Language Among North American Indians (Washington,
   [ 1972]    D.C., Government Printing Office [The Hague, Mouton],
               (=Approaches to Semiotics 15, ed. T. A. Sebeok).

Michaels, J.W.
   1923   A Handbook of the Sign Language of the Deaf (Atlanta,
          Southern Baptist Convention).

Oléron, Pierre
   1952   Études sur le langage mimique des sourds-muets, L'Année
          Psychologique 52, 47-81.

   1974   Elements de Repertoire du Langage Gestuel des Sourds-
          Muets (Paris, Centre National de la Récherche Scientifique).

Padden, Carol, & H. Markowicz
   1975   Crossing Cultural Group Boundaries into the Deaf Commun-
          ity. Paper presented at the Conference on Culture and
          Communication, Temple University, Philadelphia.

Stokoe, William
   1960   Sign Language Structure: An Outline of the Visual Communi-
          cation Systems of the American Deaf, Studies in Linguistics:
          Occasional Papers, 8 (Revised 1978, Linstok Press).

   1970   Sign Language Diglossia, Studies in Linguistics 21, 27-41.

- - - - -, & Robbin Battison
   1975   Sign Language, Mental Health, & Satisfying Interaction,
          Proceedings of 1st National Symposium on Mental Health
          Needs of Deaf Adults and Youth, eds. Mindel & Stein
          (New York, Grune & Stratton, to appear).

- - - - -, D. Casterline, & C. Croneberg
   , 1965  A Dictionary of American Sign Language on Linguistic
   [1976]  Principles (Washington, Gallaudet College Press
           [Silver Spring, MD, Linstok Press,' 2e]).

Woodward, James C.
   1973   Implicational Lects on the Deaf Diglossic Continuum.
          Ph.D. dissertation, Georgetown University.

   1976   Signs of Change..., Sign Language Studies 11, 81-94.

World Federation of the Deaf
   1975   Gestuno

# VERBS IN AMERICAN SIGN LANGUAGE

Susan Fischer
Bonnie Gough

What is    Important for the study of any language is precise
a verb?    knowledge that something is a verb and that other,
           similar things are not. In American Sign Language
(ASL), there are clues different from those in English for deciding that something is a verb. One major clue is inflection
for person, but in ASL this process is more general than it is
in many languages. Although many, but not all, ASL verbs
have distinct forms for first, second, and third persons, it is
not the subject person only that is so indicated; also, and
indeed more often, the object, source, goal, and other arguments of a sentence affect the form of a sign verb. Almost
three-fourths of the verbs we investigated for this study behave in this way. The only other parts of speech that behave
at all similarly are personal pronouns, but there is difference
between these two classes, verbs and pronouns.

The horizontal angle made by the signer's forearm distinguishes the ASL pronoun forms that mean 'you two' and
'the two of them'; it also distinguishes the ASL verb form in
'I give you' from the verb form in 'I give them.' Straight
ahead for second person and obliquely out for third, the
forearm extended moves slightly side to side for these two
pronouns; it extends as it rotates for the verb forms. Now,
the pronouns for first and second person are formed by direct
pointing with the index finger. The form of the verb in 'You
give them' requires swinging the forearm from straight away
to obliquely away as the rotation is done. Thus, it can be
seen that the person indicated determines the pronoun form,
but both subject and indirect object of a verb like GIVE
determine the verb form in ASL.

A second major clue to knowing a sign verb is context.
If it appears between two noun signs, it is probably a verb;
if it follows an auxiliary, it may be a verb; but like English
have, some ASL auxiliaries can also be main verbs. They

149

can also leave the addressee to supply a common verb appropriate to the object. If no one verb fits, the sentence is ungrammatical. In the following examples, the verb that the addressee must read in is underlined:

(1) IF YOU WANT SEE DENTIST, YOU BETTER APPOINTMENT.
    'If you want to see the dentist, you had better make an appointment.'
(2) ME CAN'T MOVIE NIGHT, MUST ALGEBRA.
    'I can't go to the movies tonight; I have to do algebra.'
(3) * ME CAN'T AFRICA. (Too many choices of verb)
(4) THAT BOY WILL DOCTOR.
    'That boy will become a doctor.' (or in context)
    'That boy will go to the doctor.'
(5) SHE CAN'T APPLE.
    'She can't eat apples.'
(6) HE CAN'T VACATION NOW YEAR.
    'He can't take a vacation this year.'
(7) YOU SHOULD CUP.
    'You should use a cup.'
(8) ME MUST PARTY.
    'I have to go to a party.'
(9) * HE WILL DEER. (Too many choices)
(10) THAT t-a-d-p-o-l-e WILL FROG.
    'That tadpole will become a frog.'
(11) * RECENTLY THAT TOWN ELECTRICITY. (Too many choices)
(12) * ME WILL HEARING-AID TOMORROW. (Too many choices)

All of the unstarred sentences are acceptable, even as the first utterances in a discourse. The starred ones and others like them cannot begin discourse but may be acceptable if the missing verb has been established as a topic. Thus, in a conversation about buying things, (12) would be acceptable and its verb understood as 'buy'.

Nouns strongly affect the acceptability. If a noun can occur as the object of only a limited number of verbs, then omission of one of these verbs is grammatical. Although our native informant says that the signs after the auxiliaries in the sentences above are nouns, and although we may be claiming that a verb is deleted by the signer and read in by the addressee, we must show that the items after the auxiliaries really do function as nouns. Let us consider eight of the examples (1,3,4,6,7,8,11,12), omitting those that deal with becoming. If we can insert a quantifier of the kind that occurs

only with nouns without changing the sign's meaning, we
can be fairly sure our claim is correct. The quantifier TWO
serves this purpose admirably, since it cannot occur with
verbs:
(13) * ME MUST TWO GO.        (14) * SHE CAN'T TWO LAUGH.
But there is an adverb, TWICE, that goes exclusively with
verb phrases:
(15) ME MUST GO TWICE.        (16) SHE CAN'T LAUGH TWICE.
What then about the nouns to be tested?
(18) YOU BETTER TWO APPOINTMENT.
    'You had better make two appointments.'
(19) SHE CAN'T TWO APPLE.
    'She can't eat two apples.'
(20) YOU SHOULD TWO CUP.
    'You should use two cups.'
(21) ME MUST TWO PARTY.
    'I have to go to two parties.'
(22) HE CAN'T TWO VACATION NOW YEAR.
    'He can't take two vacations this year.'
(23) ME CAN'T TWO MOVIE NIGHT, MUST TWO LESSON.
    'I can't go to two movies tonight; I have to do two
    lessons.'
    All these sentences are indeed grammatical, and the
only difference in meaning is the quantification of the nouns.
All these sentences can occur with TWICE as well, but then
it is the whole verb phrase that is modified. Sentences (4),
(9), and (10) are more difficult to test with a quantifier:
(24) * HE WILL TWO DOCTOR.
    However, if one can find a plausible context, this
sentence becomes acceptable:
(25) HE WILL TWO DOCTOR, DENTIST AND SURGEON.
    'He will become <u>two</u> doctors—a dentist and a surgeon.'
    We can show that in other contexts DOCTOR is indeed
a noun, but this next problem makes this kind of sentence
a class by itself. BE is a sign of ASL, but it tends to be
used either for emphasis or for signing English; i.e. using
signs as words to write, as it were, English sentences in
the air. This is not at all the same thing as signing ASL.
In the former one uses signs as substitutes for English words
and follows all the requirements of English grammar; in the
latter one uses signs as the words of ASL and uses the grammar of this language. The normal way to sign in ASL the
meaning 'He is a doctor' is
(26) HE DOCTOR.

If one signs instead

(27)     HE BE DOCTOR.

The meaning is, 'He really is a doctor.' Thus (4), THAT BOY
WILL DOCTOR simply differs from the English way of using
a copula in the normal way of ASL; its inchoative sense can
be inferred from the time frame (WILL). There is so far no
way of deciding whether BE or BECOME needs to be read in.

 Besides inflection and context, a third way to decide
whether something in ASL is a verb is the intuition of the
native signer. If our informant feels that DOCTOR is a noun
and not a verb, even though there is an implicit verbal feel
in a sentence like (4), this is a valid piece of evidence. If
she says that NO is a verb, and not always an interjection,
and if she or we can show how it is used as a verb, then we
are justified in taking the informant's judgement as accurate.

Mutability of ASL verbs.  Having established what
              signs are verbs and what
signs are not, we proceeded to investigate the mutability of
verbs in American Sign Language. We prepared a list of
verbs by picking out of The Dictionary of American Sign Language (Stokoe, Casterline, & Croneberg 1965 [1976]) any
verb that had more than one page number referred to in the
index. Then in the body of the dictionary, we picked out
all the verbs for which alternate forms were given by the
entries. The verbs so selected are shown in Table 1.

 We went over each item with our informant, asking
various questions about mutability (categories will be
discussed below). It turned out that some of the items
were not verbs; others were indistinguishable from verbs
elsewhere in the list (i.e. were two different glosses for
one sign); and also two or more signs were covered by one
gloss (e.g. SAVE names two verbs, one for keeping, the
other for rescuing). What follow are the matters we took up
with our informant for each item:

1. Strict subcategorization—How many and what kinds of
  syntactic categories the verb occurs with; e.g.
  [NP___#] for an intransitive verb.
2. Selectional restrictions—Semantic restrictions on the
  above categories; e.g. [+Anim___].

Table 1. The list of ASL verbs investigated.

| | | | | |
|---|---|---|---|---|
| ARGUE | ELIMINATE | LAUGH | RUN | TRAVEL |
| ARRIVE | ENJOY | LEAVE | SAVE | TURN |
| ASK | GET-EVEN- | LECTURE | SAY-NO | TWIST |
| BITE | WITH | LET | SCOLD | UPSET |
| BLAME | EXCHANGE | LIE | SCRAPE | USE |
| BLEED | EXPECT | LIKE | SEND | VISIT |
| BORROW | FACE | LOCK | SHINE | WADDLE |
| BRIBE | FALL-OFF | LOOK | SHOOT | WALK |
| BRING | FEAR | LOSE | SHOP | WASH |
| CATCH | FED-UP | LOVE | SHOW | WIN |
| CHANGE | FEED | MEAN | SIGN | WORK |
| CHEAT | FIND | MINGLE | SIT | WORN-OUT |
| CHOOSE | FINISH | MISS | SKATE | WORRY |
| CLASH | FLATTER | MIX | SMILE | WRITE |
| CLOSE | FLY | MOOCH | SMOKE | ZOOM-OFF |
| COME | FOOL | MOVE | SNOW | |
| CONNECT | FORCE | OPEN | SPELL | |
| CONVERGE | FORSEE | OPERATE | SPOIL | |
| CORRESPOND | FREQUENT | PAIN | STAND | |
| CRASH | FRIGHTEN | PAINT | STARVE | |
| CROSS | GET-TOGETHER | PASS | STAY | |
| CUT | GIFT | PICK-UP | STRETCH | |
| DANCE | GIVE | PITY | STUDY | |
| DECIDE | GO | POSTPONE | SUBSCRIBE | |
| DEFEAT | GOSSIP | PRACTICE | SUFFER | |
| DEFLATE | HATE | PRAISE | SUPPORT | |
| DEPOSIT | HAND | PREACH | SUPPRESS | |
| DESIRE | HEAR | PULL | SURPRISE | |
| DISAGREE | HELP | PUSH | SWALLOW | |
| DISAPPEAR | HIT | RAIN | SWEAR | |
| DISAPPOINTED | HOPE | REBEL | TAKE-PICTURES | |
| DISOBEY | INFORM | REDUCE | TAKE | |
| DIVE | INJURE | REFUSE | TALK | |
| DIVORCE | INSULT | REMEMBER | | |
| DO | INTERESTING | REMOVE | TEACH | |
| DON'T CARE | INVITE | REST | TEASE | |
| DRESS | IRON | REVERSE | TELEPHONE | |
| DRINK | JOIN | RIDE | TELL | |
| DRIVE | KICK | RIDICULE | THROW | |
| DROP | KISS | RISE | TRANSFER | |

3. Directionality—Whether the verb moves in the direction
   of one or more of its arguments, and if so which; e.g.
   SEE is directional between subject and direct object.
4. Incorporation of location—Whether the verb sign is performed closer than neutrally to the location, real or
   established, of the referent of one of its arguments.
5. Reversibility—Whether the orientation of the hand(s)
   changes depending on the location of arguments; e.g.
   SEE is [-Reversible]; LOOK is [+Reversible]; and
   OWE is also [+Reversible] but not directional.
6. Incorporation of size and shape—Whether the verb sign
   changes its handshape, location, and/or movement
   to reflect the size and/or shape of any of the referents of any of its arguments; and which arguments are
   so affected; e.g. REMOVE can incorporate the size and
   shape of the source, direct object, goal (perhaps), and
   instrument.
7. Incorporation of manner—Whether the action of the sign
   can change intensity or speed to reflect either the manner
   of the action referred to, the speaker's attitude toward
   the performance, or the mode (declarative, imperative)
   of the utterance. (Nearly all ASL verbs can incorporate
   manner in one of these ways.)
8. Incorporation of number—Whether the verb can undergo
   fast reduplication with horizontal movement, or other
   means of indicating plural in an argument; e.g. the
   number of hands or fingers used. (Any verb positive for
   this feature is also marked if it cannot form the collective plural by sweeping the hands and/or body around
   in one performance of the action; see Fischer 1973.)
9. Habitual—Whether the verb can form the habitual aspect
   by fast reduplication (without horizontal motion), and
   shows any irregularities in the change of meaning from
   the base form; e.g. DON'T-CARE is [+Habitual].
10. Continuous (slow reduplication)—Whether it is grammatical
    to perform slow reduplication to mean 'for a long time';
    e.g. FEED is [+Contin]; FEAR is [-Contin].
11. Reciprocal—Whether the verb can (or must) take two ar-
    guments that perform the action on each other and appear
    in the verb sign; e.g. GIFT allows reciprocity; HEAR
    does not, in TWO HEAR EACH-OTHER; EXCHANGE requires
    reciprocal.

12. Reflexive—Whether the sign can change to show a dis-
    tinction between, e.g., I (verb) MYSELF and SOMEONE
    (verb) ME, the verb is reflexive; LOOK is [+Reflex].

Strict subcategorization     In this section and the
rules.                       next, we will concentrate
                             on the differences in the
way the verb sign and the English word used to gloss it behave. The major syntactic difference, in general, is that
many English intransitive verbs seem to be transitive in ASL,
and conversely that some English transitive verbs can be
intransitive in ASL. There are two major reasons for this,
accounted for at least partially by the grammar of ASL. First,
ASL does not use fillers (enclitics), although some ASL verbs
incorporate directional meanings. Thus the sentences in (28)
with enclitics underlined are likely to be signed as in (29):

(28) I arrived in New York.       ME ARRIVE NEW-YORK.
     I went to New York.          ME GO NEW-YORK. (cf Fant 1972)
     John looked at Bill.         JOHN LOOK-AT BILL.
     I am ashamed of you.         ME SHAME YOU.
     George is afraid of spiders  GEORGE AFRAID SPIDER.
     The linguist got even        LINGUIST EVEN-WITH GOVERN-
       with the government.          MENT.
     The vase fell off the table. VASE FALL-OFF TABLE.
     We will not invite her       WE NOT INVITE-HER OUR PARTY.
       to our party.
     I always laugh at him.       ME ALWAYS MOCK HIM.
     Do you subscribe to Ms.?     YOU SUBSCRIBE m-s?

    The second reason for differences in strict subcategori-
zation of semantically similar verbs in ASL and English is
that some verbs that are intransitive only or transitive only
in English may be either intransitive or transitive in ASL,
with the general meaning that the transitive is the causative
of the intransitive, or that the intransitive is the passive
(or middle) of the transitive. We have cases like this in
English:

(30)   a The door opened.
       b The boy opened the door.
(31)   a The ice melted.
       b The sun melted the ice.

This is somewhat more extensive in ASL:

(32)   a   HOW MUCH BUTTER LEAVE IN COLD BOX?
           'How much butter is left in the icebox?'
       b   PLEASE LEAVE BUTTER IN COLD BOX YOU.
           'Please leave the butter in the icebox.'
(33)   a   MAN OPERATE FOR CANCER.
           'The man was operated on for cancer.'
       b   DOCTOR OPERATE MAN FOR CANCER.
           'The doctor operated on the man for cancer.'
(34)   a   PICNIC POSTPONE BECAUSE RAIN.
           'The picnic was postponed because it rained.'
       b   WE POSTPONE PICNIC BECAUSE RAIN.
           'We postponed the picnic because it rained.'
(35)   a   BABY SAVE IN BATH, CAN SWIM.
           'The baby is safe in the bathtub since it can swim.'
       b   DOG SAVE BABY.
           'The dog saved the baby.'

As these and other examples show, some form of a
case grammar might be quite appropriate for describing ASL.
This will show up more strongly in our discussion of selectional restrictions.

Selectional        Strict subcategorization rules are toward
restrictions.   the syntactic end of a syntactic-semantic
                spectrum; selectional restrictions are
nearer the semantic end. One might therefore expect the
latter sort of rules to be somewhat similar for ASL and for
English. While this is by and large true, there are some interesting differences; e.g. in English one can say (36), but
in ASL one must sign (37)—the second utterance shown in
(37) is not grammatical:

(36)   Our new furniture came yesterday.

(37)   OUR NEW FURNITURE ARRIVE YESTERDAY.
       *OUR NEW FURNITURE COME YESTERDAY.

The verb COME in ASL requires an animate agent. The verb
DISAGREE requires human agents; so while (38) is permitted
in English, (39) shows that different verb choice must be
made:

(38)      These two answers disagree.

(39)      THESE-TWO ANSWER DIFFER.
                              ... OPPOSITE.
                              ...*DISAGREE.

Similarly, <u>clash</u> can refer to people, personalities, or
colors in English, but the ASL verb CLASH can refer only
to people:

(40) a    Orange clashes with red.
     b    ORANGE RED CONFLICT.
                    ... *CLASH.

Some other differences: BRIBE implies money; one cannot
BRIBE a child with candy in ASL. Three morphologically
related verbs meaning 'support' have different selectional
restrictions in ASL. The first, made by pushing upward on
the passive arm at wrist then nearer elbow with the active
hand in fist formation, denotes physical support, often of
a large structure. The second, active fist under passive
fist thrusts upward (dez and tab 'A' in 'a' or 's' form),
selects both human patient and human agent, but the support may be moral or material. The third, which is the
second repeated, has the added restriction that the support
is monetary. The verb STAY requires an animate agent. If
one wishes to sign the equivalent of 'I want the telephone
to stay there', one must use LEAVE, not STAY. A verb that
seems to be less restricted semantically is FREQUENT,
as in 'to frequent a place, go often.' This verb can be
used not only with a location, as in English, but also with
a person as goal or direct object. The verb glossed SUB-
SCRIBE really means 'to receive regularly' and is limited
to magazines, newspapers, or money—the latter generally
in the form of pension or alimony.
      The generalization of selectional restrictions is one
of the reasons one might wish to opt for a form of case
grammar. In such a grammar, the verbs OPEN, CLOSE, FLY,
CHANGE, CONNECT, JOIN, DEFLATE, HANG, POSTPONE,
SHINE, and STRETCH would have double sets of selectional
restrictions, for transitive and intransitive uses, thus the
direct generalization about what their patient must be could
be avoided; e.g. POSTPONE has two sets of strict subcate-

gorization and selectional restrictions. For the intransitive
use these are

       [NP___]         and      +[+Event]___
  e.g.:   'I put (it) off'      'Vacation (was) postponed'
For the transitive use of POSTPONE they are

       [NP___NP]     and    [+Human]___[+ Event].
  e.g.:     'They <u>postponed</u> it' 'He <u>postponed</u> Thanksgiving'
Similarly for SHINE:

intr.  [NP___]     and    [+Concrete]___
tr.    [NP___NP]   and    [+Human]___[+Concr].
  e.g.:  'The car shines'
       'We shined the shoes'

Directionality.   Every language has strict subcategorization rules and selectional re-
strictions, but the next topics seem to be unique in those
languages that are expressed in a gestural modality—not
so much as to what the processes indicate but rather in
terms of the way they work. The first process, limited to
verbs, can be considered a process of incorporating a pronoun (or a case-marking copy of from one to three arguments)
into a verb. The pronoun copy is then deleted, leaving behind a trace—the direction in which the sign moves.

The citation form of a verb in ASL is the form with a
first person singular subject. If we simply ask our informant to give the sign for a given English verb, she will
reply with the form appropriate to use with the signer as
subject (and either YOU or some indefinite direct or indirect object). Thus the sign that means 'give (a present to
someone)' is made by two 'X' hands moving abruptly away
from the signer. For 'I give something to you', the signer
completes the sign with smoother action and ends with the
hands pointing toward the addressee. If, however, the
meaning is 'Someone gives something to me', the motion
of the sign is reversed; i.e. the hands move from the direction of the addressee toward the signer. If one wishes
to say 'You give something to her', the signer begins the
sign from the direction of the addressee and moves it toward
the location of the recipient, or the location for her that
has been established in the context. Throughout these
changes, the handshape of the verb sign remains constant;
only the direction of the motion changes to indicate the
(location of the) arguments.

Directionality is not varied on a horizontal plane only;
it varies vertically as well. If a tall adult is speaking to a
small child and wishes to say that (s)he will give the child
something, the sign action is not only away from the signer
but also downward toward the child. If the situation is reversed and the child talks of giving the adult something,
the sign moves upward as well as away from the signer.
When verb action is directed toward a person or animal, it
is usually the location of the eyes that determines the
precise angle of motion. Toward an inanimate object,
something like the center of mass seems to be used. Thus,
the verb LEAVE ('let something stay', not 'depart') is directional toward its direct object. To make this sign, one
flings the spread hands outward from the body up, down,
or to the side, depending on the location of the object.
Thus, if something is up on a shelf, the sign LEAVE is
made upward; but if it is on the floor, the action is downward. (This last verb is also partly locational; see next
section.)

GIVE is directional between the giver and the receiver;
but LEAVE is directional toward the object left. There are
other options for directionality as well. The verb BRING is
directional between source and goal. If one wishes to say
'I bring something down from a shelf over to the table',
the hands move from high up (in the direction of the shelf)
and then obliquely down toward the table. The subject (as
agent or doer of the action) is not part of this instance of
directionality.

An interesting subset of directional verbs is made up
of those that include a body part as an argument. This can
be the source, the goal (in a sense), or the direct object.
Verbs that involve directionality to or from body parts include BITE, OPERATE (surgery), HIT, BLEED, HURT, CUT,
INJECT, REMOVE, SHOOT, and AMPUTATE. If one wants
to sign 'I bumped into a door', one must specify with the
verb's movement which part of the body made contact
with the door. One generally specifies (although there is
a neutral form, the hand) the place from which one bleeds.
If one describes a mosquito bite, one shows where the
victim has been bitten, and so on. Generally these signs
(except for SHOOT) involve actual contact with the body.

In summary, directional verbs in ASL change their direction of movement to point toward the locations of various
arguments in the sentence. This process, together with
reversibility and location (next sections), is most analogous in function to inflection for person in spoken languages.
It is more extensive, however, since it inflects the verb
for arguments other than subject (agent) and/or direct object (patient); and it is also more specific.

Reversibility.    There is another way, partially related
                        to directionality, that a sign verb shows
clearly the grammatical relations among its arguments (i.e.
the noun parts of its sentence). This is the phenomenon we
are calling reversibility. If in addition to or instead of a
change in direction of movement in a verb to show who is
doing what to whom, there is also a change in the orientation of the hand(s), the verb is reversible, since the hands
can reverse or change their orientation. Not all directional
verbs are reversible, and there is at least one reversible
verb that cannot change direction.

A verb that cannot change direction is OWE; another
is LOCK. The reason for this is most likely that the action
of OWE has virtually no movement. OWE is made by (repeated)
contact of the point of the index finger (dez hand G) in the
palm of the other (tab B) hand. Except for the repeated
touching action, neither hand moves. One way of showing
the difference between 'I owe you' and 'You owe me' is by
reversing the orientation: For the former meaning, the tab
hand's palm is obliquely toward the signer, but toward the
addressee for the latter; and the touching action thus goes
appropriately in the direction of the obligation.

MEET is a very interesting verb, in terms of its directionality and reversibility. The citation form of MEET
uses both hands in index shape (G) with forefinger pointed
upward; and its action is the coming together of the hands,
palms toward each other so that the bent fingers of each
make the contact. But this is not the only form in which
MEET occurs. One way of changing it is for only one hand
to move, the other remaining in place. This will mean
'One person meets another', in contrast to citation form,
which means 'Two people meet.' With change in orientation,
change in person is indicated; thus for 'I meet you' the

passive (tab) hand is held out between the addressee and
the signer in supination (i.e. twisted so that the palm is
toward signer), and the active (dez) hand in pronation (full
opposite twist) moves outward to contact the other. The
meaning 'You meet me' reverses the orientation and also
changes the direction of this verb. The passive hand—left
hand for right-handed signers—is held close to the signer
in pronation, and the active hand, supinated, moves in
to make the same kind of contact (in all forms of MEET the
bent fingers touch, though it is usual for the fingertip of
an index hand to make the contact). These changes must
be difficult to follow in description, especially for someone unfamiliar with ASL; but they become simpler if one
thinks of each hand as a surrogate for a person involved
in a meeting situation. The upward pointing index finger
indicates the head,and the palm of each hand represents
the frontal plane. So it is in mutual meetings that both
parties converge, but otherwise one moves toward the other.

    As we have seen, in MEET and OWE both hands change
orientation for reversed relationship of arguments; but this
is not necessarily the case for all reversible verbs. In
some the tab hand stays the same and only the dez hand
changes orientation. In BEAT, for example, the dez (what
acts) is the dominant forearm. It strikes the tab (left
forearm for right-handed signers) and bends at the wrist
to continue its motion slightly. The tab is held horizontally and does not change orientation, but the dez, in a
near vertical orientation is supinated when moving inward
and pronated for outward ('I beat you') action; thus the
point of contact on the tab is respectively ulnar and radial.
In both forms the proximal (inside) surface of the dez
makes the contact. Other verbs reversible in the manner
of BEAT ('win in a contest' not 'strike') are ARREST,
FLATTER, CALL, FREQUENT, BLAME, KICK, BITE, PREACH,
COPY, and TEASE.

    There are a number of signs with optional reversibility.
The citation form of BORROW has for dez one (usually the
dominant) hand on top of the other, both hands in 'K' or 'V'
handshape; its action is motion of the whole dez configuration
inward toward the signer. Signed thus, it is the form used in
signing 'I borrow from you'. To sign 'You borrow from me'
equivalent to 'I lend to you' one can either reverse only the
direction of the motion or reverse both direction and the

orientation of the hands. CALL-BY-NAME is another of the
optionally reversible verbs. Verbs of this class are exceptions to a fairly general rule that seems to apply to reversible verbs; namely, directionality is often optional (though
not for LOOK and SEE), but once this option is taken, if the
verb is reversible, it <u>must</u> reverse as well.

Locationality.  A third way a verb sign may show its
                grammatical relations is in displace-
ment of the dez, as what acts, to the proximity of the location of one of its arguments. In contrast to directional
verbs, in which the arms move during the formation of the
sign, and to reversible verbs, in which the hands may change
orientation, in the case of locational verbs, just before
the sign is actually made the arms  are first moved toward
the appropriate location, and then the sign is performed.
Because the extension of the arms and not their action determines the grammatical relations to be interpreted, those
verbs that are prohibited by the nature of their action to
be directional can still be locational. Thus OWE, as we
have already seen, can reverse, but it cannot change direction, since it basically has no direction to change.
Similarly the basic motion of WANT is the bending of the
fingers; although in citation form the arms may move in
toward the signer slightly, this part of the sign is not
always present, especially in the unstressed form. Both
of these signs, however, can be performed near the location of one of the arguments. In the case of OWE, the
sign is performed near the location of the patient. In
the case of WANT, the verb can be signed either near
the subject (agent) location or near the object (patient)
location. With other locational verbs, the subject or the
object may be what is located by the verb (e.g. SIGN-
ONE'S-NAME), and context or the signer's eye direction
is needed to show which.

Combinations: phonological    Directionality,
and semantic considerations.   reversibility,
                               and locatability,
three means of indicating pronominal grammatical relations,
can occur in various combinations. Restrictions on which
of these combinations occur are mainly determined by the

phonology of ASL; otherwise lexically. It is also true that
not all verbs are mutable in any of the individual or combined ways. These restrictions, too, are also largely
phonologically determined.

A number of verbs can be both directional and reversible. These are largely two-handed (symmetrical)
signs; e.g. HATE, BORROW, LOOK, and FEED. Their action
is generally lateral rather than vertical, oscillatory, or
circular. Verbs that combine directionality with location
are a rather interesting set phonologically. In most of
them, the tab is a hand held stationary. This tab can be
placed toward the location of one of the arguments (thus
making the verb locational); the dez hand then moves toward that argument from the direction of (or toward)
another argument so that the action of the verb becomes
the directional part. Examples include BLAME (optionally
reversible as well), DIVE (source, not goal is locational),
and KICK.

There are very few verbs that combine only rever-
sals of orientation and location. They must be made out in
space, and the motion must be minimal; e.g. LOCK, OWE
(reversibility varies with idiolect), and PITY.

Numerous verbs can combine all three—direction,
reversal, and location—generally with the same restrictions we find in the combination of location with direction;
reversal is added. Such verbs include GET-EVEN-WITH,
FLATTER, FOOL, FREQUENT, HIT, PAINT, and sometimes
MEET (when one argument meets another only).

Exceptions.    Not all verbs in ASL can undergo all
                these processes either singly or in
combination. While there are some true exceptions (i.e.
verbs that should change direction of movement, hand
orientation, or location to show arguments but do not),
there are a number of general principles that account for
most of the verbs that do not participate in these processes. The first principle is that signs made primarily
with body tabs cannot change in these ways. This class
accounts for almost all verbs that do not participate in
these processes. The verbs HEAR, LISTEN, and EAVES-
DROP are all located on the ear or signed toward the
ear. TELEPHONE is made at the side of the face. FEAR,

ENJOY, LIKE, INTEREST(ING), LOVE, and SUPPRESS-ANGER
all have chest as tab. THINK has forehead; LOOK-LIKE is
made near the face; EAT is near the mouth; SWALLOW is
made on the throat; MISS (a bus) is near the nose; REFUSE
moves over the shoulder; and SURPRISE is made near the
eyes. None of these verbs is physically capable of incorporating location, reversal, or direction change.

A second principle is that if the movement involved
in the sign is vertical, the sign verb cannot change direction or reverse, although it may be locational; REMEMBER,
DECIDE, DISAPPEAR, PRAISE, LECTURE, ANSWER, and
SUBSCRIBE fall into this category.

As we saw with OWE, a verb that has little movement other than simple contact may be able to reverse or
incorporate location, but it cannot be directional. (We
have defined directional as change in the direction of
movement.) There are few verbs in ASL with minimal movement; examples are IRON, DANCE, SIGN (language),
MEAN (intend or signify), ASSOCIATE, TRAVEL, and DO.

There is a group of verbs (e.g. JOIN, PRAISE,
SKATE, DEPART, ARRIVE, SWEAR) that cannot reverse,
apparently because it would be awkward if not physically
impossible to do so. Thus in the sign ARRIVE (made by
hitting the back of the dez against the palm of the tab hand)
it would be impossible to reverse the orientation of the
hands unless the signer is double-jointed. Some of the
others are not impossible to reverse; but the notion of
what constitutes excessive awkwardness in signing is
still to be clearly defined; BORROW reversed is found to
be quite difficult to perform by some signers, especially
beginners, which may be why it is optionally reversible.

There are some real exceptions, verbs that are
not covered by these principles but do not reverse or
change direction. The verb RUIN, made by a fist dez
grazing the back of the tab wrist and hand pronated as
it sweeps outward, cannot reverse. The verb TEASE can
reverse, even though it is almost identical to RUIN except that the movement or action is less forceful and is
repeated. The semantic difference between these two
verbs cannot account for their difference with respect to
reversibility; nor can intensity as a feature. Other verbs
with intensity in their action do undergo reversibility;

e.g. HATE, FINGERSPELL-BIG-WORDS, and BLAME. There
are also verbs that do not repeat movement and yet can
reverse; e.g. PAY, CATCH, and LOCK. This is simply an
idiosyncratic exception such as is found for almost any
morphological rule in any language.

     Verbs of ASL that refer to time seem also to be ex-
ceptions to directional and reversible processing; e.g.
FORSEE, REMINISCE, POSTPONE. Verbs with future reference tend to have forward movement; those with past
reference tend to have movement backward. The forward
motion in FORSEE and the backward motion in REMINISCE
supersede any change in direction of movement (Nancy
Frishberg, personal communication). [An alternate explanation is suggested by the authors above, page 152; this is
to consider FORSEE and REMINISCE two glosses for but
one verb that changes both direction and orientation, depending on whether the (adverbial) argument is the future
or the past. Ed. note]

     The three processes by which ASL verbs incorporate
pronominal arguments are elaborations, it seems, of inflection for person. They operate with verbs in ASL and only
with verbs as is exemplified in one way of saying 'no' in
this language.

     The 'no' used to answer a yes-no question is a
modified form of the word no fingerspelled; but instead of
forming a "proper" 'n' (first two fingers bent down over
the thumb) and 'o' (all four finger tips meet thumb tip),
the signer of this NO first spreads apart the thumb and the
first two fingers then closes them so that just the three
tips contact. Used to answer a question, this sign does
not vary except in intensity, even when it might seem to
be appropriate; e.g. in relating a conversation between the
signer and another. The signer had reported asking the
other person a question and continued:

(41)    ME ASK-HIM, BUT HE ANSWER "NO".

In this sentence, ASK incorporates location and reverses,
but NO, even though addressed to signer, is unchanged
from its citation form.

     By contrast, there is a verb, not an interjection,
which we have glossed as SAY-NO, that is formed exactly

like NO except that the arm moves from direction of agent
toward goal (indirect object) and the dez orientation changes
so that the palm faces the same way the (imagined) no-
sayer faces. The starting point of SAY-NO also is close to
the location of the agent. Again, in describing a conversation, a signer might report:

(42)    ME REQUEST-HIM FOR NEW BICYCLE, BUT HE
        SAY-NO ME.

Here SAY-NO is directional; the arm moves from agent
toward indirect object. It is reversible; the dez in citation
form is pronated (palm out), but here supinated (palm to
signer). It is locational; the back of the dez may start
far out in the direction of the third person agent and end
almost in the signer's (recipient's) face. In this example,
then, the closing action of the thumb and first two fingers
suffices to form the interjection NO, but this sign word
is otherwise invariant. The same closing action, when it
is used as a verb, exhibits three of the defining properties
of ASL verbs.
        Even though there may be an analogous relation be-
tween directionality, locationality, and reversibility in Sign
and inflection for person in spoken languages, there is
obviously a difference between the two modalities in the
mechanics of the processes. Spoken languages use space
only insofar as air is necessary to transmit sound waves.
A gesture language, on the contrary, is laid out in space,
and uses it crucially. Indeed one can say that in its processes of change in direction, orientation, and location
ASL takes full advantage of being produced in space.

Incorporation            If the processes which have been
of size and shape.       discussed make crucial use of
                         space, the incorporation of indi-
cations of size and shape of arguments in sign verbs can be
said to mold space to fit the intended change in meaning.
The verb OPEN incorporates the shape of the patient (i.e.
direct object when transitive and subject when intransitive).
OPEN is one verb in which incorporation of size and shape
is obligatory; in many verbs it is optional, but is therefore
a stylistic change that adds color. Thus OPEN in DOOR

OPEN differs from OPEN in WINDOW OPEN; and other
changes occur if it is a sliding window that opens. The
ASL noun sign WINDOW represents a double-hung sash
window; the hands together move apart vertically and
together again. The sign DOOR represents a hinged door;
i.e. hand or hands twist open, close, open. It is interesting to note that the Japanese sign for 'door' moves
the hands horizontally apart and together, for the can-
onical door in Japan does not have hinges but slides.

The signs for opening a large box and opening
a small box are distinct, as are the signs for opening a
jar by unscrewing a lid or by prying. This brings up an
interesting point. Many of the signs that we gloss with
multiple words could be glossed more economically; e.g.
we could say UNSCREW instead of OPEN-JAR-BY-UN-
SCREWING, or SPOON-OUT instead of REMOVE-FROM-
CONTAINER-WITH-SPOON. In English there are both
specific verbs and more general paraphrases. We are
using the periphrastic alternative here because the sign
on which the variation is based is more perspicuous.

As can be seen from the previous example, the
size and/or shape of the instrument can be incorporated
in a sign verb. In REMOVE-FROM-CONTAINER-WITH-
SPOON, the shape of the signing hand is a slightly bent
'U' (i.e. index and middle fingers extended, not spread).
If the instrument is a large spoon or a scoop, all four
fingers are cupped to reflect the larger size of the instrument. If the instrument is a fork, the hand has the V
handshape (index and middle fingers extended and spread).
If the instrument is chopsticks, the sign starts with a
'V' but then closes to U as the motion is performed.

One verb that incorporates changes in size and
shape of agent (subject) is RUN. For human and other
two-legged creatures one of several variants of this sign
uses the forefinger of each hand extended downward. If
the runner has four legs, the first two fingers of each
hand are used. This can be said to be an abstraction
from an iconic representation of legs.

The size and shape of the source and goal can
also be incorporated. In the example above, REMOVE-
FROM-CONTAINER-WITH-SPOON, the size of the container is indicated by the circumference of the curved

tab hand, and the shape of the container by its orientation to represent a vertical cylinder. If the source is
not a container but a surface, the tab hand is held flat
and contact is made on its palm.

Many of the features used to indicate size and
shape of various arguments in the sentence are used and
recombined over and over again. The extended forefingers
used for iconic "legs" in RUN are also used for STAGGER,
ENTER-VEHICLE, MOUNT (horse or bicycle), LIE-DOWN,
STAND, FALL-DOWN (for quadrupeds the four iconic legs),
and CLIMB.

The use of the tab hand for the container, source,
or goal, with variation in its shape and orientation as
required, is also quite extensive. If a flat hand is used,
it can represent a plate, the floor, or any flat surface.
If a slightly cupped hand, palm up, is used, it may represent any kind of dish. The cupped hand representing
a cylinder, as noted above, can vary diameter of the indicated circle to show size; it can also be used more
generally in signs like DEPOSIT-MONEY-IN-THE-BANK,
RIDE-IN (or GET-INTO)-A-VEHICLE, as well as for the
other directionality of the dez; i.e.'withdraw', 'get out'.
More metaphorically, the curved tab hand represents the
goal in JOIN-AN-ORGANIZATION or QUIT-etc.  The B-tab
hand, rotated edge upward, in signs that depict straddling
a horse or bicycle, is also used to represent anything
that may be straddled, e.g. a chair back or a wall. These
features of the sign verbs all abstract general properties
from the physical objects they are meant to represent—
after all, a horse does not look much like a hand; and
two bent fingers may suggest a spoon, once one knows
that this is what they are supposed to represent, but
really show no  striking similarity to a piece of metal
with a handle and a bowl. Nevertheless, these are symbols that can combine with other symbols to form new signs.
Such combinations as REMOVE-FROM-WIDE-MOUTH-JAR-
WITH-SPOON could be said to be analogic with polysyl-
labic words in English; they are more complex than simple
signs.

The verb MEET discussed above is actually a special
case, incorporating size and shape, of a more general verb
COLLIDE. The performance of the general verb shows first

whether both subject and object are in motion or only the
subject; second, it shows, with size and shape incorporation, the salient dimensions of the two arguments.
If the subject or object has height as its salient characteristic, the upright index hand is used $(G_\wedge)$; e.g. for
persons, poles, trees. MEET, which is restricted to
human subjects and objects, uses two G-upward hands;
but CAR-CRASH-INTO-TALL-THIN-OBJECT uses the index
hand only as its (stationary) tab. An object considered
to have height and width will generally be represented
by a flat hand; thus, CAR-CRASH-INTO-WALL uses an
upright flat hand as tab. When the subject or object has
three relevant dimensions, e.g. a vehicle, a fist is
used to represent it. Thus, TWO-CARS-COLLIDE consists of two fists converging and meeting in sharp
contact. In the two examples just above, the dez (active)
hand, which of course represents the subject, is a fist
also. These one, two, and three-dimensional representing shapes of the hand are used as productive features
in many signs. In general, those verbs that require exclusively human subjects do not vary for size and shape,
presumably since the subjects' size and shape are already
fixed. In actual appearance, however, the handshapes
used are not even remotely suggestive of human beings.

Incorporation     The speed, intensity, and extent of
of manner.        action of a sign can be varied to
                  produce variations in meaning of the
sign. This general property is not restricted to verbs; e.g.
the sign LARGE is made with two hands starting side by
side and moving apart. If the sign is performed relatively
slowly and tensely and the hands move very far apart, the
sign translates something more like 'huge'. If it is performed even more slowly and intensely and the hands in
separating curve upward from the horizontal, it means
something more like 'enormous'.

When a verb sign changes the speed, intensity, or
size of its execution, the variation in meaning is most
often in the manner in which the action is performed. If
the verb is active, the change indicates an increase or
decrease in intensity in what the verb refers to. If the
verb is stative, change in action signals the signer's

feelings. Changes of this general kind are also used to
signal the imperative. Sometimes, depending on the lexical content of the verb, other changes in meaning will be
found. For example if the verb TAKE-PICTURES is performed
relatively fast, it means that a flash attachment was (or
is) used to take the picture. If it is performed relatively
slowly, the camera is on "bulb". If the verb THROW is
performed relatively slowly, it means that the object
thrown is relatively heavy, e.g. a shotputter's weight.
If it is performed relatively fast, it follows the regular
rule of being interpreted as throwing fast. If the verb OP-
ERATE (surgery) is performed quickly, it means 'appen-
dectomy'; if it is performed slowly, with elongated movement, it means 'caesarian section'.

Incorporation of manner into the formation of signs
seems to play somewhat the same role in Sign that intonation plays in English, except that in ASL it may be more
crucial, since often there will be only one sign where in
English there may be several words for the same thing;
i.e. words differing only in degree. In our first example,
English has besides the word large, words like big, huge,
enormous, and gargantuan. ASL has one sign, which, with
variation in execution, can cover the same semantic range.
(This is assuming that the variation in size occurs in an
object of the same kind; ASL signs for largeness in height
and in breadth or length differ.) Similarly, in English we
have words like work, slave (verb), speed-up, and goldbrick.
In ASL the one sign WORK is performed in different ways to
reflect these different meanings. The sign MEET, if performed quickly and intensely so that the hands rebound to
come apart slightly, means 'run into by accident' or 'bump
into' (i.e.'chance to meet'). Performed more slowly, it
means something like 'approach'. For more examples of
incorporation of manner, see Bellugi & Fischer (1972).

Incorporation   Verbs in ASL not only inflect for sub-
of number.        ject, direct object, indirect object,
                    goal, and location, but also for number.
There are several kinds of pluralization; these can be
termed Definite (individual), Indefinite, Collective, and
Dual. Of these only the last is not productive and fairly
regular in application. The definite plural can apply to

every verb, without exception. Its closest analogue in
English is in conjunction. This definite plural would be used
to express in ASL such a sentence as

(43) a John left and Mary left and Bill left.
     b John, Mary, and Bill left [but not together ].

Actually, a closer analogue would be (44), which is ungrammatical in English unless one is actually pointing at persons
while the sentence is uttered:

(44) He$_1$ left and she left and he$_2$ left.

The definite or individual plural is performed in such a way
that the signer's body faces the location, real or established,
of the subject (or object) while the sign is performed; it then
shifts to face the next subject or object while the sign is,
after a pause, performed again, and so on. If the verb is one
that can reverse, change direction, or show location, these
changes are made as well. It is important to note that all
verbs perform this body shift (which can sometimes be limited
to the head or even the eyes only) independently of any other
mutability factors. Further, as in sentences (43) and (44),
what is thus made plural is always definite.

        The indefinite plural could be translated into English as
'many , but not necessarily all'; but a collective interpretation
is not precluded. It consists of fast repetition, without pause,
of the verb sign, at the same time that the body, hands, or
pointing hand is moving around in a horizontal semicircle
(Phonological considerations of what moves are presented in
Fischer, 1973). This process of pluralization applies to virtually all ASL verbs, leaving few, apparently idiosyncratic,
exceptions. As in the case of the definite plural, if the verb
can reverse, change direction, or show location also, it
does so. In the case of verbs that can reverse or change
direction, in fact, it is the mutability for person that distinguishes pluralized subject, e.g., from pluralized object.
(This is also true for the definite plural.). The verb HATE
is formed by flicking the middle finger off the thumb, other
fingers extended, in the direction of the object; and it requires a change in hand orientation if the object is the first
person. In I HATE MANY, the flicking motion is directed
outward from the body and is repeated an indefinite number

of times as the hands and arms (HATE is a two-hand symmetrical sign) move in the horizontal curve. In MANY HATE
ME, the sign is repeated, the hands and arms move in the
same arc by turning the trunk, but the hands are directed
inward.

A few signs optionally form the indefinite plural with
a kind of manual sandhi; i.e. the many repetitions merge
into one sign that is formed differently from the non-plural
sign. There is a sign TAKE-A-PICTURE, made by sliding
the B hand along the palm of the other hand and closing it
to O as it slides. If this sign is repeated quickly as the
hands move around the horizontal arc, it becomes difficult
though not impossible to make a complete closure of the
active hand for each repetition. In fact, the sign TAKE-
MOVIES obviates this problem—instead of complete closure
the fingers of the signing hand perform a sort of wave, in
effect merging all the openings and closings; and now
the hand no longer moves along the palm but remains
stationary in respect to it (though the whole sign can still
sweep around in a semicircle). There a few other signs
that merge in repetition in this way, but it is by no means
a general process.

The collective plural combines elements from the
definite and the indefinite to form a new modification. It
combines the horizontal sweep from the indefinite plural
with the basically one utterance nature of the definite.
The verb sign is performed once while the hands, body,
and/or eyes are executing the horizontal sweep. This is
true even for signs whose normal utterance requires repetition; e.g. READ, ENJOY. As with the other plurals,
if the verb being modified in this way is reversible or
can change direction, it does so as well. The interpretation of this kind of plural is that the argument of the
plural verb (its subject or object) is 'everybody or everything without exception'. All verbs which can form the
collective plural can also form the indefinite plural, but
some verbs that can form the indefinite cannot form the
collective; e.g. TEASE. (This verb is formed like RUIN
except that the action repeats; since repetition or non-
repetition are neutralized to non-repetition in making
collective plurals, TEASE cannot have this plural, because any viewer would understand the sign to mean
'ruin'.) This is an apparently unallowable ambiguity,

which ASL excludes. While an explanation of avoidance of
ambiguity can account for this exception, it does not account
for others such as INSULT, JOIN-TOGETHER, POSTPONE, or
SPELL.

There are some exceptional ways in which verbs can
form plurals, both indefinite and collective, besides using
horizontal movement and/or repetition. One is to use two
hands for plural if the sign is normally made with one hand.
The difference between TELL and ANNOUNCE, 'tell everybody', is that the former uses one hand and the latter two.
This mechanism is often used in conjunction with the others
we have discussed, in particular the indefinite plural; e.g.
the sign PICK-UP is made with one hand (Citation form: in
front of body, $\emptyset$-tab, the spread hand pronated, $5_p$-dez,
closes to F as it moves upward). The sign PICK-UP-MANY-
THINGS is made by using both hands in alternation to perform the same action; at the same time, the forearms sweep
in an arc.

Another exceptional kind of plural is performed by
using more fingers than are involved in the citation form.
The verb LOOK-AT-ME is made by a V-dez pronated so that
the fingers point at the signer. The sign EVERYBODY-LOOKS-
AT-ME is made with with both hands instead of one, but also
with four fingers instead of two extended from each hand; if
only two fingers are used, the meaning is 'two look at me'
—dual forms are discussed below. The sign CLIMB also
shows this change from V-dez to 4-dez for plural agents.

The dual is formed in a limited set of verbs one of
two ways. First, if one finger is extended in citation form,
two fingers indicate dual; e.g. in PERSON-APPROACH, and
MEET. One can thus make a sign meaning 'two people meet
one person' (G-tab, V-dez; but dual in both subject and object and mutual meeting is not signed with touching V-dez
hands, because that sign means 'copulate'). Second, dual
may be made by use of two hands if citation form uses only
one; the meaning 'two look at me' mentioned above differs
from 'one looks at me' by just this one-hand, two-hand
difference.

Habitual    The habitual aspect of ASL verbs is formed by
aspect.     repeating the sign quickly but without the
            horizontal sweep used in the indefinite plural.
This addition to performance of the citation form adds the

meaning 'all of the time'. In general, only those verbs
that are point-action, or can be interpreted as such, can
form the habitual in this way. For example, READ, generally considered a durative verb, can take the habitual,
for it can be idealized as a point-action or completive
verb ( Thus, He reads a lot but he hasn't read Roots, uses
the verb first as durative then as completive). Verbs like
FEAR, MEAN, and  MISS (a person) cannot be construed
as point-action and so do not have a habitual interpretation. Some verbs can repeat in this way but have a
changed interpretation if used to mean durative; e.g.
SUFFER repeated quickly without horizontal movement
means 'suffer intensely' rather than 'suffer all the time'.
       The one point-action verb we have found that cannot
form the habitual by repetition is RUIN; its repeated form
means TEASE. This is the one sort of phonological exception we have found. All the others seem to be either
syntactic or semantic, as shown by the fact that just
those verbs that can show habitual aspect by repetition
can be embedded under the verb TEND.

Continuous        A slow, drawn-out repetition is used
aspect.           with verbs to add the meaning 'for a
                  long time'. Any non-stative, i.e.
active, verb can be thus repeated. Thus, *FEAR-FOR-A-
LONG-TIME is unallowable, since FEAR is a stative verb;
similarly with KNOW. This is not to say that one cannot
get the idea expressed of knowing or fearing something
for a long time, but only that one cannot use this particular process to indicate that meaning in the verb.
       Because the process uses drawn-out repetition, if
the sign is normally made with point contact, the point
becomes elongated as it were, so that the action of the
dez becomes a brushing rather than a tap, jab, or touch.
In addition, this continuous repetition always shows a
circular motion superimposed on the action of the sign;
e.g. TELEPHONE. Citation form of this ASL verb uses the
cheek as tab and the Y-hand in supination as dez (i.e.
the thumb is up and little finger down); the meaning
'make phone calls for a long time' or 'talk on the telephone
for a long time' is signed with a circular rather than a

straight motion to the cheek, and the hand moves along
the point of contact in each repetition instead of simply
touching it.

The interpretation of this kind of circled repetition
is continuous action for some verbs; for point-action verbs
it is interpreted as iteration. TELEPHONE is an interesting
example, since it can be interpreted either as a point-
action verb or as a durative verb. POSTPONE-FOR-A-LONG-
TIME means, roughly, 'postpone over and over again', but
PRACTICE-FOR-A-LONG-TIME means 'continue practicing
for a long time', i.e. one practice session lasts a long
while.

Reciprocal      There is a sign EACH-OTHER that can
sign verbs.     be used in sentences with any verb for
                which it is appropriate. Examples of
this type of reciprocal verb phrase are

> (45) BOY GIRL PRAISE EACH-OTHER.
>      'The boy and the girl praised each other.'

> (46) WE ENJOY EACH-OTHER.
>      'We enjoy each other.'

> (47) TWO SISTER MISS EACH-OTHER.
>      'The two sisters miss each other.'

A second reciprocal involves actually performing the verb
twice, especially if it can reverse or can change direction.
If the verb is active, this reciprocal performance carries
the implication of sequential instead of simultaneous action;
e.g.

> (48) I-FEED-YOU, YOU-FEED-ME.
>      'I feed you and you feed me' or
>      'We feed each other.'

> (49) I-FREQUENT-YOU, YOU-FREQUENT-ME.
>      'I visit you a lot, etc.' or
>      'We visit each other a lot.'

The vast majority of ASL verbs must form reciprocal meaning
in one of the two ways described. There is, however, a

third way, albeit restricted, in which signs form reciprocals with a change in sign formation; it is perhaps an analogue of infixing rather than prefixing, suffixing, or periphrasis. This is the change that is most interesting from the point of view of mutability of verbs.

In English there are numerous verbs or adjectives that require a reciprocal interpretation, what is sometimes called an "NP* subject" (Lakoff & Peters 1969); e.g. to be similar, to date, to conflict. There are also many verbs in English that allow such a construction but do not require it and other verbs that can take the addition of each other; e.g. like, call. In ASL, as in English, there are verbs that allow the reciprocal and others that require it, but the distribution of verbs that require and that allow it may be different in ASL and English; e.g. ARGUE requires a reciprocal interpretation—if one wishes to say 'I could argue with that' (reciprocal, *That could argue with me), one must use another verb. Other such ASL verbs are AGREE, CLASH (personalities, not colors), CORRESPOND (send each other letters), DISAGREE, EXCHANGE, GET-TOGETHER, MINGLE, and CONVERSE.

The ASL verbs that permit but do not require reciprocity are more interesting because they do vary. It looks as though those verbs that fall into this category are a proper subset of verbs that can change location, orientation, or direction to incorporate nominal arguments. The verb GIVE is made by X-dez (forefinger extended and crooked) moving in the direction of the recipient as the wrist slightly but sharply twists; it can be made reciprocal by adding another X-dez hand moving in the opposite direction. HATE, SHOOT, LOOK, SAY-NO, TRANSFER, and FINGERSPELL-BIG-WORDS are similarly made reciprocal.

An exception is HELP-EACH-OTHER. HELP is formed by the upward movement or pressure of the flat hand, palm up (B -dez) under the fist (A-tab). HELP-EACH-OTHER is almost like the sequential reciprocals (I-HELP-YOU, YOU-HELP-ME), but instead of there being two performances of the sign action, there is only one— the hands in contact move back and forth between the locations of the two arguments.

One can speculate as to why some verbs permit the
formation of combined reciprocals (i.e. one sign moved)
and others do not. One reason seems to be that the verb
must be mutable in at least one of the ways so far described. Another, more phonological as it were, is that in
general the sign to be made reciprocal must be made with
either one hand alone or the two hands symmetrically in
action without touching. Of course also the reciprocal must
be semantically and syntactically appropriate to the verb.

Reflexives. As in the case of reciprocals, there are
                     both internal and periphrastic ways of
expressing the reflexive in ASL. The periphrastic uses
the -SELF morpheme moved in the direction of the reflexive argument (actually touching the chest for 'myself').
This is, however, not generally used in ASL for grammatical reflexives but for emphatic reflexives; e.g.

> (50)  YOURSELF CAN OPEN-IT.
>        'You can open it yourself!'

When the -SELF morpheme is used as a grammatical reflexive, the signer is said to be "signing English" rather than
using American Sign Language.
    For most verb signs, at least for those that incorporate
location and/or reversal, the reflexive form is identical to
the first-person-object incorporating form; thus

> (51)  ME HATE-ME.
>        'I hate myself' (verb projects toward signer).

> (52)  THAT-ONE HATE-ME.
>        'Someone hates me' (verb as above).

The difference is in the subject, not in the verb; most ASL
verbs form the reflexive in this way.
    For a small set of verb signs, there is a distinct
variation from the base form to indicate the reflexive. This
variation will often look like the "someone _____ me" form
of the verb. Thus for this set of verbs too, it is true that
they form a subset of verbs that can incorporate location
and reversal. Nevertheless this variation will differ in some
respects. Generally the reflexive form will be performed

somewhat closer to the body than the first-person-object
form, but there may be some interesting differences besides
this one; e.g. CHOOSE is begun by an open spread hand,
5-dez, palm toward object, drawing away from the object
location, and finished by the change of the configuration
of the hand to 'F' (thumb, index fingertips touch, other
fingers extended). To express the reflexive, 'I choose
myself', the 5-hand begins so close to the signer's body
that the fingertips touch the chest in closing and drawing
away. [Note that this is the sign glossed VOLUNTEER in
the dictionary. B.G.] Another example of reflexive form
change is LOCK. In citation form the end of the X-dez
twists in the palm of the B-tab hand. Like OWE, this verb
is locational but not reversible in direction; it is made
closer to the signer's body if the object is first person.
LOCK, like OWE, also does reverse hand orientation to
show grammatical relations: For 'I lock you (out or in)',
the dez points outward toward the addressee, and the
tab palm is toward signer; for 'You (or someone) locks
me', the dez wrist is sharply bent and supinated to
point inward, and the tab palm is outward. Compare the
latter with 'I lock myself (out or in)'. The basic sign
is the same in action and in what acts (configuration
and orientation), but for the reflexive meaning, the whole
sign is so close to the body that sometimes the arm of
the dez hand will be touching the signer's trunk.

Although there are relatively few verb signs that
form reflexives by changing away from both the citation
form and the incorporating or reversed form, those that
do so show once again the interesting mutability of
ASL verbs.

Conclusion.    In this paper we have investigated the
                        role of verbs in American Sign Language.
Because the verb forms the nucleus of the sentence, it can
be said to form the nucleus of the language as well. We
have looked into the properties of various verbs of ASL,
particularly as they are different in distribution and process
from English verbs with similar meanings, and we have
examined how verbs in ASL change to reflect different
semantic or grammatical relations. Although there may be
a few verbs that are absolutely invariant under any of
the conditions described, the vast majority participate.

in several of the mutations we have discussed. These kinds of mutations are very different from the kinds of grammatical deformations that occur in English; indeed they are different from those that occur in spoken languages as a whole.

## REFERENCES

Bellugi, Ursula, & Susan Fischer
  1972     A Comparison of Sign Language and Spoken
           Language, Cognition 1, 173-200.

Fischer, Susan D.
  1973     Two Processes of Reduplication in the Ameri-
           can Sign Language, Foundations of Language
           9, 469-480.

Lakoff, George, & S. Peters
  1969     Phrasal Conjunction and Symmetric Predi-
           cates, in Modern Studies in English, Reibel
           & Schane eds. (Englewood Cliffs, Prentice-
           Hall).

Stokoe, William C., Dorothy C. Casterline, & Carl G.
           Croneberg
  1965     A Dictionary of American Sign Language on
           Linguistic Principles (Washington, Gallaudet
           College Press; rev. ed. Silver Spring, MD,
           Linstok Press, 1976).

Note: Research reported in the foregoing pages was supported
      by National Institutes of Health grant No. 09811-01 to
      the Salk Institute for Biological Studies.

PART TWO

# LEARNING AND USING SIGN LANGUAGE

This section of SIGN & CULTURE looks at a crucial part
of the whole age span in the community using American Sign
Language. This age range, infancy and early school years,
is of course the most important period in language development. In Chapter 7 the ideal situation for a deaf child's
language learning is described by an ideal teacher and model,
a deaf woman with both a family background of natural sign
language and an excellent linguistic education. Just as the
immediate family is source and focus of any language community, so the chapter by the late Judy Williams gets at the heart
of the sociolinguistic fact known as bilingualism.

Chapter 8 by Marina McIntire traces the stages passed
through by a deaf child of deaf parents as she learns how to
form what acts in manual signs. Like the hearing child whose
output seems to contain first intonationally correct copies of
adult utterances and then sensible strings of words, so the
child described in Chapter 8 signs understandably before she
can produce all the adult handshape forms of ASL.

In Chapter 9, Raymond Stevens considers a simple but
basic mixup in patterns. Children learn in one manner; adults
in another; yet our way of teaching deaf children has been
modeled on the adult learning pattern.

Marvin Sallop describes in Chapter 10 a practical problem
many teachers face: how to move the deaf children from ad hoc
physical action to rule-governed signing to English-ordered
sign use.

Summing up this part of the text, Bonvillian, Nelson, and
Charrow survey a wide range of language problems confronted
by deaf and hearing children and show how use of signs may
bring a desirable resolution of many of them.

PART TWO: 7

## BILINGUAL EXPERIENCES OF A DEAF CHILD

Judith Stein Williams

My husband and I had long expected that our children would have impaired hearing. Our genetic makeup showed this. Our parents, my uncle, and his four sons are deaf on my side, and four uncles on his side, and so are we. I was born deaf. My husband lost his hearing at the age of six months during an attack of whooping cough, which could be a sign that he was easily susceptible to deafness. When our son Todd was born, he showed so much alertness with his eyes and was so unresponsive to normal sounds that we knew he was like us.

My main concern was not his inability to hear (he is nearly five now and I still don't even give it a thought), but was instead how well he could live within the hearing world. His language acquisition was far more important, since this could open many channels for him including speech, lipreading, manual communication, and writing. The most important part was being able at an early age to express himself linguistically in the simplest forms. Lack of this ability can lead to personality and psychological problems. So I started talking to him like all mothers do, cooing, babbling, singing nursery rhymes, and the like—but I added signs and fingerspelling while doing all this.

It was not until he was nine months old that he finally expressed himself clearly in sign language. He loved to throw his spoon on the floor from his highchair and yell for me to pick it up. I always asked him, signing and speaking: "Where is the spoon?" at the same time pointing

181

to it before picking it up. This time he threw it again but asked me in signs, WHERE SPOON? and pointed at it. This led soon to his substituting in this frame other signs (words) like ball, light, cat, dog, and book; and we went on to using the "Pictionary" and "First Objects" and other books I read to him from while he looked at the objects pictured. By the time he was one year old he was able to identify about fifteen different things in short sentences. His vocabulary increased, but it was not until after he was toilet trained (at about twenty months) that I introduced him to fingerspelling and put a lot of stress on this way of presenting words. He mastered this kind of communication of sentences on his level in a few months, and he associated the manual alphabet with the printed alphabet. At twenty-five months he started reading, and when he was turning three, he had five hundred words in his reading vocabulary and loved to read pre-primers and beginning-to-read books. His language developed in the simultaneous sense, that is, through lipreading my speech, fingerspelling, printed matter, and signs. I see no conflict in his bilingual acquisition of English and Sign but believe that it greatly aided him. He loved nursery rhymes and was able to recite them himself. He eventually used his speech and sang some syllables out loud.

I enrolled him in the Gallaudet preschool when he was thirty months old, and its program gave him a lot of auditory training and speech work which I was not able to give him at home. His hearing aid did wonders (although he has an 85 decibel loss in both ears across the whole frequency range), and he responded more to speech and showed willingness to learn to say words accurately.

From this point everything else seemed to come naturally, and his curiosity brought him even further, until I would say that he is progressing just as normally hearing children do except that he is less vocal. He learned English very readily in expressive exercises, routines, monologues, and interpretations as well as in social responses and requests for information as the situation required. Simplification of grammatical structures was necessary in the early stages, but now at four years and ten months he simplifies them himself for his sister, Tiffany, two years younger, and elaborates them for his Daddy.

His bilingual experience is in some ways like and in others unlike that of the American-Japanese bilinguals studied by Susan Ervin-Tripp (1964). Todd has a more general knowledge of Sign, because that is the language more often used at home, and a specific knowledge of English from his education at home and in school. His is really a merger of the two languages, therefore, as in the case of the Japanese women who tend to use Japanese for social intercourse and as their base language when with other bilinguals but who do use English as the situation and the persons talked to require. Todd relies more on his Signs than on his English with his family and more on spoken English in the classroom.

As Ervin-Tripp says, "...bilinguals who speak only with other bilinguals may be on the road to merger of the two languages, unless there are strong pressures to insulate by topic or setting." Her hypothesis is that "as language shifts, content will shift." And she presents examples of the Japanese women's monologues in which moon, moon-viewing, zebra-grass, full moon, and cloud are in Japanese, and skyrocket and cloud are in English. This kind of difference needs more study in the case of Sign-English bilinguals. There may even be a trilingual situation--some words in signs, some spoken, and some in English spelled in the manual alphabet, depending on the who, where, and what of the communication.

Another observation Ervin-Tripp makes is that the Japanese women "were in an abnormal situation" when one was asked to speak English with another Japanese woman. The effects on the style of English were clear when the two situations were compared. With the Japanese listener there was much more disruption of English syntax, more intrusion of Japanese words, and briefer speech.

This is also true in cases where two deaf children are forced to speak English to each other. I notice that Todd shortens his statements and tries to add signs between them. He uses more complex ideas, structures, and words in Sign than in spoken English.

In school Todd's English is more or less that of a four-year old in a pre-school situation. But at home, when he was three years old, he asked me at the table (in signs), "Where does the meat go?" I asked him what he meant, and he replied: "Look, I swallow the meat, and where does it go?" I then explained to him in details he could understand, and he was pleased and satisfied with the answer. Another time, about six months later, he asked me where a sound he was listening to came from. I told him that I couldn't hear anything at all but that he and Tiffany and Daddy have a little hearing. He was very much hurt by this and offered me his hearing aid, hoping I would respond to sound. When he learned that it was of no help, he cried and was upset for a while. Later I told him he could help me by telling me to move the car over when he hears fire engines or ambulances passing by, because I must give them right of way. He now delights in telling me when he hears a siren, and he lets me know when he hears a sound and identifies it for me--the vacuum cleaner, someone knocking on the door, and the like. He doesn't have much hearing but uses his residual hearing well and intelligently.

Are there any deaf children this age without sign language who can express themselves this well, ask such questions, and make such distinctions? There are none that I know of. Knowing signs also helps Todd in learning English vocabulary. For example, Todd learned about a Zebra in school but not the sign for it. When he came home, he told me about the characteristics of this new animal so I could easily identify what he was trying to find out--both of us using his "base" language of signs.

For young deaf children the most important contribution of sign language is to the child's expression of his needs, questions, and responses. With it he can also develop other channels of language and expression. Without it he may have some receptive competence, if he happens to be a very good lipreader, but he will be terribly hampered in his formative preschool years. Moreover, the spoken language the teachers are trying to instill in him becomes warped because he can't really use it expressively to ask questions and to make and try out corrections after being told of his grammatical mistakes.

Sign language has advantages for the hearing children of deaf parents as well. Their bilingual experience of serving their parents by making phone calls and receiving spoken messages can be very valuable. As they use both languages they translate from one to the other. The need to interpret for deaf parents makes them listen to adult conversation with more than normal childish attention. In return they get top grades in reading, spelling, grammar, and other subjects in school, as I found when I made a personal survey of my parents' deaf friends who have hearing children, about forty children in all.

These observations agree with the results of Meadow's study (1968). She notes that many professionals warn parents against sign language in case children are motivated not to learn speechreading and speech. Her study proves these fears false and shows that deaf children that are exposed to sign language in early childhood have better reading, speechreading, and written language scores. She concludes that "the deaf children of deaf parents [who use sign language] have a higher level of intellectual functioning, social functioning, maturity, independence, and communicative competence in written, spoken, expressive, and receptive language."

Sign language is not incompatible with English. In fact, with some care about its order and by spelling English function words, it can be made into a visual equivalent of English utterance. Unfortunately, there is not a school in the United States that uses it as a medium of communication between teacher and pupil, except in the advanced department. That is too late.

## REFERENCES

Ervin-Tripp, Susan
   1964   An Analysis of the Interaction of Language, Topic, and
          Listener, American Anthropologist   66 , 86-102.

Meadow, Kathryn P.
   1968   Early Manual Communication in Relation to the Deaf Child's
          Intellectual, Social, and Communicative Functioning, American
          Annals of the Deaf 113, 29-41.

This brief paper by the late Judith S. Williams was written in 1968 when she was a graduate student at Gallaudet College. It was entered in the ERIC Document Reproduction Service by CAL/ERIC and put on microfiche (ED 030 092). It is reprinted here not only because of its combination of personal knowledge with scientific observation but also in the hope that it may encourage others to make careful studies of how deaf children acquire language and to keep as clear a grasp of differences between language and two transmission modes.

PART TWO: 8

# THE ACQUISITION OF AMERICAN SIGN LANGUAGE HAND CONFIGURATION

Marina L. McIntire

Abstract. Examination of American Sign Language — produced by a deaf child acquiring the language from deaf parents, and videotaped at age 13, 15, 18, and 21 months — shows conformity to many of the phonological rules operative for all languages. Active-hand configurations, i.e. dez handshapes, are learned in stages. A first-stage dez is substituted regularly for a dez of a later stage before second stage competence is reached. Rules specific to ASL dez substitution are posited.

Introduction. This study[1] focuses on the acquisition of one portion of American Sign Language phonology: handshape or dez.[2] The data are taken from a series of videotaped play sessions in the home of "FF" and her parents. FF has a borderline hearing loss in the right ear and is severely to profoundly deaf in the left ear. Her loss is congenital; rubella, birth trauma, and postnatal illness have been ruled out. Both FF's parents and all her grandparents are also hearing impaired. At the time of the study FF had not used any amplification. FF's parents both hold advanced academic degrees, and her father teaches at a large West Coast university. A normally-hearing son was born into the family when FF was nineteen months old.

186

The acquisition of American Sign Language as a first
language is a critical area for study within the larger field
of child language acquisition. If as most major theoreticians
have suggested, the capacity for language is part of our
human genetic inheritance, then a deaf child learning American Sign Language (ASL) as a first language should display
linguistic behavior similar to that found in children who are
acquiring other languages. The modality difference between
visual-kinesthetic and auditory-vocal systems should result
in no significant strategy differences in the normal process
of acquisition. Interesting differences related to modality may
appear between a normal hearing child and a normal deaf child,
but parallel manifestations of the universal capabilities for
human language learning should be apparent in both situations.

Initially FF demonstrated a precocity in her language
development. At the beginning of the study, when she was
one year and one month (1:1) old, she had a vocabulary of
more than 85 signs. In the fourth and last session, at 1:9,
her vocabulary had reached and passed the 200 mark. It
should be noted also that FF's syntactic development was
remarkably early and rapid. Two-sign utterances (e.g.
MOMMY SHOE; and MORE FOOD) began appearing in her
tenth month. At one year and three months, she began marking
certain question forms with a general interrogative marker,
shown herein as Q-SIGN. (This sign is made with a side to
side movement of the spread hands held up and palm-in in
front of the body — $\emptyset\ 5_{\wedge}\ 5_{\wedge}^{z}$ in the notation of Stokoe, 1960,
1965, and called "what-shrug" by Fant, 1977.)

The corpus for this study represents a noticeably constrained output, especially in length of utterances and
therefore also in syntactic complexity. Every effort was made
to maintain a casual and relaxed atmosphere in the recording
sessions; however, the presence of the videotape equipment
and two outsiders (the investigator and a video technician)
clearly had an inhibiting effect on FF's language behavior.
Phonological (i.e. formational) output is less likely to be
influenced by such constraints, and so the analysis presented
here should not be significantly affected by these limitations
of the data.

Hypothesis and model.    Boyes-Braem (1973) developed
                                   a model for describing the
process of acquiring handshapes in ASL; this was based on her
analysis of one one-hour videotape of a deaf child of two years
and seven months. Anatomical and cognitive constraints at
first control the development of baby handshapes, according
to Boyes-Braem; pointing and grasping are the functions most
commonly served by the human hand (1973: 7). Sign language
requires in addition the independent manipulation of the weaker
ulnar group, i.e. the middle, ring, and pinky fingers. The
conscious control of these fingers is acquired comparatively
late in development (Kinsbourne & Warrington 1963). This
suggests the likelihood of at least two steps in the order of
sign language development: Handshapes with features ap-
plying only to the thumb and index finger, or to the whole
hand, will be acquired earlier than those which require manipulation of the weaker fingers. Boyes-Braem's 1973 model
suggests four stages[3] of development in acquiring the production of ASL dez handshapes:

| 1. | A | S | L | bO[4] | 5 | C | G |
|----|---|---|---|-------|---|---|---|
| 2. |   | B |   | F     |   | O |   |
| 3. | I | D | Y | P     | 3 | V | H | W |
| 4. |   | 8 | 7 | X     | R | T |   |

                                        from Boyes-Braem
                                        1973

     These sequences are based on the notion that 'A' (hand
closed into fist with thumb aligned with wrist) is the unmarked
form; this is supported by anatomists and observers of child
behavior (e.g. Gesell & Halverson 1936). Dez handshapes

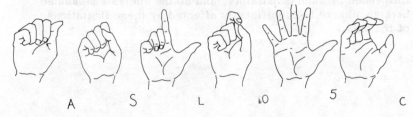

A          S          L          bO          5                    C

are defined by the positive specification of a series of features
in this model: opposition of the thumb ( S ), extension away
from the central axis of the hand of one or more fingers ( G,
5 ), the adduction of the spread fingers toward the central
axis ( B ), contact of the fingertips with the opposed thumb
( F, O ), contact of the thumb with the middle finger joint
( P ), insertion of the thumb between two fingers ( T ), and
crossing of adjacent fingers ( R ). The predicted sequence
of acquisition is based on these features.
　　　This sequence suggested by the model is based on the
gradually increasing ability, both physical and cognitive,
of the child to control the weaker fingers, making possible
the positive specification (production) of more and more
"difficult" features. The prediction, therefore, is that signs
requiring a dez handshape in a stage beyond the baby's
performance abilities (for example, a handshape from line
3) will be signed by using as substitutes dez handshapes
within her capabilities (i.e. from line 1); in this model it
is also predicted that no dez from a later stage will substitute for a dez from an earlier stage.

　　　Not all the baby's output, however, will be accounted for
by this model alone. Several secondary factors influence a
baby's performance. One is the baby's preference for (index)
finger tip contact with a tab as signing surface. This has been

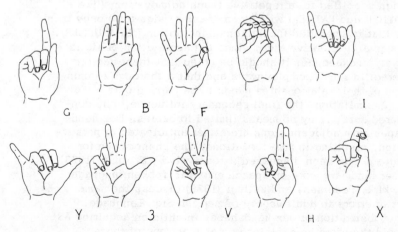

noted informally by linguists working with signing babies. It
is demonstrated most emphatically by the commonly reported
occurrence of MOTHER and FATHER being signed with a G dez
instead of a 5 dez, although the latter is well within the
limits of the babies' abilities.

Another secondary factor is miming. Often handshapes are
influenced by an action associated with the referent. For instance, FF signs BELT with an S hand rather than the appropriate
(to adult standards) H. Given the features of H, we might expect it to be replaced by a G handshape; however, FF mimes
the action of pulling a belt around her waist by using an S
hand.

A third possible influence on the output of babies'signs
is the nature of the feedback: Signs made within the visual
field (e.g. BALL, SHOE) offer potential visual feedback. In
some sense this may make it "easier" for a baby to exercise
self-correction. But if a sign is formed outside the baby's
field of vision (e.g. BLACK, MOON), she has only kinesthetic
or haptic (kinesthetic plus tactile) feedback. Thus, FF signs
BLACK with a 5 dez, rather than with a G.

A fourth factor is the complexity of the sign action or sig
required by the sign. We have no systematic, empirical evidence regarding the acquisition of sig, but it seems counter-
intuitive to believe that sig would behave very differently from
dez in the process of acquisition. It seems likely, i.e., that
a sign specified for a repetitive touching movement (like
MOTHER and FATHER) will be an "easier" sign for a baby than
one that is specified for interchanging action (HAMBURGER).
This is a speculative area, since the acquisition of sig is
largely unexamined. It should be noted that these factors
interact in fairly complex ways and that a thorough examination of their relationships needs to be carried out.

Assimilation, the final secondary influence to be considered here, is by no means limited to babies. Dez handshapes from adjacent signs are either anticipated or perseverated, resulting in mis-formations. The phenomenon for
language has been discussed extensively by Fromkin (1973)
in her landmark work on speech errors in spoken language;
Newkirk, Pedersen, and Bellugi (1976) discuss the same
sort of errors in adult users of American Sign Language.

Substitution of dez handshapes in children acquiring ASL
should therefore be explained by at least one of these
factors:

1   The dez required is from a group with feature specifications
    as yet beyond the child's cognitive and physical abilities;

2   The sign is made with fingertip contact on the tab surface;

3   The sign is pantomimed;

4   The sign occurs outside the field of vision;

5   The movement of the sign is "complex";

6   The handshape is anticipated or perseverated from an
    adjacent sign in the string.


Data and discussion.   The data discussed here are
                       taken from four different play
sessions videotaped in FF's home and described in outline
in Table 1. Participants in each session were FF, her mother,
and the investigator, with FF's father in sessions 1 and 3,
and the investigator's two sons, aged 6 and 10, in session 2.


| Session | Date     | FF's Age | Duration |
|---------|----------|----------|----------|
| 1       | 5-13-73  | 1:1      | 20 min.  |
| 2       | 8-04-73  | 1:3      | 40 min.  |
| 3       | 10-13-73 | 1:6      | 40 min.  |
| 4       | 1-08-74  | 1:9      | 30 min.  |

Table 1. Description of data sessions.


    The videotapes were transcribed in a notation based on
that in Stokoe et al. (1965), following Boyes-Braem's model.
FF's dez handshapes were analyzed to determine the percentages of successful performance of target handshapes, and to
examine substitutions (or unsuccessful tokens). The results
of the analysis are summarized in Table 2.

| Dez | Cor/Req # | Cor % | Sub # | (n, 186) % all Sub | Occ # | (n, 621) Occ % |
|---|---|---|---|---|---|---|
| A | 4/11 | 36 | 16 | 9 | 21 | 3 |
| S | 15/34 | 44 | 11 | 6 | 26 | 4 |
| L | Ø | Ø | 2 | 1 | 2 | - |
| bO | 13/16 | 81 | 35 | 19 | 47 | 8 |
| G | 28/33 | 85 | 16 | 9 | 44 | 7 |
| Index | 177/188 | 94 | - | - | 177 | 29 |
| 5 | 189/194 | 97 | 101 | 54 | 291 | 47 |
| C | 2/9 | 22 | 1 | 0.5 | 3 | - |
| B | 5/59 | 9 | 3 | 2 | 8 | 1 |
| F | Ø/7 | Ø | Ø | Ø | Ø | Ø |
| O | Ø/20 | Ø | Ø | Ø | Ø | Ø |
| Y | Ø/7 | Ø | Ø | Ø | Ø | Ø |
| 3 | 1/12 | 8 | Ø | Ø | 1 | - |
| V | Ø/8 | Ø | 1 | 0.5 | 1 | Ø |
| H | Ø/15 | Ø | Ø | Ø | Ø | Ø |
| W | Ø/2 | Ø | Ø | Ø | Ø | Ø |
| 8 | Ø/4 | Ø | Ø | Ø | Ø | Ø |
| X | Ø/5 | Ø | Ø | Ø | Ø | Ø |

Table 2. Dez handshapes required and occurring as correct or as substitutions in the data.

In Table 2, the columns show respectively, the notation
symbol for dez, the tokens correct versus tokens required, this
ratio as percentage, the number of dez handshapes substituted
for that required, the percentage of these in all substitutions,
and in the last two columns, the number and percentages of
total occurrences. Note that deictic signs or "indexing" (Index in the table) have been separated from the rest of the signs
formed with the G dez — this pointing gesture can serve as a
locative ('here', 'there'), or as a subject or object pronoun.
Since this deictic behavior is common to hearing babies as
well (see Bullowa in SLS 16, 193-218), it seems important to
take note of its prevalence as a linguistic phenomenon in the
present corpus.

One particular type of sign caused difficulties in the tab-
ulation. Some two-handed signs are symmetrical in dez shape,
dez orientation, and sig; i.e. are made in ∅ tab (e.g. Q-SIGN,
RAIN, CRY). Signs like these are commonly formed with only
one hand, as Battison (1974) points out.[4] In tabulating these
signs, there was no dependable way of judging whether the
target was the one-handed or the two-handed sign. In no case
did FF interpret this kind of sign as having different dez handshapes or different sigs. In order to maintain unity of analysis,
all these signs have been classified as if one-handed, i.e.
requiring and being signed with only one dez.

Substitution handshapes are shown in Table 3 below and
across the page:

| Session | Dez req. | Dez subs. | Sign(s) |
|---------|----------|-----------|---------|
|   | A (S) | bO | SHOE |
|   | bO | 5 | BIRD |
|   | F | 5 | CAT |
| 1 | O | bO | FLOWER, SAND |
|   | Y | 5 | YELLOW |
|   | 3 | 5 | DUCK |
|   | X | A | APPLE |
|   | A(S) | 5 | NUT |
|   |   | bO | ORANGE |
| 2 | 5 | bO | CAKE |
|   |   | G | Q-SIGN |
|   | C | A(S) | MOON |

| Session | Dez req. | Dez subs. | Sign(s) |
|---|---|---|---|
| | B | 5 | ELEPHANT, BABY, CAKE (tab hand) |
| | | bO/5 (A/A) | HAMBURGER |
| | F | 5 | CAT |
| | O | bO | FOOD/EAT, FLOWER, BALLOON, STRAWBERRY |
| 2 (cont'd) | Y | bO | STRAWBERRY (as tab hand) |
| | 3̈ | 5 | BUG, HORSE, RABBIT |
| | V̈ | bO | FROG |
| | | G | GOAT |
| | H | A | EGG (simultaneous utterance) |
| | 8 | bO | WATERMELON |
| | X | A | APPLE |
| | | B | CEREAL |
| | A(S) | bO | BICYCLE |
| | | 5 | NUT |
| | bO | 5 | BIRD |
| | C | A(S) | MOON |
| | B | 5/5 | HAMBURGER |
| | F | 5 | HAIR |
| | Y | 5 | RHINOCEROUS (non-standard) |
| 3 | 3 | 5 | BUG |
| | V | G/G - 5 | SCISSORS |
| | H | G/G -5 | CHAIR/SIT |
| | | G/5 | SPOON |
| | W | 5 | WATER |
| | 8 | 5 | WATERMELON |
| | A(S) | bO/bO | HOT-DOG |
| | bÖ | A | PEN/WRITE |
| | 5̈ | C | LION |
| | C | 5 | TURTLE |
| | | 5 - L̈ | CHURCH |
| 4 | G | 5 | -UP, BLACK |
| | B | A/5 - 5/5 | HAMBURGER, BOAT |
| | | 5/5 | BOY, BROWN, BEE, BREAD, PUPPET |
| | | G | ELEPHANT |
| | | S | BREAD (tab hand) |
| | F | 5 | BEE, CATS(UP) |

Table 3. Substitutions (continued).

| Session | Dez req. | Dez subs. | Sign(s) |
|---------|----------|-----------|---------|
|         | F        | G         | CATS(UP) |
|         | O        | A         | HOME |
| 4       | Y        | 5         | AIRPLANE, COW |
| (cont'd) | 3       | 5         | HORSE, BUG |
|         | V        | L, 5      | SHEEP |
|         | H        | S         | BELT |

Table 3. Substitutions occurring in the corpus.

Several points appearing in Table 3 are noteworthy. The first
and most significant is confirmation of Boyes-Braem's hypothesis. Stage 1 is appropriately named; virtually all of FF's
output in this corpus is from stage 1. Certainly, most of her
vocabulary is also within the signs requiring stage 1 handshapes,
but note that only four out of 186 substitutions are not from
stage 1.
     Even though Boyes-Braem's basic hypothesis (the dez
handshapes requiring control of thumb and index finger, or
the whole hand, will develop before others) is sustained,
certain patterns show in the data which are not consistent
with the distinctive features Boyes-Braem proposes. Note in
particular the interaction of A and S and the variation of these
two handshapes with bO, baby O. Lane, Boyes-Braem, and
Bellugi (1976) propose a different set of distinctive features
for dez configuration in ASL (As it would be inappropriate to
reproduce their entire system here, the reader is urged to
consult their findings). In their system, thumb opposition is
not a distinctive feature (hence A = S); rather the features
that apply to a stage 1 dez are as follows:
                    [+ compact]: no fingers extended
                    [+ concave]: at least two bent fingers
                    [+ index]: all fingers except the index closed
                    [+ touch]: one or more fingertips contact thumb
                    [+ broad]: three or more fingers extended
                    [+ full]: all four fingers extended
                    [+ radial]: (at least) the thumb extended
                    [+ ulnar]: at least the pinky extended
                    [+ dual]: only two fingers extended
This changes the feature specifications for stage 1 dez hand-

shapes considerably (Table 4). Note that certain feature
assignments are redundant and not specified; e.g. [+contact]
implies [-broad], [-full], [-ulnar], etc. Hence not all
features are specified for all dez handshapes.

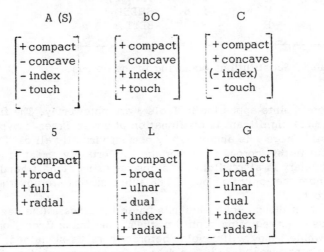

| A (S) | bO | C |
|---|---|---|
| + compact | + compact | + compact |
| - concave | - concave | + concave |
| - index | + index | (- index) |
| - touch | + touch | - touch |

| 5 | L | G |
|---|---|---|
| - compact | - compact | - compact |
| + broad | - broad | - broad |
| + full | - ulnar | - ulnar |
| + radial | - dual | - dual |
| | + index | + index |
| | + radial | - radial |

Table 4. Distinctive features for Stage 1 dez handshapes,
after Lane, Boyes-Braem, & Bellugi (1976).

Note also in Table 4 that some feature values can be changed
non-distinctively; thus, [+concave] applies to the handshape
used in certain signs and is indicated in Stokoe notation by a
superscript of three dots over the dez symbol: 5̈, WANT; L̈,
BIG-HEAD; V̈, STRICT. The new set of features facilitates the
analysis of data from the FF corpus.

For example, we can suggest three rules in FF's phonology
for the first two sessions:

$$R1. \quad \begin{bmatrix} - \text{compact} \\ - \text{index} \end{bmatrix} \Rightarrow \begin{bmatrix} + \text{broad} \\ + \text{full} \\ + \text{radial} \end{bmatrix}$$

$$R2. \quad \begin{bmatrix} + \text{compact} \\ - \text{concave} \\ + \text{index} \\ - \text{touch} \end{bmatrix} \Rightarrow \begin{bmatrix} - \text{index} \end{bmatrix}$$

R3.  $\begin{bmatrix} + \text{concave} \\ \langle + \text{touch} \rangle \end{bmatrix} \Rightarrow \begin{bmatrix} - \text{concave} \\ \langle + \text{index} \rangle \end{bmatrix}$

Rule 1 states that non-compact handshapes that are [- index]
become 5's; this includes signs requiring F, 3, and Y (e.g.
CAT, BUG, YELLOW). Rule 2 accounts for X becoming A, as
in APPLE. Rule 3 states that [+ concave] handshapes become
[- concave], and that if such a dez is also specified as
[+ touch] (O), it becomes [+ index] (bO), as in MOON, FLOWER.
     These rules will not account for all the data. This is
largely because the focus here is only on handshape, which
with orientation of the dez makes up only one aspect of the
three aspects of ASL phonology. In the phonology of a spoken
language, features must be controlled simultaneously (e.g.
voicing, tongue position, lip rounding, etc.) in order to produce sounds; and when sounds are combined to make utterances, whether words or sentences, they are produced sequentially. We have seen that for sign language handshapes
features can be posited, and that they are manipulated more
or less successfully in a baby's sign production. Note, however,
that handshapes do not exist in any sort of state separate from
the other aspects of a sign: action and location; nor separate
from the orientation of the dez. That is to say, a dez, as a
handshape plus orientation, must be produced in a certain location, with a certain action, if sign behavior is involved
(see Stokoe 1960: 40f). Presumably, the other aspects, tab
and sig, may also be organized by features, which must also
be produced simultaneously. Linearity enters the signing process only at the syntactic level. This simultaneity places a
special kind of demand on an infant whose cognitive and
physical abilities are still developing. It is for this reason
that the secondary influences previously discussed can over-
ride the systematicity of rules based on features alone.
     A preference for fingertip contact is evident in several
substitutions: SHOE, A/S ⇒ bO; BIRD, bO ⇒ 5; GOAT, V̈ ⇒ G;
and WATERMELON, 8 ⇒ bO (on the tab hand 5 instead of S'). 
Mime is evident in BELT, H ⇒ S, discussed above, and possibly in DRINK, which will be discussed below.
     Of the substituted dez handshapes occurring outside the
field of vision, virtually all are cases of stage 1 configurations
replacing more complex handshapes, as suggested by the model
(see Table 5).

| Sign | Req. | Subs. | Ses. | Other factors |
|------|------|-------|------|---------------|
| BIRD | bO | 5 | 1,3 | fingertip contact |
| CAT | F | 5 | 1,2 | fingertip contact |
| DUCK | 3 | 5 | 1 | fingertip contact |
| APPLE | X | A | 1,2 | |
| FLOWER | O | bO | 1,2 | fingertip contact, cplx. sig |
| NUT | A | 5 | 2,3 | |
| MOON | C | A(S) | 2,3 | |
| ELEPHANT | B | 5,G | 2,4 | complex sig |
| FOOD/EAT | O | bO | 2 | |
| HORSE, RABBIT | 3 | 5 | 2,4 | complex sig |
| FROG | V̈ | bO | 2 | cplx. sig, fingertip contact |
| GOAT | V̈ | G | 2 | cplx. sig, fingertip contact |
| EGG* | H | A | 2 | complex sig, * |
| CEREAL | X | B | 2 | complex sig |
| HAIR | F | 5 | 3 | |
| WATER | W | 5 | 3 | |
| LION | 5 | C | 4 | |
| CAT- (CATSUP) | F | 5 - G | 4 | |
| -UP | G | 5 | 4 | complex sign, interference |
| BLACK | G | 5 | 4 | fingertip contact |
| BOY | B | 5 | 4 | |
| BEE | B - F | 5 | 4 | complex sig |
| HOME | O | A | 4 | |
| BELT | H | A(S) | 4 | pantomime |
| COW | Y | 5 | 4 | |

* The utterance is $\begin{bmatrix} \text{FOOD} \\ \text{EGG} \end{bmatrix}$ signed simultaneously.

Table 5. Substitutions of handshape occurring outside the field of signer's vision.

Other factors also interact with these data. One would want to say that substitutions not accounted for by some rule, or by some other factor, e.g NUT, ELEPHANT in the table, are in fact explained by the unavailability of the sign for visual feedback. While the evidence seems to indicate that this may have an effect, the interaction of factors is still too opaque to make a compelling case for singling out visual feedback. Further evidence from both child language acquisition and adult errors in signing will be of some value in deciding the relative importance of the feedback factor.

A "complex sig" is a speculative matter, as has been said; many sigs, however, appear in FF's production altered from the required or adult form, and they do seem to have an effect on the handshape. For example, B/B ⇒ A/A, HAMBURGER (see Table 3). Similarly, FROG, WATERMELON, GOAT, EGG, and CEREAL may be accounted for, at least in part, by the complexity of the required sigs.

Assimilation from an adjacent dez in the string is not, strictly speaking, a factor in the present corpus. At least three signs, however, serve to show that some interference from adjacent signs does indeed influence output.

In session 2, Q-SIGN is formed twice with a G, rather than a 5. FF is looking for a pen that had dropped to the floor and disappeared. She is trying to elicit the attention of the adults present to help her find it. An admittedly rich interpretation of the passage — delivered after she had jumped to her feet — would be: "Hey! Where's that pen? It's somewhere here on the floor." It is my contention that the handshape for INDEX ('here on the floor') has intruded on the movement of the Q-SIGN ('where's/what's something'), and that this particular utterance represents a blend of the two signs. This phenomenon is not uncommon in adult experimental and error data.

An assimilation of tab (non-active) hand to (active, signing) dez  hand occurs in session 2. The target sign is STRAWBERRY, signed by twisting an O hand dez on the extended pinky finger of the other hand. The O dez is realized by FF as bO. Y is ordinarily realized as 5, but here presumably through assimilation, it becomes bO. Here also the sign changes type as well; instead of a passive tab hand held inactive while dez hand twists, FF has made it a double-dez sign with symmetrical sig:

Target: Y' O$^{\omega}$              STRAWBERRY          Ø bO' bO$^{\omega\sim}$     : FF

An actual error appears in session 4. A common sign for 'catsup' used in FF's family is performed as CAT + UP ( F$^{>}$ Ø G $^{\wedge}$). FF's attempt to produce this compound actually involves five successive signs:

$$\text{Ø} 5^{\wedge} \; \text{!:} \; )G^{X} \; \text{!:} \; )5^{X} \; \text{!:} \; \text{Ø} 5^{\wedge} \; \text{!:} \; \text{л}G^{X} \qquad \text{'up-cats' (?)}$$

It seems that the process may look something like this:

$$\begin{array}{lll} F & \Rightarrow 5 & \text{via Rule 1 (above)} \\ \text{(CAT)} & & \end{array}$$

G   ⇒ 5            via perseveration
(UP)

5   ⇒ G            dissimilation: a need to dis-
(CAT)              tinguish two parts of a compound

Session 4 offers a unique opportunity to observe the entry
of a positively-specified feature into FF's output. It also
offers some supportive evidence for the psychological reality
of the feature [+concave] in the Lane, Boyes-Braem, Bellugi
feature system. The feature has not been realized until this
point (session 4) in the corpus (see Rule 2, above; one exception, DRINK, is discussed below). Two signs in session 4,
however, indicate that FF is beginning to distinguish [+concave]
as a feature in her phonology. LION is signed with a bent spread
hand: $\ddot{5}$ (Remember that concavity as a low-level feature is
indicated by three dots over the dez symbol). FF signs LION
with a C dez. As Boyes-Braem points out, adduction of the
fingers is a natural, involuntary reflex in partially extended
position (LION is signed with the hand above the top of the
head). Added to this natural process is the fact that the sign
is formed outside the visual field of the signer. The result is
FF's over-application of the feature [+concave], perhaps mis-
taking a low-level feature for a distinctive one.

Additional evidence for the process by which the feature
is acquired is exemplified in the sign CHURCH, which is within
the visual field. FF signs:

$$\text{S' 5}^{\text{X}} \qquad \text{S' }\ddot{\text{L}}^{\text{X}} \qquad \text{S' C}^{\text{X}} \qquad \text{'church'}$$

I.e. she makes a sequence of three signs — attempts at a
correct "pronunciation" as it were. In all three, the target
forms of the tab (S hand pronated), sig (touching), and dez
orientation (pronated so that radial or thumb side of dez makes
the touch) are realized. Only the dez handshape changes.
From the left, the substitution 5 gives way to bent $\ddot{\text{L}}$ (the
feature [+concave] being applied to the thumb and index finger only); then $\ddot{\text{L}}$ gives way to the target form C, with the
feature [+concave] appropriately applied.

DRINK appears in session 2 in the adult form, with C dez.
Because this is an iconic sign, it may be that miming is a
factor in assisting FF to form a C dez handshape before the
feature [+concave] appears elsewhere. In any case, it seems
to fit the definition of a "phonological idiom: a pronunciation

which does not obey the constraints which otherwise operate
on the child's output", as given by Moskowitz (1977: 3).
Such idioms have been observed in children acquiring numerous different spoken languages; it is apparently a phenomenon that is not excluded from ASL because of the different
modality sign language uses.

More evidence regarding the feature [+concave] comes
from two occurrences of WANT. Neither token is absolutely
correct; in each case FF seems to know that the feature of
concavity must be added, but she does not yet have the competence to integrate it. In the first instance her 5 dez is
marked for laxness ($\breve{5}$), and in the second it is marked for
tenseness ($\hat{5}$):

Session 3            Ø $\breve{5}\breve{5}^{\top}$     'want'

Session 4            Ø $\hat{5}^{\perp}$     'want'

Reilly (1977) has discussed a similar phenomenon with hearing children learning spoken English; she demonstrates that
children use second turns in discourse to correct certain linguistic features that they are acquiring. While the case here
is not a second turn, it seems that this application of various
low-level features is evidence that FF is working on concavity
during the two sessions in question.

The question inevitably arises as to how much phonetic
variation is normal in any given adult sign, and how much of
FF's output falls within that range. In making judgments for
"required" dez handshapes, I have followed the <u>Dictionary of
American Sign Language</u> (Stokoe, Casterline, & Croneberg 1965
[1976]) as much as possible. The exceptions have been mainly
signs that I consider to require a baby O, bO, not a distinctive
form in the dictionary system. Some phonetic variation is apparent in adult signs. A few of the substitution of the handshapes
in the data are in fact within the acceptable range of variation.
An example is FF's TRAIN in session 4:

$$G_v^+ \, V_v^{I..}$$     'train'

This can be and is signed in adult dialects either with both hands
in H configuration or both hands in V configuration. We might predict that in FF's signing V would substitute for H, because ab-
duction, i.e. separation, of the extended fingers is more natural

than its opposite, adduction. In these cases there has been
no clear way of judging what the target was. I have systematically followed the Dictionary and counted the V, and similar
occurrences, as substitutions. In the same way, I have rated
FF's use of 5 hand configuration as substitutions of handshape
when these are realizations of B tabs in the target. In no case
do FF's substitutions block the comprehensibility of her signs.
In an adult such tokens would probably be stylistically marked
as casual or even sloppy signing, but in most cases not
'wrong'. This is a matter that requires more investigation of
both child and adult signing.

C o n c l u s i o n .    In summary, we should note that although
                        phonology in American Sign Language is in
some ways very different from phonology in spoken languages,
it obeys many of the same laws. Battison (1974) has discussed
conditions for deletion; Frishberg (1975, 1976) has demonstrated the regulating forces in historical phonological changes
of signs; Newkirk, Pedersen, and Bellugi (1976) have begun an
analysis of phonological errors in ASL, comparable to work
done by Fromkin (1973); and Bellugi and Siple (1974) have produced experimental evidence for the psychological reality of
dez, sig, and tab as the organizing principles of signs. In
the present case, we can see that it may be possible eventually to write a set of rules, abstract in nature, which will
provide a description for the acquisition of a phonology without sound.
        Moskowitz (1970) and Smith (1973) have both presented
analyses of how the phonology of English is acquired. The
children in their studies appeared to have rules in their phon-
ologies that simplified the adult, target system. Similarly,
FF's phonology appears to simplify the structure of an adult
ASL phonology. By appealing to the features proposed by
Lane et al. (1976), we are able to see how a deaf child may
make hypotheses about her language similar in nature to
those that a hearing child makes.
        In no sense is the present study to be considered con-
clusive, however; rather it should be taken as setting forth
a possible set of guideposts for future research. Many questions have been put aside or barely touched upon. However,
any future research must, I think, include the assumption
that all languages appeal to the same internal acquisition
device, regardless of apparent differences in modality and
articulators.

## NOTES

1 Supported in part by Ursula Bellugi-Klima, the Salk Institute for Biological Studies; my deepest gratitude goes to her for her consideration and encouragement. Special thanks (in alphabetical order) to Robbin Battison, Penny Boyes-Braem, Jacqueline Lindenfeld, Elliot McIntire, Breyne Moskowitz, Carol Padden, Ann Peters, William Stokoe, and Sandra Thompson. Most of all to FF and her superlative family.

2 Dez, sig, and tab are terms given in Stokoe (1960) for the three aspects of behavior into which sign morphemes were first analyzed. Subsequent work has not altered the logic of analyzing a sign into what acts, what that does, and where action occurs; but shortcomings in the original presentation and in the Dictionary (1965 [1976]) may be amended by taking dez, as what acts, to include both specification of handshape and specification of orientation, when that is distinctive. [Ed.]

3 The term "stage" indicates only the four sequential groups of the model. Nothing other than a sequential progression in dez acquisition is implied.

4 "Baby O", symbolized bO, is the handshape which appears just at the close of the adult sign TWENTY; it is not cheremic in Stokoe's notation (where it is treated as a closed variant of X, thumb opposed to index finger).

## REFERENCES

Bellugi, Ursula, & Patricia Siple
    1974    Remembering With and Without Words, in Current Problems in Psycholinguistics, Bresson, ed. (Paris Centre Nationale de la Recherche Scientifique).

Battison, Robbin
    1974    Phonological Deletion in American Sign Language, Sign Language Studies 5, 1-19.

Boyes-Braem, Penny
    1973    A Study of the Acquisition of the Dez in American Sign Language (Berkeley, MS).

Brown, Roger
    1973    A First Language: The Early Stages (Cambridge,
            MA, Harvard University Press).

Chomsky, Noam
    1965    Aspects of the Theory of Syntax (Cambridge, MA,
            M.I.T. Press).

Fant, Louie
    1977    Notes on the Grammar of American Sign Language
            (Northridge, CA, MS).

Frishberg, Nancy
    1975    Arbitrariness and Iconicity: Historical Change in
            American Sign Language, Language 51, 696-719.
    1976    Some Aspects of the Historical Development of
            Signs in ASL (University of California, San Diego,
            doctoral dissertation).

Fromkin, Victoria (ed.)
    1973    Speech Errors as Linguistic Evidence (The Hague,
            Mouton).

Gesell, Arnold, & Halverson
    1936    The Development of Thumb Opposition in the Human
            Infant, Journal of Genetic Psychology 48, 339-361.

Kinsbourne, M., & E. K. Warrington
    1963    The Development of Finger Differentiation, Quarterly
            Journal of Experimental Psychology 15, 132-137.

Lane, Harlan, Penny Boyes-Braem, & Ursula Bellugi
    1976    Preliminaries to a Distinctive Feature Analysis of
            American Sign Language, Cognitive Psychology
            8, 263-289.

McIntire, Marina
    MS      A Modified Model of Dez Acquisition in ASL (Cali-
            fornia State University, Northridge, master's thesis).

McNeill, David
    1970    The Acquisition of Language (New York, Harper & Row).

Moskowitz, Breyne
    1970    The Two-year-old Stage in the Acquisition of
            English Phonology, Language 46, 426-441.
    MS      Idioms in Phonology Acquisition and Phonological
            Change (Los Angeles, 1977).

Newkirk, Don, Carlene Pedersen, & Ursula Bellugi
    MS      Interference between Sequentially Produced Signs
            in American Sign Language (Salk Institute Working
            Paper, 1976).

Reilly, Judy Snitzer
    MS      The Second Time Around: Expansions and Refine-
            ments in Children's Second Turns (UCLA master's
            thesis in linguistics, 1977).

Smith, Neilson
    1973    The Acquisition of Phonology (Cambridge, Univ. Press).

Stokoe, William C.
    1960    Sign Language Structure, Studies in Linguistics:
            Occasional Paper 8. Revised 1978, Linstok Press.

- - - - - , D. Casterline, & C. Croneberg
    1965    A Dictionary of American Sign Language on Linguistic
            Principles (Silver Spring, MD, Linstok Press: 2$^e$ 1976).

CHILDREN'S LANGUAGE SHOULD BE LEARNED, NOT TAUGHT

Raymond P. Stevens

Children who are born deaf do not learn to speak because they cannot hear. They do not hear other people speaking; consequently they cannot imitate the sounds we call speech. They cannot hear themselves vocalize; so they cannot monitor the sounds they make. To learn speech a person must be able to hear models to be imitated and to monitor the sounds made in attempting to imitate the models.

Deaf children can be taught to speak--provided that specialized instruction presents not auditory but kinaesthetic models and guides their attempts at imitation by use of the instructors' hearing and coaching as the indirect monitoring channel. But not all deaf children are taught to speak with proficiency and intelligibility. Only a very few, perhaps five to ten percent of them, acquire speech skills sufficient for communication in a near-normal, non-frustrating way. The great majority of deaf people, both children and adults, have non-functional speech. Yet, because nine out of ten deaf children have hearing parents, speech has become the focal point in the educational process of most deaf children.

Deaf children do not learn language--the English language in America--of a kind acceptable to others, because they cannot hear. They do not hear the language and consequently do not learn the patterns that make up sentences, phrases, and idioms.

Unfortunately, learning to speak and acquiring language have often been equated and confused; as a result the ability to produce speech sounds has become more important in the eyes of many teachers and parents than the possession of language.

The consequences of mutism or quasi-mutism caused by
deafness are great and permanent for the adult. Teachers
should do all they can to teach speech, to give the deaf child
functional speech. The failure to try is a sin; the failure to
succeed is not, however, as bad as most hearing people seem
to think. Deaf people communicate in other ways than in speech.

The failure to learn English has far greater and more devas-
tating consequences than the failure to learn speech. Our
educational system depends on English much more than on
speech. The world of trade and industry, social services, and
technology depend on language which is expressed in a variety
of forms. The deaf child who cannot speak can often write or
fingerspell or sign, but the child who does not know the English
language has no way to communicate with precision. Speech is
only one form of communication; English is the only language
of our culture. The child who cannot speak is cut off from
only those people who will not take the time to use another
form of expressing English. But the child who has not learned
English and has not acquired an education in its use has nothing
to say and no one to listen to him. Unfortunately, the parrot-like
speech of the illiterate deaf child is more a reassurance for
the parents than a practical way for the child to communicate.

There are many successful deaf adults who do not have
speech. There are also deaf adults who can speak but have
nothing to say, who have gone to school but who can't think.

Education for the deaf has the talents and the energy to
succeed. Ironically, schools and classes for deaf children
could be relatively more successful than schools for hearing
children, simply because deaf children are much more dependent on the educational process than are hearing children.
Almost everything that is taught in school is new to the deaf
children. Unfortunately, however, the system has not done
well. There are many controversies and antagonisms within
the field. There is little agreement on major goals and objec-
tives.

Generally, the question, What is the most important
thing in deaf education? gets three answers. One group of
educators will say: "Speech and oral communication skills."
A second group may say: "Language or education." A third
group, deaf people themselves, often say: "Communication."

"Communication" in this answer is not to be equated with
English or spelling or lipreading or even with sign language and
fingerspelling. I believe that deaf people mean communication
not of language but through language the attitudes, knowledge,
thoughts, desires, expectations, and mores that make individuals part of their culture. I will agree with anybody who says
that deaf people get along better if they have intelligible
speech, good spoken language, or a Ph.D. in literature. But
the youngsters and adults who don't have intelligible speech,
the King's English, or educational shingles are set apart, I
believe, not because of language and speech but because of
culture. Not culture in the sense of the fine arts, sophisti-
cation, and style, but culture in the sense of socialization
and behavior patterns and social characteristics common to a
particular group of people. The most important tool or vehicle
in the socialization process of people is language. Language
is a means of socializing individuals into their culture. Parents
talk to their hearing children, not in order to teach them a
language, but rather to satisfy their needs and wants and to
teach them right and wrong as regarded by their society. The
children talking with their parents are learning the language
of their culture; they are not being taught it. They are learning
language as a tool. It is functional. It is a means to an end.
That end is satisfaction of needs and wants, the acquisition
of acceptable behavior, and the recognition of themselves as
individuals.

Deaf children, on the contrary, are taught language. True,
their teachers want them to read, but teaching language has
become the end, not the means, of the educational system. The
teachers' communication with the deaf child is too often about
language instead of about his environment, his culture, his
very life. School for the deaf has become a place to be forced
to learn a strange and foreign language and speech rather than
a place to learn about culture, and in doing so to learn language.

The consequences to the child of not being a part of the
larger culture are a low reading level, a different sense of humor,
and a different language. Deaf students who do not read, cannot
--because they are not socialized into their culture. English in
its printed and spoken forms is the language of the culture.
Until deaf children learn English in the same manner that hearing
children learn English, the majority of them will not succeed in
school, will not read, and will not hold jobs commensurate with

their innate abilities. Deaf education must communicate the culture, the attitudes, the humor, the folkways, the family traditions to deaf children. English language must become the product of that communication.

Deaf children must learn culture and language simultaneously. All that my grandmother, or that sociologists and teachers of the deaf, would call "culture" and say was important for each person to know is on the other side of the soundless barrier for each deaf child . Properly directed, education for the deaf could be devoted to breaking that soundless barrier.

All native or mother-tongue languages are learned. For too long the education of the deaf has concentrated on teaching the language. This is contrary to the natural process of language learning. Simply stated, language must be learned and not taught. Language and culture are acquired by the growing child and cannot and should not be forced into him.

Language in this sense of the word is the system of communication, whether English, French, or so-called Deaf English, that is learned through experience and use, learned out of necessity--nothing like the system that is presented in the classroom. Language is an organic, dynamic, unexplainable neurological phenomenon that can take the forms of English, French, or of anything else that people use. Some of the formal rules of grammar can be taught in the classroom, but language as communication must by its nature be learned. On that precept, deaf education must focus its energy and talents.

Some time ago someone devised the slogan, "Talk, talk, talk, talk to your deaf child." Such advice implies an understanding of the nature of language acquisition and development. Unless children, deaf or hearing, are exposed to language, they will not learn it. Unfortunately, for a deaf child, talking is an unclear, ambiguous exposure to the system of oral communication. For too many deaf children, talking simply becomes the blurred and meaningless movement of faces--sometimes perhaps communicating feelings or emotions but never communicating precise verbal messages.

Hearing children learn language through modeling as they develop conceptually. Their experiences guide and foster their command of language. As they become older they become more

skilled in communicating not only their physical needs and
wants but also in abstracting, that is in expressing themselves intellectually.

Deaf children develop language very much as hearing
children do. In a family of hearing people, deaf children
have almost no formal language, but they have simple gestures or signals, which can change from day to day. Once
the deaf child comes to school, he is exposed to a variety
of formal language expressive systems (lipreading, speech,
signs, writing), and immediately begins to learn language.
His teachers work as diligently as possible to teach him as
much as they think he can absorb. He learns to communicate
in some fashion,using any (at times all) of the forms he has
been exposed to. After eight or ten years he writes better,
takes tests, and passes silly notes to girls. He is using
language, but it is not English:

"My nose is maple syruping"

"Mr. Stevens and I scorched our way to school
this morning"

"I am my nose"

--these are communications in language, but they are not
in English in the formal sense of the name. They do not
follow the generally accepted rules of English.

Hearing children learn English because the volume of
English they hear is sufficient for them to learn the rules
of English. This critical volume of exposure has been heard
by the time the child is four years old, long before he is
independent of his parents, and before he has matured intellectually. Thus, as his independence and individuality bloom,
simultaneously his ability to communicate his own uniqueness
develops. While the language that he acquires is common to
all, the way that he uses it and what he says mark him as an
individual.

Language acquisition for the hearing child is a high-level
cognitive, thinking process. The child hears hundreds of examples of the rules; no one states to him one one-hundredth of
all the rules. From heard examples of language in practical
use the child must deduce the rules. Hearing children are able

to express themselves early in their lives in an increasingly sophisticated way. Some children can communicate simple needs before their first birthday (e.g. 'water' or 'milk', even though these sound like <u>wawa</u> and <u>mik</u>). The more complicated syntactic structures forming sentences are used by their second and third birthdays. Deaf children, however, are not exposed to enough English sentences for them to learn English. Furthermore, deaf children have to wait for years to learn simple patterns for expressing the most mundane and common things in their lives. They are not exposed to the volume of English sentences necessary for them to learn the syntax of the language. But because they have the need to communicate, they impose rules of syntax and structure on the words and phrases they know, thereby creating their own form of language (see Goldin-Meadow & Feldman 1975).

This need to communicate demands an orderly, clear, reliable system. Deaf children are no exception to this cultural, psychological, linguistic phenomenon of mankind. As the individual perceives order in his universe, he also perceives order in the language to which he is exposed. The hearing child's need for order and structure is satisfied through the process of learning the language, discovering its rules. Deaf children do not receive enough clear, unambiguous language to determine through example the rules of English. Thus to satisfy their need for order and structure in language, deaf children develop their own syntax , or language system-- often derided by educators as "Deaf English".

What some linguists have labeled as a "language freeze" --this aberrant self-created language--and a result of immaturity is actually a "language birth". Although not English, the deaf child's language output satisfies his need for system, syntax, and structure in order to communicate. The individual deaf child creates his own language based on his individual cultural and language experience. The hearing child generally has a language experience similar to that of the majority of people in his culture; thus he acquires through deductive learning the syntax of the majority. But English for the deaf child becomes a second language, while his own self-made language remains his primary means of communicating. "My nose is maple syruping" is actually the result of a creative child's communicating through language with his mother. Schools fail because they cannot teach as fast as the children

can learn. Children learn language outside the classroom too.
What they learn they bring to the classroom and subtly impose
it on what the teacher presents to them. Their instinctual need
to communicate produces a form of language that competes with
English as a language.

The deaf child in school is constantly reminded of the
"other way" to communicate; he is made aware of English not
only in the classroom, but wherever he goes: English is there
as the language of the culture. The deaf child who develops a
language does not need English to communicate to the extent
that he is taught it in the classroom. His need does not grow
because he is protected by a sheltered environment in home
and school. Hearing children have a constantly expanding linguistic environment, through radio, TV, movies, the theater,
the printed word, and most of all other people they come in
contact with. Such an expanding environment early in the
hearing child's life imposes linguistic rules and an unconscious
understanding that the culture at large dictates the language to
be used. Young deaf children do not have an expanding linguistic environment, and therefore have neither the syntax of English
nor the unconscious understanding that the culture at large does
dictate the language its members must use.

Most deaf children learn to read and write a little bit in
preschool. They learn to read their names and the sentences
which note the daily schedule:

　　　"We will go to Art."
　　　"Mr. Palmer will come today."
　　　"We will go to gym today."

When the activities are finished, the sentences are changed:

　　　"We went to Art."
　　　"Mr. Palmer came today."
　　　"We went to gym today."

Day in and day out, the schedule repeats itself, the sentences
keep coming, but the environment does not expand. Every in-
genious device, game, toy, activity, and instructional system
has been tried and will be tried again. But nothing works. The
teacher cannot compete with the live, real, gut-level communication, the signs, words, gestures, grimaces, fingerwaves,
feignings, that go on between the children. In a few years the
child will be sign-talking without regard for the rules and the
structures of English, without regard for the carefully patterned
sentences that so clearly delineated the days' schedule a few

years back. The volume of language received from the teacher
through teaching is minimal compared to the volume of language
received from other students communicating. Therefore the
learning of language becomes a game. The language with the
most input wins the affections and the attention of the pupils.
The winning language becomes the language of the children
themselves, not because human beings have a propensity for
one form of language or another, but simply because the language which is presented as the most common and the most
usable becomes the language of the community.

If any change is to come in the results of the education
of the deaf, contacts in acceptable English must outnumber
the contacts children have with other forms of language from
other students. Obviously schools cannot and should not pro-
hibit contact among students. They can and should increase
the number of meaningful contacts between student and teacher
in acceptable English. The more closely the linguistic experience and environment of deaf children approximates that of
hearing children, the more likely that deaf children will use
English as their own language. Such a language experience
and environment must provide the deaf child with the opportunity to learn English through a great volume of exposure to
syntactically consistent and semantically meaningful verbal
communications. The most likely medium for that is some form
of Manual English or signed English (see The Linguistic Reporter, 12,2,April 1970). Signed English accepts the fundamental
characteristics of sign language, and imposes English word
order and tenses on Sign in a somewhat artificial manner.
Signed English is a tool for communicating the substance of
life, culture, personal feelings, and interactions; it is not
a tool to teach English. It may be a tool through which deaf
children will learn English. Deaf children will learn to use
English as they experience English through communication.
Teachers of deaf children must teach; in fact, they have more
to teach than do teachers of hearing children. But they should
not begin by teaching language. Deaf children come to school
with little knowledge of the world around them and almost no
understanding, conception, or inkling of the world removed
from them. Polar bears and Indians, science and sewing, and
a million more things and ideas are raw material for teaching.

Language becomes an important device in teaching what
hearing children have been taught at home through communication. In the process of being taught at home, and later at
school, hearing children learn language, the English language,
in order to understand, control, manipulate, and change their
environment. Language is a tool for hearing children, but it is
never an end in itself. Mothers correct and verbalize for their
children, but only in the context of a message unrelated to
language learning itself. Children repeat the corrected or uncorrected pattern, still bearing in mind the original message.
Language (English) is a by-product of communication between
children and adults and among children themselves. Through
communication the hearing child is socialized, learns the
culture, is taught the limits of behavior, the range of expectations, the chances of success, the consequences of failure, and ad infinitum.

Culture is the substance of the communication. Language
provides the commonalty to experiences which later make it
possible for children to meet new people without a great deal
of fear, to shop and know what to expect from clerks--even
to know what to say about the loss of a loved one. Language
is the most important socialization process. Institutions,
primary groups, society depend on language for transmitting
their content to their individual members. Without language
the individual member stands apart from his culture, because
he lacks the experiences which socialize the individual.
English, reading, taxes, contracts, and the unrelated concepts of speed, independence, wealth, and sacrifice are
culturally bound. Those who are not in some degree part of
the culture cannot read. Deaf children cannot read because
they are in a cultural limbo. They are not members of their
parents' culture, nor is there a culture which they can easily
join. Reading is not looking for facts on a page, or finding
antecedents. The printed word is a verbal cue to thinking.
Unless the reader knows the culture of that particular language
he cannot read, because the printed word is an expression of
that culture. Deaf children cannot and do not read because
they are not socialized into their culture, and consequently
they do not have the command of English necessary for
reading.

Human beings communicate to satisfy needs. In the process
of communicating they learn the language of their culture, which
becomes an efficient system for satisfying present and future

needs and wants. The language and the culture are both so
complex and full of nuances that rote memory cannot serve
the individual effectively. Deaf children are taught language
in a very artificial, rote way.

"Sally run."

"What did Sally do?"

"Sally ran."

is good English but extremely poor communication. In the context
of the classroom the sentences are void of content and message.
The deaf child must memorize the structure, the syntax, and the
grammar because there are no message clues to help him learn
the language. The language that is taught is non-functional
because it does not communicate anything tangible; there is
nothing in it that the child can take hold of and use, and in
doing so learn language for future use. The language of the
classroom does not communicate, and therefore it cannot be
learned as a language. On the other hand, language that does
communicate is learned. Learned not on the first, second, third,
or even, fortieth time, perhaps, but eventually learned because
it is purposeful, because it satisfies a need and therefore becomes
a tool.

The child learns language because the experiences which
were language based communicate something that depended on
language. Such experiences become frames of reference. Such
experiences become sources of conceptual understanding and
models for language use. "The superintendent is driving fast"
implies more than just action and velocity. "The horse is run-
ning fast" likewise tells more than just whether the horse is
moving. The superintendent is probably going faster than the
horse, but is wrong in doing so. The horse is probably going
faster than all of the other horses, and thus is loved by the
track fans for doing so. Such values, judgments, and opinions
cannot be taught; they must be learned. The child who has not
learned the values, judgments, and opinions of his culture
surely cannot understand them when they are presented in the
printed word.

A frame of reference is built slowly through many unplanned
experiences and without regard for quality. Frames of reference
are created even though the child has many conflicting and con-
tradictory experiences. "Fast" is not simply a description of
velocity but an opinion about speed and its appropriateness.
Deaf children must have experiences wherein other people

around them communicate not only a description of the moment
but also their feelings, opinions, and values relating to that
experience.

Communication becomes the creator of a wealth of attitudes and opinions that help growing children understand the
culture as well as learn the patterns of the language. When
the child refers back to an experience, he does not recall
the rote memory work of the classroom, but rather the message
that was communicated through the language of the experience,
and in the process he recalls the language pattern.

Deaf children must be given language simultaneous with
their experiences, not because language necessarily helps
them understand the experience, but simply because it is a
cultural imperative that language be part of the experience.
The best thing formal education could do for deaf children
is to stop trying to make them into sentence remembering
machines--that won't work--and begin letting them learn
language as they learn about themselves and the world through
communicating with others.

## REFERENCES

Goldin-Meadow, Susan, & Heidi Feldman
    1975    The Creation of a Communication System: A Study
            of Deaf Children of Hearing Parents, Sign Language
            Studies 8, 225-234. —CHAPTER 16, below

The Linguistic Reporter
    1970    CAL Conference on Sign Language (W.C. Stokoe)
            Quotes O'Rourke's distinction of five modes:
            (1) Sign Language, (2) Signed English, (3) Simul-
            taneous Method, (4) Fingerspelling, (5) Manual
            English. Vol 12, No.2, April, 5-8. This valuable
            discussion was distributed by and may still be
            available from the National Association of the
            Deaf.

PANTOMIME & GESTURE to SIGNED ENGLISH

Marvin B. Sallop

The educational philosophy called Total Communication has
been adopted by many schools for the deaf, and more are
joining the movement each year. It was pioneered at the
Maryland School for the Deaf and is clearly stated by that
school's superintendent:

> Total Communication is the RIGHT of a deaf child to
> learn to use all forms of communication available to
> develop language competence. This includes the full
> spectrum, child devised gestures, speech, formal
> signs, fingerspelling, speechreading, reading and
> writing. To every deaf child should also be provided
> the opportunity to learn to use any remnant of resid-
> ual hearing he may have by employing the best pos-
> sible electronic equipment for amplifying sound.
> (Denton 1972)

The terms "child devised gestures" and "formal signs"
are perhaps easily understood; however, utilizing gestures
and signs as teaching tools are processes not so familiar.
First, sign language, or American Sign Language (ASL) and
"signs" should not be confused. ASL is a language with a
syntax, a grammar of its own distinct from that of English.
Manual signs, however, can be used as equivalents of
(many of) the words in grammatical English sentences.
Second, the elements of Total Communication are not seg-
mentable, separable from one another in time, but are
simultaneous and interdependent. In this paper I will focus
on one of the elements, ASL, otherwise "formal signs", and
its use within a Total Communication environment to help
pupils in one class acquire something like English word
order. I will describe the language instruction given in a
special class at the Kendall School for the Deaf, particularly
its format and the results, from a linguistic point of view.

Some idea of the initial competence of pupils in the
class can be gained from this comment by the cooperating
teacher:
> The language problems in this class are very great.
> The children are hampered by extremely limited vo-
> cabularies. In spite of the fact that most of the chil-
> dren are reading at a first grade level, their expressive
> language is much lower. In most cases they attempt
> to explain what they have seen by gestures, panto-
> mime, and a few formal signs. (Language-reading lesson
> plan, 23-26 March 1970, W. Wheatley)

A more detailed view of the pupils' language level is given
in the notes I took during the early stages of my work with
this class:
> 1    (gesture or pantomime) finger pointing to the hall,
>        child walking, face smiling with mouth open making
> grunting sounds; finger making a 90° turn to the left,
> child walking and making a turn to the left, face smiling
> with mouth open making grunting sounds; finger making
> another 90° turn to the left, child walking and making
> another turn to the left, and then another left turn, face
> smiling with mouth still open making grunting sounds;
> then the child stops walking, continues to smile, and
> lifts brows in a question.

Is this language? Hardly. Communication? Yes; in 1, the
child is pointing out the way to the school library from the
classroom. He concludes by asking, with facial expression,
if his performance is correct. His attempt just before that
noted to respond to the word library written on the blackboard
had been to point out the window. I pulled his hand down
and told him, signing and speaking at the same time to talk
to me and tell me by talking to me. The result of his next
attempt is recorded above in 1.

> 2    child makes a name sign and wrinkles the brow.

The child performing this came into the room as I was standing
at the blackboard. He looked around the room and performed
what is described in note 2, to ask me 'Where is Mr. Wheatly?'

> 3    child signs DIRTY then a name sign 'Simon' while
>        smiling and nodding his head.

The child described in 3 was addressing another pupil in the

room and making a comment about a third pupil not present
in the room, to wit, 'Simon is dirty.'

   4    child in body stance of defiance, feet apart, signs
        DIRTY and FIGHT and points to another child, YOU,
        while lipspeaking the words and speaking the words
        "dirty fight you;" her face showing anger, brows
        pushed together.
This child had been hit while she was not looking , during a
free-time mock boxing match in the room. She was saying,
in colloquial English, 'You fight dirty.'

   These examples have been selected and ordered to
show, without the need for long theoretical argument, that
children in this special class were operating at several
levels of linguistic competence. At least their performance
suggests so. Note 1 bears out teacher Wheatley's comment
about gestures and pantomime: there is hardly a linguistic
symbol in the whole performance, although the facially expressed question at the end would be correctly interpreted
by most observers from our culture. The performance in note
2 seems to be a combination of sign use (i.e. a more or
less linguistically coded motor sign) with facially expressed
questioning gesture, in this case requiring the interpretation
'where?' In note 3, "formal" or conventional signs of ASL
supply both state verb and patient (to use the terminology
and form a semantic structure as in Chafe 1970). Or to symbolize a comment and topic, or a predicate 'dirty' and a
subject 'Simon' in traditional school grammar terms. Adults
fully competent in ASL and in English might make use of the
pattern of 3 to make a similar comment; but taken with all
the other evidence provided by regular observation of this
child, what is described in 3 seems more akin to a Pivot-
Open grammar first described by Braine (1963). Note 4, with
three signs besides kinesic expression and spoken or lipspoken syllables, comes closest to full language competence.
It is a well-formed structure of ASL, presumably with the same
base as the English surface structure You fight dirty, from
which it differs in order of elements.

   The first step in designing language instruction for
this class was to recognize a hierarchy of levels in language
competence, next to identify the level of each child, and
then to pull, push, and prod him to the next higher level.

Although the instruction was directed at the individual child
and took place in the simultaneity of a full classroom, I will
try here to present it in separate steps. First, for the child
who communicated with gestures and pantomime, even though
his receptive competence was in "straight English" (i.e.
standard English spoken and simultaneously represented with
signs for words), I refused to accept from him any gestures
or pantomime that could not be considered to belong to ASL.
I gave this child negative reinforcement by not watching him
when he wanted to tell me something, unless he used signs.
When he held onto me and I could not avoid watching him,
I hit him lightly on the head or lightly slapped his hands.
This is not as cruel as it sounds, and it was the only means
effective. I would not let him get out of his seat to communicate by moving around in pantomime or acting out. He could
communicate only from his seat. I supplied signs when he
expressed a need for them and provided negative reinforcement when he did not use signs or tried to revert to gross
gestures when I knew that he knew the signs. For positive
reinforcement, I kissed him, hugged him, played with him,
gave him piggy-back rides, candy, gum, and tick marks on
the blackboard. (My cooperating teacher also discouraged
his gestures and pantomime in the same way.)

This child quickly understood that his gestures and
pantomime were no longer acceptable as means of communication and that we would accept only genuine signs. He also
learned that he was not under pressure to communicate in
speech, although we did encourage him if he tried to form the
words matching the sign with mouth and lips. Without the
pressure of being forced to produce speech, he was able to
concentrate on the acquisition of signs in structures, hence
language. At the end of six weeks, he was no longer communicating with gestures and pantomime but instead with Pivot-
open or Topic-Comment sign patterns and even a few more
elaborate patterns. (It is interesting to note that as this
pupil learned a sign, i.e. incorporated it into his production,
he subsequently lipspoke, and later spoke, the word equivalent of the sign, with speech production assistance the
teacher provided.)

The other pupils in the class seemed to know that
this child's communicative performance was below theirs,
and when they noticed that Mr. Wheatley and I were no

longer accepting his gestures and pantomimes, they too refused to accept them from him, providing him with signs from
their own level of linguistic competence. This had a snow-
ball effect on the entire class. Each pupil offered a helping
hand to the pupil on a linguistic level below him; i.e. each
was out-of-awareness aware of the linguistic hierarchy.

    The children who mixed signs and gestures were
treated with pretended misunderstanding; e.g. when a child
came up and signed WATER with a facially expressed question, I would reply that I was not thirsty, or that it was not
raining, or that I did shower last night, or I praised him for
showering last night, or I told him that I did not want the
blackboard washed, or I said, "No, we will have milk with
our lunch." His usual response to these exhibitions of my
denseness was an expanded repetition of his initial question,
often in a Pivot-Open or Topic-Comment pattern. He might
ask in signs, 'water me' or 'water me there' or 'water me go'
with a questioning face.
    Note that this pretended misunderstanding of mixed
sign-gesture or one-sign utterances was reserved for those
children who were already able to communicate thus (the
performance described in note 2 above). The child moving up
to this level from pantomime and gesture was of course more
positively responded to when he reached this sign stage. It
is interesting to note also that when I faked non-reception of
a message, the children using holophrastic (Menyuk 1969) or
mixed expressions did not revert to gesture and pantomime.
I take this as further evidence of their implicit recognition of
the hierarchy in language levels. I was prepared to give them
the appropriate negative reinforcement for reverting to gesture
and pantomime, but these children never did revert.

    At the next level, the children who were communicating
in Pivot-Open sign structures were also treated with communicative blocking. I misunderstood everything that they tried to
tell me until they added additional signs that showed they were
using a more advanced grammatical structure. For example, a
child approached me and asked in signs and speech, 'house
Washington you,' with an inquiring look. I replied that there
were many houses in Washington. He shook his head for 'no'
while lipspeaking no, and then asked again signing and lip-

speaking, 'house you sleep Washington' with the same look
of inquiry. This sequence of signs fits one pattern of sign
order in ASL, and I indicated that I understood his question
by replying that I lived at Gallaudet College. He ran off,
happy indeed, to inform the other members of the class that
Mr. Sallop lived at Gallaudet College.

These techniques were used during six weeks until
all these children learned that they could not communicate
with me or with Mr. Wheatley unless they used more appropriate
patterns of language than those they had been using.
By the end of six weeks they were all communicating with
both teachers on a level like that described in note 4 or that
in the final question at the top of this page. Unfortunately
they continued in their communicating with each other to
use the simpler Pivot-Open structures. I tried to discourage
this by butting into their conversations and misconstruing
what they had said. As long as I was in the conversation
they remained on the higher syntactic level. When I left the
conversation, however, they reverted to their Pivot-Open
patterns. I believe that if I could have been there all year
to butt into their conversations, they would have moved up
a level. Six weeks was not enough time to condition them to
drop all Pivot-Open utterances and use more elaborate structures spontaneously with each other. [Editor's note: There
may be more involved here than time and operant conditioning; in Chapter 3 there is more than a strong suggestion that
children switch codes both for age and for situation; the
presence or absence of a teacher might very well have been
the trigger for switching from a classroom-appropriate language level to an age-appropriate level—and we are told
the age of the children here.]

The most difficult language teaching problem I faced
in this class was that of three children who were already
communicating in full ASL patterns with me, Mr. Wheatley,
and each other. The task with them was to shift their ASL
syntactical patterns to those of standard English when possible, and to enrich their ASL performance by enlarging their
vocabulary and repertoire of patterns for meanings they were
striving to express. I achieved only limited success in this
task. The child who approached me with the signed, and
lipspoken or fully spoken, question WATER I GO PLEASE?

would be told in signs and speech, "Ask me in English." I
made it a point never to ask him to say it "properly;" for
his communication to me is a well-formed ASL sentence.
What I was requesting was a translation of that sentence
into another language, i.e. standard English. My position
of course constitutes a de facto recognition that English
is a second language for deaf children and that ASL may be
their first and appropriate language. Any demands made in
the form, "Repeat that properly, please;" were for an improved construction in sign language, not for English
translation.

At the end of only six weeks I doubt that many of the
children had realized that we were in fact demanding two languages from them, yet those three children who were gener-
ating appropriate constructions in ASL were being guided into
learning standard English as a second language.

English as a second language was presented to the
class in two ways, informally and formally. First, the major
portion of my language instruction was given to the class
throughout the entire school day. I signed "straight language"
to them, and by doing so provided a model (with words signed)
of standard English. I responded to their questions in standard English. I encouraged them to rephrase their questions
in standard English, to make their comments in standard
English, no matter what we were doing—math, recess, having
lunch, or even standing in the hall. Second, I had the class
for Reading, and any formal instruction I gave was in the
reading period. They also had formal language instruction
from another teacher the first hour of each day, in her classroom. There she worked on the Roberts (1958) formulas and
patterns. A side effect of this work was that the children
were exposed to the syntactic constructions of English. No
one ever told them that this was their language. They were
told only that this was English, and for that hour they would
work and reply within the Roberts frames. The children who
could make well-formed ASL sentences were here being given
models of English, which they could use when they were
required to translate from Sign to English for me. The children at lower linguistic levels were not showing any carry-
over outside the Roberts worksheets, but I do not feel that
it hurt them to have had this exposure to standard English.

The three pupils I was requiring to translate their utterances into English were also being taught to expand their
sign language capabilities. I provided them with an expansion
of their sign vocabularies whenever a sign was needed. This
was highly unstructured: I simply supplied them with a sign
or structure when the need arose in their own communication
of a message. Nevertheless an interesting thing started to
happen during my last week with the class. These three children, and no others, started to pick up and use signs of mine
that I had not been requiring them to use. Because I used
signed English continually, I had been signing, instead of
fingerspelling, was, were, is, are, am, and many other words
of English that do not have ASL signs, but which are given
sign form in Manually Coded English and signed English (i.e.
varieties near the English end of the continuum; see Chapters
1 and 2). Spontaneously the children began using these signs
in their own utterances. I had not required it of them; I had
only used the signs out of habit in my communicating with
them. Theory states that there is a lag of at least several
months between receptive competence and expressive competence; however, these three children started to give me
back these signs in only five weeks, without any pressure on
them to do so.
The fact that only these three children were using
these signs seems to offer more support for the idea that
there is a hierarchy in signing competence. The other children were apparently incapable of doing the same because of
their appreciably lower linguistic level.

To summarize the linguistic approach to language
acquisition I used with this special class, first, they were
indeed special. They had been misdiagnosed as brain
damaged and mentally retarded until they were eight or nine
years old, and until that time they had received only custo-
dial care and perfunctory teaching. At that time Mr. Wheatley,
whose background is in mental retardation, was hired specifically for this class. He found in a very short time of working
with them that they were neither mentally retarded nor brain
damaged, and that they had only some behavior problems and
learning disabilities. They then could communicate in gestures and a few signs. They could recognize their printed first
names, but did not know their last names. They could not add

one and one nor identify many colors. In the year and one
half that Wheatley worked with them, they had learned to
read at first grade level (with no exceptions) and to write
with a limited, concrete vocabulary. At the time of my six
weeks with them their ages were between nine and eleven.

Helping these children reach higher, more mature
levels of language competence began with the hypothesis
that a language hierarchy exists in signed language: at its
base is pantomime and gesture, at the next level holophrastic signs and signs mingled with gestures, at the third level
signs combined in simple Pivot-Open structures, at the
fourth strings of two or more signs in more elaborated Topic-
Comment constructions, at the fifth level signs ordered in
accordance with the grammar of ASL. This is the top of the
hierarchy for sign language. Once a child has reached this
fifth level, he is ready to move from a sign language L form
or variety to a sign language H variety (Stokoe 1970); the
latter can be identified as signed English or Manually Coded
English. Moving to this variety of output entails learning
English as a second language from the basis of ASL as the
first language, and more specifically requires knowing where
the shifts in syntactic constructions must be made and how
to make them.

This was the approach that I followed in the six weeks
that I spent with this class. There was no formal presentation
of the morphology of English, or of sign language; however,
quite a lot of morphology was presented informally. Learning
signs as units of the process of communicating ideas and as
replacements for gestures and pantomime, and seeing continually sign language from the teacher in signed English form
offers the child morphology of both Sign and English in a synthetic approach. The child receives and transmits the whole
message, gleans meaning from the parts, and is introduced
to the forms of the units of both languges without being subjected to formal instruction. This should stand him in good
stead in an extrapolation of the language approach already
begun. When the child has reached the sign linguistic level
at which he is ready to learn English as a second language,
he has already had exposure to English morphology, and this
exposure can serve as a basis for more formal instruction.
Once he has taken these first steps toward linguistic competence, the elements within Total Communication can all come

into play. The child who learned to sign FISH in class also
soon learned to write fish, to read it, to fingerspell it, and
to speak it. Although dealing here with only some of the elements of Total Communication, I emphasize in concluding
that all elements used as simultaneously as possible are
the means by which we can help the deaf pupil gain the language proficiency he needs in life.

## REFERENCES

Braine, Martin D. S.
   1963    The Ontogeny of English Phrase Structure, Language
        39, 1-13.

Bruner, Jerome
   1968    The Achievement of Codes (Harvard University Center
        for Cognitive Studies), Annual Reports 8, 55-64.

Chafe, Wallace L.
   1970    Meaning & the Structure of Language (Chicago,
        Chicago University Press).

Denton, David M.
   1972    A Rationale for Total Communication, in Psycho-
        linguistics & Total Communication: The State of the
        Art, O'Rourke ed. (Washington, American Annals).

Menyuk, Paula
   1969    Sentences Children Use (Cambridge, MA, MIT Press).

Roberts, Paul
   1958    Patterns of English (New York, Harcourt Brace, World).

Stokoe, William C.
   1970    Sign Language Diglossia, Studies in Linguistics
        21, 27-41.

PART TWO: 11

# LANGUAGES AND LANGUAGE-RELATED SKILLS
# IN DEAF AND HEARING CHILDREN

John D. Bonvillian
Keith E. Nelson
Veda R. Charrow

Introduction.   Language can be studied from widely differing perspectives, and this diversity of view-
points often forces new conceptions of the nature and use of
language. An illustration of this point is the recent experimen-
tation with teaching signs of a sign language of the deaf to
chimpanzees (Gardner & Gardner), which has focused attention
on the symbolic, developmental, and productive aspects of
language and helped to suggest criteria for deciding what constitutes language behavior. Traditionally, most linguists (e.g.
Bloomfield 1933, Hockett 1958, Sapir 1966) had stressed the
sound system (phonology) as a fundamental characteristic of
language. But evidence from recent analyses of sign languages
of the deaf requires the rejection of this kind of phonological
criterion (e.g. Hockett 1978).

The recent analyses show that a sign language may be
a "true language" (see Chapter 2 above), comparable to any
spoken language in its use of a finite, though complex, set
of units and rules that allow the generation of an unlimited
variety of sentences. Any concept, no matter how abstract,
which can be expressed in a spoken language, can also be
expressed in a sign language. The rates at which ideas are
conveyed in sign and speech transmission are also about the
same. From recent research it is becoming clear that sign languages and spoken languages are similar not only in their
fully elaborated forms—as used by fluent adults—but also in
their acquisition stages for young children.

    After a discussion of these structural and developmental
aspects of sign language, we review factors that influence
the success or failure of à child--normal or handicapped--in
acquiring either speech or sign. We then discuss the relationships among different ways of processing English or Sign [i.e.
a specific system of signing, as English is a specific system of
speech], along with the performance of deaf children in reading,
writing, and educational achievement. Finally, we consider
the implications of what is known about children's language
and cognition for theories of development and programs of
education.

Sign language structure.  The principal means of communication
in the deaf community is sign language. Actually, many sign
languages are employed (Battison & Jordan 1976). American
Sign Language (ASL) and the sign languages used in other countries differ both in the construction of individual signs and in
the structure of their sign sentences. However, each of the
different sign languages appears from informal observation and
early referential communication experiments (Jordan & Battison
1976) to be as effective as spoken languages in transmitting
messages. A study by Bellugi (1972) showed that not only
could similar information be communicated through ASL as
through English speech, but also that the information was conveyed at virtually the same rate.
    American Sign Language is the colloquial sign language
of the deaf in the United States, and it is usually the first language that a child of deaf parents in America will acquire. Two
other varieties of an ASL-related sign language, Signed English
and Manual English, are often used in schools for the deaf in
the United States and in formal settings where both deaf and
hearing persons are present. Both these language varieties depend directly on English grammatical structure, and they probably should not be considered distinct languages from English.
Fingerspelling, also widely used, is the complete spelling of
English words with a manual alphabet code. In this paper we
will center our discussion on American Sign Language, because
it has been the focus of most studies of sign language use and
structure. After discussing the formation of individual signs we
will consider what is known about grammatical structures in ASL.
    Each sign in ASL is a unique combination of a small number
of distinct aspects of visible activity which have no meaning

in themselves. Stokoe (1960) specified three different aspects
of signs that distinguish a sign in ASL from some other sign:
the place on or near the body where the sign is performed; the
configuration (including its orientation) of the hand or hands;
and the movement or the change in configuration of the hand or
hands. Stokoe called the location aspect the tabula (tab), the
hand configuration the designator (dez), and the movement
aspect the signation (sig). Altogether he identified 55 different
sig , dez, or tab aspects (or cheremes) in ASL, and viewed
their role in ASL as somewhat analogous to that of phonemes
in vocal languages. Although this classification was limited
to description of ASL, it is quite possible that there may be a
larger, universal set of gestural features from which ASL and
other sign languages draw subsets used in sign chereme formation (Fischer 1974). The cheremes used in forming ASL signs
enter only certain sorts of combinations, and thus it should
be possible to specify whether any newly-constructed sign is
a well-formed or grammatically acceptable sign in ASL. Klima
and Bellugi (1974) show that persons who know ASL are sensitive to such a notion with reasonable   cross-informant reliability.
Chinese Sign Language signs which did not closely resemble
any particular ASL sign were classified by subjects in terms of
similarity to signs used in ASL. Those signs judged as highly
dissimilar to ASL tended to be "impossible" signs within the
formational system of ASL.
    A misconception that has been shared by linguists and
laymen alike is that the sign language of the deaf is largely
pantomime, iconic. In fact, the meanings associated with
most signs in ASL are usually arbitrary, just as the meanings
of most words are arbitrary in spoken languages. Thus, an
observer unfamiliar with a particular sign language would be
unable to follow the conversation of deaf persons using that
language (Jordan 1975, Jordan & Battison 1976, Battison &
Jordan 1976). However, once the meaning of a sign is given,
in a number of cases it will appear to be iconic. An example
is the sign BIRD: The index finger and thumb are extended
and opposed with the back of the hand at the signer's chin,
in imitation conventionally of a bird's beak (Klima & Bellugi
1974). Finally, it appears that even this metaphoric aspect
of signs is gradually disappearing. Analyses of the changes
in signs over the past one hundred years indicate that many
of those signs that originally had a pantomimic or imitative
basis are becoming more conventionalized and arbitrarily
symbolic (Frishberg 1975).

Investigations of differences between speech and sign
promise to cast light on how people process information, and
perhaps even on the origins of human communication. One
difference between oral and sign language is that certain signs
and sign cheremes occur simultaneously, whereas words and
morphemes are always temporally ordered. Another difference
is that facial gestures play a much more important role in sign
language, combining with the manual signing component to
establish a dual channel kind of communication. Specific
movements of the eyes, mouth, and head are either produced
alone or simultaneously with the manual signals in order to
help convey the full meaning of the sign language sentence
(Stokoe 1972). As one example of the role of these components,
if a smile accompanies certain sentences in ASL (e.g. "I don't
understand that"), the sentences are considered ungrammatical
(Fischer 1974). It is also possible that speech and sign may
have emerged at different points in history. Several investigators
(Hewes 1973, 1974, 1976, Stokoe 1974, Kimura 1974, Kendon
1975) have suggested that man's first language was most likely
to have been a gestural one.

Studies of the grammar of American Sign Language have
usually been approached in two different ways. One approach
has been to compare ASL with oral languages, usually with
English, and to point out the many dissimilarities between the
languages. This approach has often resulted in pejorative char-
acterizations of sign language as a system with little grammatical
structure, since many syntactical forms and constraints on word
order present in English are absent from ASL. Sign language, for
example, has no signs for articles, although in certain situations
the sign THAT is used as determiner with specific objects (see
Crutchfield 1972). And only those English prepositions that
have a locational aspect have a corresponding ASL sign, while
others, such as by and of do not. Nor is there a sign for the
copula or linking verb (i.e. any form of be) in ASL, although
the sign TRUE may often be used to emphasize the reality of
something. Another easily recognizable difference between the
two languages is the absence from ASL of inflections exactly
parallel to English inflections. Since ASL does not inflect its
verb signs for tense, the sign SEAT is used where sit, sits,
sitting, and sat would be used in English. ASL is also dissimilar in that it does not indicate passive voice and different grammatical moods of verbs. It should be apparent from
the examples just considered that grammatical information
conveyed in English is transmitted very differently in ASL.

The second approach to understanding the grammar of American Sign Language has been to focus on the many unique operations ASL uses to convey syntactic and semantic information. These unique operations appear to be related to the manual and visual modes of production and reception of signs. Changes in the speed, location in space, direction of movement, and repetition of signs produce variations in meaning-- variations which in English are carried by inflections and word order. When telling a story, a signer will often attempt to develop an imaginary stage or notion of setting, establishing the location of different persons and objects within the boundaries of this "signing space" (Friedman 1975). The signer will then refer back to specific positions in this sign space in order to indicate relations between signs in a sign sentence. The development of this visual setting (spatialization) is especially important and effective when the signer is using "directional" verbs (see Chs. 1 & 6 ), as this allows the signer to compact a great deal of information in one sign. For example, the signer can vary the movement of such directional sign verbs as GIVE or HIT to indicate who is doing the acting, who is the recipient of the action, and the location of the action. (Although this directionality of sign verbs, once seen, is iconic of the direction of action from agent to patient, there is evidence in deaf children's acquisition of ASL that this neat spatial-semantic fit is a syntactical transformation neither immediately transparent to the learning child nor built into the child's utterances until a late stage; Ellenberger & Steyaert, in Siple, 1978, 261-269 [New York, Academic Press].

Spatial relations also play an important role in indicating the time of an event or action. Frishberg and Gough (1973) described an imaginary time line that runs forward and back (future and past) from the signer's mid-cheek. In addition, there are other restrictions on sign order besides those arising from reference to spatial loci. Fischer (1974) observed that ASL sentences are predominantly of the form subject-verb-object, and that, as in English, most prepositions come before objects and adjectives before the nouns they modify. The freedom of word order depends, however, on the kind of agents and objects employed. If the sentence is non-reversible in terms of agent and object roles--as in a sentence about a "man" who "pays bills"--the word order is free to vary widely, and the sentence remains grammatical. In such sentences

subject-object-verb order is allowed; whereas with reversible
subjects and objects (e.g. man and child used with a verb like
notice) subject-object-verb and other orderings of these three
elements are ungrammatical. An analysis of this sort approaches
the kind of specificity needed in descriptions of ASL syntax,
but we are presently far from having an adequate description of
the whole syntax of Sign.

Acquisition of sign language. Cross-cultural comparisons of
young children's acquisition of their native languages have
revealed many similarities and few differences in the language
learning process. This outcome might be best understood as
the result of universal underlying cognitive or linguistic capacities. However, until recently, no study had compared the
acquisition of a non-oral language (i.e. sign language) with
the acquisition of oral language. Similar patterns of acquisition for both sign language and oral language would suggest
underlying cognitive skills common to both. In addition, an
analysis of the acquisition of a visual-motor language could
help identify how each stage in the child's development of
cognitive skills and of motor and physiological capacities
affects his language acquisition.

The results of three recent longitudinal studies of sign
language acquisition in young deaf children support the conclusion that the stages there closely parallel the development
of spoken language competence in hearing children (Klima &
Bellugi 1972, Nash 1973, Schlesinger & Meadow 1972).
These conclusions are based on observations of deaf children
that include their early learning of the meanings of individual
signs, their combinations of these signs to express different
semantic relations, and finally the systematic, gradual
growth of these early combinations into more mature grammatical usage.

The youngest of four children observed by Schlesinger &
Meadow was eight months old when the study began. This
child soon acquired a large vocabulary of signs, and by the
time she was 19 months old, had used 117 different signs.
For this child and for other deaf children acquiring Sign,
the early signing was similar in two respects to a hearing
child's early word use. She often overgeneralized the referential aspect of her early signs; and, in addition, a number
of her early signs were holophrastic--expressing or sug-

gesting complex ideas or whole phrases in a single sign.
The signs DOG and BYE were among the examples of her over-
generalization. DOG referred to real dogs, to a "Doggie
Diner" restaurant, and to other animals. At first the sign
BYE was used to indicate any approach or departure--a sign
for 'hello' appeared later in her sign vocabulary. Klima &
Bellugi (1972) and Nash (1973) also noted a number of
overgeneralizations of signs in their young subjects.

Although the development of a sign vocabulary is an
important first step in a deaf child's acquisiton of language,
it is through combining signs that the child gains an ability
to convey accurately a wide range of different meanings.
And it is the data on sign combinations that provides the
strongest evidence that similar patterns of acquisition hold
for speech and sign.

The children employed a number of two-sign combinations
that closely resemble the "pivot-like" constructions reported
in Braine (1963) and Slobin (1971), in which some words (e.g.
please, my, more, come) served as "pivots" and tended to
occupy either the first or last position with regularity. Consistent with Bowerman's findings (1969), the pivot signs
occasionally occurred alone (e.g. please) or in combinations
with other pivots (e.g. more please). More detailed analyses
revealed that a full range of semantic relations were expressed
in the children's early combinations of two or more signs.
Examples below are drawn from the following children's observed performance at about age three: "Karen" (Schlesinger &
Meadow 1972), "Marc" (Nash 1973), and "Pola" (Klima &
Bellugi 1972).

    I. Agent, Action, Object Relations
        Get milk shake store.    --Marc
        Daddy (take off) shoe.   --Karen
        Boy hit boy. Man work. --Pola

   II. Dative
        Give me orange.       --Pola
        Where is woman who
        gave me balloon?    --Marc

  III. Negation
        No bed. No wet.       --Karen
        Eat no. No touch. Not fish, duck.    --Pola
        Be careful don't knock over.    --Marc

IV.   Attributive
            Bed shoes. (for slippers) Pretty lights. —Karen
            Many candy. —Pola
            Where is red ball who puppy chews? —Marc
V.    Possessive
            Move TV my room. —Marc
            Me napkin. —Pola
            Barry (Barry's) train. My sweater. —Karen
VI.   Locative
            Letty, come home school. —Pola
            Daddy come later. Daddy work. —Karen
            I think that Daddy is home now. —Marc

The sign constructions above, along with many similar constructions, appear to resemble closely the structures and the
meanings in children's early speech (cf Bloom 1970). The range
of meanings and precision in expression of meaning increased as
language developed further. With increasing age and experience
with Sign, the deaf children's vocabulary rapidly expanded—
in many cases doubling in size in the space of several months.
With this increase in vocabulary, the young deaf children also
produced and comprehended progressively longer and more complex sign sentences.

An index of the progressive development of structural complexity is the children's mastery of the signs for negation. Not
only do the techniques that the children use to express negation
change, but the changes occur in a stagewise manner comparable
to that described by Bellugi (1967) for hearing children. Marc
first expressed negation by shaking his head before a sequence
of signs or simultaneously with making a sign. Next he acquired
the sign NOT and later began to use the separate quantitative
sign NONE. Finally, Marc appropriately utilized an incorporated negative marker in signs such as WON'T and CAN'T within
his sign sentences. Similarly, Pola moved from very simple
initial forms of negation, such as head-shaking, to the use
of signs NO and NEG (Klima & Bellugi 1972) to negate sentences, as in EAT NO, DADDY RIGHT NEG, and TOUCH NO.
With further development she incorporated a wide range of
negatives in her sentences, including NOT, NO, NEG, CAN'T,
NONE, and NOTHING. Thus the progress of these children
parallels hearing children's progression from simple negation
(no eat that; eat that no) to increasing differentiation of new
words for negation together with increasingly appropriate integration of such words into sentence structures.

An interesting example of syntactic overgeneralization
by Pola was her production of a sign clearly meaning 'You
fingerspell to me'. This sign was directed in space to show
action from mother toward child, so that in the manner of
directional s.l. verbs subject ('mother') and object ('signer')
were symbolized. However, adults do not incorporate subject
and object directionally in the verb FINGERSPELL. Pola thus
appears to have created a new sign by overgeneralizing the
subject-object indicating directionality utilized in one class
of ASL verbs (see pages 66 and 67 above).

Improved sign usage by the deaf children did not seem
to be the result of specific training. Their parents usually did
not correct their arrangements of sequences of signs, their
inappropriate repetitions, or their overgeneralizations of syntactic patterns (Klima & Bellugi 1972). This failure to correct
most ungrammatical signing corresponds with the behavior of
parents interacting verbally with their hearing children's output of speaking (Brown & Hanlon 1970). However, Cicourel &
Boese (1972) observed that deaf parents do sometimes expand
their child's "telegraphic" sign utterances, filling in the in-
complete signing with what they believed were the missing
elements. In sum, the limited data available suggests that
for the child learning sign language, as well as for the hearing
child learning spoken language, parents do not give direct
feedback on grammatical correctness, but they do provide
feedback on meaning, and they produce "expansions" or
other replies which may help illustrate appropriate syntactic
structure.

Throughout the observed periods of sign development
much of the playful quality of language exchange between
mothers and children was present for these young signers and
their mothers. It is thought that playful interaction at very
early ages may contribute to the development of language.
Within the first months of life, for deaf and hearing children
alike, structured patterns of gestural and motor interaction
between adult and child have been observed (cf Stern &
Jaffe 1975). Such patterns could serve as an important basis
for later, more complex, linguistic interaction.

Aphasia and deafness. Investigation of aphasia, or language loss, in deaf persons might provide clues to the cerebral nature and "location" of sign language processing. If comparable lesions in the deaf affect sign language usage in the same manner as they affect language skills in hearing persons, then this result would be evidence of similar neurological structure and organization. But because sign language is a visual-motor language, it is quite possible that it would be processed in a different location or locations in the brain. Indeed, the existence of such a separate cerebral location for gestural communication, similar to but not identical with that for speech, was first hypothesized by Hughlings Jackson nearly a century ago. Unfortunately, the limited number of reported cases of aphasia in deaf persons, and the often accompanying lack of information about the locus of the lesions or the form of the patients' primary language do not provide an adequate basis upon which to assess Jackson's hypothesis.

Several conclusions do however follow from examination of the few reported cases. First, those deaf persons who had disorders of manual communication also had evidence of left-hemisphere damage (Kimura 1974). Such incidence of damage to the left hemisphere would of course be expected in cases of trauma induced aphasias in the general hearing population. Second, there is evidence of differential impairment of various means of communication used by these deaf patients. One subject (Douglass & Richardson 1959) showed more serious impairment in her signing than in her fingerspelling. The opposite result of less severe disruption of sign language than of fingerspelling was reported in three other cases (Critchley 1938; Sarno, Swisher, & Sarno 1969; and Tureen, Smolik, & Tritt 1951). The patient studied in the last of these recovered facility in both sign language and speech simultaneously, but differential impairment of speech and signing was evident in the other two patients and in an individual observed by Battison & Markowicz (1974). These varying patterns of deficit-after-trauma severity and modality of communication might best be explained as resulting from differences in location and severity of neural damage. A third conclusion is that the overall patterns of loss of language and then the gradual progress toward recovery of it are quite similar in both deaf and hearing patients. Finally, several of the cases revealed an absence of general motor impairment, or apraxia, in the presence of sign impairment. This finding suggests that a sign aphasia should be considered a genuine language loss and not a motor disorder.

One further implication of the finding of differential impairment of communication modalities in deaf persons is that, if hearing persons lose some or all of their ability to use speech, they may still be able to acquire some facility in the gestural sign expression of language. And, similarly, it is conceivable that when ability in signing is lost, language therapy might be effective in another mode; e.g. writing or geometric symbols.

Sign acquisition by speech-limited hearing children. When a hearing child fails to acquire spoken language, the reasons for the failure may lie in factors that specifically concern speech. At present it is not possible to make even an educated guess about the numbers of children who have language-learning difficulties that block speech acquisition but may not block development of language in another mode. Accumulated observations on retarded, autistic, and other speech-limited children show that when little or no progress in speech acquisition has been made, progress in sign language acquisition is sometimes possible. We shall review programs demonstrating such progress and also give a brief account of prior work on teaching speech to autistic children.

Ideally, accounts of sign acquisition by speech-limited children should provide clear detail of the children's level of speech production and speech comprehension before acquisition of signing begins. In addition, progress in constructing sign sentences should be related to context--as in the above described accounts of acquisition for deaf children--so that emerging semantic relationships can be determined. Since these conditions rarely have been met, it is often not possible to know either the theoretical implications or the practical implications of reported results.

In infantile autism the failure of the child to develop communicative language skills has long been recognized as a symptom. Indeed, the disturbance in language and symbol use has been considered by some investigators to be the primary handicap of autism, from which the social and behavioral abnormalities arise (Churchill 1972, Rutter & Bartak 1971). Lovaas, Berberich, Perloff, & Schaeffer (1966) reported speech in previously mute autistic children gained through a behavior modification program emphasizing reinforcement of imitative speech. However, children who received this therapy seldom went beyond the trained utterances to spontaneous generation of new sentences comparable

to those of normal young children. More generally, autistic
children typically have shown only limited progress toward
the full acquisition of speech. Spontaneous, rule-governed
sentences at the level of production attained by normal
five-year-olds have rarely been the result of such programs.

Two recent studies examined the progress in sign
acquisition made by autistic children. In each study teachers
used both speech and sign language, but the children made
significant advances in productive language only in sign
language. Creedon (1973) reports on 21 children. Estimates
of their language levels ranged from 4 to 24 months at the
onset of extended training, when the children were four to
nine years old. From the information provided it is not possible to determine clearly for any child the achieved level
of language mastery in signing nor how it relates to initial
speech skills; although there is a rough indication that
children who were relatively advanced in signing were also
relatively advanced in initial speech skills. What is clear
is that the children learned many signs and sign combinations
which appear to reflect many different semantic and syntactic
aspects of language. Some spontaneous uses of sign sentences
are reported, but there is no separate analysis of spontaneous
sentences as opposed to those involving direct instruction
or imitation.

In the second study (Bonvillian & Nelson 1973, 1976)
considerable progress in sign language was made by a mute
nine-year-old autistic boy. Earlier, unsuccessful attempts
to teach this boy speech included a computer-interaction
language program and operant-conditioning techniques.
Although the child initially lacked any productive language
and any comprehension skills beyond the one word level,
in six months of sign training he acquired a vocabulary of
more than 50 signs. More significantly, these signs were
combined in spontaneous statements reflecting a range of
semantic relationships comparable to that shown by young
hearing children acquiring speech or young children acquiring
sign language. In addition to his acquisition of sufficient
components of a language system to allow frequent dia-
logues with others, this boy also showed improved behavior
on a number of other dimensions. His incidence of soiling
and of temper tantrums declined dramatically; his attention
span and social relationships improved also (cf Creedon 1973);

he showed a gain of 17 months on a vocabulary intelligence test;
and his speech comprehension advanced. During the six months
of this study such two-sign combinations as SWIM SCHOOL,
TOMORROW PLAY, BOY DRINK, and RED BALL were common.
There were also many more complicated sentences composed
of three, four, or five signs. Among these were EAT, TURKEY, TO-
MORROW and NO MOTHER CAR PLAY SCHOOL (when his
mother was not coming to pick him up because he was going
to play at school). This boy's training in signing continued
after the six-month study, and the complexity of his sentences
and his vocabulary size continued to increase (the latter to
over 200 signs). Recently informal reports of his sentences
included many grammatically sophisticated structures: A
remarkable instance was WHEN I GET BIG LIKE DADDY AND
HAVE WHISKERS I'M GOING TO BE A STREET CLEANER OR A
DOCTOR.

Sign language is just one of the several visually-based
communication systems which have been tried with speech-
limited children. Ratusnik & Ratusnik (1974) provided a
brief but interesting account of an autistic seven-year-old's
progress in learning visual methods of communication. He
first learned to write individual words and to use plastic
letters to spell words. Communication in these modes gradually improved. Then a new instructional system was started
in which the child formed sentences on a visual "communication board." Questions and directions were given orally,
but the child responded by using word-blocks on the communication board. Suppose the child has four blocks which show
the four words  the, Mother, is , eating; a teacher could
then show a picture card related to this set of words and
then ask questions which the child could answer by choosing
the appropriate words and arranging them to form a sentence.
Using this highly structured system, the child made advances
in understanding the uses of an increasingly large set of
syntactic forms. In addition, a few sentences were generated
spontaneously and a broader range of communication opened
up between the child and others. This child was still a long
way from full mastery of a productive or receptive language
system, but the technique facilitated progress for him, and it
may have application for other children with severe language-
learning difficulties.

Some mute retarded children also have recently acquired components of sign language. They have succeeded in learning a large lexicon of signs and have used these signs in simple combinations (Briggs 1974, Wilson 1974). Insufficient detail has been reported to allow comparison of these children's language acquisition with that of hearing or deaf children. However, it could well be that the pattern of sign acquisition for non-speaking retardates resembles the acquisition of oral language skills in speaking retardates. If so, we would anticipate that the pattern of acquisition in the former would also mirror that of normal children, except for a much reduced pace of development. In addition to being an effective means of communication for the retarded child or autistic child with severe oral language handicaps, sign language or other forms of visual language may facilitate the acquisition of speech or of comprehension of spoken English by these children (Bricker 1972, Miller & Miller 1973, De Villiers & Naughton 1974).

The success of sign language and graphic language training with autistic children and nonverbal retarded children might be attributed to some extent to the special characteristics of a motor coding system. This interpretation is suggested in part by two studies that investigated brain damage and motor coding in adults (Milner 1965, Starr & Phillips 1970). Whereas brain damage made the learning of verbal and visual information impossible, it had little effect upon the learning of motor sequences. Two further studies show successful acquisition of signs or mimic gestures by severely subnormal cerebral palsied children (Levett 1971, Peters 1973) and underline again the conclusion that a visual-motor system for language transmission is a promising avenue of communication for many nonverbal children.

A Theoretical Discussion of Success and Failure in Acquiring
a Language

In trying to understand why some children succeed and others fail to master sign language or a spoken and written language, we have already reviewed much evidence that provides useful clues. Here we will try to integrate these previous observations with additional information on factors that may influence language acquisition. We will consider some interesting possibilities of difference between various "learners" of language--deaf, blind, autistic, and retarded children, and sign or symbol-using chimpanzees--in the pace and manner in which they achieve possible cognitive prerequisites to language acquisition, and also in the ways in which early linguistic activity may be combined with other actions.

At first glance it might be assumed that there would be extensive mutual interference between signing about the world and acting upon the world. After all, the young child can simultaneously pull the cat's tail and comment verbally; though a simultaneous comment in sign might be difficult. But when rattles, people, pacifiers, food, thumbs, and other referents available to the young child are considered, it becomes quite evident that, depending upon what the child tries to express at what time, either sign or speech might be at a "disadvantage." On the whole, either sign or speech will be generally available without interference from other ongoing actions of the child. Further, it is clear from Schlesinger & Meadow's observations of hearing children of deaf parents that signing and speaking can develop concurrently without either adversely affecting development in the other mode. The question then is what circumstances and prerequisites are involved when a child succeeds rather than fails to acquire language.

A child certainly might fail to master language or might move toward mastery on a delayed schedule because he or she failed to master a cognitive prerequisite or mastered it only belatedly. But what milestones in cognitive development have been established as prerequisites to language? At present there is no conclusive evidence for any clear cut prerequisite, and we shall argue that there is good reason to doubt some common speculations about prerequisites. Piaget (1951), Sinclair (1971), Bruner (1966), and Brown (1973) have suggested in very general terms that the infant's sensorimotor schemes serve as a foundation for language acquisition. Any adequate theoretical account must move beyond broad generalities, however; and the concept of object permanence has much appeal as a possible prerequisite to symbolic use of words or signs. Yet it can be argued that there is no logical necessity that a general understanding of objects' stability should be prerequisite to the child's use of symbols to represent some aspects of some objects, actions, and events. In addition, recent evidence on blind children and deaf children

casts doubt on any crucial role of object permanence as a
prerequisite to symbol mastery. For blind children, object
permanence mastery may be delayed by as much as two
years, compared with sighted children; but the language
growth of blind children seems to proceed on a normal time-
table (Fraiberg 1968). In contrast, deaf children succeed
in object permanence situations at the same ages we would
expect for hearing children; but they may show appropriate
use of signs even earlier than hearing children begin using
words. Witness the deaf child who signed MILK in appropriate
fashion--and made sure she got milk and no other food--at
the age of $5\frac{1}{2}$months (Schlesinger & Meadow 1972). From what
we have seen and heard of early sign acquisition, it seems
that children learning sign often fully master individual signs
before they have mastered object permanence. A similar emergence of some signs before object permanence, seems probable
for the chimpanzees that are reported to have used appropriately
ASL signs such as DRINK and MORE and TICKLE when they were
about 3 months old (Gardner & Gardner 1975).

We have just argued that even though object permanence
often may precede mastery of words or symbols, the first is not
prerequisite to the second. A similar analysis may also be
appropriate for the concepts of "hierarchical structure" (Bruner
1966) and "agent, object, location" (Brown 1973). It has been
suggested that these concepts are necessarily attained nonver-
bally before they are expressed in language. Again the evidence
available tentatively indicates only a rough empirical correlation
in time between nonlinguistic mastery of such concepts and clear
linguistic differentiation. The present evidence is too weak to
allow specification of what is prerequisite to what. But whether
or not specific nonverbal prerequisites exist for these early linguistic concepts, linguistic and nonlinguistic meanings are
in most cases very tightly interrelated (Nelson 1974, Strohner
& Nelson 1974).

Especially in the symbolic play of the young child, it is
clear that linguistic and nonlinguistic action are very freely
and flexibly interrelated. The absence of complex symbolic
play may help explain the failure of some children to learn to
communicate in spontaneous, rule-governed sentences. A
similar lack of complex play may explain why most chimpanzees
who have learned to use signs have not achieved the fluency
even of young deaf children who are acquiring sign language.

Perhaps the ability to use combinations of words (signs) or
actions in two senses, the playful and the goal-directed, may
be essential to the generation and revision of successively
more sophisticated sets of rules for sentence structures.

Other conditions necessary for language. In order to acquire
any first language, a child undoubtedly must interact with at
least one user of the language. We assume that the child's
"model" for the language must fulfill three conditions: (1)
The model must be physically and psychologically available
for communication. (2) The model(s) must use a wide range of
grammatically appropriate sentences and must do so from the
outset of word use until the child has mastered the syntactic
system. (3) The model must both initiate conversations with
the child and reply sensibly and grammatically to some of the
child's own sentences. This last condition would not be met if
the child merely listened to or observed the use of language by
models on television programs. In one remarkable instance--
in which deaf parents wanted their hearing child to learn spoken
English but not sign language--the primary source of language
available to the child was reported to have been American
television (Sachs & Johnson, in press). Neither sign nor speech
was used extensively with this child by adults or by other children. Only when the child began interacting regularly with
normal, speaking children (at about age 4) did he form any rudi-
mentary sentences. Even then, progress toward adult speech
remained very slow. Usually, of course, a fluent model (adult
or child) is available and interacts extensively with a child,
using many grammatical sentences that are varied in form but
that generally are less complex and shorter than the sentences
that adults use when conversing with each other (cf Phillips 1973).
    In addition to the general characteristics of an adequate
model, it seems likely that particular kinds of replies and examples may be required if the child is to succeed in mastering
syntax. However, for the moment we can just briefly sketch
some first steps toward a full analysis of the role of child-
adult interaction patterns. The available positive evidence
comes from two studies (Nelson, Carskaddon, & Bonvillian
1973, and Nelson 1975) in which adult English speakers used
selected kinds of replies to normal $2\frac{1}{2}$ to 3-year-olds. In
each study, children interacted individually with an adult who
used the following strategy: Reply to a child's sentence with a
sentence which keeps the same basic meaning but expresses

this meaning in a new sentence structure. The reasoning was
that the child would compare the successive sentences and
notice new aspects of sentence structure. Advances in syntax
were made by children in both studies, and the second study
provides the only evidence we have seen that specific syntactic forms (e.g. tag questions) can be induced by specific
kinds of adult-child interaction. Extensions of research along
these lines may eventually identify the patterns of interaction
necessary for syntax acquisition in speech or in sign. Efficient
educational intervention programs may then become feasible
for some children who have experienced little success in mastering syntax but who lack none of the motor, cognitive, or
perceptual abilities needed for language acquisition.

Even though a child may have deficiencies that hinder
language acquisition, appropriate "detours" around these difficulties may make language acquisition possible. Consider
deficiencies in the following areas: perception, recognition,
and recall of speech sequences; programming or executing a
series of articulatory movements; and precise motor movements
that are not visually guided. Any of these deficiencies would
be severe handicaps to the acquisition of spoken language. But
a child might have any or all these deficiencies, and still
possess all the cognitive capacities necessary for fully compre-
hending and producing meaningful grammatical sentences in a
medium other than speech. If so, such a child might be able to
"detour" past these deficiencies if sign language or some form
of written language were the medium of communication between
the child and an appropriate adult user of the language. Detours
of this general kind may have been involved in the recent success
of many autistic children in acquiring aspects of sign language
(e.g. those described in Bonvillian & Nelson 1976, and Creedon
1973). The studies mentioned here will, it is hoped, spur a
broader search for ways to bypass deficiencies that block certain routes to language mastery while leaving other routes open.

The processing and use of English by the deaf. One of the most
dramatic indicators that the deaf usually deal poorly with English
is this fact: The reading performance of most deaf 16-year-olds
is at least five years below grade level.(Bornstein & Roy 1973).
For many individuals there is more than just a developmental lag
--they commonly reach a plateau at a low level of reading skill
that will continue throughout adulthood (Reich & Reich 1974). In
comparison with hearing persons, the deaf typically show marked

developmental lags and low eventual plateaus not only in
reading skills but also in written English skills, English vocabulary size, and level of educational achievement (Bonvillian, Charrow, & Nelson 1973).

Patterns of English usage. Nearly all comparisons of deaf
and hearing persons' English usage have revealed significant
differences between the two groups. In patterns of word association the groups overlap only slightly. Furthermore deaf children do not show the same systematic changes in word-to-word
association patterns over time as those reported for hearing
children (Jacobson 1968). However, Bonvillian & Charrow (1972)
argue that developmental changes in deaf children's sign-to-
sign associations would parallel the developmental shifts in
the word associations of hearing children. This prediction was
supported in a recent experiment by Tweney & Hoemann (1973).
    Studies of recall and recognition of English sentences
demonstrate that deaf students, in marked contrast to hearing
controls, are not assisted by the grammatical constraints provided by word order or phrase structure (e.g. Odom & Blanton
1967, Fremer 1971). These differences suggest that the deaf
and the hearing are using different rules or strategies in processing English sentences. Work on reading comprehension
of the deaf provides additional backing for this conclusion
(Odom & Blanton 1970). A related finding from this work is
that deaf students show lower comprehension for standard
English sentences than for sentences designed to approximate
the syntax of American Sign Language.
    A final indication that deaf children show less sensi-
tivity than hearing children to the properties of English is
seen when the groups are matched on reading achievement
scores. Even when this matching is done, the hearing children demonstrate higher skills on tests of semantics and
syntax (of English) (Moores 1970).
    Why should deaf students, even after extended instruction
in the use of English, show such marked deviance from hearing
students in sensitivity to grammatical structure and in the
mastery of reading and writing? At least part of the answer
may be in the role which sign language plays for many deaf
children and adults in the coding and learning of English.
This is our next topic, together with a more general discussion
of coding processes.

Multiple codes and their combinations. How the deaf student
codes information has been the central question of many recent
investigations. In these studies, analyses have been made of
the different coding and retrieval strategies which deaf students
use with visually presented letters, words, and sentences. It
is now clear that there are at least five codes which the deaf
may use: speech based, fingerspelling based, shape based,
visual imagery based, and coding in terms of signs. In addition
it is clear that combinations of these codes and further elaborated coding and organization also occur. Variables that affect
which codes are used include the age of onset of the child's
hearing loss, the degree of the loss, educational techniques,
experimental tasks, and the language environment of the child's
home or residential institution.

Coding letter sequences. In recalling visually presented sequences of letters, deaf and hearing subjects usually exhibit
widely different response patterns. Deaf children and adults,
especially if they have profound hearing loss and only limited
speech skills, are apt to confuse letters which are similar in
visual appearance or similar in terms of their fingerspelling
equivalents. In contrast, hearing subjects or deaf subjects who
with available speech skills code letters in terms of their
phonological (or articulatory) characteristics should recall
well the letter sequences which are dissimilar phonologically,
and phonologically similar sequences should lead to confusions
for them and therefore to more frequent error in recall. Conrad
(1973) found that this expectation was confirmed for hearing
adults and for deaf college students with relatively limited degrees of hearing loss. For deaf college students with relatively
more severe hearing loss, errors in recall were equally frequent
whether or not the letter names were phonologically similar.
Wallace (1972) also compared deaf students with hearing controls on recall of visually presented letter sequences. The deaf
students made predominant use of visual coding while hearing
students relied on articulatory coding. Wallace (1972) further
reported that orally trained deaf subjects used some articulatory
coding, but that manually trained subjects appeared to use a
dactylic or fingerspelling code along with visual shape cues.
Similar conclusions fit data obtained by Locke & Locke (1971).
    Despite the evidence of differential code use by deaf
subjects with differing skills and backgrounds, much remains
to be clarified. As yet no studies have firmly demonstrated

that a deaf subject who initially produces a pattern of errors
indicative of a certain kind of coding (e.g. fingerspelling)
will no longer show this pattern of errors if such coding is
selectively blocked or if the subject is instructed to use a
different means of coding. And in most research to date, the
levels of speech, signing, and fingerspelling skills of the
deaf subjects are not measured in detail independently of
the recall tasks used to infer the subjects' coding strategies.
Clearly, for both theoretical and educational reasons, it
will be important to distinguish in future research between
unavailable coding skills and coding skills which are available
but unused.

Coding words. Two coding strategies, sign language and
visual imagery,  appear to play especially important roles
in deaf students' word processing. However, the relative
importance of these two factors in word recall by deaf students is not yet well described either in general terms or in
terms of the variations from student to student and from task
to task.

Craig (1973) proposed that the deaf store verbal information almost exclusively in the form of visual imagery. A
number of previous studies with hearing subjects had shown
that words with easily imaged meanings (e.g. concrete
nouns) were more easily learned or recalled than words that
were difficult to image (e.g. abstract nouns). The deaf subjects in Craig's experiment exhibited greater retention of
high imagery than of low imagery words, but the relative difference in overall retention for the deaf was comparable to
that of normally hearing subjects. This result contradicted
Craig's expectation that the deaf students would have particular difficulty in recalling words hard to image.

In addition to visual imagery, many deaf students are
likely to use other codes, especially sign language or
fingerspelling. With this possiblilty in mind, the two
factors  of ease of expression in sign language (cf Odom,
Blanton, & McIntyre 1970) and of rated visual imagery
were systematically varied in experiments by Conlin and
Paivio (1975) and Bonvillian (1974). In both studies, deaf
students recalled words with high imagery values and words
with sign language equivalents significantly more often than
words which were neither easily signed nor imaged. Conlin
and Paivio found that a high imagery value for a word had a

greater facilitating effect on paired-associate recall than a
word's signability. In contrast, Bonvillian found that the
dimension of signability had the more facilitative effect on
free recall of words. In a second experiment, Bonvillian
presented highly signable words and instructed half the
deaf subjects to form visual images of the experimental
words. The remaining subjects rehearsed the sign equivalents for the words. Those subjects instructed to use sign
language recalled more low imagery signable words than
those subjects instructed to form visual images. This result
suggests that when deaf students use a code for words that
are not well-suited for that code, then performance may
suffer. However, switching to another code allows excellent
recall of the same words (cf Conrad 1971).

The work of Klima and Bellugi (1974) also adds to our
picture of word and sign coding processes in the deaf. The
investigators examined confusion errors made in the recall
of individual signs by deaf persons who know American Sign
Language but who indicated recall by writing English word
equivalents. Their results suggest that the deaf subjects
were coding in terms of sign parameters and decoding into
English words at the time of recall.

Coding sentences. The literature reviewed above regarding
deaf students' coding of English letters and English words
establishes that, among deaf students, differences in coding
can be related, at least roughly, to relative skills in sign,
fingerspelling, and speech, and also to degree of hearing
loss. What then can be expected for the processing of English
sentences? In the case of a sentence, each word can be
coded in terms of sign, speech, fingerspelling, shape, or
visual imagery. But in addition, the grammatical structure
of the sentence must also be represented. On this level also
it is clear that English is processed in contrasting ways by
hearing students and deaf students.

"Deafisms" are grammatical errors in written language
that rarely occur among hearing students but commonly among
deaf students. Charrow (1974) suggested that there may be
enough commonalty among deaf adolescents' English errors
to justify the existence of a "Deaf English" non-standard
dialect or of a regular pidginization of English. In an experiment based on this idea, students were tested on recall of
sentences in the hypothesized "Deaf English" and of corres-

ponding standard English sentences. Hearing subjects had
more difficulty in recalling "Deaf English" sentences than
in recalling standard English sentences, but deaf subjects
found the former as easy to recall as the latter. In addition,
it appeared that the sentences were processed in different
ways by the deaf and the hearing children, since they com-
mitted different kinds of errors. Charrow proposes that
whereas hearing persons rely on obligatory grammatical
rules of English, the deaf have inconsistent or variable
rules for certain English constructions.

One explanation for certain difficulties that some deaf
students encounter in English reading and writing tasks may
be that they have learned English as a second or foreign
language. Charrow and Fletcher (1974) administered the Test
of English as a Foreign Language (a test designed to identify
special difficulties of second language learners) to two groups
of deaf students with some skills in English: One group contained children of deaf parents who had acquired American
Sign Language in infancy; the other contained deaf children
of hearing parents who had learned to sign from peers and
teachers after age six. In general, the performance of a
large comparison sample of foreign students more closely
resembled the performance by deaf students with deaf parents
than it did the performance of deaf students with hearing
parents.    Charrow and Fletcher conclude that for deaf children who acquire sign language in infancy many aspects of
English are learned as aspects of a second language. This
study, like numerous previous studies, also demonstrates
that overall English skills were higher for deaf children of
deaf parents than for deaf children of hearing parents. In
sum, we might conclude from this study and related work
that: (1) In most instances, a deaf child who learns sign
language at an early age--compared with a child who does
not--will more easily master English skills. (2) Special
patterns of errors and special ways of coding may be involved when children learn English after learning sign language.
(3) It may be necessary to change current instructional programs in order to teach these children English more effectively.

Cognitive abilities. The proposition that deaf persons possess
cognitive abilities comparable to those of most hearing persons
rests upon a broad pattern of recent evidence. A differentiated
analysis of cognitive abilities is provided by Furth's reviews
(1964, 1971). In each of the following areas, the deaf and the
hearing show similar cognitive processing abilities: perception,
memory, rule learning, and a series of problems related to
concrete and formal operational thinking--conservation, seri-
ation, transitivity, logical symbols, and propositions (Furth
& Youniss 1971). For many deaf students, as compared with
hearing students, there were two kinds of differences that
indicate somewhat slower mastery of the same concepts. One
difference was that in learning logical symbols and propositions, the deaf subjects required more training than did the
hearing subjects. A more widespread difference was that concepts or skills were typically attained at a slightly earlier
age in the hearing than in the deaf children. In terms of educational factors and more specifically the opportunity of using
one's first-learned language (sign or speech) in classroom or
study assignments, the deaf have been disadvantaged in ways
that could easily account for such differences in the pace of
cognitive growth or learning. Regardless of the explanations
for the observed temporal lag between the deaf and the hearing
in cognitive development, the conclusion stands that most
deaf persons demonstrate the same set of cognitive abilities
which hearing persons demonstrate. This conclusion is supported also by the finding that both the rate and the pattern of
language acquisition are similar for young deaf children who
are learning to sign and young hearing children who are learning to speak.  The cognitive abilities required for language
use are further evidenced by the fact that a few deaf persons,
despite enormous practical and educational obstacles, master
written language or speech.
       The deaf and the hearing may use comparable cognitive
abilities in specialized ways, resulting in distinct patterns
of performance. This suggestion awaits exploration for the
most part, although we have reviewed above some differences
in the language coding processes of the deaf and hearing. In
one additional study on this topic, deaf subjects performed
significantly better than hearing subjects on tests of spatial
memory and memory of designs, but performed more poorly
on the tests of memory span for visually presented digits
(Blair 1957). It is quite likely that an auditory rehearsal

strategy facilitated the hearing subjects' performance on the
memory span tasks. Finally there is the question in much
research as to whether the deaf are distinctive in the sense
that they show thought "without language." In fact, there is
little good evidence on language-thought relationships in
the deaf, as most research on thinking in the deaf is highly
ambiguous about the sign language or English skills of the
subjects studied (Bonvillian, Charrow, & Nelson 1973).
Accordingly, at present even less is known about language-
thought relationships in the deaf than in the hearing.

Since deaf children usually possess "normal" cognitive
abilities but fail to master many aspects of their school cur-
riculum and especially the culturally crucial skills of reading
and writing, the question arises as to how to help the deaf
child better to use his cognitive abilities to learn these
skills. One approach would be to rely more heavily on sign
language in instructional programs for the deaf. This has
been urged by many scholars, as well as by former students
of schools for the deaf (see Reich & Reich 1974). A related
consideration is that in the first six years of life some deaf
children have inadequate opportunities to learn any language.
Our view is that deaf children's optimal use of their cognitive abilities will occur when two conditions are met: Sign
language is learned and used freely during the period between
birth and age five; and, instruction in reading, writing,
speaking, and lipreading, and any content areas relies upon
sign language as an essential component of instruction.
Some further thoughts and evidence along these lines are
taken up in the next section.

Languages for Education and Research. Deaf children who
know and are encouraged to use manual communication generally show equally favorable or more favorable educational
outcomes when compared with deaf children whose instruction
has come primarily through speech and speechreading. "Manual" subjects, those who had early childhood background in
manual communication or who were given instruction using
some manual techniques, have shown superiority in comparisons to subjects with oral language backgrounds on a wide
range of skills and tests. Such comparisons have included
overall academic achievement, psychosocial adjustment,
mathematics, reading, written language, responsiblity, and
independence (see Bonvillian, Charrow, & Nelson 1973,
Mindel & Vernon 1971).

The observation that a child can acquire Sign without
any harmful effect (and possibly beneficial effect) on progress
in spoken language appears to be true not only for deaf
children but also for hearing children (Schlesinger & Meadow
1972). This finding carries some interesting implications. One
is that a hearing child who has deaf parents can be expected
to acquire the two languages concurrently in the period between
birth and age five, sign language for communicating with deaf
relatives and friends and speech for communicating with the
larger, hearing community. Another implication is that some
young hearing children who do not require sign language for
communication with parents might nevertheless be given the
opportunity for learning to sign. Such children will then have
a fluent second language available and valuable for communication with the significant minority of deaf persons in their
community.

Another issue in discussion of deaf education has been
the efficacy of simultaneous presentation of information in
oral and visual modes. Klopping (1972) and Moores, Weiss,
& Goodwin (1973) compared deaf children's comprehension
of stories or information presented in various modes and mode
combinations. The results indicated that the most accurate
means of communication involved the simultaneous use of
sign or fingerspelling together with sound and speechreading.
The single modes tested--written words or voice--and the
combinations of modes that excluded signs and fingerspelling
were much less powerful techniques. But further research is
needed better to assess the contribution of each mode in
various mode combinations.

On the level of psychological theory, a number of
additional questions arise about the ways in which languages
in different modes can be combined with each other and used
to aid cognitive performance. From the research on aphasias
it is established that many components of language processing
can be isolated. An ability to receive or to produce speech,
to read, to write, to sign, to fingerspell, or to process Braille
--each of these has been isolated to some extent in different
individuals who suffered traumatic cerebral injury. This diversity of specific losses indicates that the representation of
each mode may be distinctly different at some level. But the
additional fact that individuals who are fluent in any two of
these modes can translate easily between the two modes
would seem to indicate a similarity at least at an abstract

level. For some pairs of modes an additional variation is
possible--simultaneous reception of two modes (possibly
more) or simultaneous production of two modes (possibly
more). Thus one can read and speak, or write and speak,
simultaneously in one language. But what about combinations of sign language and speech? A definitive analysis
of the processing possibilities in this case would tell
much about the nature of language, of attention, and of
speech and sign. The few informal observations known to
us on this topic all suggest that simultaneous sentences
in speech and sign are possible only when the sign language used borrows syntactic structure directly from the
spoken language; e.g. spoken English in conjunction with
signed English is easily accomplished by those who know
both well. But American Sign Language, with its own distinctive syntactic system (see above), may be impossible
to produce simultaneously with equivalent spoken English
sentences. [Unless, of course, there are short, simple
sequences in both ASL and English which happen to have
the same number and order of parts, i.e. signs and words;
see Introduction above.]        Full processing (at least
in production) of a complex message in two syntactically
distinctive languages simultaneously may well be beyond
the capacities of most or all individuals fluent in the two
languages. In any event, the ways in which various sorts
of simultaneous processing differ from reception-and-trans-
lation    situations should be fascinating to work out.
      When a child has fully mastered a first language before
the age of five, the language has always been either a
spoken language or a sign language (or in rare instances
both concurrently; see Chapter 7above). If one assumes that
man is biologically endowed with speech-specific capacities (Chomsky 1965), the cases of sign language acquisition pose a problem. Perhaps then the capacities of man
that make language possible are specific to the structures
of sign or speech. We doubt it. Rather it seems probable
that man, and possibly some other primates, possesses or
develops a set of cognitive capacities that make the tasks
of learning complex, socially-embedded cognitive systems--
including languages--both interesting and surmountable.
To be less abstract, it certainly seems possible that the
child's first language could be written English or French.
For a few deaf persons this is likely to have been the case

(after age five), even though firm documentation to this
effect is lacking. Our argument also implies that a new
tactual or visual or auditory language could be invented,
learned by adults, and then acquired by children who
interact with the adult language users. To fulfill such a
possibility we would argue, there is nothing lacking in
the child's cognitive ability.

In part, our interest in the possibility of the young
child acquiring linguistic and conceptual systems besides
sign and speech rests upon an interest in developmental
theory. But practical implications are also involved. If
there are clear alternatives to speech or to sign as a first
language, then some children with specific difficulties
which hinder acquisition of these languages may achieve
greater success in the mastery of another language.

In this review, there has been much more discussion
of deaf children than of other speech-limited children,
primarily because less is known about language and cognition in the latter. Unquestionably, though, many speech-
limited children have cognitive deficits much less rarely
found in deaf children. Thus we would urge some caution
and discrimination in attempted extensions of sign language
programs to autistic, retarded, and other speech-limited
children. Instead, two strategies seem in order. One is to
try multiple approaches, with signing as just one possiblity.
Often the cognitive capacities of children become evident
only when new approaches are tried, as the few instances
of progress in sign acquisition by mute autistic children
demonstrate. The other strategy is to try to match technique
to the particular cognitive strengths and deficiencies of
the child. In some cases sign alone may be a highly logical
choice of technique, but for other children completely new
techniques (as we have just argued) or combinations of
speech, sign, writing, and other techniques may be more
suitable. Looking to the future, we will need lucid and
specific formulas for choosing languages and techniques
for educating language-limited children. But for the moment,
what is both shocking and hopeful is that so much "firm
knowledge" of five years ago about speech and language has
been revised to incorporate new theoretical and educational
elements.

Conclusion. Children's language acquisition and use has
usually been discussed solely in terms of a child's oral
language and its written version. This paper establishes
that the many languages of children--sign language, speech,
written language, and other possible languages or language-
like systems--require investigation if children's cognitive
and linguistic processes are to be understood.

Ten years ago few psychologists, linguists, or educators would have predicted that today so much would be
known about the sign language of the deaf. But from current
evidence four broad conclusions about sign language emerge.
It is clear, first, that sign language is a true language, comparable in complexity to oral language. Second, deaf children
and hearing children appear to bring the same general cognitive
capacities to language acquisition and to the development of
cognitive skills. In addition, there are strong parallels between
the rates and processes of acquisition for sign language and for
speech. However, in the coding and retrieval of written language the differences in language modalities of deaf and
hearing children result in strikingly different performance patterns.

It is argued that if a child is to acquire successfully
either speech or sign (or any other first language), similar
conditions must be satisfied. There are certain to be some
cognitive prerequisites for language acquisition, although
they remain to be specified. The qualities of interaction
with a model that are required for acquisition of any language
are beginning to be understood.

Educational issues for the deaf have focused on the place
of speech, sign language, and fingerspelling in instruction.
Studies of educational outcomes, of information processing
in experimental tasks, and of language acquisition, all
imply that increased emphasis on sign language would aid
the majority of deaf students. Sign language could be acquired
by young deaf children before age five and then used as the
primary (but not exclusive) medium for interaction in schools.
If sign is mastered as a first language, and is accepted by
teachers who also know and use it, the next generation of
deaf students may well approach levels of reading and writing
comparable to those of the hearing.

Methods of educating autistic, retarded, and other
speech-limited children are beginning to reflect the recent
insights into children's language processes generally,
and particularly into the visually transmitted sign languages
of the deaf. Sign language acquisition has progressed to
complex stages in some autistic and retarded children who
have normal hearing but lack speech. As the research continues, there is an excellent chance that full mastery of
signing will prove possible for some hearing children who
cannot master speech.

## REFERENCES

Abbott, Clifford F.  (This is Chapter 2, above)
    1975    Encodedness and Sign Language, Sign Language
            Studies 7, 109-120.

Battison, Robbin M., & Harry Markowicz
    1974    Sign Aphasia and Neurolinguistic Theory. Unpub-
            lished MS, Ling. Research Lab, Gallaudet College.

Battison, Robbin M., & I. King Jordan (This is Chapter 5, above)
    1976    Cross-Cultural Communication with Foreign Signers:
            Fact and Fancy, Sign Language Studies 10, 53-68.

Bellugi, Ursula
    1967    The Acquisition of Negation. Unpublished doctoral
            dissertation, Harvard University.
    1972    Studies in Sign Language, in Psycholinguistics &
            Total Communication: The State of the Art, O'Rourke
            ed. (Washington, American Annals of the Deaf), 68-84.

Blair, Francis X.
    1957    A Study of the Visual Memory of Deaf Children,
            American Annals of the Deaf 102, 254-263.

Bloom, Lois
    1970    Language Development: Form and Function in
            Emerging Grammars (Cambridge, MA, MIT Press).

Bloomfield, Leonard
    1933    Language (New York, Holt, Rinehart).

Bonvillian, John D.
    1974    Word Coding and Recall in Deaf and Hearing Students.
            Unpublished doctoral Dissertation, Stanford University.

- - - - -, & Veda Charrow
    1972    Psycholinguistic Implications of Deafness: A Review.
            Tech. Report No. 188, Institute for Mathematical
            Studies in the Social Sciences, Stanford University.
- - - - -, Veda Charrow, & Keith E. Nelson
    1973    Psycholinguistic & Educational Implications of
            Deafness, Human Development 16, 321-345.
- - - - -, & Keith E. Nelson
    1973    Sign Language Acquisition in a Mute Autistic Boy.
            Paper at Peninsula Children's Center, Palo Alto.
    1976    Sign Language Acquistion in a Mute Autistic Boy,
            Journal of Speech & Hearing Disorders.

Bornstein, Harry, Howard L. Roy
    1973    Comment on "Linguistic Deficiency and Thinking:
            Research with Deaf Subjects 1964-1969," Psycho-
            logical Bulletin 79, 211-214.

Bowerman, Melissa F.
    1969    The Pivot-Open Class Distinction. MS, Harvard U.

Braine, Martin D. S.
    1963    The Ontogeny of English Phrase Structure: The
            First Phase, Language 39, 1-13.

Bricker, Diane D.
    1972    Imitative Sign Training as a Facilitator of Word-
            Object Association with Low-Functioning Children,
            American Journal of Mental Deficiency 76, 509-516.

Briggs, Terry L.
    1974    Sign Language in Alingual Retardates. Paper at
            American Association of Mental Deficiency meeting,
            Toronto.

Brown, Roger
    1973    A First Language (Cambridge, MA, Harvard Univ. Pr.)

Brown, Roger, & Camille Hanlon
    1970    Derivational Complexity and Order of Acquisition
            in Child Speech, in Cognition & Development of
            Language, Hayes ed. (New York, Wiley), 1-53.

Bruner, Jerome S.
    1966    On Cognitive Growth, in Studies in Cognitive Growth,
            Bruner et al. eds. (New York, Wiley), 1-67.

Charrow, Veda R.
    1974    Deaf English: An Investigation of the Written English
            Competence of Deaf Adolescents. Unpublished
            doctoral dissertation, Stanford University.
    1975    A Psycholinguistic Analysis of Deaf English, Sign
            Language Studies 7, 139-150.
- - - - -, & J. D. Fletcher
    1974    English as the Second Language of Deaf Children,
            Developmental Psychology 10, 463-470.

Chomsky, Noam
    1965    Aspects of the Theory of Syntax (Camb., MA, MIT).

Churchill, Don W.
    1972    The Relation of Infantile Autism & Early Childhood
            Schizophrenia to Developmental Language Disorders
            of Childhood, Journal of Autism & Childhood
            Schizophrenia 2, 182-197.

Cicourel, Aaron, & Robert J. Boese
    1972    Sign Language Acquisition & the Teaching of Deaf
            Children, in Functions of Language in the Class-
            room, Cazden et al. eds. (NY, Teacher's College
            Press), 32-62.

Conlin, Donna, & Allan Paivio
    1975    The Associative Learning of the Deaf: The Effects
            of Word Imagery & Signability, Memory & Cognition
            3, 335-340.

Conrad, R.
    1971  The Effect of Vocalizing on Comprehension in the
          Profoundly Deaf, British Journal of Psychology 62,
          147-150.

    1973  Some Correlates of Speech Coding in the Short-Term
          Memory of the Deaf, Journal of Speech and Hearing
          Research 16, 375-384.

Craig, Ellis M.
    1973  Role of Mental Imagery in Free Recall of Deaf, Blind,
          and Normal Subjects, Journal of Experimental Psycho-
          logy 97, 249-253.

Creedon, Margaret P.
    1973  Language Development in Nonverbal Autistic Children
          Using a Simultaneous System. Paper at the Society for
          Research in Child Development, Philadelphia.

Critchley, MacDonald
    1938  Aphasia in a Partial Deaf-Mute, Brain 61, 163-169.

Crutchfield, Paul
    1972  Prospects for Teaching English Det + N Structures to
          Deaf Students, Sign Language Studies 1, 8-14.

De Villiers, Jill G., & Joseph M. Naughton
    1974  Teaching A Symbol Language to Autistic Children,
          Journal of Consulting & Clinical Psychology 42, 111-117.

Douglass, E., & J. C. Richardson
    1959  Aphasia in a Congenital Deaf Mute, Brain 82, 68-80.

Fischer, Susan D.
    1974  Influences on Word-Order Change in American Sign
          Language. MS. Salk Institute, La Jolla, California.

Fraiberg, Selma
    1968  Parallels and Divergent Patterns in Blind and Sighted
          Infants, in The Psychoanalytic Study of the Child 23,
          Eissler et al. (eds) (New York, International Univer-
          sities Press).

Fremer, John J., Jr.
    1971  Recognition Memory for Approximations to English
          in Deaf and Hearing Subjects at Three Age Levels.
          Test Development Report TDR-71-1. Educational
          Testing Service, Princeton.

Friedman, Lynn A.
  1975  Space, Time, & Person Reference in American Sign
        Language, Language 51,940-961.

Frishberg, Nancy
  1975  Arbitrariness and Iconicity: Historical Change in
        American Sign Language, Language 51, 696-719.

Frishberg, Nancy, & Bonnie Gough
  1973  Time on our Hands. MS. Salk Institute, La Jolla, CA.

Furth, Hans C.
  1964  Research with the Deaf, Psychological Bulletin 62,
        145-164.

  1971  Linguistic Deficiency and Thinking: Research with
        Deaf Subjects 1964-1969, Psychological Bulletin, 74,
        58-72.

- - - - - & James Youniss
  1971  Formal Operations & Language: A Comparison of Deaf
        and Hearing Subjects, International Journal of Psycho-
        logy 6, 49-64.

Gardner, Beatrice T., & R. Allen Gardner
  1971  Two-Way Communication with an Infant Chimpanzee,
        in Behavior of Nonhuman Primates 4, Schrier & Stollnitz
        (eds) (New York, Academic Press), 117-184.

  1975  Early Signs of Language in Child and Chimpanzee,
        Science 187, 752-753.

  1969  Teaching Sign Language to a Chimpanzee, Science 165,
        664-672.

Hewes, Gordon W.
  1973  Primate Communication and the Gestural Origin of
        Language, Current Anthropology 14, 5-24.

  1974  Language in Early Hominids, in Language Origins,
        Wescott, Hewes, & Stokoe eds. (Silver Spring, MD,
        Linstok Press), 1-34.
  1976  Introduction, and The Current Status of the Ges-
        tural Theory of Language Origin, in Origins & Evo-
        lution of Language & Speech, Harnad, Steklis, &
        Lancaster eds. (NYAS 280), 3 & 482-504.

Hockett, Charles F.
    1958    A Course in Modern Linguistics (New York, Macmillan).
    1978    In Search of Jove's Brow, American Speech 53, 243-313.

Jacobson, Dorothy L.
    1968    Word Associations and Usage of Parts of Speech by
            Deaf Children. Unpublished M.A. thesis. University
            of Minnesota.

Jordan, I. King
    1974    The Referential Communication of Deaf Adolescents,
            Paper at Eastern Psychological Association, Phila.
    1975    A Referential Communication Study of Signers and
            Speakers Using Realistic Referents, Sign Language
            Studies 6, 65-103.
- - - - -, & Robbin M. Battison
    1976    A Referential Communication Experiment with Foreign
            Sign Languages, Sign Language Studies 10, 69-80.

Kendon, Adam
    1975    Introduction, in The Organization of Behavior in
            Face-to-Face Interaction, Kendon, Harris, & Key
            eds. (The Hague, Mouton).

Kimura, Doreen
    1974    The Neural Basis of Language qua Gesture. Research
            Bulletin Number 292, Department of Psychology,
            University of Western Ontario, London, Ontario.

Klima, Edward S., & Ursula Bellugi
    1972    The Signs of Language in Child and Chimpanzee,
            in Communication and Affect, T. Alloway ed.
            (New York, Academic Press), 67-96.
    1974    Language in Another Mode, in Language and Brain:
            Developmental Aspects  Lenneberg ed. (Neuro-
            sciences Research Program, Bulletin 12, 539-550).

Klopping, Henry W. E.
    1972    Language Understanding of Deaf Students under
            Three Auditory-Visual Stimulus Conditions, American
            Annals of the Deaf 117, 389-396.

Levett, Lisbeth M.
   1971  A Method of Communication for Non-Speaking Severely
         Subnormal Children--Trial Results, British Journal of
         Disorders of Communication 6, 125-128.

Locke,  John L., & Virginia L. Locke
   1971  Deaf Children's Phonetic, Visual, and Dactylic Coding
         in a Grapheme Recall Task, Journal of Experimental
         Psychology 89, 142-146.

Lovaas, O. Iver, et al.
   1966  Acquisition of Imitative Speech by Schizophrenic Chil-
         dren, Science 151, 705-707.

Miller, Arnold, & Eileen E. Miller
   1973  Cognitive Developmental Training with Elevated Boards
         and Sign Language, Journal of Autism & Childhood
         Schizophrenia 3, 65-85.

Milner, Brenda
   1965  Brain Disturbance after Bilateral Hippocampal Lateral
         Lesions, in Cognitive Processes & the Brain, Milner
         & Glickman, eds. (Princeton, Van Nostrand), 97-111.

Mindel, Eugene D., & McCay Vernon
   1971  They Grow in Silence (Silver Spring MD, National
         Association of the Deaf).

Moores, Donald F.
   1970  An Investigation of the Psycholinguistic Functioning
         of Deaf Adolescents, Exceptional Children 36, 645-652.

- - - - - , Karen L. Weiss, & M. W. Goodwin
   1973  Receptive Abilities of Deaf Children across Five Modes
         of Communication, Exceptional Children 40, 22-28.

Nash, Jeffrey E.
   1973  Cues or Signs: A Case Study in Language Acquisition,
         Sign Language Studies 3, 79-92.

Nelson, Katherine
   1974  Concept, Word, and Sentence, Psychological Review
         81, 267-285.

Nelson, Keith E.
    1975  Facilitating Syntax Acquisition. Paper at Eastern
          Psychological Association, New York.

- - - - - , G. Carskaddon, & J. Bonvillian
    1973  Syntax Acquisition: Impact of Experimental Variation
          in Adult Verbal Interaction with the Child, Child
          Development 44, 497-504.

Odom, Penelope B., & Richard L. Blanton
    1967  Phrase Learning in Deaf and Hearing Subjects, Journal
          of Speech and Hearing Research 13, 54-58.
    1970  Implicit & Explicit Grammatical Factors & Reading...,
          Journal of Reading Behavior 2,47-55.
    1970  (with C. McIntyre) Coding Medium & Word Recall...,
          Journal of Speech & Hearing Research 13,54-58.

Peters, Leslie J.
    1973  Sign Language Stimulus in Vocabulary Learning of a
          Brain-Injured Child, Sign Language Studies 3, 116-118.

Phillips, Juliet R.
    1973  Syntax & Vocabulary of Mothers' Speech to Young
          Children: Age & Sex Comparisons, Child Development
          44, 182-185.

Piaget, Jean
    1951  Play, Dreams, and Imitation in Childhood (New York, Norton).

Ratusnik, Carol M., & David L. Ratusnik
    1974  A Comprehensive Communication Approach for a Ten-
          Year-Old Nonverbal Autistic Child, American Journal
          of Orthopsychiatry 44, 396-403.

Reich, Peter A., & Carol M. Reich
    1974  A Follow-up Study of the Deaf. Toronto Board of Edu-
          cational Research Report, Toronto, Ontario.

Rutter, Michael, & Lawrence Bartak
    1971  Causes of Infantile Autism: Some Considerations from
          Recent Research, Journal of Autism & Childhood Schizo-
          phrenia 1, 20-32.

Sachs, Jacqueline, & Marie L. Johnson
    1975  Language Development in a Hearing Child of Deaf Parents,
          Proceedings of the International Symposium on First
          Language Acquisition.

Sapir, Edward
    1966  Culture, Language, & Personality (Berkeley, University
          of California Press)

Sarno, John E., Linda P. Swisher, & Martha T. Sarno
    1969  Aphasia in a Congenitally Deaf Man, Cortex 5, 398-414

Schlesinger, Hilde S., & Kathryn P. Meadow
    1972  Sound & Sign: Childhood Deafness & Mental Health
          (Berkeley, University of California Press).

Sinclair, Hermine
    1971  Sensorimotor Action Patterns as a Condition for the
          Acquisition of Syntax, in Language Acquisition: Models
          & Methods, Huxley & Ingram eds. (New York: Academic
          Press), 121-135.

Slobin, Daniel I.
    1971  Psycholinguistics (Glenview, Scott, Foresman).

Starr, Arnold, & Laura Phillips
    1970  Verbal & Motor Memory in the Amnesic Syndrome,
          Neuropsychologia 8, 75-88.

Stern, Daniel N., & Joseph Jaffe
    1975  Vocal & Visual Interaction between Mother and Infant.
          Paper at Conference on Developmental Psycholinguistic
          and Communication Disorders, New York Academy of
          Sciences, New York.

Stokoe, William C.
    1960  Sign Language Structure: An Outline of the Visual Communi-
          cation Systems of the American Deaf, Studies in Linguistics:
          Occasional Paper 8 (reissue, Silver Spring, Linstok Press).

    1972  Semiotics & Human Sign Languages (The Hague, Mouton).

    1974  Motor Signs as the First Form of Language, in Language
          Origins, Wescott, Hewes, & Stokoe eds. (Silver Spring,
          MD, Linstok Press), 35-50 -- also, Semiotica 10, 117-130.

Strohner, Hans, & Keith E. Nelson
    1974  The Young Child's Development of Sentence Comprehension:
          Influence of Event Probability, Nonverbal Context, Syntactic
          Form, & Strategies, Child Development 45, 567-576.

Tervoort, Bernard M.
    1968  You Me Downtown Movie Fun? <u>Lingua</u> 21, 455–465.

Tureen, Louis L., Edmund Smolik, & Jack Tritt
    1951  Aphasia in a Deaf Mute, <u>Neurology</u> 1, 237–244

Tweney, Ryan D., & Harry W. Hoemann
    1973  The Development of Semantic Associations in Profoundly
          Deaf Children, <u>Journal of Speech & Hearing Research</u>
          16, 309–318.

Wallace, Graeme
    1972  Short Term Memory & Coding Strategies of the Deaf.
          Unpubl. Doctoral Dissertation, McGill University, Montreal.

Wilson, Paula S.
    1974  Sign Language as a Means of Communication for the
          Mentally Retarded. Paper at the Eastern Psychological
          Association, Philadelphia.

PART THREE

## (SIGN) LANGUAGE AND CULTURE

Linguistics when too rigorously interpreted and practiced as a
study of verbal codes loses the vigor it had when each language
of the New World was studied as part of the culture of its users.
The more recent alliance of linguistics with psychological
theory and experiment has produced insights, but perhaps because the larger and older discipline has top billing in "psycholinguistics," it also opens a never ending search to explain
mind-and-language. The reappearance, however, of the anthropological spirit of Boas and Sapir in the form of sociolinguistics
unites the study of language not just with the people who use it
but also with their institutions, belief and value systems, and
special circumstances.

In Chapter 12 Harry Markowicz examines this bicultural
bilingual situation. Deaf people have to "live in the hearing
world," as educators of the deaf are fond of saying without a
thought about how it is to be done. Deaf people in fact do not
have to or choose to and often are not able to use all the hearing
world's tacit assumptions, including unquestioned reliance on
hearing and speaking to form life patterns. Instead, most deaf
people live in contact with others like themselves, forming one
of the many subcultures within each general culture—but one
that is special because its signed unspoken language helps to
shape it.

Chapter 13 takes us deep (or rather way up) within the
Deaf world. The 33 subjects of this network study are top leaders
—though they are only some of the Deaf elite. Their work puts
them into communication with hearing persons to varying degrees, but they all communicate more with one another (and with
their deaf families and constituents) than outside the Deaf
world. They lead and shape a special world "within" the hearing
world; they are much alike in many respects and vary in others;
but the one characteristic they all share is use of American Sign
Language; and no one who does not use it is admitted to their
group.

PART THREE: 12

# SOME SOCIOLINGUISTIC CONSIDERATIONS OF AMERICAN SIGN LANGUAGE

Harry Markowicz

Author's note. The sign language situation has changed somewhat in the United States since this was written in 1970. A growing number of linguists are now engaged in ASL research, including deaf linguists who have made major breakthroughs; for instance finding that inflectional systems, not previously recognized, have an important role. Sign language has also gained a greater degree of public acceptance through artistic ·productions, its exposure on television, and the efforts of deaf people on behalf of their language and culture. In the schools, oralism has largely given way to the total communication philosophy, thereby making room for a variety of signing that retains some English structure or for one of the sign codes invented to teach English to deaf children.

In the mid-eighteenth century, a controversy developed over the instruction of deaf children, pitting against each other the founders of two opposed methods of instruction. In 1775, the Abbé Charles Michel de l'Épée established the first public school for deaf children in Paris. The method of instruction consisted of the language of signs. A German contemporary, Samuel Heinicke, became known as the originator of the oral method, by which deaf children are taught through speech and lipreading. The controversy between the two schools—the manual and the oral—was never resolved and is still today a central issue in the bitter debate between the proponents of each method.

A search through the literature indicates that the

267

debaters, professionals concerned with the education and
the welfare of deaf children, have only rarely looked to linguistics for support for their positions. On the other hand,
it appears that until very recently, linguists have not
shown any interest in the development and use of language
by deaf persons. Interest in the modes of communication employed by those who are deaf seems to have arisen following
the establishment of the field of psycholinguistics. Recent
studies by Blanton (1968), Lenneberg (1967), McNeill (1965)
indicate a concern with the language problems of the deaf
person and the implications for the education of deaf children. Sometimes the approach is from the point of view of
advancing theoretical knowledge of linguistics, and other
times from the practical aspect of helping deaf persons overcome a very large handicap.

Sign language            Sign language constitutes the most
communication.           important means of communication
                         for the majority of the deaf popu-
lation in North America. At the same time the general community and some deaf people themselves consider it inferior to
and more primitive than spoken languages. Linguistic studies,
whose results indicate that sign language is not fundamentally
different from other languages, can contribute to giving it the
legitimate status that it deserves and that may be necessary
for the welfare of the community to which it belongs. Sign
language and its acquisition by deaf or hearing children may
have important implications for linguistic theory. However,
this paper will not deal with them as much as with describing
the status of signs as a language used by a substantial number of deaf people.

     Herbert Kohl (1966) writes, "As adults, deaf individuals
use sign language exclusively, or a combination of signs and
words....This is true regardless of/ whether the individuals
went to college or not, and is also independent of intelligence."
While sign language does permit communication with hearing
people (Very few non-deaf persons know this language, these
usually the children of deaf parents), the facts indicate that
sign language is the preferred means of communication within
the community of the deaf. Social scientists have observed
the existence of a subculture of deaf people:
     Because most deaf persons are happier in association

with other deaf persons, and because of the concen-
tration which results, there develops a subculture of
the deaf within the larger community. This subculture
is a direct result of their deafness, a result of the
difficulty they have in communicating with the hearing
society around them as opposed to the ease with which
they interact among themselves. (Boese 1964: 4)

A quotation of the demographer Anders S. Lunde in Stokoe
(1978: 22) reveals the extensive use of sign language in the
subculture of the U.S. Deaf population:

Although oral schools emphasize speechreading and
speech, the plain fact is that the deaf as a group use
the sign language among themselves. According to
Best [Deafness & the Deaf in the U.S., 1938], 78.2
percent of the deaf used sign language and only 1%
used speech alone.

Concerning language acquisition by the congenitally
deaf, Lenneberg writes:

In America it is not until the child is four or five that
intensive language training is begun, and during the
first year the training is merely preparatory, that is,
readiness for the instruction in articulation, lip
reading, and reading and writing. (1967: 320)

Lenneberg is referring to deaf children whose parents are
hearing people and who are naturally unfamiliar with the language of signs. Deaf children of deaf parents who communicate manually learn to sign in the same manner as hearing
children learn to speak. Their linguistic development seems
to parallel that of hearing children, say Stuckless and Birch
(1966: 454). Lenneberg continues:

Thus there can be no doubt that the deaf come in contact with language at an age when other children have
fully mastered this skill and when, perhaps, the most
important formative period for language establishment
is already on the decline. (1967: 321)

Today the proponents of the manual method are waging a
battle from the sidelines, or from the underground, because
there does not exist in North America a school for deaf
children where the children are taught through the medium
of sign language. Neither is sign language included as a
subject matter in any school (Stokoe 1960: 25f). All deaf
children at present are brought up by the oral method, or

in a few schools by a modified oral method, which involves
the use of fingerspelling. In some schools, after an initial
stage in the oral system, children who fail to make satisfactory progress are relegated to the manual department
(Getz 1953: 51).

McCay Vernon, like other social scientists, writes
about the deaf population as a suppressed minority. He points
out that deaf children, like Puerto Rican, Indian, and Black
children, "tend to be forced into segregated schools over
which they have little control" (1969: 3). He expresses the
psychological relation between the deaf child and the language of the community of which he will probably become
a member in this way:

> The consequence of the almost exclusive use of "out-
> side" educators has often been teachers and adminis-
> trators who cannot fathom the life circumstances of
> their pupils....The National Association of the Deaf
> has long supported the use of the language of sign and
> fingerspelling. Yet the child is taught that these mo-
> dalities, the only ones he can master for purposes of
> communication with other deaf persons and with his
> family, are bad. This negative value is transmitted by
> its being forbidden to him and his family by the school.
> His teachers rarely know the language and frequently
> refuse to use it if they do. (1969: 3)

Robert Boese, in a study of the deaf community of Vancouver,
British Columbia, found that almost unanimously, the edu-
cators favor oralism for every child (1964: 14). Most educators
of the deaf in North America seem to hold the same view.
Commenting on the state of education for deaf children, Don
Campbell, a psychologist, writes:

> Paradoxically, the very teachers who embrace the
> idea that most profoundly deaf children, can through
> speech acquisition, learn to relate well in a hearing
> world, often themselves studiously avoid involve-
> ment with the deaf community other than during the
> school day when they are paid to do so. This is par-
> ticularly interesting in view of the fact that these
> teachers might be expected to be among the first to
> promote true social integration of the deaf. In prac-
> tice this is usually not the case. (1970: 2).

In many schools the use of signs is discouraged or punished, while in others it is tolerated. Without the benefit of instruction, the vast majority of deaf people acquire sign language and fingerspelling by association with other deaf persons (Furth 1966: 9). Croneberg (1965) points out the difference between a "native" signer and a "non-native" signer. The native signer is typically a deaf or hearing child of deaf parents, or a deaf person who has had extensive contact with sign language users "since early childhood or early youth" (1965: 297). The non-native signers include a few teachers of deaf children and other deaf persons with only limited intercourse with native signers.

E d u c a t i o n   w i t h o u t   a   w o r k i n g   l a n g u a g e . It is revealing to note the results obtained by the schools which claim to be educating deaf children by means of the oral method. A study done by Boatner showed that only about 5% of the deaf students aged 16 or over leaving the 88 schools surveyed in the study, had attained 10th grade or higher (cited in Quigley 1969: 13). In another study, Furth found that

> ...the percentage of deaf pupils who have linguistic competence...reaches a maximum of only 12%, a number which may be somewhat inflated by the presence of pupils in the norming sample who had lost their hearing after the acquisition of language, or who were not profoundly deaf. (1966: 14)

Furth's evaluation was based on reading skills of the pupils. Quigley points out that reading achievement is not a reliable indicator of a deaf child's linguistic competence and suggests that the ability to write in English is a more reliable measure (1969: 13). Commenting on the writing done by the students of Gallaudet College, Stokoe writes:

> When we look at the literally tons of evidence—we have files of students' writing going back to 1954— just one conclusion is to be drawn. If one objective of our profession is to teach the language of his culture to the deaf child, we have failed. Looking only at the top 10th of the products of our teaching of the deaf child, we can hardly see that we have tried. The language patterns of the other 90% hardly bear looking at. (1963: 967)

Furth, among others, suggests that the education of
deaf children has not been adequate. He points out that "a
four-year old hearing child masters language and so does an
adult with an IQ of 40" (1966: 15). Thus, a high intelligence
level is not a prerequisite for the acquisition of language,
while the majority of deaf children in schools for the deaf do
not acquire it as well as do retarded individuals. According
to Furth, "The true 'language' of the deaf is the sign language,
as one can readily observe" (1966: 15). Blanton agrees and
expresses the opinion that signing will continue to serve as
the medium of communication in the Deaf community (1968:
166).

The suggestion that sign language is the 'true' language of the deaf is not a recent one. Épée, who is best
known as the founder of the manual method for the education
of deaf children, wrote:

La langue naturelle des sourds et muets est la langue
des signes: ils n'en ont point d'autre, tant qu'ils ne
sont point instruit, et c'est la nature même, et leurs
différents besoins, qui les guident dans ce langue.
Il importe peu en quelle langue on veuille les instruire:
elles leur sont toutes également étrangères, et celle
même du pays dans lequel ils sont nés, n'offre pas
plus de facilité que toute autre, pour réussir dans cette
enterprise. (1776: 12)

[The natural language of the deaf and mute is the language of signs: they have no other, so that they are
are not taught it, nature and their own different needs
guide them into this language. It matters little in which
language one wishes to teach them; whatever it is they
are all foreigners to it, and even the language of the
very country in which they are born provides no more
facility than all the rest for use in teaching them.]

Recorded history indicates that there had been attempts to
educate the deaf long before Épée started his school. Pedro
Ponce DeLeón, a Spanish monk born in 1520, educated the
children of several noble families "by associating objects
with the printed word and then introduced speech by associating movements of the vocal organs with the printed char-
acters" (Quigley 1969: 4). [For more recent scholarship on

early Spanish teachers of deaf children, see Chaves & Soler
(1974, 1975).] Another approach was taken by Juan Martin
Pablo Bonet, who also taught the deaf children of several
Spanish noblemen. He described his method in a book published in 1620, Simplification of <u>Sounds and the Art of</u>
<u>Teaching the Dumb to Speak</u>. Bonet's method, which is
similar to the "Rochester Method" employed in some schools
in the past and today, consisted of teaching a one-handed
manual alphabet, which was associated with the printed
letters. Speech was then taught by associating movements
of the vocal organs with printed and fingerspelled letters
(Quigley 1969: 4). Morkovin (1960) cited in the same work
by Quigley reports that this approach is presently in vogue
in the Soviet Union, where it is claimed to obtain excellent
results in developing speech and speechreading.

In the initial stages of his instruction, Épée made use
of a fingerspelling alphabet associated with the printed letters,
and he also made some attempts to teach his pupils speech.
However, he differed from his predecessors, as is indicated
above. He believed that sign language was the natural language of the deaf and that it should be the medium for their
instruction.

He set out to expand the sign language then in use by
adding what he called <u>les signes méthodiques</u>, which had the
effect of creating a one-to-one relationship between grammatical items in the French language and in sign language. He
imposed the French grammatical structure on sign language
so that deaf people would have access to French language and
culture (Stokoe 1978: 5). This elaborate system of methodical
signs was seen by Épée as the natural language of the educated deaf person for their thinking processes and for their
communication. [He was doubtless shrewd enough to have
realized that in everyday use the elaborate system would
undergo curtailment and change. Editor's note]

At the same period that Épée was operating his school
in Paris, Samuel Heinicke became the proponent of what became known as the oral method. Heinicke adopted a philo-
sophical position derived from Locke, the founder of empiricism
(Garnett 1967: 123). Locke rejected the concept of innate
ideas and principles; according to him, all knowledge comes
from experience, the mind initially being a blank. Thinking
takes place in words (sounds) which form part of experience.

Inspired by Locke, Heinicke claimed that thinking is not possible without spoken language, since it is conducted in the
mind by means of the sounds which we make when we talk.
A person who has not learned to talk, therefore cannot think,
at least not in abstract terms; as a consequence of this belief, Heinicke became the proponent of the oral method of
educating deaf children. He opposed manual communication
as being harmful to the intellectual development of the deaf
person. Reading, for someone unable to speak, he relegated
to the same position as manual communication, since for
such an individual a written text cannot evoke the sounds of
the language in his mind. Heinicke wrote, "it is a mistake
to believe that the sense of sight, through written speech,
can replace the sense of hearing for deaf mutes. Abstract
concepts cannot be developed through the aid of writing"
(quoted in Garnett 1968: 23). Heinicke represented written
communication in the following manner in the exchange of
letters between himself and Épée:

> Through sight we obtain always (inner?) impressions
> of colors, shapes, and surfaces which are then pre-
> sented as abstracted in our imagination; yet, we must
> not believe that because words permit themselves to
> be represented on paper that they therefore can be sim-
> ilarly presented inside ourselves. No, this in no way
> follows. Written or printed words are like heaps of
> flies' feet or spiders' legs; they are not forms or figures
> that can be presented as fixed or abstracted in our im-
> agination; and we are hardly able to represent individ-
> ual letters to ourselves subjectively with any continuity.
> (Garnett 1968: 23)

In his criticism of Épée, Heinicke thus claimed that a deaf
person unschooled in the oral method cannot remember, beyond a short period of time, the spelling of words or the
configuration of signs representing abstract concepts. In
a letter to the editor of a Viennese newspaper, Heinicke
wrote: "Clear thinking is possible only in spoken language"
(Ibid., 47).

It naturally followed for Heinicke that if deaf people
are to be able to think abstractly they must be taught to speak
and to speechread. He was of course aware that even through
speechreading, the deaf do not perceive auditorially the
sounds of a conversation. He resolved this problem by sugges-

ting that the sense of taste somehow provides the deaf with
the sound data necessary for thinking to take place (Garnett
1967: 126). Although this bizarre suggestion has not been
adopted by Heinicke's followers, his method is today the
prevailing one. Young deaf children are not taught in sign
language, and signs are generally not used by their educators to communicate outside of the classroom with their
pupils. The two centuries of debate about which method to
utilize in the education of the deaf often seems to lack the
advantage of any scientific evidence. Furth points out the
basic fallacy in the educational philosophy of our schools
for the deaf: "They [the deaf] feel instinctively that without
sign language most of them would indeed be unable to communicate anything but the most primitive and obvious needs"
(1966: 16). The same view is held by others who have had
extensive contact with deaf individuals; Pintner, quoted by
Getz, asserts that

> Some deaf children's speech is comprehensible only
> to their hearing associates, and it is a bitter disap-
> pointment later on in life to find that what they have
> acquired through long years of hard work is useless
> when they meet a stranger. (1953: 56f)

In the same work, the opinion of J. Keith is similar:

> Speaking from my own observations of lip reading
> classes, methods, teachers, and students for more
> than thirty years, I have still to meet a single one
> of the lip reading students or graduates who could
> understand ordinary rapidly spoken speech.

And R. T. Brill points out one reason why deaf people form
their own subculture:

> Even when they are fairly good speakers and lip-readers,
> which is true of only a small percentage, there is a
> difficulty in the means of ordinary communication, and
> the result is that they will isolate themselves.

The National Association of the Deaf speaks for a large number of deaf adults when it states:

> The many intelligent deaf who are confused and help-
> less in classes where oral instruction and nothing
> else is allowed resent the fact that their education is
> restricted in this way. Through no fault of their own
> they have been denied all the workable types of com-
> munication which should be open to them. . . . Time which

could have been well invested in acquiring knowledge
has been wasted in forcing children to concentrate on
the unreliable arts of speech and lip reading.
Don R. Campbell, a psychologist employed by the Western
Institute for the Deaf, in Vancouver, writes:

Not enough thought is given by administrators of most
oral programmes to the fact that while many ten year old
deaf children are struggling to say simple sentences on
the two or three year [old's] language level, they may
also be lagging farther and farther behind in their ability to cope socially and emotionally in a hearing world.
They may, at the same time, be falling dramatically
behind in their intake of general information. (1970: 4)

Explanations.    From the point of view of linguistic
                 competence only, leaving aside all
matters of psychological and sociological concern, such as
the deaf individual's adjustment to his handicap, his educational achievements, his relations with the deaf and
hearing communities, his employment potential, etc., one
finds it hard to understand why the professionals who deal
with the deaf attempt to impose one mode of communication
over another. The deaf turn to sign language as their "natural"
language in the same way that a hearing individual acquires
and uses the language of the community in which he grows up.
Commenting on the educators' viewpoint, Furth writes:

The fixation on the secondary aspect of language,
namely speech, in preference to everything else, including linguistic competence, is indeed baffling.
This oral preoccupation must strike a neutral observer as irrational. It is like some strange custom or
institution which is encouraged within a community
although perceived as harmful by an outsider.
(1966: 209)

A review of the literature on the education of the deaf
and their social and employment problems written by teachers,
school administrators, psychologists, and social workers,
indicates almost complete denial of the existence of sign language and fingerspelling—the manual means of communication. The whole emphasis of the educators is directed toward the learning of speech and lipreading, generally confusing
this activity with the teaching of language. They are also often

convinced that they are creating in the deaf the possibility
to think. A teacher comments: "These 'wordless' children
are at the same time without any adequate thinking process"
(Dumitrescu, in Fusfeld 1967: 63). Another teacher explains
how she attempts to overcome her pupils' linguistic problems:

> Some have good speech, others try so hard, though
> we can hardly understand them and there are still
> many others who have no speech at all. In this case,
> I emphasize in the child the power of lipreading and
> the ability to express himself in writing. I try my best
> to develop in him all the possibilities that will help
> him in his struggle for existence—his speech, lip-
> reading and writing abilities—for all these put toge-
> ther will help him a great deal in the daily contacts
> which enrich life. (Alvarez, in Fusfeld 1967: 89)

For this teacher, like so many others who are well-meaning
and sincere in their efforts to help deaf children become
part of society, there is no awareness that sign language,
the language of the Deaf community, can be the means by
which deaf children can be educated.

Campbell points out that

> ...several extensive research studies (Meadow 1967,
> Montgomery 1966, Stevenson 1964, Quigley & Frisina
> 1961, Quigley 1969, Stuckless & Birch 1966, and Vernon
> 1969) have shown that children with early manual communi-
> cation not only are more advanced when they enter school,
> but maintain this advantage throughout their school age
> years. (1970: 15)

The results of these studies indicate that in a comparison of
them with children who have been brought up orally only, the
former generally have a better command of language, not only
in manual communication, but also in lipreading, reading, and
writing. There was no difference in speech intelligibility between the two groups. In most cases, the early manual group
showed better psychological adjustment and higher educational
achievements. Stevenson's study found that four times as
many students from the early manual group went to college
as students from the oral group.

The lack of sensitivity shown by some educators toward deaf children equals their ignorance about the deaf
community and their prejudice against sign language. This

insensitivity is illustrated by this comment from a teacher
quoted above:

> Speech and speechreading may mean nothing at first
> to a deaf child, just like talking to a newborn baby.
> But in every way, we have to keep on and be deter-
> mined to work on it. The time used cannot all be
> wasted for we even talk to animals and to our pets,
> which after numerous repetitions, learn to respond
> to commands, etc. (Alvarez, in Fusfeld 1967: 89)

The view that a deaf child who does not learn to
speak and lipread is less than a human being seems to be
quite prevalent among educators of deaf children. The
following provides another example:

> Not long ago I spoke with the lady director of an oral
> school. She was telling about her program, dispara-
> ging signs as "glorified gestures." Finally she
> pointed to a little Black girl, hearing aids sprouting
> from both ears, who was sitting on the floor and
> staring at us: "Look at her; she's such a well-
> trained little animal. (Ridgeway 1969: 20)

The view against signing can be best understood as
prejudicial in nature, due to the empirically based belief
that only speech is language and that thinking is possible
only through speech:

> Underlying this general emphasis on verbal learning
> was the ready association of thinking and language
> which prevailed in one form or another throughout the
> history of Western thought and education. The history
> of the deaf stands out as one exceptionally glaring
> instance of man's inability to see beyond the confines
> of his own theoretical assumptions. (Furth 1966: 212)

Furth has investigated extensively the relationship between
conceptual and verbal skill. On the basis of his studies he
concludes that "The basic ability to conceptualize and reason
is seen as largely independent of [spoken] language and
mainly subject to the general experience of living" (1963:
482). Thus, while deaf people may have poor vocal language
skills, they may have a normal distribution of intellectual
abilities.

The educators' prejudice is akin to the ethnocentrism
shown by numerous teachers of English who claim that only
standard English is correct, while nonstandard dialects are

ungrammatical corruptions of the "pure" language. In the process of teaching "correct" English, they make the speakers of nonstandard English feel that their dialect is inferior (La-bov 1970). The educator of the deaf claims that the spoken language, English, is superior to the language of the Deaf community. The following statement taken from a report on the education of the deaf made to the Canadian Department of Education and Science in English illustrates that point:

> There was agreement that deaf children signing among themselves out of class, and deaf adults communicating by signs, are both using forms which are ungrammatical and bear little relationship to normal usage.

The Commission, which itself was not familiar with sign language, listened to the testimony of individuals, both deaf and hearing, whose opinions were sought because of their contact with sign language, without considering the fact that they were not qualified to make objective observations about language. A study based on an informant's opinions of his language certainly would not be considered scientific by a linguist. It is hard to comprehend why this is the practice when it comes to sign languages. The claim that sign language forms are "ungrammatical" refers to the fact that sign language has a structure which is different from English, but then so do Chinese, Turkish, and Swahili. It would be ludicrous to call these languages ungrammatical because they are structured superficially unlike English. However, cultural and linguistic chauvinism does exist; the claim that the French language is the most logical and the most precise of all languages is still heard. The Commission's report continues:

> One witness pointed out that when good and fluent signing is used, it is not, in fact, a self-sufficient language but **parasitic** upon well-developed mastery of conventional language. (p. 27)

The relationship between signing and English is a complex problem which will be somewhat illuminated by a proposal made by Stokoe and to be presented later in this paper.

When recognition is given to manual communication, it is usually by the social workers and psychologists who work with deaf adults and are therefore aware of the limitations imposed on the communication with their deaf clients by lipreading, synthetic speech, and writing. Stephen K.

Chough, a deaf social worker, explains deaf people's preference for signing and fingerspelling over other modes of
communication: "Just as hearing people prefer spoken communication to written communication, so do almost all deaf
people prefer manual communication" (in Fusfeld 1967: 352).
Most deaf people acquire sign language and fingerspelling
from others in their subculture, although the community at
large does not approve of manual communication. Some deaf
individuals who have not acquired linguistic competence in
English, and who have been prevented from acquiring the
ability to communicate by manual means by the emphasis
placed on oral communication in their schools, do not share
a language with anyone and therefore live in virtual isolation from all human contact. "Because of difficulty in, or
in some instances lack of, means of communication there can
be nothing for some but a life of deprivation, loneliness and
dissatisfaction" (Chough, loc. cit., 350). Another social
worker points out the importance to the individual of communication with others:

> An inability to communicate creates barriers to the
> satisfaction of basic needs. Since the individual's
> well being depends in large part on his ability to sat-
> isfy his own needs harmoniously with the needs of
> others, the deafened person may experience consider-
> able frustration both from inner emotional sources and
> from outer, social situations. (Ibid.)

This explains in part why deaf people associate for the most
part with other deaf individuals and form a subcommunity in
which communication takes place with almost the same facility as in the hearing world.

When it is accepted as a system of communication,
sign language is often not considered equal to other natural
languages. Chough makes the following statement:

> While the characteristics of the sign language are more
> colorful, lively, and dramatic than other means of communi-
> cation, it has some disadvantages, especially those of
> grammatical disorder, illogical systems, difficult ex-
> pression of abstract ideas, and linguistic confusion. (p. 351)

This kind of unscientific observation, literally nonsense, is
based on comparison with English grammar, English word
order, English word classes and forms, and English semantics,
instead of treating a sign language as an independent natural

language. Bernard M. Tervoort, a native of Holland, who has
studied language development of American and Dutch deaf
children, provides an example of the kind of research done
by those who consider sign language only a manual representation of some spoken language:

> ...until he [Stokoe] definitely proves differently, the
> author of the present study warrants to set forth the
> hypothesis that at least among well educated deaf adults
> English is the communication system used, be it through
> speech and lipreading only, through fingerspelling or
> through signs, or through a combination of these. (n.d.: 4)

His implication is that less educated deaf adults use a form
of broken or ungrammatical English. Another observation made
by Tervoort is that the material he recorded on film for his
study on young deaf children contained very few instances of
metaphoric, ironic, or humorous usage (1961: 460). It is
apparent from the anecdotes he introduces as evidence, that
it is beyond his capacity to determine what constitutes meta-
phor, irony, or humor in a language in which he has less than
native ability. [See also Chapter 4 above.] To prove that abstract and idiomatic usage requires special teaching to deaf
children Tervoort shows that they must have the expression
'to hold open house' explained to them, otherwise they understand 'to keep one's door open' (1961: 471). By the same
token, a French pupil learning English in school would also
need an explanation for such an idiomatic expression. However, on the basis of that particular evidence, one would
hardly claim that Frenchmen do not employ idiomatic expressions in their own language. It is correct that deaf children
must be taught English—a language that is foreign to them;
but it does not follow that their own language is therefore
impoverished, as Tervoort indicates.

Herbert Kohl, following a non-partisan investigation
of the literature on the education of the deaf, concluded that
the schools have failed to do what they set out to do; namely
to educate deaf children. Like others, he notes that while
deaf individuals generally use sign language for their interpersonal communication, none of the methods of education
for deaf children involves the use of that mode of communication (1966: 10). Although Kohl is entirely sympathetic to
the use of sign language—he believes that it is the missing
element in the education of deaf children—he holds certain

reservations regarding its status as a full-fledged language.
He expresses the view, based on his study of the literature,
that:

> ...sign language is limited in scope and expressive
> power compared to oral language. It is bound to the con-
> crete, and with difficulty rises to abstraction, metaphor,
> irony, and humor. The various relevant studies seem to
> imply that this concreteness generalizes to the learning
> of English, and it is an interesting question as to whether
> this limitation may be responsible for some of the deaf
> child's behavior and maturational problems. (Kohl 1966: 18f)

It appears that all such opinions originate from those who
either are not familiar with sign language or are linguistically
naive and therefore unable to make scientific observations of
any language.

Sign language      To date [1970] very little linguistic
as a language.     work has been done on sign language.
                   What is available tends to indicate
that it is an independent language, with its own grammatical
and semantic structure. It appears to share general linguistic
principles with [vocally] articulated languages. Elizabeth
McCall, concludes from her study of sign language:

> Results of the analysis show that Sign has a syntactic
> system that can be systematically described in a gene-
> rative grammar. Constructions generated from the gram-
> mar that was defined in this investigation are structurally
> different from English in most cases. It is believed that
> taken as a whole, Sign is grammatically unique from any
> other language. (1965: 83)

Unlike such observers as Fusfeld, McCall found that sign
language "is a true language" with a "sequential grammatically ordered sentence structure: independent of other languages" (1965: 77f). She suggests a hypothesis concerning
the relation between sign language and the spoken language
of the community at large:

> It is highly probable that the sign language, or languages,
> are grammatically distinct from any others, although it
> may be hypothesized that the structure of Sign in any given
> country shifts somewhat in the direction of the grammar of
> the native oral language. This question, however, awaits
> further investigation. (McCall 1965: 78)

Another investigator, Stokoe, has dealt with this matter. His writings include a structural description of the "cheremic" (phonemic) system and the morphocheremics, or morphophonemics, of American Sign Language. In a work published in 1960 [revised in 1978], Sign Language Structure, he describes an orthography he devised for the units of this sign language. In 1965 he and two colleagues published a sign language-English dictionary in which the signs are listed "in the order of the symbols used to write them" (1965: xxiii), using the orthography described in the earlier work.

Stokoe's analysis of sign language structure is based on the Trager and Smith (1951) model of linguistic description. It describes the combination of cheremes into signs (i.e. the morphocheremics of sign language) and to a limited extent the equivalents of morphological and syntactic levels in spoken languages. The actual syntactic structure of sentences had not yet been analyzed, but several nonmanual elements were isolated and assumed to be part of the syntactic patterns in the same way that the suprasegmentals of speech enter into the structural makeup of spoken sentences. Stokoe writes:

> The sign language, as the term is understood in this study, requires only a small, though radical, change in the definition of language given by Trager in his "Paralanguage" (Studies in Linguistics 13, 3): 'It is the cultural system which employs certain of [the visible actions of the face and hands], combines them in recurrent sequences, and arranges these sequences into systematic distribution in relation to each other and in reference to other cultural systems.' (1960: 30 [1978: 25])

The sign, according to Stokoe in this early analysis, corresponds to the morpheme, the smallest meaningful unit in any language;

> The sign morpheme, however, unlike the word, is seen to be not sequentially but simultaneously produced. Analysis of the sign cannot be segmented in time order but must be aspectual. The aspects of the sign which appear to have the same order of priority and importance as the segmental phonemes of speech are the aspects of configuration, position or location, and motion [action]...

Like consonant and vowel, the aspects position,
configuration and action may only be described in
terms of contrast to each other. (1960: 40 [1978:
37f])

The three aspects have been called tab, dez, and sig by
Stokoe (respectively position, configuration, and action),
and he proposed at the same time the terms chereme and
allocher for the concepts corresponding with phoneme and
allophone (1960: 30). Signs are formed by the combination
of the three aspects, requiring movements of the hands and
arms of the signer. Facial expression and other bodily
activity, Stokoe suggests (1960: 40), function like suprasegmentals. In conclusion he states that

...the work so far accomplished seems to us to
substantiate the claims that the communicative activity of persons using this language is truly linguistic
and susceptible of microlinguistic analysis of the most
rigorous kind. (1960: 67) [1978: 79]

Croneberg, a deaf colleague on the dictionary project, has
also observed that sociolinguistic variations found in spoken
languages occur in sign language:

ASL (American Sign Language) exhibits both horizontal
and vertical variations. So far, only obvious and easily
recorded vocabulary differences have been observed.
(Stokoe, Croneberg, Casterline 1965: 314)

In different geographical areas, different signs are sometimes
used to represent the same thing. Or else, in the same area,
different signs are used by the young and the older, the
Whites and the Blacks. Stokoe suggests that investigations
of sign language will eventually require a change in the
definition of language so that it will read (with the deletion
of the word vocal that used to appear before symbols): "A
language is a system of arbitrary symbols by means of which
persons in a culture carry on the total activity of that culture"
(1960: 67) [1978: 80].

Stokoe (1970b) has applied the features of diglossia,
discovered and described by Ferguson (in Word, 1959, 15,
325-340), to sign language. Diglossia occurs when the same
speakers use two or more varieties of the same language under
different conditions. This approach to sign language contributes
to linguistic knowledge, since Stokoe shows that in most
respects, sign language diglossia occurs in the same fashion

as in the languages that Ferguson used in his investigation:
Arabic, Modern Greek, Swiss-German, and Haitian Creole.
Secondly, but of more importance to the Deaf community,
Stokoe's study by showing the similarity of ASL to other languages and mixed language situations could lead to a changed
attitude toward sign language and its use by deaf people for
their interpersonal communication and for the education of
deaf children.

One of the two varieties of sign language used in
North America (excluding areas where English is not spoken
in the general community) consists of English represented
visually by means of signs and fingerspelled words. In diglossia this form is called 'H' and in the deaf community it
is referred to as "correct signing" or "(grammatical) sign language," the name "manual English" having also been suggested (Stokoe 1970b: 28). Sign language H is used in more
formal occasions such as in church, for lectures, for all forms
of written communication, etc. For deaf people who sign, as
for the speakers of the other languages Ferguson studied, H
is the prestige form. It is considered by the users of both
superior to variety L, the conversational language in use for
most everyday communication; it is called "signs" or "signing"
by deaf persons. The sign for 'conversation' also refers to L
(Ibid.). Stokoe points out that diglossia would present no
problem for the Deaf community, except for the fact that outsiders—i.e. professional educators—have made deaf people
feel that only H is a respectable language, assuming without
benefit of any knowledge of linguistic science that L "is no
language at all, has no grammar, is but a collection of 'gestures...suggestive of ...ideas'" (1970b: 30). As in the case
of the four languages used by Ferguson, sign language L is
grammatically simpler than H, in which signs or fingerspelled
words are in a one-to-one relation with spoken words, and in
which English morphology is represented and its word order
followed. Sign L has its own syntax and does not have most
grammatical features found in English, such as inflections and
subject-verb concord (33f). H and L share most of their vocabularies; H contains "the whole technical and learned vocabulary
of English," which does not have any equivalent in L, since
the subjects requiring technical vocabulary are discussed only in
H (34); although L can and does borrow vocabulary from H when
necessary for conversational use.

In diglossia as described by Ferguson, "The sound systems of H and L constitute a single phonological structure ..." (1970b: 36). The "gestemic" (i.e. phonological) systems of H and L in American Sign Language are described by Stokoe as " a single gestemic structure of which the L gestemics is the basic system and the divergent features of H gestemics are either a subsystem or a parasystem....In using H the signer 'refines' his L gestemics" (37). These differences amount to "the substitution of one allocher for another. The cheremic (phonemic) system embraces them both" (37). In another interesting suggestion worth pursuing further, Stokoe considers fingerspelling a subsystem of sign language, which could be accounted for as "a divergent feature of H gestemics" (37-38).

The lack of interest in sign language shown by linguists in the U.S. where the deaf population is now estimated at one third of one million individuals can be attributed at least in part to the behavioristic basis of American structural linguistics.

> The tone of behavioristic theory was set by its founder, Watson, who proposed that what is called thinking may be nothing but subaudible speech. In other words, thinking is just silent [spoken] language. (Furth 1966: 37)

The non-mentalistic approach taken by the linguist Bloomfield also led him to see thinking as identical to language. He called thinking "talking to oneself;" and he explains further how "thinking" develops as a process of socialization:

> As children we talk to ourselves a lot, but under the correction of our elders, we soon learn to supress the sound producing movements and replace them with very slight inaudible ones: we "think in words."(Bloomfield 1933: 28)

Referring to gesture languages such as those used by monks who have taken a vow of silence and by American Indians as an auxiliary language, Bloomfield states: "It seems certain that these gesture languages are merely developments of ordinary gestures and that any and all complicated or not immediately intelligible gestures are based on the conventions of ordinary speech" (1933: 39). He also writes that "deaf and dumb language," like writing, is merely a derivative of language (1933: 144). While this claim holds true for variety H of ASL, the facts indicate that variety L is not derived from spoken language, and that it has its own independent structure and lexicon. The influence of the dominant culture, the hearing community, must also be recognized over the linguistic expression of the Deaf community, particularly on the level of vocabulary. However, Bloomfield does not refer to any empirical evidence that sign language is derived from spoken language; he appears to make this claim on theoretical grounds so as to avoid a contradiction with his assumption that we "think in words."

Sapir, the anthropological linguist, wrote that possession of a language is a universal fact of human nature. In his words:

> One may argue as to whether a particular tribe engages in activities that are worthy of the name of religion or art, but we know of no people that is not possessed of a fully developed language. The lowliest South African Bushman speaks in the forms of a rich symbolic system that is in essence perfectly comparable to the speech of the cultivated Frenchman. (1921: 22)

However, the kind of symbolic system acceptable to Sapir for language and thinking was restricted to that found in speech:

> We shall no doubt conclude that all voluntary communication of ideas, aside from normal speech, is either a transfer, direct or indirect, from the typical symbolism of language as spoken and heard or, at the least, involves the intermediary of truly linguistic symbolism... auditory imagery and the correlated motor imagery leading to articulation are, by whatever devious ways we follow the process, the historic fountain-head of all speech and of all thinking. (1921: 21)

With these a priori conceptions of the nature of linguistic symbolism and of thinking, it is not surprising that Sapir rejects the possibility that gesture languages, including that used by deaf people, possess independent systems suitable for the thinking processes of those who use them. He states that "The intelligibility of these vaguer symbolisms can hardly be due to anything but their automatic and silent translation into the terms of a fuller flow of speech" (Ibid.). Aside from the fact that this statement contradicts the native signer's intutition (communicated to the writer by several native signers both deaf and hearing), the claim does not seem tenable in light of the fact that 88% of deaf adults do not achieve linguistic competence in a spoken language (Furth 1966: 14). Sapir would have us believe that the signer who expresses himself fully and freely in sign language, translates from or into another language in which his level of expression—in speech, lipreading, reading, writing, and fingerspelling—may be less adequate than that of a four year old hearing child. For deaf people Sapir's claim leads to an important implication concerning their education, their employment potential, and their social status in the community of hearing people; viz., that because of their inability to hear and to acquire spoken language, they are forcibly limited in their intellectual capacities.

Sociolinguistics and status. We have seen earlier how Heinicke developed the oral method for the same reasons; i.e. he felt that unless deaf people learned to speak and lipread, they would have no language and they would be unable to think, or at best they might think in concrete terms only. The concept that articulated words are the necessary medium through which thought can occur is said to be an idea held by the Greek philosophers (DeLand 1968: 8). Although references to deaf persons exist from early times, not much information is given about them. One thing they do indicate, according to DeLand, "they were considered incapable of being educated" (Ibid.). The deaf, with occasional exceptions that were often recorded with exaggerations, were left in ignorance. Methods for the instruction of the deaf began appearing toward the end of the sixteenth century in different parts of Europe. The change in attitude toward the deaf resulting from the awareness that they could be educated to take part in the culture around them was extremely significant. It was no longer thought that "dumbness," in the sense of lack of intellectual capacity, was the necessary correlate of deafness. After almost two hundred years of instruction, the lot of deaf people has been much improved and they have gained a certain degree of acceptance in the society at large. However, Furth points out:

Our educational and scientific atmosphere does not permit us really to accept deafness.... As stated before, the deaf are now accepted as being possibly equal to the hearing in intelligence, but only insofar as they succeed

in learning the language of the hearing. Common opinion
about the interdependency of language and thinking has
hardly changed. (1966: 28)

Just as in the case of other minority groups, North American
society is willing to accept the deaf on condition that they
accept its values, here represented by its language. Furth
points out that "This attitude is constantly nourished by
theories of scholars who extol language as the source and
medium of civilization and intelligence" (1966: 203). In this
regard, Labov, a critic of recent programs for teaching the
"culturally disadvantaged," states:

> For many generations, American school teachers have
> devoted themselves to correcting a small number of
> nonstandard English rules to their standard equivalents,
> under the impression that they were teaching logic.
> This view has been reinforced and given theoretical
> justification by the claim that nonstandard Negro English
> lacks the means for the expression of logical thought.
> (1970: 22)

The similarity between the criticisms levelled at sign language and at nonstandard Black English is striking. Labov
points out that

> linguists have endeavored for many years to show
> that differences in language are matters of social
> convention established by historical processes which
> shift continually the social prestige of dialect vari-
> ants. (1970: 1)

Apparently linguists have not been very successful in establishing this point of view, since the opposite opinion still
prevails in our society. The argument for equal status of sign
language is more difficult to present than that for nonstandard
English, because in one extreme it is an independent language
and in the other it can be a visual representation of English—
both L and H varieties making use of signs. The prejudice
against nonstandard English dialects is caused by "ignorance
of basic facts about human language and the people who speak
it" (Labov 1970: 34). To make sign language acceptable requires, in addition, overcoming the long-standing assumption
concerning the relation of thinking and spoken language. In
this respect, structural linguists (Stokoe excepted) have been
of no help, because to do so would cause them to contradict
their underlying assumption; i.e. that thinking is a silent expression of speech.

Sign language offers two different areas of research
to the linguist. The first one involves doing basic investigations on the nature of sign language: linguistic description
and analysis. This type of study would add to the store of
knowledge of natural languages used by humankind to communicate with one another. It may also contain implications for
linguistic theory for which less exotic languages would not
provide evidence. At the very least, the existence of languages that make use of visually rather than auditorially perceived symbols would require the redefinition of some basic
concepts in the science of linguistics. Of more importance,
research on sign language acquisition among children of deaf
parents offers possible evidence for the hypothesis advanced
by Chomsky and others that there is an innate language
capacity in human beings (Chomsky 1965, Lenneberg 1967,
McNeill 1966). Their assumption is based on a rationalist
approach to linguistic theory, in which language is seen as
species-specific and a result of man's unique biological
make-up (Lenneberg 1967: 28). The empiricist view, which
holds that language is acquired as a result of conditioning of
the individual by his environment and his experience (Skinner
1957), may obtain support from the work being done by Allen
and Beatrice Gardner with a chimpanzee who is acquiring signs
of ASL (Science, 1969, 165, 669-672).

A conference on sign languages, sponsored by the
Center for Applied Linguistics, was held on the 5th and 6th of
December 1969 (Stokoe 1970a). Its unstructured discussions
dealt mainly with problems of definition and classification
(Stokoe 1974: 346-371) among nine participants, including two
deaf persons in the secretariat of the National Association of
the Deaf. This conference reveals a growing interest by linguists and sociolinguists in sign languages.

The second area of interest for the linguist in sign
language is directly in the field of applied linguistics. One
of the problems requiring attention is how to make sign language acceptable as a mode of communication for deaf adults
in the community at large; and of greater importance for the
welfare of the Deaf community, to make it acceptable as the
medium for the educating of deaf children. In relation to this
problem, psycholinguistic investigation of language acquisition will, it is to be hoped, shed some light on how linguistic competence is established in an individual. This knowledge

could then be applied to determine ways of educating deaf
persons so that ultimately they can achieve true bilingualism:
sign language competence for interpersonal communication in
the Deaf community, and linguistic competence in English,
at least in written English, so that they can also partake of
the common culture of the society in which they live.


## REFERENCES

Blanton, R. L.
   1968   Language Learning & Performance in the Deaf, in
          Developments in Psycholinguistics Research, Rosen-
          berg & Koplin eds. (New York, Macmillan), 121-176.

Boese, R. J.
   1964   Differentiations in the Deaf Community. Unpublished
          study submitted to the Department of Sociology,
          University of British Columbia.

Bloomfield, L.
   1933   Language (New York, Holt, Rinehart & Winston).

Campbell, D. R.
   1970   A Look at Education of the Deaf, and the Respon-
          sibilities of the Medical Profession. Unpublished
          study, Western Institute for the Deaf, Vancouver, B.C.

Chomsky, N.
   1965   Aspects of the Theory of Syntax (Cambridge, MA,
          MIT Press).
   1967   The Formal Nature of Language, in The Biological
          Foundations of Language, Lenneberg (New York,
          Wiley), 397-442.

DeLand, F.
   1968   The Story of Lip-Reading, Its Genesis & Develop-
          ment (Washington, A.G.Bell Association for the Deaf).

Department of Education & Science
   1968   The Education of Deaf Children: The Possible Place
          of Fingerspelling & Signing (London, HMSO).

Épée, Abbé C. M. de l'
    1776    L'institution des sourds et muets, par la voie
            des signes méthodiques (Paris).

Furth, H.
    1963    Language & the Development of Thinking, in
            Proceedings of the International Congress on
            Education of the Deaf, and 41st Meeting of
            the Convention of American Instructors of the
            Deaf (Washington, Gallaudet College)
    1966    Thinking Without Language, Psychological
            Implications of Deafness (New York, The Free Press).

Fusfeld, I. S.
    1967    A Handbook of Readings in Education of the Deaf
            and Post School Implications (Springfield, IL,
            Charles C. Thomas).

Gardner, R. A., & B. T. Gardner
    1969    Teaching Sign Language to a Chimpanzee, Science
            165, 669-672.

Garnett, C. B., Jr.
    1967    The World of Silence: A New Venture in Philosophy
            (New York, Greenwich).
    1968    The Exchange of letters between Samuel Heinicke
            & Charles Michel de l'Épée (New York, Vantage).

Getz, S.
    1953    Environment & the Deaf Child (Springfield, IL,
            Charles C. Thomas).

Kohl, H. R.
    1966    Language & Education of the Deaf (New York
            Center for Urban Education).

Labov, W.
    1970    The Logic of Nonstandard English, Report of the
            20th Annual Round Table on Languages & Linguistics,
            Alatis ed. (Washington, Georgetown University)

Lenneberg, E. H.
    1967    The Biological Foundations of Language (NY, Wiley).

Lenneberg, E. H.
  1969    On Explaining Language, Science 164, 636-643.

McCall, E.
  1965    A Generative Grammar of Sign. Unpublished M.A.
          thesis, University of Iowa.

McNeill, D.
  1965    The Capacity for Language Acquisition, in Pro-
          ceedings of the National Conference on Behavioral
          Aspects of Deafness, pp. 11-28/
  1966    Developmental Psycholinguistics, in The Genesis of
          Language: A Psycholinguistic Approach, Smith &
          Miller eds. (Cambridge, MA, MIT Press), 15-84.

Quigley, S. P.
  1969    The Influence of Fingerspelling on the Development
          of Language, Communication, & Educational Achieve-
          ment in Deaf Children (Institute for Research on Ex-
          ceptional Children, University of Illinois).

Ridgeway, J.
  1969    "Dumb" Children, The New Republic 161, 19-21.

Sapir, E.
  1921    Language (New York, Harcourt Brace & World).

Skinner, B. F.
  1957    Verbal Behavior (New York, Appleton Century Crofts).

Stokoe, W. C.
  1960    Sign Language Structure: An Outline of the Visual
  [1978]  Communication Systems of the American Deaf,
          Studies in Linguistics: Occasional Papers, 8.; o.o.p.
          (Revised, 1978, Sign Language Structure, Silver
          Spring, MD, Linstok Press).
  1963    Language Structure & the Deaf Child, in Proceedings
          (see Furth 1963 above).
  1970a   CAL Conference on Sign Languages, The Linguistic
          Reporter 12 (2), 5-8.
  1970b   Sign Language Diglossia, Studies in Linguistics 21,
          27-41.
  1974    The Classification & Description of Sign Languages, in
          Current Trends in Linguistics 12(1), 346-371.

Stokoe, W. C., D. C. Casterline, & C. G. Croneberg
    1965    A Dictionary of American Sign Language on Linguistic
    [1976]  Principles (Washington, Gallaudet College Press)
            Revised 1976 (Silver Spring, MD, Linstok Press).


Stuckless, E. R., & J. W. Birch
    1966    The Influence of Early Communication on the Lin-
            guistic Development of Deaf Children, American
            Annals of the Deaf 111, 452-462.


Tervoort, B. M.
    1961    Esoteric Symbolism in the Communication Behavior
            of Young Deaf Children, American Annals of the
            Deaf 106, 436-480.
    n.d.    Analysis of Communicative Structure. Report, project
    (1965)  No. RD-467-64-65 of the Vocational Rehabilitation
            Administration of the Department of Health, Education,
            & Welfare, Washington, DC.


Vernon, M., & B. Makowsky
    1969    Deafness & Minority Group Dynamics, The Deaf
            American 21 (11), 3-6.


Added in this revision:


Chaves, T. L., & J. L. Soler
    1974    Pedro Ponce de Leon, First Teacher of the Deaf,
            Sign Language Studies 5, 48-63.
    1975    Manuel Ramirez de Carrion (1579-1652?) and his
            Secret Method of Teaching the Deaf, SLS 8, 235-248.


Trager, G. L., & H. L. Smith, Jr.
    1951    An Outline of English Structure, Studies in Linguistics:
            Occasional Papers, 3.

PART THREE: 13

# AN ELITE GROUP IN DEAF SOCIETY

William Stokoe
H. Russell Bernard
Carol Padden

"Any large society must have an elite group
to lead it and manage its affairs.... Small
societies can get along without any social
stratification at all. Therefore the principal
evolutionary trend has been toward increasing
power and authority in the elite."
—Driver 1973: 358

Deaf society is no exception to the dictum that "any
large society must have an elite group..." Schein (1968)
estimates the adult deaf in the Washington, D.C., metropolitan area alone to number between 1,132 and 1,492.
Schein and Delk (1974) find the "prevocationally" deaf to
number as many as 203 per 100,000 in the nation's population, and they cite Health Examination Surveys (HES) and
Health Interview Surveys (HIS), which put the incidence of
those who "can hear and understand a few spoken words or
who cannot... understand any" at 1,100 (HES), and 1,000
(HIS) per 100,000 (1974: 32). By any measure then, the five
hundred thousand to one and one-half million deaf persons
in the United States may be seen to constitute a large society.
But more than demographers' numbers are needed to
make a society. It has been common practice for authorities
concerned with the delivery of education and other services
to deaf persons to deny that a Deaf society exists. (For a
typology of some of those who reject "the deaf experience,"
see Nash 1975). These authorities suppose instead that deaf
persons form a handicapped minority that needs a special
group of hearing professionals to lead it and manage its affairs. In some countries, unfortunately, this self-serving
view of the hearing specialist has become a self-fulfilling
prophecy, and as a result many deaf persons in those countries have become almost totally dependent. Deaf society in

the United States is large enough to wield power and authority through its own elite.

The purpose of this paper is not primarily to substantiate the claims that the deaf population forms a society, a
large society, a society with its own elite group. These facts
are self-evident, as the original presentation attests—this
was one of seven studies composing the Symposium "Culture
and Language in the Deaf Community" at the 73rd Annual
Meeting of the American Anthropological Association in Mexico City, November 1974. Its purpose instead is to examine
the power and authority structure in the Deaf community as
it is revealed by the communication network of an elite group,
the better to understand some of the characteristics of the
group and of the wider society it serves.

There is little difficulty, as a rule, in finding those
individuals who lead and manage. What headdresses and
white horses do in some societies to distinguish leaders is
done in other societies by titles, offices, and positions.
But if the elite are easy to identify, they are notoriously hard
to study. It is easier indeed to get their permission to investigate hundreds or thousands of their constituents than to
probe the structure of the group in authority. Since knowledge
is power, any elite group carefully guards the real knowledge
of its structure and function.

We present here, therefore, an unusual glimpse of how
power and authority are regulated. In part this is possible
because two of us bring to the task an accumulation of forty
years of participating, observing, and otherwise interacting
with or in deaf society. One of us is deaf (70db better-ear
loss from birth), has deaf parents, a deaf sibling, and many
deaf friends—in short is a member of deaf society. The other
of these two has direct professional contact with several members of the elite group that has extended over many years. In
part too, the technique developed by the third author and a
colleague makes this investigation possible.

KBPAK (Killworth & Bernard 1974) produces a sociogram
like picture of a network in any closed group of 40 to 150 persons, but unlike most sociograms, the matrix $CAT_{ij}$ at the base
of KBPAK has as its input 100% ranked data of unlimited choice.
The distance matrix, which is the input to the program, is
manipulated to produce a matrix of minimum distance from any
$\underline{i}$ to any $\underline{j}$, using as many intermediaries as are required. The

number of intermediaries used to achieve this minimum distance is given as the "cognitive category of interaction" between any i-j pair; hence $CAT_{ij}$ (Bernard & Killworth 1973:
145-184). KBPAK output contains information of two kinds:
(1) any individual in the group may or may not be in a subgroup; and (2) linkage may be reciprocal, one-way, or non-
existent between any two individuals. [This means that
members of a group may be characterized as a clique in the
traditional sociometric sense; however, subgroup membership obviously depends on internal perceptual or external
ethnographic factors; thus, unlike other similar techniques,
$CAT_{ij}$ produces real cliques only as an artifact or consequence
of operant interactional or cognitive factors within the larger
group.]

Procedure.    Our investigation of the deaf elite group had
                     four steps. First we pooled experience,
direct knowledge, and intuition to assemble a list of the
likeliest persons for inclusion in a hypothesized elite group,
which finally numbered thirty-three. The question of their
constituency (i.e. what society or societies they represented and what were their dimensions) were left unanswered.
All 33 reside in the capital metropolitan area; all are well
known to many of the area's other residents; several are
officers of state, national, and international deaf groups of
various kinds. While we cannot claim, therefore, that these
33 persons are the elite of a particular deaf society that is
geographically or otherwise determined, we are sure that the
elite group of national deaf society is somewhat larger at
least, and that among these 33 are to be found local, national,
and international leaders.
         Second, a personal interview enabled each person in
the 33 to rank the other 32 according to communicative contact. Frequency, length, and importance of communication
with the others were lumped in the ranking, as were both
professional and social interaction. When this step was completed, we had input data for KBPAK in the form of a 33 X 33
matrix of numbers (one for each person) showing the distance
from any i to any j. The third step was computer processing
of this data. Finally the output was analyzed by all three of
us; linkage and subgrouping shown in the program readout
were converted from tables of numbers into several sociograms

differing in fineness of detail; then the structure of the elite
group as shown in the sociograms was related to extensive
ethnographic data.

The $CAT_{ij}$        The program output shows a network of
sociograms.     seven subgroups plus six individuals not
                contained in the subgroups. Four of the
six clearly fit the role of "broker" and stand outside all the
subgroups but with links to and from them. Each of the four
"brokers" has seven to ten links with members of four or
five subgroups. A fifth member of the six has nine links in
all, but these are all with just two subgroups. This person
is not needed as a broker, because both these subgroups
have more than twice as many direct links between them as
he provides. This first brief survey of the data accounts for
32 of the whole group of 33, 27 lying in the seven subgroups
and 5 outside. The remaining member stands really outside
the main group as well. Linked reciprocally with only two
others and with a link to but not from two additional others,
this person represents our error in compiling the original
list in step one. Despite a position that entails regular professional contact with several members of the elite group,
this person is not cognitively perceived by its members as
one of them.

Subgroups        We have begun by considering the excep-
and brokers.     tional instance in the network and will
                 proceed to the more and more typical; i.e.
in the opposite way from the $CAT_{ij}$ program, which progressively identifies and removes from the matrix whatever will
most reduce the variance. After the non-member or marginal
member of the group we find one who appears potentially a
member of either of two subgroups, but who stands between
them with links to both. From this member we come to several
who have the position of broker. Bernard and Killworth (1973)
find any broker under strong pressure to be included in a subgroup, and predict that a broker will preserve independent
status only when there is a structurally well-defined liaison
function to be performed in the communication of the group.
Details of the brokers' positions in this network will come to
light when subgroup characteristics are examined; here it is
possible to predict that two of the brokers, '5' and '25' in

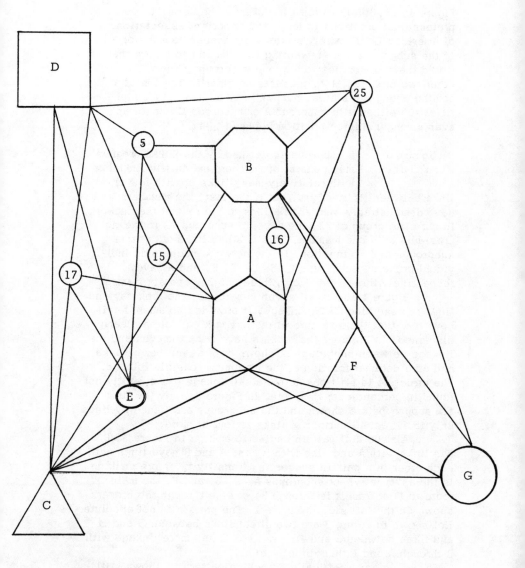

Figure 1. The seven subgroups (A-G) of the 33-member elite group, the brokers, and other individual members, with lines to show $CAT_{ij}$ linkage.

Figure 1, are likely to remain brokers. The nature of their
professional positions in large and important associations
of American Deaf society makes their access to many or all
of the subgroups more rewarding to them and to others than
would their closer ties to any one subgroup. One of the
other two brokers, '15', presents no clear indication of a
coming change in status, but '17' may be headed for identification either with subgroup A or subgroup D, or for an
even stronger liaison position between them.

Subgroup        A subgroup as defined by the KBPAK program
structure.      may consist of members maximally linked or
                with relatively many links or with few or no
links between its members, but if the last, the members will
have demonstrably similar relations to the rest of the network.
In our elite group of 33, the seventh subgroup (G in the figures) has only one member. This one has links with other
subgroups and so functions in the network much as do individual brokers. Subgroups F, E, D, C, B, and A have,
respectively,three, two, four, three, eight, and six members.
        Figure 1 shows all seven subgroups, the brokers, and
lines representing $CAT_{ij}$ linkage. It provides so much detail,
however, that the structure of the network cannot be clearly
discerned. In Figure 2 the brokers have been removed and the
linkage between subgroups is shown both as number of links
and as a decimal fraction of the maximum possible linkage.
The structure is still obscure. Actual linkage has a reality not
found in percentages; therefore, in Figure 3, only the first
six subgroups are shown and the subgroups are joined by lines
only if the actual number of links is four or more.
        A structural pattern begins to emerge in Figure 3. E
has links with A and also with B, and A and B have links with
each other in a pattern suggesting transitivity. More striking
is the asymmetry: for subgroups A, C, E, and F, the main
route to D or from it is through B, or else through the brokers
shown on the left side in Figure 1. The pattern is not absolute.
Not shown in Figure 3 are two direct links between C and D
and three between E and D. Even so, C has more linkage with
B through A and F than directly to B.
        This asymmetrically branching pattern is shown still
more clearly in Figure 4. Although only four of the seven subgroups are shown in Fig. 4, 22 of the 33 members are included,

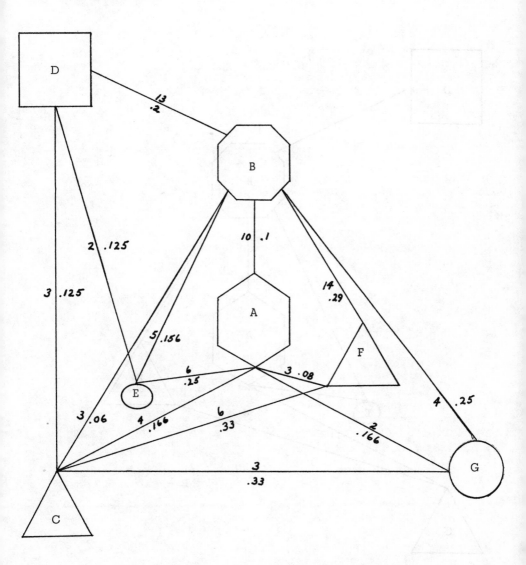

Figure 2. The subgroups only (28 of the 33), with numbers of direct links
and decimal fraction of maximum linkage possible shown.

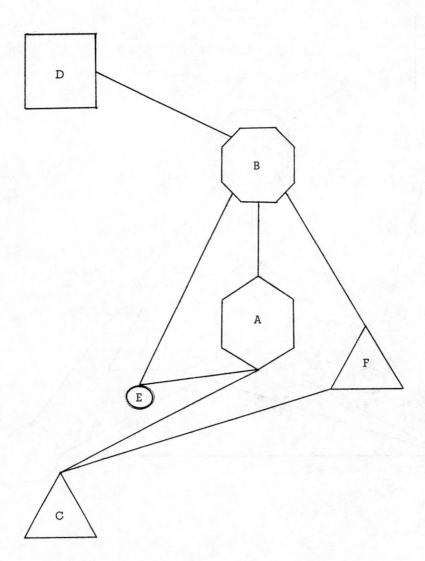

Figure 3. Six of the seven subgroups of the network, containing 78.78% of
population, with lines showing four or more links.

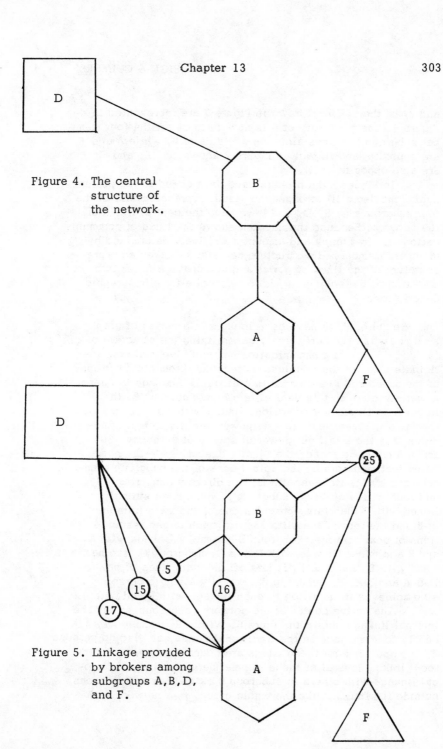

Figure 4. The central
structure of
the network.

Figure 5. Linkage provided
by brokers among
subgroups A, B, D,
and F.

and 37 of the 62 links drawn in Figure 3 are represented in
Figure 4. The centrality of B is now quite clear: the four member subgroup D stands alone on one side of B, while A and F
are opposite (and in fact as Figure 2 shows, C, E, and G
are also opposite to D).

In Figure 5 the brokers have been added to the picture
again, making still stronger the visual impression that in the
four subgroups A, B, D, and F we have the central frame of
the network. Because the network shows the lines of communication—its frequency and amount cognitively determined by
all of its members—its structure can also be taken as representative of the lines of power and authority. A fuller interpretation of the sociogram, however, calls for ethnographic
description.

Inside the       We have been looking at a series of graphs
subgroups.       progressively generalizing the structure of
                 a communication network. We will now an-
ticipate some of the conclusions reached through ethnography
of the group and sketch here in colloquial language the general
power structure in this deaf elite group: Subgroup B, the
largest, is the center of action, linked with more subgroups
than is any other, and drawing power directly from D. Subgroup D is the small but powerful source of authority. Subgroup A might be termed the "junior executives"—the name
being justified both by the actual ages of the subgroup members and by A's linkage with D, not directly but through B,
and four or five brokers. Subgroup F, even more strongly
linked with B than is A, provides one of the main liaisons
of B and the rest of the elite 33 with much larger associations of deaf persons. Subgroup E has major linkage with A
and B and minor linkage with D and C. Subgroup C also has
links with D, but like E, it lies off the main lines of power—
D-B-A and D-B-F. Subgroup G, actually a single person,
also achieves its position through linkage with B and with A.

The active center of the network, subgroup B, has the
internal linkage shown in Figure 6. Within B, members 1, 2,
and 14 form a clique in the traditional sense, as also do persons
7, 10, and 32; both these triads are bound together by reciprocal links. Several of these six members also have reciprocal linkage with others in subgroup B as well as with persons
outside it. Thus B, like the whole group, is a network with

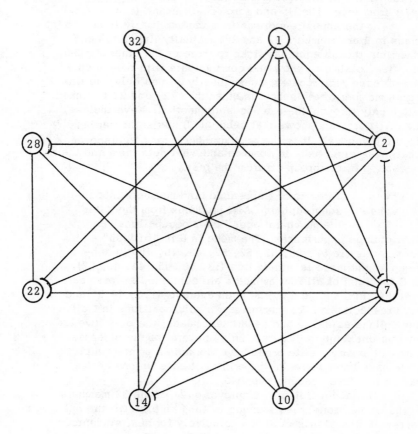

Figure 6. Linkage within the eight-member subgroup B.

Legend:   Mutual linkage between members -- ⬡——⬡

Link <u>from</u> r. member <u>to</u> l. member -- ⬡——(⬡

all four kinds of linkage: <u>mutual</u> (e.g. 1↔2); <u>to</u> or <u>toward</u> (e.g. 2→7); <u>from</u> (e.g. 10←1); and <u>zero</u> or no linkage (e.g. 1 / 32).

At the opposite extreme from the maximally linked triads in B are members 22 and 28, mutually linked to each other; but though each has links to three of the other members of B (i.e. claims to know and communicate with them), only one of these reciprocates; consequently 28 has only one link <u>from</u> a member of the subgroup other than 22, and 22 is linked into B only through 28—a tenuous connection. Nevertheless, the $CAT_{ij}$ program shows that subgroup B has eight members (Figure 6, above). It is the ethnographer's task to discover what these eight have in common and what sets them and their perception of the group off from the rest.

Linking       Three forces appear to bind members into the
factors.      subgroupings $CAT_{ij}$ produces from the data:
              the members' ages, their occupations, and
their college experiences. The mode in B is "fiftyish"—
actual ages are 57, 55, 52, 52, 52, 48, 46, 40. In subgroup A, the mode is mid-forties (53, 50, 45, 44, 40, 37).
In D the ages of all four members are contained in four years
—61-64. In C, E, and F, the ages average 41.3, 40.5, and
42.3 respectively. Six members of B hold positions in Gallaudet College as deans and department heads; the other two are
government printers—interestingly, several of the older members of the whole elite group have worked as printers and
some have been active in the printing trades unions before
having full time academic positions.

Gallaudet College, employer of 21 of the 33 members
of the whole group, was founded in 1864 and is still the only
four-year liberal arts college exclusively for deaf students.
(It now includes also programs in which a deaf person may
earn an advanced degree.) The college therefore has a much
more pervasive influence than that simply of employer on the
communication network, the power structure, and the ordering
of affairs in the Deaf community. Not surprisingly 29 of the
33 members of the group have earned degrees at Gallaudet and
two have bachelor's degrees from other colleges or universities.

The importance of college in the lives of all deaf
persons is unusual as well. Schein and Bushnaq (1962) found
that there was one deaf person in college for 68 in school (the
year 1960) but in the whole population, comparing school and

college numbers, the ratio is 1 to 11 instead of 1 to 68. The denominator of the latter fraction was certainly much larger in the 1930's and 1940's, when half the present group of 33 were in college. The number of those who having entered college continue to a degree is of course considerably smaller. Add to this the fact that 23 of the 33 have master's degrees, and 11 have earned doctorates or have all but the dissertation completed, and it becomes strikingly clear that a high educational level is a key characteristic of the deaf elite.

But this is not the whole account of how Gallaudet College affects the structure of this elite. What happens is that age and the associations afforded by this unique institution work together to produce strong bonds indeed. Half of the members of subgroup A have been interacting with each other for more than 20 years; six of the eight members in B have been in close contact for more than 30 years; and all four members of subgroup D have known each other for at least 45 years. A few in each subgroup, as classmates, have shared both sides of the initiatory rites of hazing and all the rest of class rivalry and other college activities. Many have been in close touch with each other since sharing one to five years (Gallaudet students often begin with a preparatory year before the freshman year) in college. These then are more than cognitively and communicatively linked subgroups of deaf individuals; they are "cohorts" proceeding through life in a social formation that resembles the age-sets described in classic anthropological studies.

Subgroup A (Figure 7), like B, has two maximally linked triads (or cliques): 6-11-31, and 6-23-31; it misses by one link (23's link to 11 is not reciprocated) a four-way saturation of linkage. The members' ages show a wider spread (37 for the youngest to 53) than in B, and although three of the six share overlapping college years, one member of A did not attend Gallaudet. Their years of graduation range from '51 to '76. In other respects A is a homogeneous group: all its members have the same employer, and four of the six work in offices near each other. Yet the remaining two, about as far removed when at work from the others as the campus layout permits, are not on the edges but in the center of this maximally linked subgroup network. There is more to linkage than the three forces so far examined.

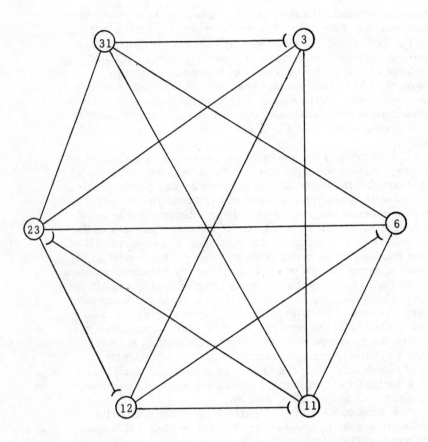

Figure 7. Linkage within the six-member subgroup A.

Legend:  Mutual linkage between members -- ◯——◯

Link from r. member to l. member -- ◯——(◯

Subgroups C and F (Figure 8) both consist of a triad, with two members mutually linked but the third with no row-one $CAT_{ij}$ linkage to the pair. In C, the ages might suggest such a structure (47, 42, 35); but in fact the linked pair are the eldest and the youngest members. Professional positions rather than age seem to explain the subgroup relationship in C. All three members of C have other than Gallaudet College employment, and their duties and contacts would seem to provide them with a similar cognitive perception of the rest of the whole group. In structure F is quite like C; the ages are 53, 44, and 30, with linkage reciprocal between the eldest and youngest; and the professional positions they hold and the nature of their work seem to be major factors in their relationship.

The members of subgroup E number only two; they have mutual linkage, work in close proximity, and are professionally in similar relationship to the activities of subgroups A and B.

Members of subgroup D (Figure 9) have the closest years of birth and college graduation (1910-1913 and 1932-1935). Three of the four members hold positions in the Federal government, with positions like Chief of Branch, Head of Division, Senior Consultant; the fourth is a department chairman in Gallaudet College. The positions of the first three with a powerful government department literally connect deaf society through this entire elite network with the power that federal funds, grants, programs, policies, projects, and agencies can provide. The location, activity, and organizational expertise of the remaining member supply direct linkage to other parts of the network. This member has mutual linkage with a broker and a member of B, has links to three other members of B and to a second broker, and has links from members of C and B—all this of course in addition to his internal linkage with the others in subgroup D.

To recapitulate what the graphs show: D is at the source of power. B directly wields much of that power, has 13 direct links with D and 6 more through brokers, controls important deanships and chairmanships within Gallaudet College, which since 1864 has both served and been served by the deaf elite. Subgroup A derives power from D through B and through brokers, and controls top positions in the newer precollege programs of Gallaudet College; viz. the Model

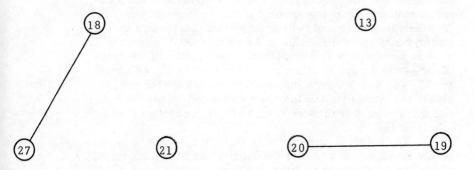

Figure 8. Linkage within subgroups C (on left) and F (on right).

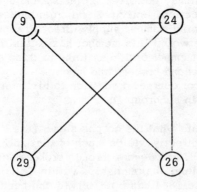

Figure 9. Linkage within  subgroup D.

Secondary School for the Deaf and Kendall Demonstration
Elementary School. The other subgroups and the brokers
connect closely with A and B. They also extend the power
of the elite group to outside networks; e.g. to such formal
groups as the National Association of the Deaf and the
National Fraternal Society of the Deaf. But this outward
connection of the whole elite is noteworthy; only four of
the 33 list fewer than four such organizational affiliations.

The list of organizations tied into this network and
the power it wields strengthens the demographers' contention that Deaf society is large and moreover already well
organized. Some organizations the 33 belong to or direct:

American Athletic Association of the Deaf
Alexander Graham Bell Association
Capital City Association of the Deaf
Comité International des Sports Silencieux
    (Familiarly, "The Deaf Olympics")
Conference of Executives of American Schools for
        the Deaf
Convention of American Instructors of the Deaf
Episcopal Conference of the Deaf (National)
Gallaudet College Alumni Association
International Association of Parents of Deaf
        Children
International Catholic Deaf Association
Maryland Association of the Deaf
Minnesota Association of the Deaf
National Association of the Deaf
National Congress of Jewish Deaf
National Fraternal Society of the Deaf
National Rehabilitation Association
Professional Rehabilitation Workers with the
        Adult Deaf
Registry of Interpreters for the Deaf
Southeastern Athletic Association of the Deaf
Union League of the Deaf
World Federation of the Deaf

The network of $CAT_{ij}$ linkage has helped select and
assemble some of the pertinent information about this elite
group and its structure, yet what has been related here is but
a glimpse of a societal structure. The 33-member group in-

cludes only one woman and one Black, though deafness occurs
indiscriminately; it is not at all certain that even these two
representatives of deaf minority groups would have been found
closely linked into an elite group a few years earlier. Although
the members of the elite group are not then representative of
the variety in the deaf population, the kinds of information
pulled together by the $CAT_{ij}$ technique can be used to deal
with other important ethnographic questions.

The language of      False and disingenuous statements
the network.         are commonly made about deaf society,
                     as they are about other linguistic
minorities. Falsehoods achieve wide circulation and general
acceptance long before their falsity can be revealed by careful
study of the characteristics of the group. This statement, often
heard by those who work with deaf persons in educational
settings, is an example: "In our schools we must teach proper
—or correct or 'straight'—language (i.e. English); sign language is useless to the deaf person who wants to get on in
the world; the deaf had better forget sign language and concentrate on learning proper English."
        Nothing could be more mistaken. Among the 33 deaf
persons in the elite group here described, the level of proficiency in English, especially written English, is high as
the educational attainment and present positions of the members would lead one to expect. However, there are members
of this group whose positions and successful functioning in
them call for clear and effective communication, which is not
always the same thing as correct formal English; many of
them deal daily with persons whose competence in the English
language is indeed slight. More important, though, is than
in the network and even more so within the subgroups, the
language used for the all-important internal linkage is some
variety of American Sign Language (Stokoe, Woodward). ASL,
moreover, may be accounted the native or first language of
13 of the 33, who began signing before age 6. Nineteen of the
33 report that their deafness occurred before their sixth year,
so that even if some of the 19 may not have acquired ASL until
after age 6, it may still be the first language in which they
could have unhampered, comfortable communication with their
peers, whatever the language native to their parents.
        A more powerful indicator that ASL is the central

interactive system, the language, of the elite group is a
product of the $CAT_{ij}$ analysis. Interviews to obtain the $CAT_{ij}$
input data (i.e. the ranking of all by each) were conducted
in ASL—in most cases, admittedly, a variety of ASL closer
to English in structure than unpidginized ASL (see Woodward
& Markowiz, chapter 1 above). One of the 33, however, did
not allow the interviewer to use signs or fingerspelling, used
no manual action in his responses, and insisted on the use
of spoken English by the interviewer. Although his first contact with some members of this group was made fourteen
years before the study was made, it often happened that one
of the others being interviewed, on seeing this person's name
on one of the cards to be ranked, would ask, "Who's that?"
The effect of this on the output has already been referred to:
the person in question has but three links to others, one link
from, and one reciprocal link. In the program output from its
processing of 33 arrangements of 33 numbers, the cognitive
category of interaction was almost non-indicated. Cognitively,
that is, the other members of the elite group did not consider
this person to be a member.

Furthermore, a converse example confirms that the
use of ASL as primary interactive language is essential to
the elite communication network. Another member of the 33
person group would be expected, because of factors already
looked at, to be an outsider also or a marginal member. Becoming deaf only two years before the study was made, he
had used sign language for only a few months before the first
interview. Not only was his acquaintance with the others of
short duration, but his experience with sign language was
equally new. Nevertheless, instead of showing up in the output as one on the perimeter or tenuously linked with a subgroup or two, he is to be found in the vital, young-executive
subgroup A. More than that, he belongs in both of the maximally linked triads of A and has additional linkage with those
outside this subgroup. His tragic death little more than one
year after the study began—from the same illness that caused
his deafness—was treated as a signal loss by the whole
group and a great personal loss to the Deaf community.

The importance of sign language as the channel for
communicating in this network is shown powerfully but
oppositely by these two instances. Early deafness, long
acquaintance with the group, or one's contemporaries in it,

the special educational experience of Gallaudet College, a
key position in the special institutions concerned with the
education of deaf persons, and even regular professional
contact with several members of the elite group—all these
do not suffice to tie one into the elite network, if one does
not use its language. Yet another person, with only a single one of these qualifications (professional position) but
who had a willingness to use and communicate in ASL, not
only belongs in the group but may even hold a special and
central position within it.

Sign language and its importance to the elite and the
whole Deaf society it serves are therefore not as they are
commonly represented by some who profess to "serve the
deaf." There are other misconceptions as well which the combination of ethnography and network studies can clear up.

**Who will
lead them?**     One misconception deals with the nature of
the deaf elite group itself. One of the
writers can recall hearing often, during his
introduction to the Gallaudet College milieu, this pontifical
refrain (here slightly paraphrased): "Oh, yes; so-and-so is
bright and able; but you're wrong if you think he is deaf. The
leaders among the deaf are the hard of hearing and the ones
who lost their hearing in their teens after they had language."

This often was the response to the writer's praise of
a deaf colleague, and was only thinly veiled contempt for the
deaf (usually pronounced "deef" in this context). And yet,
like other sociological generalizations based on little or no
study, it might contain truth as well as error and the very
objectionable patronizing tone.

Examining the elite network has brought to light a
strong age-set solidarity; it also reveals a dynamic: the composition of the group may be seen to change in time. If we
look at those among the 33 who are over sixty, we find one
who became deaf in childhood and the rest deafened in their
teens, with the average age of onset of deafness a little more
than 15 years. But in subgroup B, the next age cohort, the
average age at onset of deafness is 4.3 years, with three of
the eight members of B born deaf. And when all those in the
whole elite group under 40 years of age are considered, a
total of eight, we find four were born deaf, two others lost
their hearing at five and six, and none could hear after age
eight.

If it was once true, say thirty or forty years ago, that
the leaders in the Deaf community were deafened, not deaf, it
is quite clear from this study that those who lead tend to be
those born deaf or becoming deaf in infancy. And if hard of
hearing persons once had roles of importance in the affairs of
Deaf Americans, it is not true now. Only one of the 33 considers "hard of hearing" a more appropriate description than
"deaf" (but this goes with other indications of non-member-
ship in the group considered above). Decibel ratings of loss
of hearing, where available, bear out this self-judgment. The
sociograms presented here confirm recent evidence that there
is an emerging awareness of and pride in the community and
its control of power (Vernon 1974). Although looking at the
ages of onset of deafness in the age groups (over sixty to
under forty) represented in the study seems to show a tendency
for fewer late-onset and more early-onset members in the elite
group, this is probably not a direct function of passing time
but much more likely a return to the situation in American (and
in French and other continental) Deaf society that obtained
before the late nineteenth century oralist movement banished
sign language instruction and literally wiped out a considerable
educated community of deaf persons in one or two generations.
     One of the most interesting areas for further study is
that portion of the Deaf community in which the acquisition of
the group's language and acculturation can take place earliest
and most naturally; i.e. among families in which deafness is
inherited and present in every generation. Among the great
majority of deaf persons—nine out of ten deaf children have
hearing parents—full socialization into the group is likely to
take place later, at school age, or at school leaving age
(Meadow 1972). The powerful effect of enculturation within
the child's immediate family instead of at school and of
learning the language and standards of the group in infancy
instead of much later can be seen clearly in the elite group:
six of the 33 have deaf parents; this is about twice the proportion in the deaf population generally. All six of these and
seven more members of the whole group began signing before
the age of 6. From the structure, composition, and dynamics
of the elite deaf network, it appears not only that the deaf
are increasingly leading and managing their own affairs but
also that those deaf from birth or infancy, those with deaf
parents, and those who began signing with others early in

life are emerging as leaders in this society. The inference
that ought to be made by teachers and parents of deaf children is very clear: those deaf children not enculturated
naturally in a home with deaf signing parents will have the
best chance of rising in the society to which they will
inevitably belong if they begin learning and using sign
language as a natural language as early as possible.

## REFERENCES

Bernard, H. Russell, & Peter D. Killworth
   1973    On Social Structure of Ocean-going Research
           Vessels & Other Important Things, Social Science
           Research 2, 145-184.

Driver, Harold E.
   1973    Cross Cultural Studies, in Handbook of Social
           & Cultural Anthropology, Honigman ed. (Chicago,
           Rand McNally), ch. 8.

Killworth, Peter D., & H. Russell Bernard
   1974    $CAT_{ij}$: A New Sociometric Technique Applied to a
           Prison Living-Unit, Human Organization 33:4.

Meadow, Kathryn P.
   1972    Sociolinguistics, Sign Language, and the Deaf
           Sub-Culture, in Psycholinguistics and Total Communi-
           cation, O'Rourke ed. (Washington, American Annals
           of the Deaf), 19-33.

Nash, Jeff
   1975    Hearing Parents of Deaf Children: A Typology,
           Sign Language Studies 7, 163-180.

Schein, Jerome D.
   1968    The Deaf Community (Washington, Gallaudet College).

- - - - -, & Sulieman Bushnaq
   1962    Higher Education for the Deaf in the United States,
           American Annals of the Deaf 107, 416-420.

Schein, Jerome D., & Marcus Delk
   1974    The Deaf Population in the United States (Silver
           Spring, MD, National Association of the Deaf).

Stokoe, William C.
   1970    Sign Language Diglossia, Studies in Linguistics 21,
           27-41; repr. in Semiotics & Human Sign Languages
           (Mouton, 1972), 154-167.

Vernon, McCay
   1974    Deaf Militancy (editorial), American Annals of the
           Deaf 119, 15.

Woodward, James C.
   1973    Inter-Rule Implication in American Sign Language,
           Sign Language Studies 3, 47-56.

   1974    A Report on the Montana-Washington Implicational
           Research, Sign Language Studies 4, 77-101.

PART FOUR

BIOLOGICAL AND INTERACTIVE ROOTS OF SIGN LANGUAGES

Studying languages as they connect with cultures and connect
and separate members of cultures adds a necessary social
dimension to the study of linguistic codes. But just as important
and possibly prior logically is studying the psychophysical
functions that make language possible at all. The fields of
perception and of voluntary and involuntary muscle action,
not to mention cognition and communication, are too immense
for this last section; but there are good reasons to believe
that studies in these areas will be especially rewarding.

Patricia Siple in Chapter 14 reminds us that how we see
is fundamental to how we use vision to see language expressed—
especially when hearing is inoperative; that handshapes and
action are seen by different structures (compare pp. 14-17 above);
and even that signers' eyes may be telling us to look harder at
faces than at hands.

Adam Kendon's chapter clearly shows that the roots of sign
expression lie deeper than those of spoken expression, and
hence that gestural behavior may have shaped the internal parts
of language more and earlier than did vocal output. Chapter 15
also introduces a new area of study, interaction: beneath language is communication and beneath both is interaction, the
behavior of organisms controlled by a feedback system.

The last chapter could well have been first, for it shows
us an aboriginal model of language. The children described by
Susan Goldin-Meadow and Heidi Feldman heard no language
spoken and saw no language signed, yet by the end of the study
they "had language" in their gestures. Two factors explain:
like all children they were born with human language propensity;
and like no others in their circumstances they could interact
with fellow beings ready and able to treat their gesturing attempts
from the first as language becoming.

PART FOUR: 14

# VISUAL CONSTRAINTS for SIGN LANGUAGE COMMUNICATION

Patricia Siple

Language        Production of the signals of any language
& modality.     must to some extent depend on the modality
                of that production. The vocal apparatus can
produce only a limited range of all the sounds that a human
ear can detect, and there is certainly a limit to the possible
duration and sequencing of these sounds. Similarly, the production of language signals must be related to the perceptual
system receiving them. A difference between two sounds must
be a difference that the hearer can immediately, accurately,
and automatically detect before that difference can be used to
convey a distinction between two elements of a language. The
production of language signals, therefore, must be constrained
by the apparatus used to receive them. We would expect that
sign  languages of the deaf would evolve in such a way that
their units would become less perceptibly ambiguous. Since
sign languages are received and initially processed by the
visual system, we would expect that the rules for the formation of signs of a sign language would be constrained by
the limits of the visual system.

One of the important limits of human vision is that
it is not equally acute in all parts of the field that it takes in.
When we focus on a point, we can see a great deal of
detail in the area immediately surrounding that point, because the image of the point and its area falls on the most

319

sensitive part of the retina of the eye, the fovea. Farther
away from the fixated point, we can see less and less fine
detail.[2] We might then expect the formation of signs in a
sign language to depend on where they are located in the
visual field of the sign receiver. Further, if the person to
whom the signs are addressed watches the signer by focus-
ing on a particular spot, we might expect fine detail in
the signs to be important in that location. Signs in that
location should differ minimally from other signs made there
by smaller changes than do signs made in places farther
away from the point of fixation, where such fine detail
would not be detected.

Our observations indicate that signers do indeed
have a fixed place of focus. When deaf signers are conversing, the receiver tends to look at the sender's face.
Eye movements that do occur tend to be small excursions
about the signer's face. This may seem strange, given
that sign is a gestural language in which the hands have a
large role, until we realize that the face gives very important cues to the meaning of a signed utterance (Bellugi &
Fischer 1973, Liddell 1977, Baker 1976). We can use this
information about where a person attending to signing
habitually looks, along with the knowledge that we have
about the human visual system, to make predictions about
the form that signs will take in any sign language.

Relative acuity.    In order to recognize a sign, a
                    viewer must be able to discrimi-
nate that sign from others similar to it. Stokoe (1960: 41f)
posited three aspects as constituting the ways in which
one sign (morpheme) can differ from another: configuration
of the hand or dez, location or tab, and motion or sig.
[More recently, what acts, where it acts, and its action
(see Chapter 1.)]    We should expect the limits of the
visual system for perception of fine detail to affect the degree to which these aspects of signs themselves are finely
or grossly different.

---

[2] This is easily tested: Focus on a word in the middle of this
page; words immediately around can be read easily without a
shift in fixation, but those farther away are indistinct.

Visual acuity, one limit of the system, is measured by various methods. Most familiar is the Snellen chart of letters of graduated sizes, commonly found in most doctors' offices. Optimal acuity occurs when the observer looks straight at a letter to focus the figure on the fovea. Acuity is then reported as what the eye sees at 20 feet relative to what the normal eye sees; thus, 20/20 acuity is normal, and an eye with 20/80 acuity sees the same detail at 20 feet that the normal eye sees at 80 feet. Another method of measurement uses a broken circle, known as the Landholt C, presented at a given distance and under a standard level of illumination. Acuity is then defined as the size of the gap necessary in order for the observer to determine whether the gap is at top, bottom, left, or right.

Acuity is best at the point of fixation; it drops off rapidly as the distance from that point increases. Visual acuity across the visual field has been measured as a function of this distance from the fixation point by Mandelbaum and Sloan (1947), using the Landholt C. Their data for photopic illumination (like that of a normally lit room) is shown in Figure 1 as the relation of acuity to angular distance. The distance from foveal fixation is measured in degrees of angle, since this method relates distance from the eye to distance away from the center of fixation however near or far the visual field. Thus the relative acuity is the same 20 inches away from center at ten feet of distance as 4 inches away from center at a distance of two feet. A relative acuity of 0.5 means that the size of the gap in the Landholt C must be approximately twice that needed to be perceptible in central vision. Figure 1 shows that this level of acuity is only about 2 degrees from the center of vision, and that acuity 10 degrees from center is reduced to one-tenth that at the point of fixation. Other methods of measuring acuity, e.g. use of the Snellen chart, produce similar findings (Ludvigh 1941).

These findings have direct implication for the reception of sign language. Suppose a person receiving a sign language communication is placed six feet from the signer. (Six feet is chosen here because observation shows that this is a good approximation of the distance signers actually choose when in conversation. This six foot

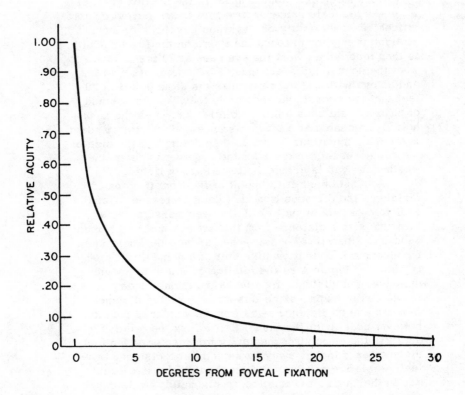

Figure 1.   Relative visual acuity as a function of degrees
of eccentricity from the center of the fovea
(From Mandelbaum & Sloan 1947).

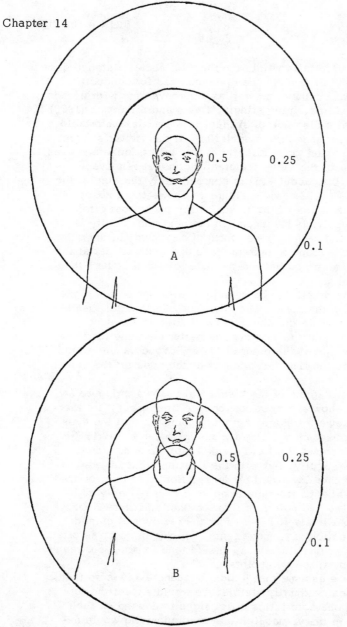

Figure 2. Zones of relative acuity around two different
fixation points: 2A, point of fixation between eyes,
2B, point of fixation assuming a downward cast
of the viewer's eyes.

distance also falls within the range of social distance described by Hall (1966), the distance used for conducting
impersonal business as well as for conversing with friends
and associates. Interestingly, Davis and Silverman (1970)
report that a distance of six feet is the most comfortable
distance for speechreading.) Now, if the viewer six feet
from the signer looks directly at the latter's nose and eyes,
the center of the face, the area of greatest relative
acuity (1.0 to about 0.5) is approximately the size of the
face (sin $4^{\circ}$ X 72" = 5"). Figure 2a shows three zones
around the center of the face. Within the inmost circle
relative acuity is maximum. In the next zone acuity is
between one half and one fourth of maximum. In the outer
zone acuity drops to one fourth to one tenth of that at the
fixation point; and beyond the outer circle it is less than
one tenth.

Fine detail can be seen by the viewer on the signer's
face and in the zone around the face. Some detail can be
picked up out to the shoulders and down to the upper
chest, as acuity in this zone is better than one fourth of
maximum. But at the outer circle or beyond, a line would
have to be ten times as wide as at the nose for the signer
to see it.

The diagram of the visual field shown in Figure 2a
does not show the most comfortable line of sight for the
normal viewer. Design engineers point out that the eyes
naturally assume a downward cast (Morgan et al. 1963).
Figure 2b shows the field divided into the same zones
of relative acuity, but with the fixation point lowered to
allow for this downward tendency. Note that this lowered
gaze still keeps the face in an area of reasonably high
acuity. The two points of fixation used in Figure 2 are
those most likely to be used by the receiver of signed
communication. Eye movements, which can occur as often
as every 200 milliseconds, should tend to occur between
and around these two points.

If we assume that a sign language evolves so that
it becomes maximally visible, we would expect the formational characteristics of its signs to depend on their
location in the visual field. In particular, we would expect differences in fine detail to be more important in the

regions of higher acuity. Small differences in position, in
motion, in number of fingers and overall handshapes can
be easily detected in such areas. Farther out from fixation
point, only gross differences in these aspects of a sign
can be detected. We would expect to find pairs of signs
made in the areas about the face or upper chest to be
visually more similar, i.e. to differ  in a less detailed
way, than signs made in the areas of lower acuity. Thus
in high  acuity areas, we might expect to find pairs of
signs that differ only by the number of fingers extended
(e.g. G-hand versus H-hand, or RED/SWEET in ASL). We
would also expect to find a small difference in location
(e.g. chin to cheek or nose to upper lip) to be a minimal
distinction between signs in the area of highest acuity.
The set of signs made in the regions of lower acuity
should not contain such pairs. We would expect to find
there only gross distinctions like the difference between
a closed hand and an open hand (A/B or 5). In addition,
we know that many signs in ASL are made in the open
area in front of the signer's body. It is assumed that
most of these signs are made above some plane as lower
limit. While it might be thought that a reasonable lower
bound for these signs might be the plane of the forearm
resting horizontally, acuity data would lead us to predict
a slightly higher plane—one nearer the end of the sternum.
A look at the Dictionary of ASL (Stokoe, Casterline, &
Croneberg 1976 [1965]) will show that these predictions
are confirmed.

Conditions of      The amount of information that can
low acuity.        be taken in from peripheral areas of
                   vision is small compared with that
gathered near the point of foveal vision. Yet signs are
made in these peripheral areas. As we have seen, perception of these signs can be enhanced by keeping minimal
distinctions large. Perceptual data indicate, however,
that other properties of the visual sign stimulus can be
utilized by the sign system to maximize information that
the eye can gather in areas of low acuity.

It has been shown that large motions increase the
probability of perceiving the less-detailed information to

be obtained from peripheral areas (Kulikowski 1971).
Such large motions may, however, detract from information
received in areas of high acuity, where small motions
enhance the perception of this more detailed information.
Thus we would predict that signs made on or about the
face and upper body will have small motions and that
signs made off and to the sides of the body will have
large motions. Furthermore, when these large motions are
made, we would expect them to be made along the vertical and horizontal axes, since acuity is greater along
these axes than for other orientations (See Springer 1972).

Another variable that will increase the amount of
information obtainable in an area of low acuity is the
amount of redundancy in the information presented. Cherry
(1966: 308) has broadly defined redundancy as "a property
given to a source by virtue of an excess of rules...
whereby it becomes increasingly likely that mistakes in
reception will be avoided." Redundancy can occur as the
repetition of elements or as the addition of elements to
convey information already implicit in the stimulus.
There are two ways that redundancy can affect the communication of information (Coombs et al.1970). First,
there can be redundancy within a stimulus; i.e. an overlap of information can be produced by increasing the
number of elements or features in the stimulus so that
more than one element conveys the same information.
Such redundancy will increase the ability to receive the
information over and above the deficit produced by increasing the number of elements making up the stimulus.
This is accomplished by incorporating within the recognition system a  set of rules that allow it to use the
incoming information more efficiently. For example, in
the phonetic alphabet used for voice communication
(e.g. saying "Able, Baker, Charlie..." for 'A, B, C...'),
the complexity of each of the stimuli has been increased
over that of the names of the English letters; i.e. a
multi-syllablic word has been substituted for each letter
name. The listener has a chance of recognizing one or
more parts of the word, each one of which will help in
inferring the letter represented. The probability of
recognizing individual letters has thus been increased

by increasing internal stimulus redundancy.

Redundancy can also be thought of with respect to the entire set of possible stimuli. Redundancy between two stimuli is determined by the proportion of elements of one stimulus that can overlap with (convey the same information as) the other stimulus. This concept can be extended to a larger set of stimuli. While a great amount of redundancy within a stimulus will aid in its recognition, redundancy among stimuli will decrease the ability to discriminate one stimulus from another and thus decrease recognition ability. In the English alphabet, for example, many letter names have common acoustic elements: BCDEGPTVZ.

Such sound similarities have been eliminated from the phonetic alphabet; no syllable can be found in more than one letter name. Lack of this type of redundancy enables the listener to discriminate letters in a sequence, provided the listener gets some information about each letter presented.

Both these aspects of redundancy can be directly applied to the transmission of information in a sign language. We would expect these considerations to become especially important in areas where acuity is greatly reduced. First, we would expect a greater amount of internal redundancy within a sign in these areas. There are at least two ways that this redundancy can be incorporated: elements can be added by using two hands instead of one; and information presented to one side of the visual field can be duplicated on the other side. The latter doubling of information requires that the handshapes and movements on each side are symmetrical. If the viewer expects this symmetry (i.e. if it is a rule of sign formation), then the probability of correctly receiving the information and recognizing the sign will be increased. We would expect therefore the signs made in peripheral, low acuity areas to be two-handed symmetrical signs. Because signs are produced sequentially at a rapid rate in natural conversation, the sign receiver also needs to discriminate very quickly between similar signs. Therefore, as in the phonetic alphabet, we should expect to find in the large peripheral two-handed symmetrical signs more redundancy than in those signs made on or near the face and upper chest.

Considerations of redundancy may also help to explain certain characteristics that have been noted in ASL.
There is often a great deal of repetition of individual signs
in signed discourse. While some kinds of repetition have
been shown to serve grammatical functions (Fischer 1973,
Supalla 1977), others remain puzzling. Nevertheless, repetition is an easy way to increase redundancy. An examination of non-syntactic repetition in a sign language might
be expected to show that it occurs most often within a
set of signs that are difficult to recognize or predict, but
which are important for understanding a signer's meaning.
We would also expect more of this kind of repetition
under adverse signing conditions or when the message is
very important.

Signs in ASL are sometimes formed from the combination of two existing signs; e.g. the sign for 'brother' was
formerly signed by successively signing BOY and SAME.
Such a compound originally maintained the locations and
hand configurations of the two constituent signs and joined
them with smooth transitional motion. As sign language
has changed, however, the forms of these compounds have
changed in systematic ways. In their original form, compound signs tended to be large signs, since they comprise
two different signs; over time the location of one or both
parts tends to change so that the two locations are closer
or become one. Often too the new location or locations of
the sign are in an area of higher visual acuity. In other
cases, the sign becomes more symmetrical, both hands
assuming the same hand shape and movement changing
toward symmetry. (For confirmation of these predictions,
see Frishberg 1975) Such changes, by increasing the internal redundancy, make the sign more easily recognizable.
To the extent that a sign language makes use of compound
signs, we should expect to find similar changes toward
increasing internal redundancy in any sign language.

Illumination   Two other variables are known to affect
& contrast.    acuity: overall illumination (Pirenne 1962)
               and the contrast in luminance between
different parts of the visual stimulus. In fact, the amount
of contrast necessary for perception can be viewed as a

measure of visual acuity (Westheimer 1972). Since these
variables tend to be environmentally controlled and to some
extent random over a wide range during signing situations,
we would not expect them to provide constraints on the formation of signs in a sign language. We might, however,
expect that the behavior of the signer and perhaps that of
the viewer would be affected by them.

      Below a certain limit, when illumination decreases
visual acuity decreases, but this decrease in acuity is not
constant across the visual field (Mandelbaum & Sloan
1947). In fact, at some point the periphery becomes more
sensitive than the fovea, because the rods, the receptor
cells in the periphery of the retina, are more sensitive at
lower light levels than are the cones in the central portion
of the eye.[3] There are several reasons why we should not
expect this reversal to affect sign formation. First, it does
not occur until illumination is very low—below the level of
illumination on a starry moonlit night. Also, while the periphery is more sensitive than the fovea at these light levels,
actual acuity at the most sensitive part of the periphery is
less than 8 percent of the acuity for the center of the eye
under the light conditions shown in Figure 1. Because we
see so poorly in such low illumination, we would expect
very little signing to occur, and thus would not expect sign
formation to adapt itself to such viewing conditions. For
the most part, a sign language will be used under conditions
like those for which Figure 1 holds. If a language evolves so
that it is efficient under conditions in which it is most likely
to be used, the curve of Figure 1 should be of use in predic-
ting the form of the language. On those rare occasions when
signing must occur in low levels of illumination, we would
expect the signer or the viewer to compensate for this reduction in visual sensitivity. Westheimer (1972) has pointed
out that such compensation can occur by increasing the time
duration of the stimulus. He states that increasing duration
can increase acuity for durations up to two seconds under
some conditions. We would therefore expect the signer to

---

[3] You can demonstrate this to yourself on a starry night. First
fixate on a star and note a dim star nearby; then try to fixate
on the dim star. Surprisingly it will disappear as it comes
into the center of vision!

slow down the rate of sign production. We might also expect the viewer to move closer to the signer. However,
this distance is often strongly controlled by physical and
social conditions. If no compensation were made for the
low level of light, we would expect the viewer to make
errors in interpreting the signs.

Contrast, as noted, may be viewed as a measure
of acuity; instead of widening the gap in a C or the width
of a line, it is possible to increase the contrast between
figure and ground to make a pattern (e.g. stripes) easily
detectable. Such contrast data, if determined from fovea
to periphery, would take the same form as the acuity relation
shown in Figure 1. Data from Campbell and Gubisch (1966)
indicate that the kind of information picked up by the peripheral area of the eye requires much higher contrast for
detection than that picked up in the central area. Thus, we
would again make the same predictions as for those based
on acuity data. We would expect the sign system to require
finer discriminations to be made to detect signs seen in
the central portion of the visual field than for peripheral
signs.

Contrast level certainly varies from  one signing
situation to another. As with luminance, we would expect
a sign language to have reached a maximum efficiency for
the normally found range of contrast levels. If for some
reason the contrast were lower than usual, we might expect
the signer to slow the rate of sign production in order to
increase acuity for the viewer. If the signing rate were
not reduced, we would expect the viewer to make more
errors in recognition. When it is important that the viewer
understand the signer with low or zero error rate, the
signer can increase contrast by wearing dark, solid-color
clothing. This is most important in situations where the
signer has little control over rate of signing, as when interpreting spoken discourse for deaf audiences. Instructions
to interpreters usually suggest that they wear dark clothing.

Summary.  The. assumption has been made that a language
               will be shaped to some extent by the sensory
system used to perceive its signals. A sign language is received by the human visual system, and so knowledge about

that system can be used to predict certain constraints that
may operate in a sign language. From data on visual acuity
we predict much finer distinctions will be made in the handshape, location, and movement of signs performed near the
center of viewer vision, i.e. signer's face and upper body,
than in the same aspects of signs farther away from center
of fixation. We predict that signs made in the outer, more
peripheral zones will have large movements tending to follow
horizontal or vertical axes, in order that the viewer's ability
to detect differences may be enhanced. In addition, from
data on redundancy in information transmission and reception
we predict that signs made in peripheral areas of vision will
be or will tend to become signs made with two hands instead
of one and symmetrical in handshape and movement; signs
with these characteristics are not very similar to one another.
Luminance and contrast are not expected to affect the sign
production system itself except in the sense that the system
should make itself understandable under normal viewing
situations. Abnormal situations would be expected to affect
either the rate of signing or the amount of information obtained by the viewer.

## REFERENCES

Baker, C.L.
    1976     What's Not on the Other Hand in American
             Sign Language. Papers from the 12th Regional
             Meeting of the Chicago Linguistic Society.

Bellugi, U., & S. Fischer
    1973     A Comparison of Sign Language and Spoken
             Language, Cognition 1, 173-200.

Campbell, F. W., & R. W. Gubisch
    1966     Optical Quality of the Human Eye, Journal
             of Physiology (London) 186, 558-578.

Cherry, C.
    1966    On Human Communication, 2nd edition (Cam-
            bridge, Massachusetts, M.I.T. Press).

Coombs, C.H., R.M. Dawes, & A. Tversky
    1970    Mathematical Psychology: An Elementary Intro-
            duction (Englewood Cliffs, N.J., Prentice-Hall).

Davis, H., & S.R. Silverman
    1970    Hearing and Deafness (New York, Holt).

Fischer, S.D.
    1973    Two Processes of Reduplication in American Sign
            Language, Foundations of Language 9, 469-480.

Frishberg, N.
    1975    Arbitrariness and Iconicity: Historical Change
            in American Sign Language, Language 51, 696-719.

Hall, E.T.
    1966    The Hidden Dimension (New York, Doubleday)

Kulikowski, J.S.
    1971    Some Stimulus Parameters Affecting Spatial &
            Temporal Resolution of Human Vision, Vision
            Research 11, 83-93.

Liddell, S.F.
    1977    An Investigation into the Syntactic Structures
            of American Sign Language. Ph.D. dissertation,
            University of California at San Diego.

Ludvigh, E.
    1941    Extrafoveal Visual Acuity as Measured with
            Snellen Test Letters, American Journal of
            Opthalmology 24, 303.

Mandelbaum, J., & L.L. Sloan
    1947    Peripheral Visual Acuity, American Journal of
            Opthalmology 30, 581-588.

Morgan, C.T., J.S.Cook, A.Chapanis, & M.W.Lund
    1963     Human Engineering: Guide to Equipment Design
             (New York, McGraw Hill).

Pirenne, M.H.
    1962     Visual Acuity, in The Eye, Davson ed. (N.Y.,
             Academic Press), Volume 2, 175-195.

Springer, R.M.
    1972     Neural Factors in Visual Anisotrophy.
             Unpublished manuscript.

Stokoe, W.C.
    1960     Sign Language Structure: An Outline of the
             Visual Communication Systems of the American
             Deaf, Studies in Linguistics: Occasional
    [1978]   Papers, 8. [Revised, Silver Spring, MD, Linstok]

- - - - - , D.C.Casterline, & C.G.Croneberg
    1976     A Dictionary of American Sign Language on
             Linguistic Principles (Silver Spring, Maryland,
             Linstok Press). (First edition, Washington,
             D.C., Gallaudet College Press, 1965)

Supalla, T.
    1977     Verb/Noun Distinctions in American Sign
             Language. Paper presented at the National
             Symposium on Sign Language Research and
             Teaching, Chicago, May-June.

Westheimer, G.
    1972     Visual Acuity and Spatial Modulation Thresh-
             olds, in Handbook of Sensory Physiology,
             Jameson & Hurvich eds. (New York, Springer-
             Verlag), Volume 7, part 4, 170-187.

PART FOUR: 15

GESTICULATION, SPEECH, & THE GESTURE THEORY OF
LANGUAGE ORIGINS

Adam Kendon

The gesture      Gordon Hewes (1973a) has revived the argu-
theory.          ment that speech is a late development in
                 human evolution and that the first manifes-
tations of a language capacity were in systems of gesture. He
adduces several different lines of evidence in support. First
he points out that language in its first form would have made
use of such neurological and anatomical equipment as the
prelinguistic hominid already had available to it. The neurological and anatomical specializations associated with speech
(Lenneberg 1967, Geschwind 1972) would have evolved only
after the evolutionary shift in the direction of linguistic-like
behavior. As Mayr (1968) has pointed out, behavioral change
is always the first kind of change to take place in evolution—
morphological change following later. Hewes argues that the
findings of the Gardners (1971),in which the chimpanzee Washoe
has been shown capable of learning some elements of a gesture
language, support the contention that in terms of brain structure the pre-linguistic hominid would have had the cognitive
capacity for a linguistic form of communication, even though
it did not have the anatomical specializations suitable for
speech. Hewes also points out that chimpanzees exhibit naturally much behavior that could be regarded as a substrate
for gestural language; e.g. they orient to and address behavior
towards specific other individuals, they show certain limited
amounts of gestural communication, and they can make use
of each other's postures and incipient locomotory movements
in gaining information from one another about the environment
(Menzel 1971). Hewes also refers to the work of Lieberman (1973)
and colleagues, which suggests that the vocal tract of Neanderthal man was not suitable for the production of fully articulated
speech. Yet evidence of burial practices, tool making, and hunting
among these people makes it highly likely that they were capable

334

of linguistic communication of some sort. Hewes suggests that it is plausible to suppose that this was a predominantly gestural form.

Hewes further points out that comparative study of the vocal systems of primates and humans, both of their functions and of the neurological apparatus that controls them, has made it clear that the call systems of primates that have been regarded in earlier treatments as a possible substrate for the emergence of speech (e.g. Hockett and Ascher 1964) are not related to the vocalizations used in speech by humans (Reynolds 1968). On the other hand, the later-alization of both the speech function in the brain and of the control of skilled movements as suggested by the development of handed-ness suggests that we should consider the possibility that there is a close association between the development of speech and the development of skilled manipulation of the environment. In another paper (1973b) Hewes has elaborated on this point, suggesting that there is a close relationship between the development of tool use and the development of language, a relationship that becomes much easier to comprehend if language first emerged as a gestural system. In a summary of some recent studies of lateralization, Kimura (1973) has pointed out that the dominant hand is involved not only more heavily in skilled movements but it is also used predominantly in the hand movements that accompany speech. Furthermore, there is some indication from the literature on brain damage that the same lesion may affect both motor skill sequences and sentence construction, thus providing further support for the intimate relation between environmental manipulation and language, a relationship much easier to understand if language first appeared in gestural form.

Hewes' position depends upon the view that the communicative functions of language are not intrinsically bound up with the pro-perties of the linguistic code that is made use of by speech. If it were shown, therefore, that linguistic communicative functions carried out by bodily movement or other means besides speech were secondarily derived from speech and did not function as systems in their own right, his argument would be greatly weakened. There are many different functions of language. However, the most dis-tinctive of its communicative functions seems to be that it enables users to _tell_ each other things. That is, it enables users to give accounts of their thoughts, feelings, perceptions, and memories, and of things that may not be happening at the time of the telling and which may not be witnessed directly. This function, which we shall here call the _reportive_ function, combined with a capacity

to communicate reportively about virtually anything, would appear
to be the feature of language which sets it off most distinctly
from all other communicative systems. For Hewes' position to be
sustained, it is of great importance to know whether systems of
gesture can function reportively in this sense and whether they
do so after their own fashion, and not as a system derived from
speech, as writing clearly is, for example.

It has been well known for some time that sign languages have
been used by such peoples as the North American Plains Indians
(Mallery 1881, 1972) and the Australian Aborigines (Roth 1897,
Mountford 1938, Berndt 1940, Meggitt 1954). Also well known are
the sign systems used by the deaf; and extensive and sometimes
apparently autonomous use is made of gesture in communication
by Latin peoples, especially in Southern Italy (di Jorio 1832, Rosa
1929, Lyall 1956). Recent intensive work on some of these systems
has made it clear that while in some cases (such as the sign
systems used by Trappist Monks; see Barakat 1975) such sign languages are derived from spoken language, so that they may be
thought of as a kind of "gesture writing; " in other cases the gesture system is organized according to its own principles that have
little in common with spoken language and yet the system is able
to operate, because of sufficient elaboration both in vocabulary
and syntax, with much the same effectiveness. Thus La Mont West
(1960) undertook a very detailed study of a version of a North American Plains Indian sign language and showed that it could be seen
as an almost wholly autonomous system. He pointed out that its
grammatical structure makes use of spatial rather than temporal
relations and that extensive use is made of visual onomatopoeia.
It seems highly likely that the sign languages of the Australian
Aborigines are similarly elaborate and autonomous (West 1963).

Extensive work has now been done on sign languages of the
deaf. From this it has become clear that here also we encounter
systems that are organized according to principles quite different from those of spoken languages, and that also function fully
as effectively (Stokoe 1972, Cicourel and Boese 1972, Schlesinger
1971).

These findings lend strength to the view that the capacity to
communicate reportively is not dependent upon specific ability
of speech, though it might be argued that these sign languages,
autonomous in their organization though they may be, are but
manifestations of an inventiveness that has arisen as a result of
capacities made available through the development of language
and that they tell us nothing about how language itself may have

first emerged. However, if it could be shown that a proclivity to communicate reportively by gesture is spontaneously present in the human species, this would make it much less likely that sign languages are consciously developed artifacts designed to meet particular situations. It would suggest that reportive communication by gesture is at least as fundamental a process as is speech and that, at the very least, reportive communication in gestural and vocal form emerged concurrently.

Tervoort (1961) has described how reportive communication by gesture arises quite spontaneously among very young deaf children. He shows that they very readily invent mimetic forms in movement to represent things they wish to refer to and that these forms, in some circumstances, come to be used by several children. As they do so they undergo a rapid process of simplification and conventionalization and they may become fully incorporated as a part of a shared sign system which functions in a fully reportive fashion. This would suggest that human beings will fashion a language out of whatever behavioral materials there are to hand, and that this will be done gesturally if no spoken language or the capacity to produce or receive one is available.

Another line of evidence will be pursued in this paper. We shall review findings from some detailed studies of the organization of bodily movements that occur concurrently with speech. As we shall see, this work shows that this bodily activity is so intimately integrated with the activity of speaking that we cannot say that the one is dependent upon the other. Speech and movement appear together, as manifestations of the same process of utterance. That is, in the translation of "ideas" into observable behavior, typically addressed to specific others and which is read by those others as reportive of these ideas, the output that results is manifested in both speech and movement. Circumstances of utterance may affect the degree to which either is enhanced, but where gesture is used to the exclusion of speech we see but a special emphasis of an ability all of us possess, an ability as fundamental, if not as usually well developed, as speech itself.

Speech and body motion relationships in the utterance. When a person speaks there is always some movement in the body, besides the movements of the jaws and lips that are directly involved in speech production. This speech-associated movement may be slight and comprise not more than a minor bobbing of the head or occasional movements of the eyes and eyebrows. Quite often,

however, movement may be observed in other parts of the body
as well, most notably in the arms and hands. These movements
may become more complex and extensive and, when they do, we
shall speak of the one making them as <u>gesticulating</u>.

Ekman and Friesen (1969) have distinguished this kind of movement with the use of the term "illustrator". We shall use the term
"gesticulation" in preference, however, for it is a more neutral
term and it implies nothing about the possible relationship between
these movements and concurrent speech. Furthermore, "illustrator"
suggests a discrete entity. "Gesticulation", on the other hand,
refers to a process of activity and as such seems more appropriate
for what is, after all, a very fluid and dynamic phenomenon.

Gesticulation is to be distinguished from movements such as
those engaged in when the individual scratches his head or adjusts
his clothing. Movements of this sort, referred to as "body focus-
sed movement" by Freedman and Hoffman (1972) and as "self adap-
tors" by Ekman and Friesen (1969), though they do occur in speakers,
may also be observed in individuals at other times. Gesticulation,
however, only occurs when someone is actively engaged in an utterance, usually within a focused interactional event. Body focused
movements of course may be quite revealing of the individual's
motivational or organismic state (see Krout 1935), but they appear
to occur in spite of the individual's participation in an utterance
exchange and are not part of it. To use Goffman's terminology
(1974), they are treated as part of the "dis-attend track" in face-
to-face interaction.

As has just been noted, an individual engaged in an utterance
typically is also a participant in an utterance exchange within a
focused interactional event. He is thus a participant in a complex
of systems of behavioral relationship;and much of his behavior
that can be observed, often intimately intertwined with the behavior of utterance, functions in the maintenance and management
of these systems. Thus there are aspects of posture and orientation, patterns of head movement and gaze, movements of the
hands and arms, and vocalizations which play a crucial part in
the organization of the interactional event. These aspects of behavior have been dealt with by Scheflen (1963, 1964,1973), Kendon
(1967, 1973), and Duncan (1972, 1973), among others. In any full
treatment of the behavior of language they must be considered in
detail, for they comprise an important part of the way utterances
are managed as acts of interaction. For the present, however,

we shall leave these aspects of the behavior of language to one side. As Goffman (1974) has put it, these aspects function in the "directional track" of interaction. Here we are concerned exclusively with the behavior that is directly involved in what Goffman calls the "story line" of the interaction.

The movements of gesticulation and their relationship to speech may be analyzed by a close inspection of examples recorded on 16mm sound film. By use of a hand-crank operated time-motion analyzer, it is possible to examine and re-examine the film frame by frame or by short stretches of several frames at a time. A detailed map may be made of the movement patterns observable, which can be plotted on a chart to show their development in time to the nearest frame. Using standard sound-film rates, this means that we can analyze the behavior to the nearest twenty-fourth of a second. Such a map of the movement patterns may be matched with a phonetic transcription of the concurrent speech, which can also be plotted against the frames of the film it matches. In this way, the relationship between body motion and speech may be examined to the nearest twenty-fourth of a second (or to smaller intervals of time, if the appropriate film speed is used). Details of these procedures were first described by Condon and Ogston (1966, 1967), and an account may also be found in Kendon (1970, 1972).

The first work in which this approach was used was that of Condon and Ogston (1966, 1967). In this work an extremely detailed study of the flow of movement in relation to the speech flow was undertaken. This showed that as the speaker speaks his bodily movement is rhythmically coordinated with his speech rhythm. One of Condon's principal concerns, in this work, has been to explore the degree to which this synchrony of speech and movement is precise. Its significance for our present concern is that it shows that the individual, in speaking, acts as a whole, that speech is not a disjunct action system but that it continuously mobilizes the muscular systems of the whole body.

Condon's work has been conducted at very fine levels of organization. He has examined the synchrony of bodily movement with speech at the verbal, syllabic, and phonic levels of the organization of speech. Here we shall be concerned with much higher levels of organization. As Condon (1974) himself has pointed out, at the level of the phrase and above, we tend to observe parts of the body differentiated out in movement, so that the head, the arm, or the hand, or at times the whole trunk performs phrases of movement that are sustained over syllabic groupings at the level of phrases and, as we shall see, at still higher levels of organization.

In the first study to be considered here, fully reported in
Kendon (1972), an extended utterance was analyzed, which was
taken from a film made in London. In a London pub, eleven
people, who had gathered over drinks with an American anthropologist, were discussing the differences between British and
American national character. In the utterance analyzed the
speaker maintained a continuous discourse for about two minutes. He directed his utterance to the anthropologist, but in
such a way that it also served as an address to the whole group.

The speech stream was segmented into intonation tune
units, following criteria given by Roger Kingdon (1958). This
yields units which are the equivalent of Tone Units, as these
are defined by Crystal (Crystal and Davy (1969). The relationship between these Tone Units was then examined, and they
were found to participate in four levels of organization. First,
the Tone Units were found to combine into groupings termed
Locutions. These generally comprised complete sentences.
Locutions were found to combine into Locution Groups, and
these in turn were organized into Locution Clusters. Locution
Clusters may be thought of as the paragraphs of the discourse.
They are set off from one another by a pause or by a marked
change in voice quality, loudness, or pitch range, and there
is generally a clear shift in subject matter. The Locution Clusters are themselves combined into the highest level of organization of all, the Discourse, which is here the equivalent of
one speaker turn.

It was found that each level of organization distinguished in
the speech stream was matched by a distinctive pattern of organization of bodily movement. Thus for the duration of the Discourse,
the speaker sustained a bodily posture that contrasted with the
posture he sustained before and after it. For each of the Locution
Clusters within the Discourse, he used his arms differently.
Over the first of the three clusters distinguished he used his
right arm only; over the second cluster he used his left arm only;
while over the third he used both arms together. Within each
cluster, each Locution Group was contrasted in the way in which
the head moved over each of the Locutions within it. Each Locution
began with the speaker's head held erect or raised and tilted to
one side. As the Locution unfolded the head was lowered to be
brought to a low central position or to a lowered left-tilt position.
Locution Groups were distinguished according to whether the head
movement pattern was a forward lowering or a forward lowering

combined with a leftward tilt over each Locution within the Group.
Successive Locutions within a Group were distinguished from one
another not only by the head movement cycle we have just des-
cribed--each Locution starting with the head in a raised position--
but also in the pattern of movement in the hand and arm employed.
For example, in the second Group in the Discourse analyzed,
over the first Locution the left arm was fully extended and retracted;
over the second Locution gesticulatory movement was confined to
the forearm rotation and movement in the wrist and fingers; over
the third Locution the forearm was raised by flexion at the elbow
and a succession of lowering movements were then observed.
Finally, at the level of the Tone Unit, distinctive movement patterns could again be observed. Thus over the first Tone Unit in
the first Locution of the second Group, the left arm was fully extended, it was retracted over the second Tone Unit, and extended
again over the third.

The paralleling of organization in the speech stream and gesticulatory stream revealed in this example, together with certain
details having to do with the relative timing of the nuclei of the
Tone Units and the nuclei of the gesticulatory phrases, led to the
conclusion that it is "as if the speech production process is manifested in two forms of activity simultaneously: in the vocal organs
and also in bodily movement" (Kendon 1972:205). Analyses of other
examples, taken from other sources, have served to reinforce this
conclusion. Furthermore, some additional features of the speech-
gesticulation relationship have become apparent that allow us to go
further in our understanding of how far back in the speech production
process the organization of concurrent bodily movement has its origin.

We shall now consider some findings from some other analyses of
gesticulation structure in relation to utterance structure. Space does
not permit a full presentation, which will be reserved for another
publication. In this new work a number of examples of extended
utterances have been analyzed, all of them taken from a film made
in Philadelphia at the Eastern Pennsylvania Psychiatric Institute.
The film, known as ISP 001 63, is of five psychiatrists and a social
worker meeting to discuss a patient the social worker and one of
the psychiatrists had been interviewing. The film contains many
examples of extended utterances, with a good deal of gesticulatory
activity.

In this work the speech in selected extended utterances has
been analyzed into Tone Units and their various groupings according to procedures already described (Kendon 1972) and outlined

briefly above. In analyzing the structure of the gesticulation,
however, we made use of the concept of the Gesticulation Phrase.
This will be more fully presented elsewhere, but the basic criteria
for distinguishing it may be summarized briefly.

In forelimb gesticulation the limb is typically lifted away
from the body as it performs one or more complex movement
patterns, and then is returned to what may be called its rest
position. Gesticular Units thus may be demarcated as extending
from the moment the excursion of the limb begins to the moment
when the limb is fully at rest again. Within such an excursion
the limb may perform one or more Phrases of gesticulation. A
phrase of gesticulation, or G-Phrase, is distinguished for every
phase in the excursionary movement in which the limb, or part
of it, shows a distinct peaking of effort—"effort" is used here
in the technical sense of Rudolf Laban (Dell 1970). Such an
effort peak (less technically, such a moment of accented movement) is termed the stroke of the G-phrase. It is usually preceded by a preparation, i.e. a phase in which the limb moves
away from its rest position to a position at which the stroke
begins. The stroke is then succeeded by a recovery or return
phase in which the limb is either moved back to its rest position
or in which it is readied for another stroke.

Gesticular Phrases, like Tone Units, may be grouped in
various ways, so that a Gesticular Unit (G-Unit) may contain
more than one G-Phrase. Description is further complicated by
the fact that both limbs may be used simultaneously, at times
performing in unison, but at other times showing considerable
differentiation in the way they are employed.

Several of these features will now be illustrated with a
specific example. In Figure 1 a G-Unit and its internal structure is diagrammed in relation to the speech it co-occurred
with. In Figure 2 three sketches of S are presented to show
his general posture and two main features of his gesticulation.
The example is taken from the film ISP 001 63 already mentioned.
In this example, the psychiatrist, S, who is presenting the
case is commenting on the difficulty he has had in getting the
patient in question to give a coherent account of herself. The
passage we are concerned with is as follows, transcribed to
show its organization into tone units:

this patient has been a problem/ so far as a history is
concerned/ uh y'know a very formal one/ uh or any kind
of a history/ cos she talks very very rapidly/ and and
moves very quickly/ from one area to another/

We are concerned here with the gesticulation that occurs in association with the last five tone units in this passage.

It will be seen from Figure 1 how a single G-Unit extends during the passage of speech in question. It is recorded as beginning at frame 11084, the earliest point in which gesticulatory movement can be observed, in this case in the left hand, to frame 11250, when both limbs have returned to a stable, non-gesticulatory position. This G-Unit, however, will be seen to contain three manual G-Phrases, regarded as being organized into two groupings or Parts, the first Part containing two G-Phrases, both enacted by the left hand; the second Part contains one G-Phrase only, enacted by the right arm. These G-Phrases are regarded as belonging together in a single G-Unit because, in the first place, between G-Ph 1 and G-Ph 2 the hand does not return completely to its rest position. Secondly, as will be clear from Figure 1, G-Ph 3 begins before the recovery phase of the preceding G-Phrase is completed. G-Ph 1 and G-Ph 2 are grouped into Part I be÷ cause they are very similar in form and in the space they make use of. G-Ph 3 is regarded as belonging to a separate Part, in this case because it is enacted by a different limb. In other examples, where the gesticulation is confined to one limb only, distinct Parts are recognized if the limb moves to an entirely new spatial area for enactment, or if it engages in a sharply distinctive movement pattern.

G-Phrase 1 and G-Phrase 2 are very similar. For both the fingers of the left hand are extended and spread to assume an "umbrella" hand form (i.e. with palm facing down, all digits are extended and abducted, but all are partly flexed at the A-joints). At the same time this development of the "umbrella" form occurs, the wrist extends slightly, lifting the hand away from the chair arm on which it has been resting (see Figure 2). In each of the two G-Phrases, this development of the hand posture and the concurrent wrist extension is regarded as constituting the preparatory phase of the G-Phrase ($p_1$ and $p_2$ in Fig. 1). In the Stroke ($s_1$ and $s_2$) in each G-Phrase, the wrist is flexed rapidly, moving the "umbrella" hand sharply downwards. In both the stroke is followed by a hold ($h_1$ and $h_2$) in which the hand, still in its "umbrella" form, is held still in the position it reached at the end of the stroke. Thereafter, in G-Phrase 1, the fingers slowly flex and draw together into a "loose bunch" form. This is regarded as a

partial recovery (pr$_1$) because the hand does not return all the
way to the position it was in before the onset of the G-Phrase.
After the hold (h$_2$) following the stroke in G-Ph 2, however,
the fingers are drawn fully together, but at the same time the
arm is moved off the chair arm into S's lap. The forearm is then
supinated and the hand spread, to form a support for the folder
that S is holding (see Fig. 2). Note that in this case the limb
is moved, not to a rest position, but to a position in which it
is employed in a non-gesticulatory activity.

G-Phrase 3 is likewise analyzed into a preparatory phase
(p$_3$), in which the arm is lifted upwards through flexion of the
upper arm (at the shoulder joint); a stroke (s$_3$) in which the
upper arm is rotated inwards and outwards twice, serving to
sweep the hand in to the center of S's gesture space and out
again; and a recovery phase (r$_3$) in which the arm is lowered
again, and then moved to reassume the position it had before,
supporting the folder. The stroke in this case is a complex
stroke, analyzeable into four components.

Finally, note should be taken of the segment marked
GH 1, which occurs during h$_1$ in G-Phrase 1. This is a gesture
of the head, in this case a head-shake. As may be noted from
the diagram in Figure 1, it is integrated with the gesticulatory
activity in the limbs, and as we shall observe later, it bears
the same relationship to the speech structure as do the other
gestural units. For the present, however, it is convenient to
treat head gestures separately, and we have not considered
this as part of the gesture phrase organization described for
the forelimbs.

A detailed analysis of the relationship between the phrase
structure of the gesticular flow and the organization of the speech
flow has been carried out on five extended utterances from the
film ISP 001 63 from three different participants. There are three
general statements that may be made from these analyses:

First, just as we found in the analysis summarized earlier
and reported (Kendon 1972), so here, in the two examples in
which there were divisions in the discourse at the Locution Cluster level, these Clusters contrasted in their concurrent gesticulation in terms of the way the limbs are involved in gesticulation
Thus in F 42, an extended utterance by the social worker, which
divides into four Clusters, over the first she uses only her left
arm in gesticulation; over the second she uses both arms equally;
while over the third she uses both arms, but the right arm is

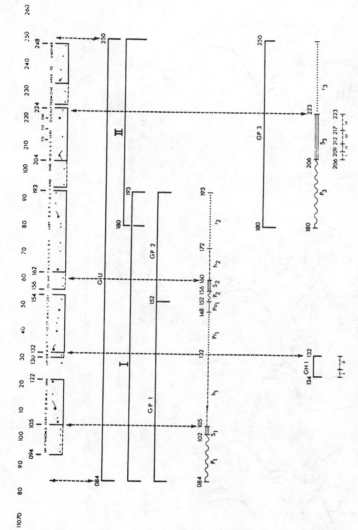

Figure 1.  Diagram to show the organization of a Gesture Unit and its relationship to the vocal aspect of the utterance. The utterance is taken from the film ISP 001 63, frame nos. 11070-11270. The boundaries of tone units are shown by solid vertical lines immediately below the text. The head section of each tone unit is marked by a continuous horizontal line, the pre-head section by a dotted line. Intonation patterns for each tone unit are written below the text. GU - Gesture Unit; GP - Gesture Phrase; p - preparation; s - stroke; h - hold; Pr - partial recovery; Pa - pause; r - recovery; GH - Gesture Phrase in Head. Vertical broken arrows indicate relationship of components of the gesture phrases with components in the vocal aspect.

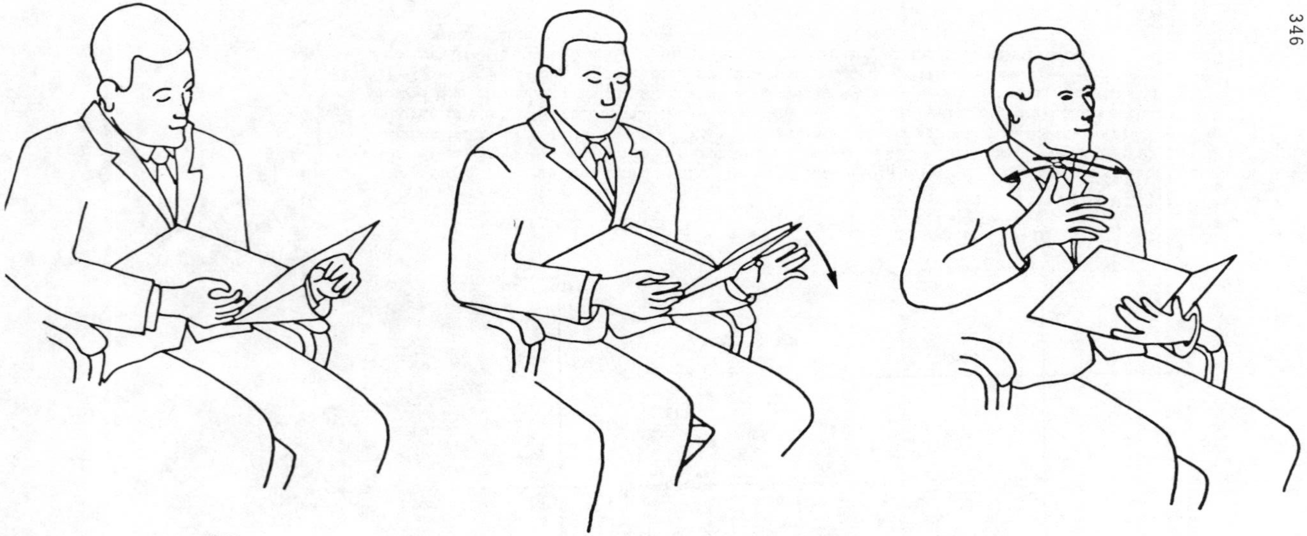

2(a)

2(b)

2(c)

(a) position of hands prior to the Gesture Unit

(b) "umbrella" form of left hand in G-Phrases 1 & 2; arrow shows direction of movement in stroke phase

(c) position of right hand in G-Phrase 3; arrows show pattern of movement in the stroke phase of this G-Phrase

Figure 2.   Tracings from film ISP 001 63 to illustrate hand position in the G-Unit shown in Figure 1.

dominant. Similarly in S 134 (an utterance of the psychiatrist who presented the case to the group), the discourse is divisible into three Clusters. Over the first, which is very short, S uses his left arm; over the second he uses his right arm; and over the third he again uses his left arm.

Second, in all of the examples we have analyzed so far, each Locution has its own G-Unit. That is, boundaries of Locutions are associated with the gesticulatory limb either at the rest position, or with it being in the phase of return to that position. Furthermore, within each G-Unit, the pattern of movement observed is different. This also confirms what was found in the previous analysis: each Locution is associated with a distinctive Unit of gesticulatory activity.

Third, whereas in the previous example, as we saw, each Tone Unit was differentiated with a distinct pattern of gesticular organization--each Tone Unit was found to be matched with a distinct G-Phrase--in the other examples we have analyzed this relationship between Tone Units and G-Phrases has been found to be somewhat more complex. In F 42, for example, in which there are twenty-six Tone Units, twenty of these had a corresponding G-Phrase. Of the other six Tone Units, three, occurring in succession, shared a single G-Phrase (which extended over the entire sequence of the three), while the other three Tone Units each had associated with them not one, but two G-Phrases. Likewise in D 43 and in S 134, we found groupings of Tone Units covered by a single G-Phrase.

An examination of just which Tone Units are grouped by a single G-Phrase and which co-occur with one or with more than one G-Phrase, suggests that the G-Phrases are manifestations of the "idea units" the utterance is giving expression to and are linked to the output of Tone Units only as closely as this itself is linked to the expression of "idea units". For example, in F 42, Locution 4 is as follows:

     (10)           (11)             (12)

/but all through/ you you sensed/ that she and father/ are
     (13)             (14)
being very seductive/ with each other/ (nuclear syllables of

each Tone Unit are underlined). A single, though complex, G-Phrase occurs over Tone Units 11 to 14, in which the forearm is moved back and forth in front of the body, with the hand held palm inward. This movement would seem to embody two items in interplaying relationship with one another. Thus, though it takes a succession of Tone

Units to specify "patient" (she) and "father" and their "relationship", a depiction of their relationship is here given in a single
G-Phrase. On the other hand, also in F 42, we have the Tone Unit
"and supposedly re<u>buffs</u> her", and in association with this two
G-Phrases are performed. In association with "re<u>buff</u>" the hand is
held with the palm facing the body, the upper arm rotated inward
at the shoulder so that the forearm crosses the body. As the nuclear
syllable of "rebuff" is uttered, the thumb is moved rapidly outwards in a pushing-away movement. This, however, was preceded
by a movement of the whole arm, in which the arm is raised and
then lowered slightly and also moved towards the body. However,
as it is so moved it also is moved in a series of rapid, in-out
motions of small amplitude. Such rapid back and forth movement
is not uncommonly seen in association with expressions such as
"partly", "more or less", or "somewhat". Here it appears, thus,
that in the single Tone Unit in which the idea of "rebuff" and of its
<u>supposed</u> character is given expression, these two aspects are
given separate expression in two G-Phrases.

In D 29 and D 43 we find examples of a single G-Phrase, here
taking the form of a sustained hand position, being held over two
or three Tone Units which are all linked by a common theme. In
D 43 and also in S 134 we find groups of Tone Units in which only
one conveys new information, the others serving to link this piece
of new information with the previous or succeeding argument of the
discourse. Here a G-Phrase associated with the new information
is performed, but it co-occurs with the Tone Unit grouping (Locution) as a whole, and does not mark out the separate Tone Units.

The degree to which the different levels of organization in discourse are marked by separate G-Phrases appears to be a matter
of some variation, at least below the level of the Locution, and
further analyses will be needed before we will be in a position to
specify anything about what factors might be related to this.
However, it would appear that whereas the structure of the movement pattern in gesticulation is closely integrated into the
rhythmical structure of the co-occurring speech stream (Condon
and Ogston's work has shown how very close this is), in terms of
the phrasal organization of the gesticulation a distinct phrase of
gesticulation is produced for each unit of meaning or "idea unit"
that an utterer deals with. This means that the phrases of gesticulation that co-occur with speech are not to be thought of either as
mere embellishments of expression or as by-products of the speech
process. They are, rather, an alternate manifestation of the process

by which "ideas" are encoded into patterns of behavior which
can be apprehended by others as <u>reportive</u> of those ideas. It is
as if the process of utterance has two channels of output into
behavior: one by way of speech, the other by way of bodily
movement.

<u>Further analyses of the relationship between Speech Units and
Gesticulation Units and Phrases</u>. An examination of the relationship in time between the nucleus of a Tone Unit and the stroke of
its associated G-Phrase shows that the stroke of the G-Phrase is
completed either before the Tone Unit nucleus, or just at its onset. This phenomenon was reported in Kendon (1972) and it is confirmed in our later analyses. Thus in F 42, in which there were
22 Tone Units with a matching G-Phrase, in fifteen instances the
stroke was completed either before or simultaneously with the
onset of the tonic syllable; there were six instances in which the
stroke was completed by the end of the tonic syllable; and only
one instance in which the stroke continued after the tonic syllable. In all instances the gesture phrase <u>began</u> well before the
tonic, and in most instances it began before the onset of the head
of the Tone Unit. In none of the material we have analyzed is
there a single instance of a G-Phrase <u>following</u> its associated
Tone Unit. It either co-occurs with it or precedes it. Where we
are dealing with the first Tone Units of a discourse, furthermore,
if gesticulation occurs during the first such Unit it always begins before speech begins. Usually only the preparatory phase
of a G-Phrase is enacted before speech, but occasionally complete phrases are enacted. An example of this was described in
Kendon (1972).

The appearance of G-Phrases somewhat in advance of the appearance of speech phrases with which they are associated means,
of course, that the G-Phrase must have been organized at least at
the same time, if not a little in advance of its associated speech
phrase. Thus the G-Phrase must be seen as originating simultaneously with the origination of speech and not as a product of the
speech production process.

Further indication that the gesticulation associated with speech
is an alternate manifestation of the same encoding process is provided by an examination of the relationship between G-Phrases and
speech phrases in which there are pauses or hesitations. For example, in many cases where a Tone Unit has already begun, and a
pause occurs between the prehead and the head onset; if a G-Phrase

is also under way, it may continue to completion despite the
interruption in the flow of speech. Indeed from several examples
we have analyzed, it seems that the speech is only resumed
once the stroke of the G-phrase has been completed. Here it
would seem that, despite the pause, the speaker had already
organized the semantic structure of the next part of the utterance,
for the G-phrase that is performed in the pause is well formed,
clearly embodying the content of what is also produced in speech.
Such within-Tone Unit pauses where kinesis continues reflect,
thus, an interruption in the speech production process but not an
interruption in the process of utterance.

An example to illustrate this (full details must await another
publication) is F2, taken from the beginning of film ISP 001 63,
where the participants are settling in their seats and discussing
in an informal way what is going to happen in the main part of
the session. F makes a joke based on a scene in Wilder's film,
Some Like it Hot. She says: /they wheel a big table in/ with a
big with a big [pause] cake on it/ and the girl/ jumps up/ —here
someone else fills in for her with the phrase, "with a machine gun."

This speech, here comprising but one Locution, may be
divided into four Tone Units. For the first three of these there
are three corresponding G-Phrases, and the form of movement
in the stroke in each has a clear relation to the content of what
F is saying: thus in G-Phrase 1, F sweeps her left arm inward
in a horizontal motion—associated with "they wheel a big table
in." In G-Ph. 2, co-occurrent with Tone Unit 2, F makes a series
of circular motions with the forearm pointing downwards and with
her index finger extended, here describing in movement the shape
of the cake. In G-Ph. 3, she raises her arm rapidly until it is
fully extended vertically above her. This is clearly a "jumping
up" movement, the action of the girl F is referring to, though
the action, it will be seen, is not referred to verbally until the
last Tone Unit, during which F is not producing a new G-Phrase
but is recovering from the previous G-Phrase.

Looking at the relationship in time between the components
of these G-Phrases and the flow of speech, it appears first that
the stroke of G-Ph. 1, the horizontal inward movement of the
left arm, commenced precisely at the same moment that F's speech
began, but its preparation, the lifting of the arm to the position
from which it commences the inward sweep, began just 19/24ths
of a second before this. Second, it will be noted that the second
Tone Unit is broken up: its pre-head is spoken twice and then
there is a pause of 26/24ths of a second before the rest of the

phrase is uttered. It is during this pause that the rotary movements of the second G-Phrase are produced. The head section of
the Tone Unit "cake on it" is uttered as the limb recovers from
the stroke. Here, then, though speech was arrested, this part
of the utterance was continued to completion kinesically.

In the next G-Phrase, as we have see, F raised her arm
rapidly to a vertical position. This movement matched precisely
the tonic of the Tone Unit—the word girl—but as we have already
noted, the form of the movement referred not to the girl but to
her action of jumping up, which is nevertheless given verbal
expression in the next and final Tone Unit. Thus although in
phrasal organization F's speech and gesticulation become once
again aligned, in semantic content the gesture was performed
well in advance of the verbal reference.

As we have seen, phrases of gesticulation tend to appear
a little in advance of their associated speech phrases, and
their preparation begins sometimes well in advance. This suggests, as we have said, that the processes of speech utterance
and gesture utterance begin at one and the same time. The
temporal priority of gesture may partly be due to the fact that
for a given idea to be expressed in words it must be strung out
in time, whereas the same idea may be expressed in a gesture
within a single movement or pose of the hand. However, the
observation that speech production may be interfered with while
gestural production is not, may also suggest that the process of
gestural encoding is more readily accomplished than that of
verbal encoding and so may be faster for this reason.

Conclusion. We have argued that gesticulation is a second
product of the process of utterance. Insofar as utterance makes
use of the vocal channel, use is made of a complex code,
language. In the kinesic channel, however, the movement
patterns that are employed in gesticulation do not appear to have
properties that are like the lexical and syntactic character of
spoken language, though they do appear to share in the dynamics
of their organization some of the prosodic features of speech,
at least in the speakers of English to which this sort of analysis
has been confined. Thus we have seen how gesticular phrases
may be distinguished in terms of nuclei of kinesic emphasis,
much as Tone Units may be distinguished in terms of nuclei
of vocal prominence. There is when the whole is considered some

reason for thinking that intonation tunes may have their parallel
in kinesic organization. Thus Birdwhistell (1970) has reported
that a lowering of a gesticulating body part co-occurs with a
falling terminal juncture in speech, and that where a gesticulating body part is sustained or held at the end of an utterance,
the pitch of the voice is also either sustained or raised.
Several examples of our own, which will be reported in detail
elsewhere, show that in questions in which the pitch of the
voice is raised or held, concurrently the head or hand is also
raised or sustained.

   However, gesticular movements, although shaped in part
in parallel to the prosodic structure of the concurrent speech,
also are patterned in ways that are clearly related to the content
of what is being expressed. Furthermore, in the various poses
the hands may assume, we can also see manifestations of aspects
of the content. The relationship between the content of the gesticulation and the content of the speech is a highly complex one
and we cannot undertake a detailed review of this here. To date
the most thorough treatment of this still remains that of Efron
(1941). Here we will cite a few representative examples from our
own material to show that the mode by which ideas are encoded
in gesticulation is quite different from the way in which they are
encoded in language.

   First, the speaker may depict in gesture some object or action
he is referring to in speech. Thus in the "cake" example, F 2, given
above, F performed movements that were analogous to movements
that would be made of wheeling in a table or jumping up; she also
made a movement that outlined the shape of the cake she was talking
about. Movements characteristic of aspects of action are indeed
very common. In F 42, which we already have alluded to, F continued her description of the patient's relation to her father by saying
"and she doing things to annoy him, to attract his attention, to
outrage him." Over each of these three Tone Units she moves her
hand outward in a rapid "slapping" movement, which has the dynamic character of actions that, addressed to another, would pro-
voke or tease. In D 43, in asking why both the psychiatrist and
the social worker F had had difficulty in getting the patient to tell
her history, D says "...maybe it's because Pete doesn't want to
nail down this attractive bit of fluff or something." As he says
"nail down" he raises his right arm, hand posed as if it is holding
something, and he performs a series of forward thrusts, an action
sequence which has the character of knocking nails into something,
as one mi ght if one were nailing a notice to a door.

In these examples the speaker seems to be creating a gestural
form de novo to suit the immediate utterance. Sometimes, however,
he makes use of a gestural form that is more or less conventionalized. Thus, in the example just mentioned, when D says "bit of
fluff" he raises both hands, palms facing inwards, and performs
sinuous in-out movements, thus performing a well known gesture
which means 'shapely woman'. Such conventionalized patterns
may take on the status of gestures which can be given a meaning
when presented in isolation. These have been termed "emblems"
by Ekman and Friesen (1969).

Gesticulation does not only depict objects, actions, or behavior styles of others being described. It may also be used to encode
more abstract features of the utterer's discourse. For example, it
may refer to the overall theme of the utterer's discourse, rather
than to particular parts within it. Thus, in the first part of D 43,
D says: /How about this history business/ you Pete's havin'
trouble getting a history/. As he says this, his hands are held
forward, palms facing each other in a "framing" arrangement. This
double hand frame was sustained throughout the series of tone units
in this part of the utterance, which are linked together by the theme
of "getting a history". In other instances a sustained hand position
may be observed which appears to mark the kind of utterance that is
being produced. Thus we have collected many examples in which a
sustained position of an open palm extended forward marks a question or an utterance in which the performer is putting forward an
example for discussion.

Gesticulation may also in various ways make visible the organization of the discourse. We have already referred to the way in
which body use is differentiated in association with different segments of the discourse. However, at times one may observe gesticulatory patterns that appear to have this function particularly. In a
discourse recorded in the film TRD 009 (not described in Kendon,
1972) the utterer, X, describes certain features of the British Nor-
therner. As he does so, each Tone Unit is marked by a distinct
rotary movement of the right arm, while he holds his left arm forward and slightly bent at the elbow. This is sustained for this
segment of the discourse, apparently framing or tying together the
separate statements he is making.

The foregoing is intended to suggest that there are many different ways in which gesticulation may be related to the content of an
utterance. Gesticulation and speech work together in an intimate
relation of great flexibility and subtlety. However, as we have already suggested and as these examples make clear, the mode of

encoding of content is quite different in gesture from the mode of
encoding in speech. Whereas in language highly conventionalized
forms from an already established vocabulary are used, which are
organized sequentially according to grammatical rules, in gesticulation encoding is presentational. Though conventionalized forms
may be used, the utterer has considerable freedom to create new
enactments which do not then pass into any established vocabulary.
As far as can be seen at the moment, gesticulation is not composed
of elements which are formed into constructions according to a
syntax. They occur, rather, as a succession of enactments which
express in presentational fashion, the ideas which may also be
given discursive expression in speech. The sequencing of gesticular phrases and units is governed by the order of presentation of
ideas in the discourse.

We have also seen how gesticular phrases must be constructed
in advance of their performance, just as speech phrases are, and
that they appear to originate at a very early stage in the process of
utterance. Recent developments in linguistic theory have led many
to the view that it is the semantic organization of an utterance that
is the starting point for the processes by which its surface structure
is eventually generated (Maclay 1971, Leech 1974). Most particularly
in this connection we may mention the views of Wallace Chafe (1970)
who has argued explicitly for the position that the process of utterance generation proceeds through a series of stages, starting with
the organization of semantic structures. The work on gesticulation
we have reviewed here would suggest that this earliest stage in the
process of utterance formation has, or can have, a direct expression in behavior.

If we accept the view that in producing an utterance a speaker
starts with something which he wishes to say--we may call this an
"idea complex"--in order to translate this into a behavioral form
which can be "read" by a recipient as a report of this idea complex,
the idea complex first has to be organized in some way into packages
or units which can form the basis for the planning of actions which
will function for a recipient reportively. Because of limitations imposed upon expression both by the way in which actions themselves
may be executed and by the way in which they can be taken cogni-
zance of by a recipient, the organization of an idea complex into
packages which must then be enacted sequentially is inevitable.
Clearly, however, this process of linearization proceeds furthest
in the production of speech. In gesticular expression, thus, we
have an output that reflects an earlier stage in this process of

translation from idea complex to report. The further analysis of
gesticulation, thus, may provide a means of gaining much insight
into the process of utterance.

Let us now return to the theme with which we began. Hewes
(1973) remarks at the end of his paper, as a further point in support of the theory that language was originally gestural in form,
that "gesture did not wither away, but persisted as a common accompaniment to speech, either as a kinesic paralanguage for
conveying nuances, emphasis, or even contradiction of the spoken
message...or in situations where spoken language fails...(p. 11).
The work we have reviewed here would suggest that a much
stronger statement is warranted. Our observations suggest that
gesture is not so much a common accompaniment to speech but
that it is an integral part of the whole act of uttering; that it is not
just a kinesic paralanguage but that it may be employed, even in
the apparently highly verbal situations we have studied, to encode
many different aspects of the ideas being given expression. The notion
that gesture may convey nuances, emphasis, or contradiction is
correct. However, it also may encode the most central and abstract
ideas also being encoded in speech.

It is obvious that gesticulation is not an invariable accompaniment
of speech, at least not in an overt and readily observable form, and
it would be extremely useful to have much more detailed information
on the circumstances in which it does or does not occur. Systematic
work on this question is surprisingly scant, however. It has been
suggested (Ekman and Friesen 1972) that gesticulation increases
with excitement and enthusiasm or where the speaker has a dominant role in the interaction. Gesticulation also increases where
feedback from the listener suggests difficulty of comprehension and
also where the speaker himself has difficulty in finding the right
verbal forms for what he has to say. This last point has also been
suggested by De Laguna (1927) and by Werner and Kaplan (1963).
Cohen and Harrison (1973) compared the frequency of gesticulation
when speakers give directions to someone over an intercom and
when they gave similar directions to the other person face-to-face,
and they found an increase in gesticulation in the latter situation.
Baxter, Winter, and Hammer (1968) found that speakers speaking
fluently on a subject with which they were familiar, gesticulated
more frequently than did those who spoke on subjects they were not
so familiar with. For our immediate purposes, however, it is sufficient to note both the immediate and universal availability of
gesticulation as a mode of utterance and its intimate and deep con-

nection with speaking. Speakers, indeed, are usually hardly aware that they gesticulate, so spontaneous a part of the whole process of utterance does it appear to be.

This intimate connection between gesticulation and speech would seem to be consonant with the idea that in its emergence language, or reportively functioning behavior, was at least as much gestural in form as it was vocal. What is striking is the fact that though gesticulation operates as a mode of expression even as speech is also operating, it is encoding ideas in a completely different manner. Theories of the evolution of language must be able to account for this as well as be able to account for the emergence of speech. A much fuller and closer look at the mode of encoding in gesture would appear to be warranted.

The fact that gesticulation tends to anticipate speech, that speech may be disrupted though concurrent gesticulation continues to go forward smoothly, and the fact that on occasion a gestural response may be given first before any speech whatever is begun, does perhaps provide a hint that the gestural channel is easier and more readily called upon, that the process by which an idea is transformed into public behavior of a reportive character is more swiftly accomplished gesturally, that there are fewer steps to the process than there are when formulation of the "idea" into speech is to occur. The least we can say about this is that we would not, perhaps, expect a more elaborate and time-consuming method of utterance to be the one that was first developed in language evolution.

In conclusion, we would urge that a distinction be drawn between speech and other modes of idea expression which may nevertheless be seen as manifestations of the process of utterance. In formulating theories about the origin of language, thus, we must attend to two great questions: First, how did the human species acquire the ability to engage in reportive behavior? Second, how did this reportive behavior become specialized in the form of speech?

## REFERENCES

Barakat, R. A.
   1975   The Cistercian Sign Language: A Study in Non-Verbal
          Communication (Kalamazoo, MI, Cistercian Publications).

Berndt, R. M.
   1940   Notes on the Sign Language of the Jaralde Tribe,
          Transactions of the Royal Society of South Australia
          64, 267-272.

Birdwhistell, R. L.
    1970      Kinesics and Context: Essays on Body Motion Com-
           munication (Philadelphia: University of Pennsylvania
           Press).

Chafe, W. L.
    1970      Meaning and the Structure of Language (Chicago:
           University of Chicago Press).

Cicourel, A. C., & R. Boese
    1972      The Acquisition of Manual Sign Language and Genera-
           tive Semantics, Semiotica 5, 225-256.

Cohen, A. A., & R. Harrison
    1973      Intentionality in the Use of Hand Illustrators in
           Face-to-Face Communication Situations, Journal
           of Personality and Social Psychology 28, 276-279.

Condon, W. S.
    1974      Communication and Order: the Micro "rhythm hier-
           archy" of Speaker Behavior, in Harries & Nichenan
           (eds) Play Therapy in Theory and Practice.

Condon, W. S., & W. Ogston
    1966      Sound Film Analysis of Normal and Pathological Be-
           havior Patterns, Journal of Nervous and Mental Dis-
           ease 143, 338-347.

    1967      A Segmentation of Behavior, Journal of Psychiatric
           Research 5, 221-235.

Crystal, D., & D. Davy
    1969      Investigating English Style (Bloomington: Indiana
           University Press).

De Laguna, G.
    1927      Speech: Its Function and Development (New Haven:
           Yale University Press).

Dell, C.
    1970        A Primer for Movement Description Using Effort-Shape
                and Supplementary Concepts (New York: Dance Notation
                Bureau).

di Jorio, A.
    1832        Mimica Degli Antichi Investigata nel Gestire Napoli-
                tano (Napoli: Stamperia del Fibreno).

Duncan, S. D., Jr.
    1972        Some Signals and Rules for Taking Speaking Turns
                in Conversations, Journal of Personality and Social
                Psychology 23, 283-292.

    1973        Towards a Grammar for Dyadic Conversations,
                Semiotica 9, 29-46.

Efron, D.
    1941        Gesture, Race, and Culture (New York: King's Crown
                Press); reprinted as Approaches to Semiotics 9, ed.
                T. A. Sebeok (The Hague: Mouton).

Ekman, P., & W. Friesen
    1969        The Repertoire of Nonverbal Behavior: Categories,
                Origins, Usage, and Coding, Semiotica 1, 49-98.

    1972        Hand Movements, Journal of Communication 22, 353-374.

Freedman, N., & S. Hoffman
    1972        The Analysis of Movement Behavior during Clinical
                Interviews, in A. Seigman & B. Pope (eds.), Studies
                in Dyadic Communication (Elmsford, NY: Pergamon).

Gardner, R. A., & B. Gardner
    1971        Two Way Communication with an Infant Chimpanzee,
                in Schrier & Stollnitz (eds.), Behavior of Nonhuman
                Primates IV (New York: Academic Press).

Geschwind, N.
    1972        Language and the Brain, Scientific American 227, 76-83.

Goffman, E.
    1974        Frame Analysis (New York: Harper and Row).

Hewes, G. W.
     1973a      Primate Communication and the Gestural Origin of
                Language, Current Anthropology 14, 5-24.

     1973b      An Explicit Formulation of the Relationship Between
                Tool Using, Tool Making, and the Emergence of
                Language, Visible Language 7, 101-127;

Hockett, C. F., & R. Ascher
     1964       The Human Revolution, Current Anthropology 5, 135-168.

Kendon, A.
     1967       Some Functions of Gaze Direction in Social Interaction,
                Acta Psychologica 26, 22-63.

     1970       Movement Coordination in Social Interaction, Acta
                Psychologica 32, 100-125.

     1972       Some Relationships Between Body Motion and Speech,
                in Seigman & Pope (eds.) Studies in Dyadic Communi-
                cation (Elmsford, NY: Pergamon Press).

     1973       The Role of Visible Behavior in the Organization of
                Social Interaction, in von Cranach and Vine (eds.),
                Movement and Communication in Man and Chimpanzee
                London & NY: Academic Press).

Kimura, D.
     1973       The Assymetry of the Human Brain, Scientific American
                228, 70-78

Kingdon, R.
     1958       The Groundwork of English Intonation (London: Longmans).

Krout, M. H.
     1935       Autistic Gestures: an Experimental Study in Symbolic
                Movement, Psychological Monographs, No. 208, 46,
                1-26.

Leech, G.
     1974       Semantics (Harmondsworth: Penguin Books).

Lieberman, P.
    1973        On the Evolution of Language: a Unified View,
                Cognition 2, 59-94.

Lenneberg, E. H.
    1967        Biological Foundations of Language (NY: Wiley).

Lyall, A.
    1956        The Italian Sign Language, Twentieth Century
                159, 600-604.

Maclay, H.
    1971        Overview for Part II, Linguistics, in Steinberg &
                Jakobovits (eds.), Semantics: An Interdisciplinary
                Reader in Philosophy, Linguistics, and Psychology
                (Cambridge: Cambridge University Press).

Mallery, G.
    1881        Sign Language Among North American Plains Indians
                (Washington: Smithsonian Institution); reprinted as
                Approaches to Semiotics 14, ed. T.A. Sebeok (The Hague:
                Mouton).

Mayr, E.
    1968        Population, Species, and Evolution (Camb., Mass:
                Harvard University Press).

Meggit, M.
    1954        Sign Language Among the Walbiri of Central Aus-
                tralia, Oceania 25, 2-16.

Menzel, E. W., Jr.
    1971        Communication About the Environment in a Group of
                Young Chimpanzees, Folia Primatologica 15, 220-232.

Mountford, C. P.
    1938        Gesture Language of the Ngada Tribe, Oceania
                9, 152-155.

Reynolds, P. C.
    1968        Evolution of Primate Vocal-Auditory Communication
                Systems, American Anthropologist 70, 300-308.

Rosa, A.
   1929        Espressione e Mimica (Milano: Hoepli).

Roth, W. E.
   1897        Ethnological Studies Among the North-West-Central
               Queensland Aborigines (Brisbane: E. Gregory, Gov-
               ernment Printer).

Scheflen, A. E.
   1963        Communication and Regulation in Psychotherapy,
               Psychiatry 26, 126-136.

   1964        The Significance of Postures in Communication
               Systems, Psychiatry 27, 316-331.

   1973        Communicational Structure: Analysis of a Psycho-
               therapy Transaction (Bloomington: Indiana University
               Press).

Schlesinger, I. M.
   1971        The Grammar of Sign Language and the Problem of
               Language Universals, in Morton (ed ), Biological
               and Social Factors in Psycholinguistics (London:
               Logos Press).

Stokoe, W. C., Jr.
   1972        Semiotics and Human Sign Languages (The Hague:
               Mouton).

Tervoort, B. T.
   1961        Esoteric Symbolism in the Communication Behavior
               of Young Deaf Children, American Annals of the Deaf
               106, 436-480.

Werner, H., & B. Kaplan
   1963        Symbol Formation (New York: Wiley).

West, La Mont, Jr.
   1960        The Sign Language: An Analysis (Ph.D. Dissertation,
               Indiana University).

   1963        Aboriginal Sign Languages, in Stanner & Sheils (eds.),
               Australiana Aboriginal Studies (Melbourne: Oxford Press).

PART FOUR: 16

THE CREATION OF A COMMUNICATION SYSTEM IN DEAF
CHILDREN OF HEARING PARENTS

Susan Goldin-Meadow
Heidi Feldman

Problem. Common knowledge has it that when you talk to
a child in English the child learns to speak
English, and when you talk to a child in Japanese the child
learns to speak Japanese. It is also now well known that
when you sign to a child in American Sign Language the child
learns to sign in American Sign Language. But what if you
neither talk nor sign to a child? Will the child be able to
communicate with others, and if so will the child's spontaneous communication have any or all of the properties of natural languages?

To answer these questions about the role of linguistic
input in the development of symbolic communication systems,
we have observed a population that, in some sense, has been
neither talked to nor signed to at all. Our subjects are deaf
children, whose severe hearing losses prevent them from
acquiring any spoken language in the natural way. Furthermore
they are deaf children whose hearing parents have consciously
decided not to let their children see a standard manual system
or sign language and to concentrate instead on oral education.
At the time of our study, our subjects had benefitted very little
from their oral training. Our study was designed to observe the
symbolic systems that our subjects might spontaneously create
in order to communicate despite their lack of an obvious linguistic model to guide their communicative development.

362

Method.     Our sample included four children ranging in age
            from one and one-half to four years. We visited
each child in his home at intervals of approximately six weeks.
Data from two of the children, David and Dennis, are reported
on in this paper (see Table 1). At each visit we gave the child
a variety of toys to play with, and we taped his activity with
the toys in the presence of other hearing participants—the investigators and the child's parents. Although we recorded both
the spoken and the gestural behaviors of our subjects and the
parents, we became interested primarily in the gestural output of the deaf children. We concentrated on the gestural behavior simply because these children seemed to make very
little systematic and spontaneous use of vocalization, unquestionably as a result of the hearing impairment.

| Subject's name | Taping session | Age in yrs; mos |
|---|---|---|
| David | I | 2 ; 10 |
| | II | 2 ; 11 |
| | III | 3 ; 0 |
| | IV | 3 ; 3 |
| | - | |
| | VIII | 3 ; 10 |
| Dennis | I | 2 ; 2 |
| | II | 2 ; 3 |
| | III | 2 ; 4 |
| | IV | 2 ; 6 |

Table 1. Summary of videotaped data.

      We used our videotapes to develop a coding system of
the form and meaning of the gestures employed in communication. Our first task was to pull the gestures out of the
stream of ongoing motor activity. To accomplish this we set
up two criteria for a gesture: (a) the gesture must be directed
to another person (this criterion is met if the child makes
some attempt to establish eye contact with the person); (b)
the gesture must affect the partner through its symbolic meaning
and not as a direct motor act (e.g. if a child physically re-
strains the partner, we do not consider this a gesture, but if

the child holds up an open hand in a stop-like gesture, he is
indirectly restraining the partner through the symbolic meaning
of the gesture).

After discriminating gestures from other motor acts, we
characterized the form of each gesture along the dimensions
used to describe the phonology of American Sign Language (ASL)
(Stokoe 1960, 1978). We also coded the number of gestures
contained within each gestural phrase. The assignment of
gestural phrase boundaries was done with reference to the
time interval between gestures, the continuity of movement,
and the return to neutral position (hands in a relaxed position
in front of the body), as is done in marking boundaries in ASL.
Spot checks of reliability between two independent observers
yielded 86% agreement on the isolation of gestures from the
behavioral stream and the assignment of gestural form and
gestural phrase boundaries.

In addition we coded the children's gestures according
to the meanings they conveyed. Following Bloom (1970, 1973)
we relied on context both to determine the meanings of single
gestures and to determine the semantic relations represented
by gesture phrases. Each gesture in a combination or phrase
was assigned to a semantic role or case (cf Fillmore 1968)
according to its referent's relationship to the referents of the
other gestures in the combination. Thus, if the child produced
the gestural combination signifying 'mommy doll' when mother
dressed the doll, then we considered the gesture for mother to
be the agent and the gesture for doll object or patient. The same
combination could be produced after the mother had received
the doll. In this case the gesture for mother was classified as
person (or dative case) and that for doll would again be object.
An independent observer using our context code agreed with
our assignment of meanings to 94% of the gestural phrases.

Results.    We find that the deaf child does indeed develop
a gestural system for the purposes of communication. The developmental course of this gestural system is
remarkably similar to the early stages reported for the hearing
child learning to speak. At this point in our study, we have
isolated three phases of development from cross-sectional
data. We have data on two children in the first phase and on
two different children in the second phase; one child in this
second phase has progressed during our period of observation
to give us data on the third phase.

In the first phase of development the deaf child uses
very few different gestures and is limited to single-unit or
single-gesture phrases. The deaf child produces these single
gestures in the same contexts in which are found the hearing
child's early single words (Bloom 1970, 1973). For example,
the hearing child may say "More" when he wants an additional
cookie; the deaf child extends his hand, palm up, toward the
potential agent of giving and the desired object. When the
hearing child sees a rabbit hopping across the room, he may
say "See" or "Dat"; in this situation the deaf child will point
an index finger at the object. At this moment in development,
both the deaf and the hearing child's symbols are ambiguous;
we cannot determine from the child's word or gesture which
aspect of the whole situation he is referring to. In the example
given we cannot decide whether he is referring to the rabbit-
ness, the hopping-ness, or the tail-ness of the situation. The
child lacks specificity in his communication, a lack that both
hearing and deaf child remedy in the next phase of development.

In the second phase there are two developments of the
communication system; our data suggest they are simultaneous:
(a) the deaf child creates lexical items to specify individual
objects and actions; (b) the deaf child specifies the relations
between objects and actions by combining gestures into two-
unit phrases according to his own gesture-ordering rule.

In his lexicon the deaf child symbolizes an action with
an action gesture; e.g. if the child wants someone to open a
jar for him, he moves his hand in a twisting motion in the air
—in this case the gesture specifies an action he would like
done. However the deaf child also uses gestures involving
action to symbolize objects; in other words, in a different
situation when no action has been, can be, or will be performed,
the child uses the same twisting motion to specify the jar itself.
[Since the original publication of this paper, Supalla has made
it clear (Supalla & Newport 1978) that characteristic regular
difference in gestural action distinguishes ASL verbs from ASL
nouns; as yet we have no information on how early deaf children in an ASL environment make this grammatical distinction.]
This motor iconic representation system allows the deaf child
to be fairly precise in his symbols. For instance, he can distinguish the symbol for banana ( a fist at the mouth accompanied by opening and closing of the mouth) from the symbol for
ice-cream cone (a fist at the mouth accompanied by tongue

licks). These motor iconic gestures continue to be used by older deaf children.

Table 2 presents a summary of the specific lexical items produced alone and in combination by the two children we have observed in the second phase of development. The data in this table provide us with three interesting facts about the deaf child's lexical development. First, both children produce a number of different specific lexical items; i.e. a number of types (col. 1). Second, these different lexical items often occur more than once in the sample; i.e. the number of tokens (col. 2) is larger than the number of types. Third, the specific lexical items do occur in gesture combinations, i.e, as part of the entire symbolic system (col. 3, Table 2).

| Subjects | TYPES[a] | TOKENS[b] | |
|----------|----------|-------|-----------------|
|          |          | Alone | In Combination |
| David    | 56       | 107   | 62             |
| Dennis   | 25       | 50    | 19             |

Table 2. Lexical items produced by David and Dennis in sessions I-IV.

In addition to these lexical gains, the deaf child at this time also begins to combine gestures to symbolize semantic relations; e.g. he points at the hat he desires (object) and then, without breaking the continuity of his movement, points at the top of his head (location). He has explicitly coded two arguments, or cases, of the relation, and from the context we infer the implicit relation 'put'. In Figure 1 we see a summary of the pairs of cases coded in each child's two-gesture combinations. The children expressed three predominant relations in their two-gesture combinations: action, location, and possession. Furthermore, they expressed these most frequent relations by using the same simple ordering rule: semantic object first, then action, location, or possessor. Figure 2 presents only those combinations that occurred more than five times during an observation period.

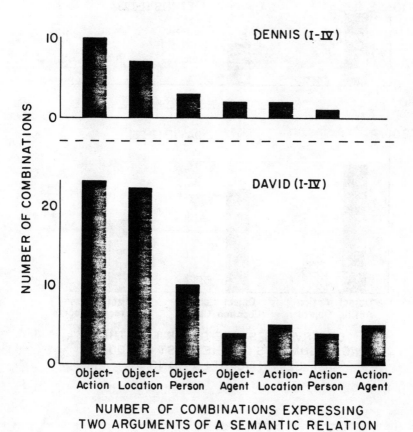

NUMBER OF COMBINATIONS EXPRESSING
TWO ARGUMENTS OF A SEMANTIC RELATION

Figure 1.

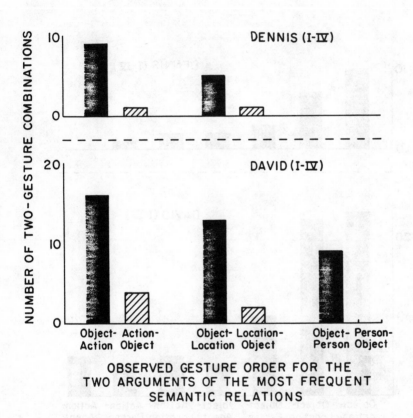

OBSERVED GESTURE ORDER FOR THE
TWO ARGUMENTS OF THE MOST FREQUENT
SEMANTIC RELATIONS

FIGURE 2.

In this second phase of development, the deaf child has created a means of specifying objects, actions, and the relations between them. The hearing child at a comparable point in his language development also begins to produce specific lexical items and to combine words (Nelson 1973, Goldin-Meadow, Seligman, & Gelman 1974); he thus uses linguistic structures much like those the deaf child with no linguistic model uses to attain the same level of specificity in communication.

There is a third phase of development in which the deaf child combines more than two gestures in one phrase in order to symbolize more than one semantic relation; e.g. the child points at the picture of a bird beak on a puzzle piece, then points at his own mouth to denote the similarity between the two, and then points at the spot in the puzzle where the bird-beak fits. Thus the child has specified two aspects or relations to the bird beak: similarity and location. In another example, the child symbolizes in one phrase that the shovel is used to dig outside when it snows, is associated with boots, and is kept downstairs. The data at the moment suggest that the child may be conjoining semantic relations in one phrase in a rule-governed, as opposed to a random, fashion. An increased data base is necessary to determine the reliability and the nature of these potential rules.

In summary, we have isolated three phases of development that the deaf child goes through in creating a gestural communication system in the absence of any linguistic model presented to his working senses. It is possible that the deaf child bases this communication system on some input model however. One hypothesis is that the child's parents generate this gestural system of phrases, which the child then imitates.

To test this hypothesis we observed and videotaped the mother's spontaneous gestures and subjected these gestures to the same analysis we used on the child's gestural output. We found that although the mothers generated as many names for objects and actions as the children generated during the sessions (see Table 3, columns 1 & 2), they did not develop the same lexical items that the children developed. Furthermore, the mothers very rarely produced their specific lexical items in combinations encoding semantic relations, while the deaf children frequently did (Table 3, col. 3). Even when the mothers did combine gestures, their combinations were

| Subjects | TYPES[a] | | TOKENS[b] | | | |
| | | | Alone | | In Semantic Relation Combinations | |
| | Child | Mother | Child | Mother | Child | Mother |
| David | 56 | 54 | 107 | 90 | 47 | 9 |
| Dennis | 25 | 23 | 50 | 58 | 18 | 3 |

[a]Types = Number of different lexical items.

[b]Tokens = Number of lexical occurrences across types.

Table 3.   Lexical, items (gestures) produced in sessions
I-IV by child and mother.

not rule-governed as the children's combinations were (Figs.
3 & 4). In general, we found that the mothers developed the
combinatorial skill several recording sessions after the children already had exhibited this skill in their gestural output.
Thus, the deaf children have not even been exposed to a
spontaneous gestural system that might have served as a rule-
governed model for their symbolic development.

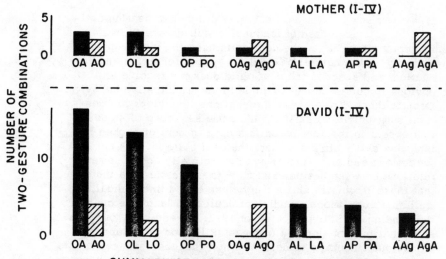

SUMMARY OF MOTHER-DAVID COMPARISON
OF GESTURE ORDERING RULES FOR
TWO ARGUMENT SEMANTIC RELATIONS

FIGURE 3 (above).                    FIGURE  4.  (below).

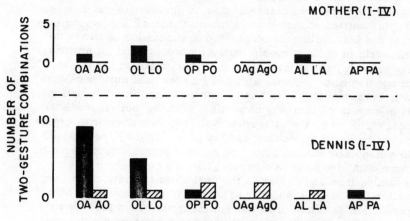

SUMMARY OF MOTHER-DENNIS COMPARISON
OF GESTURE ORDERING RULES FOR
TWO ARGUMENT SEMANTIC RELATIONS

Discussion.   Our deaf subjects differ from hearing chil-
                      dren of language acquiring age in two
important ways: first, the deaf child uses the visual-gestural
modality as the natural channel for symbol reception and production; and second, the deaf child does not receive an
obvious linguistic model to guide his communicative behavior.
Despite these differences, the deaf child develops his gestural communicative skills in the same sequence of stages
that appear in the hearing child's development of spoken
language skills. In particular, the deaf child invents names
for actions and for objects, and syntactically codes semantic
relations between actions and objects. Thus our data indicate
that these linguistic skills can be expressed in a manual, as
well as a vocal mode. Studies of adult sign language confirm
this finding (cf Bellugi & Fischer 1972). In addition, our data
show that the ontogenesis of these skills does not depend on
an obvious linguistic model. We know that the child can create
a simple system of communication with no input model; however
it is not clear from our present data exactly how far the child
can progress without the benefit of such a model.
          Of course, if the child is supplied with a model in either
the manual or vocal mode, he will by and large conform his
particular names and syntactic orderings to that model. But
where does the deaf child who has no obvious linguistic model
get his particular names and syntactic orders? We hypothesize
that the deaf child generalizes and abstracts from actions in
the world in order to create names for objects and for actions.
For example, the twisting motion of the wrist used in the act
of opening a jar becomes stylized into the deaf child's gesture
with both meanings, 'jar' and 'open'. Abstracting from actions
is a process particularly compatible with the motoric mode the
deaf child uses. Young hearing children, who sometimes create
names by using speech sounds, even though they are exposed
to a linguistic model, often use an onomatopoeic process, e.g.
"num-num" for food. We suggest that the hearing child is abstracting from sound just as the deaf child is abstracting from
action. Presumably sound is as natural to the vocal mode of
production as action is to the motoric mode. Thus here we have
an example of how the modality by which the symbols are expressed alters the form that the symbols take.
          Similarly, we hypothesize that the deaf child's rule of
ordering object first may be induced from his motoric acts on

the world; e.g. if a child wants to relocate an object, he
must first situate that object and then move it to its new location—the object occurs before the location in the child's
motor action schema. We suggest that the child uses this
ordered motor action schema as a basis for his symbolic representation of the same event (cf McNeill 1974).

In summary, we have shown that symbolic communicative behavior is a resilient skill that develops in children
of normal intelligence who interact with human beings and
with objects. Symbolic communication can begin to develop
despite severe auditory impairment and in the absence of an
obvious linguistic model.

Our study, in conjunction with current work in sign
linguistics, allows us to consider how certain variables affect the particular form a language will take. The modality
through which a language is produced and received (e.g. the
vocal apparatus and the ear) is one variable that in part shapes
the form of the language. Since contemporary sign languages
differ from spoken languages in modality, a comparison of the
two different systems points to the effects of modality on
linguistic structure (cf Bellugi & Fischer 1972, Stokoe 1974,
Battison 1974, Siple ch. 14). Language change over generations
comprises a second variable that shapes the form of a language (Bever & Langendoen 1971). American Sign Language,
like spoken languages, has undergone historical change
(Frishberg 1975). Our deaf subjects, however, do not have a
historically based linguistic model available to them. The
communication system they have created illustrates the influence of modality on linguistic structure without the
influence of historical change. Thus our data suggest how
two factors, modality and lack of historical model, contribute
to the design features of a language.

## NOTE

This paper was originally presented at the Society for Research
in Child Development meeting in Denver, April 1975. The data
for the paper are preliminary and are extended in doctoral
dissertations submitted to the University of Pennsylvania:
The Development of a Lexicon in Deaf Children of Hearing

Parents by Heidi Feldman, and Symbolic Representation of
Semantic Relations: A Study of a Spontaneous Gestural Language by Susan Goldin-Meadow. We thank Lila Gleitman for
her assistance in developing many of the points in this paper,
Rochel Gelman for her criticisms of an earlier version, Lisette
Tefo and Barbara Gray for their help in coding videotapes, and
finally our subjects and their families for their continued coop-
eration throughout the study. We wish to acknowledge the
support we have received  from The Spencer Foundation grant,
the NSF Graduate Fellowship awarded to Heidi Feldman, the
NICHHD Grant (HD 00337) under the direction of J. Aronfreed,
and the NICHHD Grant to R. Gelman (HD 52744).

## REFERENCES

Battison, Robbin
     1974     Phonological Deletion in American Sign Language,
               Sign Language Studies 5, 1-17.

Bellugi, Ursula, & Susan Fischer
     1972     A Comparison of Sign Language and Spoken Language,
               Cognition 1, 173-200.

Bever, Thomas, & D. T. Langendoen
     1971     A Dynamic Model of the Evolution of Language,
               Linguistic Inquiry 2, 443-463.

Bloom, Lois
     1970     Language Development: Form & Function in Emerging
               Grammars (Cambridge, MA, MIT Press).
     1973     One Word at a Time (The Hague, Mouton).

Fillmore, Charles J.
     1968     The Case for Case, in Universals in Linguistic
               Theory, Bach & Harms eds. (New York, Holt).

Frishberg, Nancy
     1975     Arbitrariness and Iconicity: Historical Change in
               American Sign Language, Language 51, 696-715.

Goldin-Meadow, Susan, S. Seligman, & R. Gelman
   1974   Language in Two-Year-Olds. Unpublished MS,
          University of Pennsylvania.

McNeill, David
   1974   Semiotic Extension. Paper at Loyola Symposium on
          Cognition, Chicago.

Nelson, Keith
   1973   Structure and Strategy in Learning to Talk, Mono-
          graphs of the Society for Research in Child Develop-
          ment 38.

Siple, Patricia A.
   1978   Visual Constraints for Sign Language Communication,
          Sign Language Studies 19, 95-110. (Part Four: 14)

Stokoe, William C.
   1960   Sign Language Structure, Studies in Linguistics: O.P.
   [1978]  8; revised (Silver Spring, MD, Linstok Press).
   1974   Motor Signs as the First Form of Language, Semiotica
          10, 117-130; & in Language Origins, Wescott, Hewes,
          Stokoe eds. (Silver Spring, MD, Linstok Press),35-49.

Supalla, Ted, & Elissa Newport
   1978   How Many Seats in a Chair: The Derivation of Nouns
          and Verbs in American Sign Language, in Understanding
          Language through Sign Language Research, Siple ed.
          (New York, Academic), 91-159.

Tervoort, Bernard
   1967   Esoteric Symbolism in the Communication Behavior of
          Young Deaf Children, American Annals of the Deaf
          106, 436-480.